SINGAPORE: CITY-STATE IN SOUTH-EAST ASIA

PHILIPPE REGNIER

Singapore

City-State in South-East Asia

Translated from the French by Christopher Hurst

UNIVERSITY OF HAWAII PRESS
HONOLULU

First published in 1987
as *Singapour et son environnement régional:*
Étude d'une cité-état au sein du monde malais
by Presses Universitaires de France, Paris
(Publications of the Graduate Institute
of International Studies, Geneva)
© Presses Universitaires de France, 1987

This translation and updating © C. Hurst & Co.
(Publishers) Ltd., 1991

Published in North America by
University of Hawaii Press
2840 Kolowalu Street
Honolulu, Hawaii 96822

Published in the United Kingdom by
C. Hurst & Co. (Publishers) Ltd.,
38 King Street, London WC2E 8JT

Printed in Hong Kong

Library of Congress Cataloging in Publication Data

Régnier, Philippe.
    [Singapour et son environnement régional. English]
    Singapore, a city-state in South East Asia / by Philippe Régnier.
      p. cm.
    Translation of: Singapour et son environnement régional.
    Includes bibliographical references and index.
    ISBN 0–8248–1406–1. — ISBN 0–8248–1407–X (pbk.)
    1. Asia, Southeastern—Foreign economic relations—Singapore.
    2. Singapore—Foreign economic relations—Asia, Southeastern.
    3. Asia, Southeastern—Foreign relations—Singapore. 4. Singapore—Foreign
relations—Asia, Southeastern. 5. ASEAN. I. Title.
HF3790.Z7S656   1991
337.5905957—dc20   91–13257
                                                       CIP

FOREWORD

The city-state of Singapore is one of the wonders of the post-colonial world. It has been transformed from a declining entrepot ejected into sovereign statehood into a remarkable model of successful modernisation. It has become a by-word for efficiency and excellence — exemplified by the reputation enjoyed by its international airline. Singapore has been personified through the dynamic role assumed by its first prime minister Lee Kuan Yew who gave up office in November 1990 after more than thirty years of tenure. He gave up office but not politics, remaining in the cabinet with the portfolio of senior minister and with his authority unimpaired.

That reluctance to let go politically reflected a political philosophy based on worst-case calculations. Lee Kuan Yew is driven by an obsession with the innate vulnerability of Singapore, sea-locked and air-locked between Malaysia and Indonesia, and whose principal assets other than its port are the industry and intelligence of its people. The need to cope continually with geopolitical and economic vulnerability explains why politics in Singapore is made subordinate to collective economic and social priorities and also to questions of human rights. Success has its price in terms of constraints on individual liberty, which Lee Kuan Yew does not try to conceal. Indeed, he proclaims its necessity.

The success story of Singapore is told and explained well by Dr Régnier in a timely English translation of his original French text. He sets his study of the rise of this remarkable trading emporium in historical context demonstrating in its development how an intrinsic vulnerability, which remains Lee Kuan Yew's obsession, has been recurrently overcome. The signal contribution of this volume is the author's ability to encompass within a single set of covers illuminating accounts of Singapore's industrial growth, its assumption of a regional economic and political role and the nature of the city-state's paternalistic political system.

Dr Régnier is an optimist as well as a skillful chronicler of the life and times of modern Singapore. He regards Singapore as a latter-day Venice of South-East Asia, and expects it, unlike its historical forebear, to survive as a prosperous independent state.

London School of Economics and Political Science   MICHAEL LEIFER
December 1990

CONTENTS

TABLES

MAPS

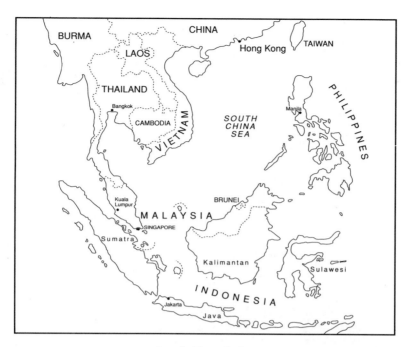

South East Asia.

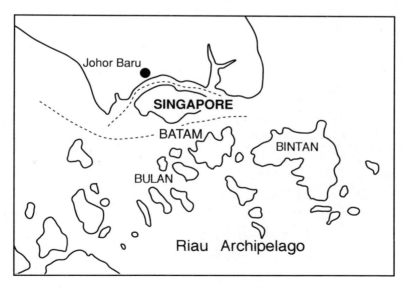

Singapore and its closest neighbours, Johor
Baru (Malaysia) and Batam (Indonesia).

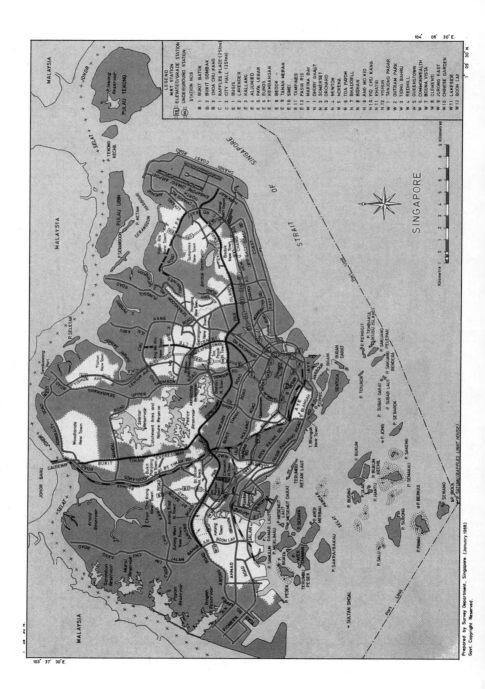

104° 05′ 30″ E.

1° 09′ 30″ N.

103° 37′ 30″ E.

SINGAPORE

STRAIT OF SINGAPORE

MALAYSIA

LEGEND

MRT STATION
ELEVATED/GRADE STATION
UNDERGROUND STATION

STATION NOS

B	1	BUKIT BATOK
B	2	BUKIT GOMBAK
B	3	CHOA CHU KANG
C	1	RAFFLES PLACE (2Stns)
C	2	CITY HALL (2Stns)
E	1	BUGIS
E	2	LAVENDER
E	3	KALLANG
E	4	ALJUNIED
E	5	PAYA LEBAR
E	6	EUNOS
E	7	KEMBANGAN
E	8	BEDOK
E	9	TANAH MERAH
E	10	SIMEI
E	11	TAMPINES
E	12	PASIR RIS
M	1	MARINA BAY
N	1	DHOBY GHAUT
N	2	SOMERSET
N	3	ORCHARD
N	4	NEWTON
N	5	NOVENA
N	6	TOA PAYOH
N	7	BRADDELL
N	8	BISHAN
N	9	ANG MO KIO
N	10	YIO CHU KANG
N	11	KHATIB
N	12	YISHUN
W	1	TANJONG PAGAR
W	2	OUTRAM PARK
W	3	TIONG BAHRU
W	4	REDHILL
W	5	QUEENSTOWN
W	6	COMMONWEALTH
W	7	BUONA VISTA
W	8	CLEMENTI
W	9	JURONG EAST
W	10	CHINESE GARDEN
W	11	LAKESIDE
W	12	BOON LAY

Kilometre 1 0 1 2 3 4 5 6 7 8 9 Kilometres

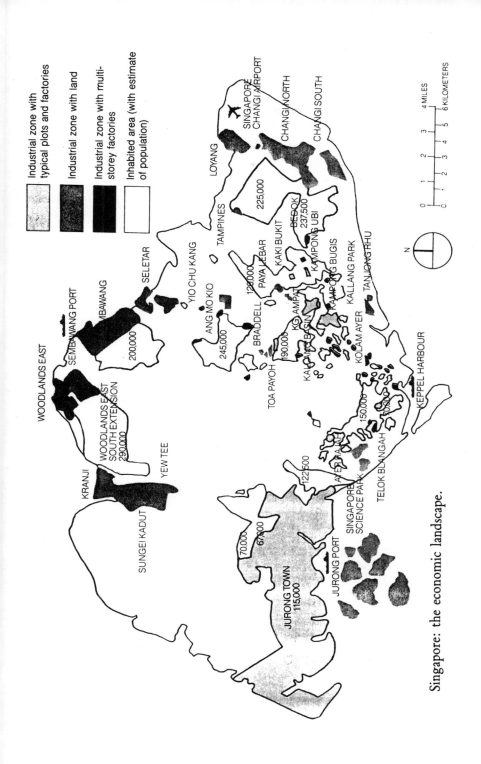

Singapore: the economic landscape.

Industrial zone with typical plots and factories

Industrial zone with land

Industrial zone with multi-storey factories

Inhabited area (with estimate of population)

N

0   1   2   3   4 MILES
0 1 2 3 4 5 6 KILOMETERS

WOODLANDS EAST

KRANJI

SUNGEI KADUT

WOODLANDS EAST SOUTH EXTENSION
290,000

YEW TEE

70,000

67,000

JURONG TOWN
115,000

JURONG PORT

SINGAPORE SCIENCE PARK

TELOK BLANGAH

KEPPEL HARBOUR

AYER RAJAH

122,500

150,000

100,000

KALLANG BASIN

KOLAM AYER

TANJONG RHU

KALLANG PARK

KAMPONG UBI

KAMPONG BUGIS

KG AMPAT

190,000

TOA PAYOH

BRADDELL

245,000

ANG MO KIO

YIO CHU KANG

120,000

PAYA LEBAR

KAKI BUKIT

BEDOK
237,500

TAMPINES

225,000

LOYANG

SEMBAWANG

SEMBAWANG PORT

SELETAR

200,000

SINGAPORE CHANGI AIRPORT

CHANGI NORTH

CHANGI SOUTH

SINGAPORE, A TRADING EMPORIUM
Basic elements and historical continuity

The chief concern of this book is with the changes — at least, the visible ones — which have occurred in South-East Asia since the middle of the 1960s. It sets out to establish the character of the network of economic relationships between a newly-independent city-state and the mainly very young states that surround it, within the framework of a regional association which is itself only in an early stage of construction. The period that concerns us begins with the independence of Singapore in 1965 and the creation of the Association of South-East Asian Nations (ASEAN) two years later in 1967. These events are related to the separate evolution of the Federation of Malaysia and the extraordinary sovereignty of this emporium with an overwhelming Chinese majority yet situated at the very heart of the Malay world, to which it appears to be indissolubly bound.

This primary fact could lead one to examine the regional attributes of Singapore at the present time purely on the basis of the developments that have stemmed from the 'new' situation of 1965–7. However, if one were to limit oneself in this way, there is a danger of overlooking the lessons of history which are indispensable in order to identify the functions of Singapore fully and accurately. Even if our essential purpose in this work is to concentrate on the regional role which Singapore has played since its independence and accession to ASEAN, this should be set in a much longer perspective if one is to distinguish elements that represent change from those which are continuations from the past. To examine the precolonial and colonial history of South-East Asia, not in a linear and descriptive way but with a deliberate selectivity, is to link up with this forgotten or unappreciated continuity, and to appreciate certain basic ideas that form a unifying thread through our investigation.

There has been an uninterrupted succession of commercial emporia in South-East Asia belonging to a system of intra-regional and inter-national relations that is more than 2,000 years old, and the Republic of Singapore inherits its functions precisely from this succession of state organisations based on the typical economic structures of an emporium. In this introduction we draw attention — in relation to Singapore and its regional environment — to the remarkable continuity over the centuries of certain forms of state power and the interaction between them, and this helps us to evaluate and compare the transformations that have taken place in recent times.[1]

The character of states in South-East Asia: the coupling of trading emporia with vast agrarian hinterlands

When Singapore was founded in 1819, this did not represent either an artificial creation by the British coloniser or an isolated phenomenon in the history of the region – where, on the contrary, sea-based emporia have appeared down the ages. A glance at the map of South-East Asia makes it clear how great is the geostrategic importance of the Strait of Malacca linking the Indian Ocean and the South China Sea,[2] which would confer great maritime and commercial power on any form of state organisation capable of controlling this pivotal zone.[3] At least since the second century AD, this attribute has caused a series of state organisations, definable as maritime commercial emporia, to emerge and then disappear in the vicinity of the Strait. Singapore is only the latest in this series. Clearly, this type of occupation of coastal and maritime space is not peculiar to South-East Asia, since other great sea-routes throughout the world have given birth to such renowned examples of the same phenomenon as Venice and the medieval Hanseatic ports.

The existence of commercial emporia on the southern coastline of South-East Asia is remarkable in that throughout history they have flourished alongside state organisations of another kind: those based on agriculture. These, in contrast to the emporia which control maritime trade, dominate the interior — that is to say, the vast hinterlands on either side of the Strait: the Malay peninsula and the Indonesian archipelago, but particularly Java and Sumatra.[4] This dichotomy has

1. Charles D. Cowan, 'Continuity and Change in the international history of maritime Southeast Asia', *JSEAS*, IX (1968), pp. 1–11.
2. 'In South East Asia, perhaps more than anywhere else, the geographical environment determines human history' (Paul Isoart, *Les états de l'Asie du sud-est*, Paris: Economica, 1978, p. 1).
3. 'In retrospect it can be seen that any dominance exercised over the Strait of Malacca had been derived from a position of economic strength located either on the east coast of Sumatra or on the west coast of the Malay Peninsula' (Michael Leifer, [156], p. 8). *Les grandes voies maritimes dans le monde, XV–XVIe s.*, Paris: Ecole Pratique des Hautes Etudes, Bibl. Gén., section VI, 1965.
4. Hans-Dieter Evers, *Traditional trading networks of Southeast Asia*, Univ. of Bielefeld, Sociology of Development Research Center, 1984. R.B. Smith & W. Watson (68), pp. 181–2.

continued in the region since ancient times right up to ASEAN today. The difficult co-existence of these two types of state has produced an unstable equilibrium which exerts a pervasive influence over the nature of economic and political relations within the region. This has been the case before, during and since the colonial era.[5] The resulting ties of natural economic complementarity (agriculture and commerce) and interdependence (in the political sphere among others) can be a possible source of conflict — between the sea-based emporia, which are open to the region and to the world, and their neighbours whose internal order is largely based on agriculture. Confrontations at various levels were the unavoidable destiny of the first historical empires in the region – Srivijaya and Majapahit, just as they affected Singapore and Malaya much later when they were ruled by the British and the Dutch East Indies during colonial rule: the two rival colonial systems competed keenly with one another.

The economic relationship which subsists today between the commercial and industrial emporium of Singapore and its two immediate partners, Malaysia and Indonesia, is unquestionably a result of this powerful legacy from the past. We look below at some aspects of this ever-present heritage, the object being to place the economic functions of modern Singapore within the coherent system of intra-regional relations which existed in the past and has so deeply influenced South-East Asia's evolution.

The pre-colonial commercial emporia in South-East Asia

There is no need here to look back into the distant past — the domain of the archaeologist. The succession of trading emporia and vast agrarian empires can be illustrated by a number of significant examples.

Ancient history and the first Indianised kingdoms

Apart from the famed overland Silk Route, the Straits of Malacca and Sunda and the northern and north-eastern coasts of Sumatra, the Malay peninsula and southern Indochina constituted the inescapable maritime trade route between India, China and South-East Asia from earliest

---

5. 'The continuing theme of an unstable and changing balance between the influence of a policy based on a populous and agricultural Java, on the one hand, and that of the commercial and maritime power of a rival system in or near the Straits area on the other, can be observed throughout the colonial era as before it' (Cowan, op. cit., p. 9).

times, and gave a particular slant to the entire precolonial history of South-East Asia.[6] Of the first Indianised kingdoms established in the region, the rapid rise of its pre-Angkor civilisation gave Funan ascendancy in the Mekong and Menam deltas approximately between the 2nd and 7th centuries AD. According to the accounts of Chinese travellers, the Funan kingdom had a double vocation: maritime activity along the coast[7] — which was particularly well developed — and agriculture that was in the process of being established and at the same time was spreading through the interior, anticipating the Khmer kingdoms of Chenla and subsequently Angkor from the 7th–8th centuries onwards. Funan was described as the meeting-point between India and China, benefiting from the alternation of the monsoon winds which both its own large merchant fleet and traders from abroad had learned to master. George Coedes writes that 'Funan occupied a privileged position on the maritime trade route, and constituted an unavoidable staging-post, as much for navigators who passed through the Strait of Malacca as for those crossing the isthmus of the Malay peninsula. Funan was perhaps the farthest point for shipping from the eastern Mediterranean.' It probably also had relations with Persia.[8]

In the 3rd and 4th centuries, these developments favoured the establishment of a chain of ports along this much-frequented sea route. Tunsun was a typical example, a kind of commercial outpost close to the south-eastern tip of the Malay peninsula. A second 'crossroads' for trading — Ko-ying, on the west coast of Java or perhaps on the southeast coast of Sumatra — seems to have been where Indian vessels anchored after their passage through the Strait of Malacca, and the point from which their cargo was redistributed throughout the region.[9]

These characteristics anticipated the role of regional entrepot which the sultanate of Malacca and later Singapore were to inherit.

6. 'There grew up throughout the greater part of the Malaysian archipelago a geopolitical pattern remarkably similar to that of maritime Europe in medieval times, with political power organised in units of sea rather than land, so that a state's territory consisted of a series of scattered ports and bases, strategically placed on both sides of the waterway which it sought to dominate' (Charles A. Fisher [26], pp. 106–7). For antiquity see G.E. Gerini, *Researches on Ptolemy's geography of Eastern Asia*, London, 1909.
7. Kenneth R. Hall (35), pp. 1–77; Smith & Watson, op. cit., pp. 286–7. On the first Chinese traders, see Wang Gungwu, *The Nanhai trade: A study of the early history of Chinese trade in the South China Sea*, Kuala Lumpur: Printcraft, 1959.
8. G. Coedès (17), pp. 83, 93–4.
9. O.W. Wolters (83), pp. 47, 60, 70, 80.

The trading empire of Srivijaya

From the 7th century to the 13th, a vast trading empire, Srivijaya, became established in Sumatra around Palembang and Jambi, its hegemony embracing the Malacca and Sunda straits. After the fall of Funan around 627, the two kingdoms of Chenla and Angkor grew up parallel to each other; the latter was the first large state system in South-East Asia based on agriculture. The first agrarian kingdoms in Java were formed in the 8th–10th centuries in the centre and then the west of the island, to form the empire of Majapahit.

The commercial power of Srivijaya derived from its control of the two straits. This enabled it to form a vital link in the network of sea routes linking the Arab world and India and the East Indies and China, and to exercise its suzerainty over both the Malay peninsula and West Java.[10] Srivijaya manifested certain characteristics in common with those found later in Malacca and Singapore: a small population and workforce, a lack of agriculture (rice was imported from Java), a scarcity of marketable goods produced locally (a typical feature of outward-looking entrepots), and a pervasive materialism (it produced hardly any important artistic or architectural monuments).[11]

For their part, 'the early states of Java were not so much rivals of Srivijaya as neighbours operating within a different system.'[12] These states looked towards the interior of their lands, and ruled vast agricultural regions: there a hierarchical administrative and religious bureaucracy became established, and left behind such monuments as the (still surviving) temples of Borobudur and Prambanan.

At this time, there was genuine complementarity between the two systems, one commercial and the other mainly agrarian, right at the heart of the Malay world. But this was not a stable equilibrium.[13] Initially the Javanese kingdoms were not much interested in external trade and were content to pay tribute in kind to Srivijaya by means of the sea routes which it monopolised, but this situation was reversed from the 10th/11th centuries onwards. Following attacks on Palembang by Tamil raiders, covert hostility from the Javanese, and the appearance

10. Brian E. Colless, 'The early western ports of the Malay peninsula', *J. of Tropical Geography*, Dec. 69, pp. 1–9; Hall (35), pp. 78–102; Leifer (156), p. 7; Karl Polanyi, *Trade and market in the early empires*, Glencoe, Ill.: Free Press, 1957.
11. Smith (68), pp. 403–4; Wolters (83).
12. Cowan, op. cit., p. 13.
13. Nicholas Tarling (72), pp. 21–2.

of new emporia conveniently close to Java's agriculture (on the north coast), Srivijaya could no longer check various initiatives to open up direct trade with Arab and Chinese merchants, by-passing its own entrepots.[14] In the 13th century, after numerous hostile expeditions against the two islands, the second capital of Srivijaya, Jambi, was compelled to declare its allegiance to the rulers of Java. This was the beginning of the Majapahit empire (*c.* 1293).

In this phase of South-East Asian history, trade and agriculture had underpinned the creation of, respectively, Srivijaya and Angkor; the former had dominated the archipelago and the latter the Indochinese peninsula. Their successors were Majapahit and Siam. In contrast to the specialised function of Srivijaya, Majapahit was built on both types of territorial organisation discussed so far. It came into existence as a federation of agrarian kingdoms, successors to the first Javanese states which had coalesced after a long series of civil wars and the incursion of a Chinese fleet in 1292. But it also included several large ports – Makassar, Tuban, Gresik, Surabaya and the island of Madura — which were in simultaneous contact with the agricultural regions inland and the spice islands, thus assuring them of commercial services.

Majapahit anticipated the Dutch colonial empire in two important respects. It did so, first, by this double vocation which the Portuguese were also to assume before they were driven out by the Dutch, and secondly by making the first attempt to unify the archipelago. However, it was not destined to last for longer than about a century; it does not seem ever to have succeeded in obtaining more than periodic control over the Strait of Malacca and the commercial interchange resulting from the revitalisation of Jambi and Palembang and the activities of numerous traders from outside the region.[15] On the shifting frontiers of Majapahit, a complementary system of commercial organisation was being set up, even without its knowledge.

First mention of Tumasik and the rise of the sultanate of Malacca, the true precursor of Singapore

Tumasik

The history of Singapore did not begin when the British installed themselves there in 1819, but much earlier when the Malacca sultanate was

---

14. Coedès (17), p. 371; Smith (68), p. 474.
15. Cowan, op. cit., p. 5; Hall (35), pp. 103–35; Jacob C. Van Leur, *Indonesian trade and society*, The Hague: Van Hoeve, 1955.

created in the early fifteenth century. The extent of trading activity in the island of Tumasik (or Temasek) was mentioned around the 1490s, when Paramesvara, prince of Palembang, was taking refuge there so as not to submit to the rule of Majapahit. He founded the new emporium of Malacca a few years later.

It is difficult to give a precise date for the beginnings of Tumasik, which could be very ancient due to its privileged position as an island.[16] Srivijaya, to the extent that it held sway over the Strait and the Malay peninsula, probably had a well-established presence there – there is no doubt that the same is true of Majapahit, of which 13th/14th-century remains have been found.[17] Tumasik appears to have been the focal point of a contest between Majapahit and Siam for the control of the Malacca Strait, and it gave allegiance to Siam until the governor sent there by the Siamese was assassinated by Paramesvara. It is from this prince that the word '*Singapura*', city of the lion, is said to derive: in time, it came to replace the island's earlier name, and entered into legend.[18]

Around 1400, Siam intervened again, precipitating the departure of Paramesvara and the end of the island's commercial activity. For some time it continued to be a centre for piracy, in close relations with the Malacca sultanate, until it sank into the obscurity of regional history, only re-appearing in the 19th century.

Malacca

Like Raffles much later, Paramesvara had a geostrategic instinct which caused him to establish himself at the entrance to the Malacca Strait. Seeking Chinese protection against the ever-present covert threat from the Siamese, and desirous of opening a free port for Arab traders as the result of his marriage and conversion to Islam, he founded the sultanate of Malacca. Inheriting the attributes of Srivijaya, it became a major new

16. Brian E. Colless, 'The ancient history of Singapore', *JSEAS*, X, 1 (1969), pp. 1–11. Mary Turnbull (78, pp. 1–33) indicates that an island probably corresponding to Tumasik was mentioned under different names from the beginning of the Christian era. See also Jacques Dupuis (23), p. 26.

17. Jewels and a large stone covered with Javanese characters from the time of Majapahit were found at the mouth of the Singapore river. Turnbull, loc. cit.; Coedes (17), p. 371; Tarling (72), p. 14.

18. The term '*Singapura*' is attributed (among other opinions) to Paramesvara or one of his ancestors who, arriving at Tumasik, saw a strange animal similar to a lion. It is also possible that these princes wished to restore the throne of the lion of Srivijaya.

commercial power at the very heart of the Malay world, and was the true forerunner of Singapore.[19]

In the 15th century, the sultanate expanded on an unprecedented scale. Having become the chief trading centre in South-East Asia for Arab and Chinese merchants (the latter being supported by the presence of armed Chinese fleets), it drew its wealth from its activity as an entrepot for spices and other rare and sought-after products of the region — and likewise for similar products from abroad.[20] This international meeting-place, which the British faithfully imitated in the 19th century, was a forerunner of the organisation of Singapore. Apart from adopting the status of a free port and thus advertising its willingness to trade with all comers (even Siam), the economy of Malacca was based on a system of uniform customs duties of 3–6% raised on goods in transit. When its commercial and territorial power was at its height (in 1477–90 it had control of both sides of the Strait and, against competition from northern Siam, of much of the peninsula), Malacca had no less than 5,000 foreign residents, speaking eighty-six different languages or dialects but all using a lingua franca related to ancient Malay (as they use English today), and bringing into existence several distinct autonomous neighbourhoods, each devoted to a particular speciality. The same phenomenon occurred in Singapore under British rule.[21] As master of the sea routes and of various key points in the archipelago and the peninsula — regional staging-posts that were necessary for it to function as a trading centre — Malacca represented a focus for the Islamisation of the Malays, in which Arab and Gujerati merchants played the principal role.[22]

This last great emporium of the precolonial age fell to the assault of

19. 'The state based on maritime commerce reached its fullest development after the establishment of Malacca around 1400. The models of Srivijaya and Majapahit clearly inspired the founder of the last pre-colonial trading empire, just as the example of Malacca was later to serve the Portuguese and their successors' (Lea E. Williams [81], p. 47). See also Onghokam, 'The decline of indigenous commodity trade', *Prisma* (Jakarta), Dec. 83, pp. 3–21.

20. 'Malacca thus appeared, at the end of the 15th century, as the capital of a sort of trading empire in which Muslims of all races were the agents. It anticipated the future role of Singapore' (Dupuis [23], p. 28). A. Reid, *Trade goods and routes in Southeast Asia, c. 1300–1700*, paper of SPAFA workshop, Jakarta, Nov. 1984.

21. Tan Ding Eing (70), pp. 1–11.

22. The role played by Malacca in the 15th century as a religious and cultural centre in the region appears to have been important in view of its function as a staging-point for pilgrimages to Mecca and a place where books of significance in the world of Islam were printed.

Albuquerque in 1511, and like the fall of Srivijaya this event is highly instructive concerning the life-cycle of this type of state. As with its predecessors, Malacca's wealth and its very viability were fragile. This was manifested in two complementary ways. Among Malacca's internal weaknesses, the lack of cohesion in its ruling élite was inevitably dangerous for a trading city that faced mounting external threats — a lesson taken to heart by those ruling Singapore today. At the beginning of the 16th century, the absence of a system of hereditary succession, and the rivalries this caused in the sultan's court, was aggravated by the fickleness of the foreign traders. Whether residing permanently or only transitorily in the sultanate, these were ready to offer their loyalty unreservedly to any newcomer who could show naval or military superiority. In the event, the beneficiaries were the Portuguese.

The external weaknesses were not circumstantial but mainly structural. Having no agricultural base, Malacca was dependent for most of its food supplies on Java and Siam, and the sultanate was therefore in no condition to withstand a Portuguese blockade from the sea. Soon after Vasco da Gama landed in India in 1498, Lisbon showed that it knew how to profit from one of Malacca's principal resources, the spice trade — a strategy recalling that of the Javanese kingdoms against Srivijaya. The capture of Malacca in 1511 was a striking illustration of this process.

The 'new' trading emporia of the colonial period and the founding of Singapore

There is no need here to examine the history of colonisation in South-East Asia. However, it is helpful to demonstrate how commercial entities were set up at the will of successive European regimes, and how these entities fitted into a pre-established regional and international order ('historical continuity') and perpetuated the formation of emporia which were vital for seafaring and for trade.

The first chain of colonial trading posts

By virtue of the papal award under the treaty of Tordesillas in 1494, Spain and Portugal, fortified by their European experience of seafaring, and coveting the spices and precious metals of distant lands, were authorised to divide up the world according to their discoveries.[23]

23. A. Kammerer, 'La Mer Rouge, l'Abyssinie et l'Arabie depuis l'Antiquité', *Les guerres du poivre* (vol. 2), Cairo, 1935, quoted in Ch. Robequain (62), p. 11.

Setting out in opposite directions, they met eachother in South-East Asia, in the Moluccas — Ternate and Tidore — and strove to connect the producers of spices there with Europe through a commercial system based on chains of trading posts along the intercontinental sea-lanes which they had just identified.[24]

Portugal

The conquest of Malacca was not a chance event. The Portuguese were hunting down the Arab traders with a view to taking their place, and they tried to make use of the trading circuits which the Arabs controlled. After the sultanate had fallen, they succeeded in revitalising the economy of Malacca by making it one in a series of staging ports — Hormuz, Goa, Ceylon, Amboina (today Ambon in Indonesia) and Macau. For more than a century, Malacca continued to enjoy a solid prosperity by imposing taxes on the numerous vessels that passed through the Strait.[25]

Like Batavia and Singapore in the 19th century, Malacca was an essential link between Europe, India and the South China Sea, used successively by the Portuguese, the Dutch (from 1641) and the British (from 1824), and administered by a captain-general under the authority of the viceroy in Goa. A similar structure was used by the British, who administered Singapore from Calcutta.

The Portuguese did not break up the pre-existing system of intra-regional relations, but partly adapted it to their own purposes. Parallel to it, rival emporia linked to the spread of Islam developed as an alternative source of commercial activity. The Portuguese gained an advantage with the founding in 1522 of Sunda Kalapa in western Java (the future Batavia, renamed Jacatra in 1527 by the Islamised state of Bantam) and by securing control of Ambon, Ternate and Tidore in 1575–8. However, they came up against the power of Acheh in northern Sumatra and of Johore at the southern end of the Malay peninsula, where the successors of the sultanate of Malacca had taken refuge (other branches had spread throughout the region — in Brunei, Bantam, Makassar, Tuban, Demak, Madura and Surabaya). At the end of the 16th century, the expansion of Acheh had covered both shores of the Strait, as well as various anchorages in the Malay peninsula (Kedah and Perak). Defeated around 1629 by a Portuguese-backed coalition con-

24. Milton Osborne (56), p. 75.
25. D.G.E. Hall, (34), p. 199. 'Commerces et navires dans les mers du sud', *Archipel* (Paris), 1979, pp. 105–94.

sisting of Malacca, Patani and Johore, Acheh was able to withdraw strategically, and showed a remarkable vitality right up to the beginning of the 20th century.[26]

Spain

A similar strategy of commercial penetration was applied by the Spanish colonisers. When the struggle for control of the spice trade between Ternate (Portugal) and Tidore (Spain) was over, the treaty of Zaragoza in 1529 confirmed the papal award of 1494, recognising Portugal's ascendancy in the Moluccas and Spain's in the Philippines.

In 1570 the Spaniards founded Manila as an advance post for trade between their American conquests and China — American gold and silver for Chinese silks and other local products. Henceforward the Philippines became, irrevocably, a peripheral part of South-East Asia, set apart from the rest of the Malay world, partly by its geographical location but above all by the actions of its Spanish overlords. The Spaniards set up a system of control that was monolithic and durable: it lasted till 1898. It took the great agricultural properties of Spain as a model, and introduced Catholicism throughout the archipelago, which remained largely immune from Indianisation and the inroads of Islam, except for Mindanao and the Sulu islands. Spain also linked Manila to a trading network that reached across the Pacific to Acapulco in Mexico and ultimately to the mother-country itself; it did not pass through South-East Asia at all. In the 20th century the link was with the United States. Manila's local trading activities were oriented towards China, in competition with its Portuguese rival, Macau, and then Hong Kong.

Manila was certainly not atypical of this succession of maritime and commercial centres in South-East Asia, but the factors just mentioned are intertwined with the historical reasons why the Philippines have played a rather peripheral role on the regional scene right up to the 20th century. This applies also to its relations with ASEAN at the present time.[27]

26. Cowan, op. cit., p. 7. Hall follows the same line in drawing attention particularly to the incessant triangular conflicts between Malacca, Acheh and Johore which prevented the Portuguese from gaining close and permanent control over the flows of trade through the Strait. A.B. Lapian, *The maritime network in the 14th century*, paper to the SPAFA workshop, Jakarta, Nov. 1984.

27. The economic relations between Manila and Hong Kong are much closer than those between the Philippines generally and Malaysia, Singapore or Indonesia, all of which have been members of ASEAN since 1967.

Batavia and the Dutch East Indies (18th–20th centuries)

The Dutch were set to profit from the attachment of Portugal to the Spanish state in 1580 and the closure to foreigners in 1594 of the port of Lisbon, where they had obtained their supplies of spices. They now proceeded to conquer the sea routes that had been identified by the earliest colonists.[28] As heirs of the mercantile tradition of the Hanseatic cities, they set up the East India Company (VOC) in 1602, and from 1616 onwards occupied some fifteen trading posts east of Malacca which the Portuguese had continued to occupy.

Jan Pieterszoon Coen, appointed governor-general of the Dutch Indies in 1614, had the single ambition of re-building a commercial empire on the model of Srivijaya and Malacca. With his establishment of the new trading centre of Batavia in 1619 on the site of the old native fort of Jacatra, he began a new phase of Dutch expansion in South-East Asia, based essentially on trade. Batavia was inserted at the heart of a polity which sought to achieve a tight control over the sea lanes by means of a network of fortified trading stations scattered through the archipelago. It used this instrument of control in preference to dominance of the interior of the islands, which did not form part of Dutch policy till the mid-19th century at the earliest.[29]

Batavia was now a magnet for all the most important commercial transactions — a tendency which could only increase when the Dutch captured Malacca from the Portuguese in 1641. It was on the basis of their possession of these two ports, dominating the archipelago and the Straits, that the Dutch adopted the 'Statutes of Batavia' in 1642, which claimed a total commercial monopoly over trade between Europe and the Dutch Indies and within the region. This objective was largely fulfilled, since the Dutch put in place a military-industrial system

28. The first expedition of Cornelis Houtman, which was able to make use of maritime charts made by the Portuguese, reached the Sunda Strait. For their part, Francis Drake and Cavendish made the voyage to Ternate in 1577–9, but the English were driven out by the Dutch (the massacre of Amboina in 1623). A sort of *status quo* then became established up to the end of the 18th century. The Dutch decided to settle Java, while the British contemplated the extension of their influence in India as a first move, except for its trading posts of Bantam and Bencoolen.

29. Cowan, op. cit., p. 7, and Robequain (62), p. 13. For this period one should consult C.R. Boxer, *The Dutch sea-borne empire, 1600–1800*, London: Hutchinson, 1965; Kristof Glamann, *Dutch-Asiatic trade, 1620–1740*, The Hague: Nijhoff, 1958; and Meilinck Roelofsz, *Asian trade and European influence in the Indonesian archipelago, 1500–1630*, The Hague: Nijhoff, 1962.

erior to any that had been attempted earlier by the Portuguese.[30]
ᵉ Islamised trading emporia, which scored notable successes in their
lings with the first colonists, entered a phase of relative stagnation
r 1660, and in some cases the process of disintegration went so far
: they were compelled to make various concessions to the Europeans.
ʰe following century saw the growth of a keen rivalry between the
:ch and the English. In 1784 the treaty of Paris ended the exclusive
ᵐercial monopoly of the Dutch in the Indian Ocean. The British
ved in Penang in 1786 and from that year till 1816 were in effective
trol of the Dutch Indies; in 1798 the Dutch East India Company
ed to exist. With these events a second phase in the colonisation of
Indies began, and a certain equilibrium returned to the traditional
ᵉs of the region.[31] Of the Dutch, Charles Cowan has written:
ᵉy gradually transformed their system into a Java-based polity,
ᶜentrating more and more on the exploitation of Java's natural
urces. . . . We may perhaps say that they had exchanged the mantle
rivijaya and Malacca for that of Majapahit. In these circumstances
ᵉ appeared at the end of the century a new Straits maritime system,
ɔrmidable a competitor to the Dutch Java-based polity as Malacca
been previously to Majapahit. This new system was centred on the
ish settlements of Penang and (after 1819) of Singapore.'[32]
fter the initial, commercial dominance of the Dutch had declined,
ᵢ symbiotic economic systems took their place in the 19th century.
:se were both complementary and in rivalry with eachother, and
sistent with the historical evolution of the Malay world. The Dutch,
their part, colonised the agricultural lands of the Javanese interior,
ing henceforward on a system of forced cultivation (devised by Van
Bosch), from which the surplus was exported through Batavia. The
:ish, on the other hand, returned to ᵗhe early practices of the Dutch
the mercantile tradition of Portugal, Malacca and Srivijaya by
anising a single emporium out of the three colonies on the Straits:

'In effect such a policy was a logical continuation of the traditional monopolistic
control exerted in turn by Sri Vijaya, Malacca and the Portuguese over the
maritime commerce passing between the Indian Ocean and the South China Sea,
though the Dutch flow of trade was more effectively controlled, thanks to their
command over major sources of the principal commodities involved' (Fisher
[120], p. 137). See also Holden Fuber (120), p. 19, and P. Devillers *et al.* (22),
pp. 156–258.
. Nicholas Tarling (71).
. Cowan, op. cit., p. 8.

Penang, Singapore and Malacca. The rise of this new entity owed much to the doctrines of free trade and free navigation.[33]

This situation was ratified by the Anglo-Dutch treaty signed in London in 1824, which exchanged the British possessions in Sumatra for the Dutch ones, such as Malacca, on the Malay peninsula. Now, for the first time, a clearly defined frontier divided the differing legal and political systems of the peninsula and the archipelago, a difference also manifested in their respective economic systems: the one predominantly maritime and commercial and the other wedded to the land and to agriculture.

This distinction was already deeply rooted in the history of the region, and once again it was playing a crucial role. It remains, even today, the key to understanding the essential nature of economic relations in the Malay world, and particularly those between Singapore and Indonesia.

The rise of Britain's South-East Asian empire: the succession of 'world economy' systems

Besides this dualistic typology of state formation as the determinant of South-East Asia's evolution, there are other analytical criteria for assessing how commercial emporia have functioned down the ages. Before we turn to the characteristics of Singapore in their own right, we can glean from the structure of the British empire and even its European predecessors some material for preliminary consideration of how these vast 'world economies' worked, and the devolved role of trading emporia in this context.[34]

Throughout history, economic systems have been created, with their centres in great mercantile capitals like Venice, Genoa, Lisbon, Bruges, Amsterdam and London, but with vital chains of warehouses, of which certain links were in South-East Asia. One world economy — i.e. 'an economically autonomous piece of the planet, essentially self-sufficient and with its external links and its trade conferring an organic unity upon it' (F. Braudel) — followed another in succession.

Whether one is talking of Venetian and Arab power turning to the riches of the East, or the Portuguese and Dutch colonial empires exporting the model of the first European maritime centres, or the

---

33. 'For some decades, the Dutch combined two roles that had been exercised separately in the past by competing poles of power based on alternative economic systems' (Leifer [156], p. 9).
34. F. Braudel (8).

British empire built on a string of trading posts extending from the Mediterranean to South-East Asia and China, each of these world economies has strewn the great sea routes — their nervous systems — with local emporia of which the latest to appear in the Malay world was Singapore.[35]

With the passage of time, these world empires were replaced by 'world cities' entities whose entire vocation was international — as subsidiary centres and staging-posts in a process of wealth accumulation, through which the main currents of goods, capital, news and human talent flowed. Singapore, at once a world staging-post (formerly for the business of the British empire and today for that of Japan, the United States and Europe as a whole) and a regional centre (of the Malay world and, today, of ASEAN), is hemmed in by a hierarchy of zones in varying stages of economic development, which — to varying degrees — trade with it. It was thus with Palembang and Malacca in earlier times. The whole ensemble constitutes a regional economy tending in the direction of a form of integration of its own, at the same time as taking its place in a world economy which largely transcends national frontiers.[36]

Beyond all these concepts and the specific nature of Singapore, it may be said that the regional space and the regional division of economic activities are organised between a major urban metropolis (a powerful magnet for regional development), secondary cities (other emporia and regional communication centres) and peripheral zones (remote and relatively inaccessible agrarian hinterlands little affected by the rise of the regional metropolis and its satellites).[37]

This analytical framework underpins any examination of Singapore's attributes as a colony and of the relations at the present time between the city-state, ASEAN and the rest of the world.

The founding of Singapore and the expansion of a new commercial emporium, 1819–1965

Raffles and the choice of Singapore

The development of British trade with China at the end of the 18th century and the need to protect it against the Dutch navy and local

35. 'In a strategic sense the parallel with the Mediterranean sea later in the century is suggestive, and the series of British footholds at Penang, Singapore, Labuan and Hong Kong may be compared with Gibraltar, Malta, Suez and Aden' (Fisher [26], p. 85).
36. I. Wallerstein (79).
37. J.-C. Perrin (191), p. 85.

pirates served as a signal to Britain of the urgent necessity for it to establish a staging-post on the long sea route between India and Canton. Penang was the first such port to be founded– it was ceded by the sultan of Kedah to Francis Light in 1786 — but it was too far from the Malacca Strait to have the advantages which the East India Company in London required. Taking advantage of the eclipse of Dutch power in Java since 1795 and the decline in Anglo-Dutch rivalry, the governor-general of India, the Marquis of Hastings, took possession of the southern extremity of the Malay peninsula and entrusted Thomas Stamford Raffles, governor of Bencoolen and formerly (1811–16) lieutenant-governor of Java, with the mission of founding a new trading post at the most central point possible in the neighbourhood of the Strait. This was to be done without provoking the slightest armed conflict with the Dutch, who had just installed themselves in the Riau islands.[38]

On 28 January 1819, Raffles, who was familiar with the legend of Tumasik, and could appreciate its remarkable geostrategic position, disembarked at Singapore. After involving himself in a succession dispute in the sultanate of Johore, in which he assisted Sultan Hussein to gain the throne, he negotiated an agreement which permitted him to establish a trading post in the island. There were vehement protests from the Dutch, but Lord Castelreagh and influential circles in the City of London were aware of its importance and refused to evacuate it; a close collaborator of Raffles, named Farquhar, was appointed as the first resident-general in Singapore (1819–23), under the authority of the former. The inspiration for Raffles's commercial ambitions came both from the ancient emporia of the region and from Britain's contemporary imperial ambitions. He wrote in 1819 to the governor-general in Calcutta: 'What Malta is in the West, that may Singapore become in the East.'

The year 1824 proved decisive. As we have already seen, the British and the Dutch shared out the Malay world between them in the treaty of London — which exchanged Bencoolen for Malacca. At the frontier of these two spheres of colonial power, and at the meeting-point of great sea routes, the sultan of Johore ceded Singapore island to Britain with a ten-mile belt of territorial waters around it.

38. G.S. Graham (32) and D.G.E. Hall, *From Mergui to Singapore, 1689–1819*, paper to the Siam Society, Bangkok, Sept. 1952. Sir Thomas Raffles has been the subject of a number of works, e.g. M. Collis (18); Emily Hahn (33); H. Marks (49); K.G. Tregonning, *The British in Malaya, 1786–1826*, Tucson: Univ. of Arizona Press, 1965; and C.E. Wurzburg (84).

From that time onwards, the status of the island closely reflected its economic rise. Of the three colonies in the Strait, Singapore alone had the capacity to receive large ships: Penang had no timber, and Malacca was silting up. In 1832 Singapore took the place of Penang as the seat of the governor.[39] It continued to be administered from Calcutta by the East India Company up till 1858, and then by the India Office in London till 1867. In that year it finally assumed the direction of the three colonies, now styled Crown Colonies and under the direct authority of the Colonial Office. In that capacity it directed the colonisation of the interior of the Malay peninsula during the second half of the 19th century, just as the Dutch did in Java.

The birth of a regional and international economic crossroads

The economic history of Singapore could be summarised in an impressive series of statistics and achievements. Its rapid growth recalls the development of the earlier emporia, and prefigures that of the independent republic from 1965 onwards.[40]

In 1825–40, the sheltered deep-water harbour established itself as a rendez-vous for large European merchant vessels and the boats of Chinese and other local owners, the former with goods from India (textiles, arms, opium) for redistribution in the region, and the latter with spices, silks, tropical woods, tea and tin. Sailing ships proceeding both to and from Singapore benefited from the seasonal rhythm of the monsoon winds, and gave a truly complementary character to the exchange of goods, making use of the two circuits: the Europe-India-China run and the regional inshore network.[41]

In agreement with the East India Company, Raffles and his successor Crawfurd founded in Singapore a free port that was destined to loosen the trading monopoly of Batavia and attract the greatest possible number of traders of all nationalities.[42] Till 1853 no tax was levied on commercial transactions, the authorities obtaining the greater part of their revenue from the consumption of opium. The first duties based on tonnage and the stamping of harbour documents were introduced in 1853–63, and these remained modest. At the same time, the Dutch

39. Charles D. Cowan, 'Early Penang and the rise of Singapore', *JMBRAS*, XXIII (1950), pp. 113–203.
40. K.R. Hall (35), p. 60.
41. Tan Ding Eing (70), pp. 65–6; C.A. Trocki (76).
42. C.B. Buckley (10); John Hall-Jones (36).

discriminated strongly against goods which had passed through
Singapore before being landed in Batavia, and excluded foreign citizens
from free access to Sumatra, Borneo and Celebes. This policy encouraged a major contraband trade, which continues to this day and is a
perpetual bone of contention between Singapore and Indonesia.

   This confrontation illustrates the competition not only between two
rival empires in the 19th century, but also — as between that pair of
irreconcilable opposites, Singapore and Batavia — two economic concepts: on the one hand, free trade in the service of a country in the process
of industrialisation, hungry both for primary products and for outlets,
and on the other hand, the protectionist trading system of the Dutch
who, in analogous ways, reproduced the errors of their predecessors the
Portuguese, and withdrew within their own frontiers (e.g. with large-
scale cultivation in Java).[43] This dichotomy in the economic history of
the Malay world in the 19th and 20th centuries, anticipated by differing
state structures of the pre-colonial period, encouraged the development
of deep divergences in the region, reaching right to the very heart of
ASEAN at the present time — notably between Singapore and
Indonesia.

   The existence of a free port and a policy of laissez-faire gave an
immediate stimulus to Singapore's mercantile economy, to which the
island's demographic evolution bore eloquent witness: from 15,000
inhabitants in 1824 to more than 50,000 in 1850 (the village seen by
Raffles in 1819 had had a population of about 150 fishermen). In the
1830s, fully half of the goods carried through the Strait of Malacca also
passed through the control of the island authorities, and Singapore
enjoyed a corresponding boom. The volume of this traffic was swollen
by the opening up of China, through the Nanking treaty of 1841 and
the Opium Wars, and the creation of new free ports in Hong Kong,
Labuan and Makassar. Thus Singapore, with no significant manufacturing industry till 1959–63, made its mark on the economic scene in
the region purely through its dynamic performance in the commercial
and tertiary sectors.

   As regards communications and transport, the opening of the Suez
canal in 1869 gave a boost to steam navigation, and Singapore became
the premier staging-post in South-East Asia, providing water and coal,
and docks, unloading jetties and repair yards capable of handling several
dozen ships at one time (in 1870 there were 3,000 harbour buildings).

---

43. S. Arasaratnam, 'Monopoly and free trade in Dutch-Asian commercial debate . . .
    within the VOC', *JSEAS*, Mar. 73, pp. 1–15.

The travelling time from London had been halved, and numerous shipping lines established services on the island.[44] The telegraph played a part in this revolution: links with Batavia and Calcutta were inaugurated in 1859 and 1870 respectively. Thenceforward commerce in Singapore grew in tandem with the development of communications.

Even if Singapore had to yield pride of place to Hong Kong where exchange with China was concerned, its entrepot trade still made progress with forty-three agency houses (twenty were British), handling most flows of goods after 1846. Banks and chambers of commerce, both European and Chinese, made their appearance, and thus were born the local financial empires with branches reaching throughout the whole region.[45]

In the later nineteenth century, the colonisation of the Malay peninsula (1874–1909) continued Britain's interrupted territorial growth in the region, and Singapore became the outpost for London's financial interests involved in the exploitation of the tin and natural rubber production of the interior. To coal storage in the port was now added petroleum, for which the demand grew steadily during the First World War.

As a result of the often indispensable intermediary role played by the Chinese merchants of Singapore between the European dealers and the indigenous peoples of the region, the development of Malaya's natural wealth was accompanied by a massive influx of Chinese labourers (mainly Hokkien, Teochew, Cantonese and Hakka). Singapore organised and oversaw these migratory movements into the hinterland:[46] this process gave birth to the division, at all levels, between the predominantly Chinese urban civilisation of Singapore, with its links to mining sites, plantations and the ports handling the flow of exports (Ipoh, Taiping, Kuala Lumpur, Georgetown, Butterworth, Port Swettenham, Malacca, Port Weld) and tne world of the traditional rural economy in the rest of the peninsula, where the population was mainly Malay.[47]

At the same time, like Malacca in an earlier age, Singapore became

44. In 1837, the following companies were involved: Oriental Steam Navigation Co., Norddeutscher Lloyd, Messageries, Dutch Rotterdam Lloyd, East India Steamship Co., Indo-China Navigation Co., China Navigation Co. and Ho Hang Co.
45. The Straits Chinese Association and the Chinese Chamber of Commerce were founded in 1900 and 1906 respectively.
46. Joyce Ee, 'Chinese Migration to Singapore, 1896–1941', *JSEAH*, 2 (1961), pp. 33–51.
47. Dupuis (23), pp. 48–51.

a cultural centre in the region, a place where Arab and Malay merchants and men of learning came together, from which pilgrims set out for Mecca, where Islamic religious literature was distributed, where Malay sultans and chiefs took refuge and engaged in political intrigue, and where close ties were maintained with the Kuomintang party in China.[48]

In the years following the First World War, Singapore failed to recover its former prosperity. Being dependent on a British economy weakened by four years of conflict in Europe and then by the effects of the economic crisis of 1929–32, which eroded the principles of free trade (through the adoption of the new imperial system of trade preferences) and free immigration, its recovery was long delayed. However, a large-scale programme of public investment went some way at least towards mitigating the bad turn events had taken. In order to guarantee the security of the British possessions in South-East Asia and respond to Japanese expansionist tendencies, the imperial conference which took place in 1921 decided to build a powerful naval base in Singapore. The project was completed twenty years later, just as air transport was coming fully into its own; Singapore's airport was opened in 1937. Right up to 1965–70, these infrastructural installations continued to be a major centre of activity, and reinforced Singapore's position as a regional and international crossroads.

The stakes for survival and viability: the experience of 1938–45 and 1963–65

Rapid, externally-conditioned economic development and then a sudden and usually definitive decline due to external changes have characterised the rise and fall of many commercial emporia. Like Srivijaya and Malacca, ancient Tumasik — destroyed by the intervention first of Siam and then of Portugal — was not immune to this historical law. The example of Singapore, in its turn, raises similar questions to those presented by the fate of its vanished predecessors.

Many observers since the early nineteenth century have believed the basis and *modus operandi* of this little colony to be transitory. The threat posed by the Dutch became less immediate after 1824, but a fear inspired

---

48. Singapore was a magnet for the wealth of rich Overseas Chinese merchants. Sun Yat Sen visited the island no less than eight times between 1900 and 1910, and established a branch of the Kuomintang there in 1912. Ho Chi Minh, in his turn, founded the Malay Communist Party in Singapore in 1930.

by the opening of other free ports in South-East Asia and in the Far East (notably Hong Kong), and by the possible building of a canal across the isthmus in southern Siam, took its place. However, these factors had the effect of stimulating Singapore's development.

The absence of agriculture because of insufficient space, and of industry because no workforce or vocation for manufacturing existed, bred anxiety: Singapore's dependence on the outside world and on imports was considered excessive and therefore a danger.[49] The absence, too, of any military base (except the modest Fort Canning, built in 1860) to reduce its vulnerability as an island, together with internal disorder (caused by the weak interventionism of the authorities in public housing, by financial red-tape, and by the Chinese secret societies whose machinations long remained unchecked), added to this first wave of anxiety about the viability of Singapore. Of course the formidable economic expansion of the second half of the nineteenth century swept these doubts away.[50]

However, if certain doubts were removed with the passage of time — with the help, especially, of the building of the British naval base and the growth of a more diversified socio-economic system — others remained. These were of a kind which are inherent in the conditions which influence the destiny of commercial emporia, and in Singapore's case they have reappeared throughout its history. This fact is well illustrated by the Japanese occupation and the difficult years around the time of independence.[51]

The Japanese occupation

Singapore cannot be viewed in isolation from its external environment, as is well exemplified by its vulnerability in the face of Japanese expansionism in 1941–2. In spite of having fortifications, completed in great haste in 1932–41 but believed to be impregnable, the port of Singapore none the less did not have a fleet to defend it or any aerial defence. At the last moment, London sent out two of the mightiest capital ships of the Royal Navy, the *Prince of Wales* and the *Repulse*, without considering the danger to which they were exposed from the Japanese air force, which sank both of them. London also did not envisage the possibility of a Japanese invasion — not by sea but from the Johore jungle which was only separated by a narrow stretch of water from the

49. Fisher (26), p. 147.
50. Mary Turnbull, (78), pp. 92, 155, 332.
51. Turnbull, ibid., p. 332.

island's virtually undefended northern shore. On February 15, 1942, the pearl of the British empire in South-East Asia fell to the Japanese without a struggle.

The Times in London carried the headline 'More than the evacuation of a town, it was the end of an era'.[52] That truth was finally recognised by Britain three decades later, in 1969–71, when it shut down the naval base. This bitter demonstration of the fragility of Singapore made a profound impression at the time on several people. One was Winston Churchill, who called it 'one of the greatest disasters in British history', and another was Lee Kuan Yew. Once Lee attained power, he was to show that he had learned the lessons of 1942 in regard to his defence policy.[53]

Another lesson came from the fact that between 1942 and 1945 the Japanese conquerors placed Syonan (as they called Singapore) at the centre of their 'Co-prosperity Sphere' in South-East Asia. As the new masters of the island, they knew how to benefit from its exceptional geographical situation and obtain the collaboration of the Overseas Chinese who, like the merchants of ancient Malacca, were able to adapt themselves to political changes as one invader was succeeded by another.[54] Apart from the mythical concept of trying to transform Singapore into a self-sufficient economy (the city suffered severe food shortages during the war), the Japanese chose Syonan as the base for their administrative and military command in Malaya (to which they attached Sumatra) and throughout the region. The visit of Prime Minister Tojo in 1943 confirmed Singapore as the cornerstone in the construction of 'Grand East Asia' and as the communications centre for the New Order.[55]

The troubled years leading to independence, 1963–65
The years immediately before independence offer another example of the nature of the challenges which can imperil the survival and viability of this emporium. When Britain granted Singapore an autonomous

52. V. Thomson, *Post mortem on Malaya*, New York: Macmillan, 1943, p. 7, and Ph. Richer (61), p. 85.
53. 'We decided that from then on our lives should be ours to decide, that we should not be the pawn and playthings of foreign powers . . . Such was their [the Japanese] blindness and brutality. They never knew what they did to a whole generation like me' (Lee Kuan Yew in Alex Josey [439], pp. 29 & 41).
54. Turnbull (78), p. 205.
55. F.C. Jones, *Japan's new order in Southeast Asia, 1937–45*, London: OUP, 1954, p. 383, which quotes the *Syonan Tribune* of 6 July 43. Turnbull (78), p. 213.

status in June 1959, this marked the starting-point of a new period of disturbance against the backdrop of the anti-Communist state of emergency (in force since 1948) and the riots of 1956 which had seriously threatened the internal security of the island.

In 1961, the moderate wing of the People's Action Party (PAP), led by Lee Kuan Yew (Chief Minister since the elections of May 1959), had to face a new onslaught from the left and a split in the party when the left-wing Barisan Socialis party broke away in May of that year and joined the opposition. Fearing that the Communists would try to seize power, the Prime Minister of Malaya, Tunku Abdul Rahman, proposed on May 26, with support from London, a grand federation of Malaysia — to include Singapore so that the island should no longer be at the mercy of political developments which could destroy its flourishing economy.[56] Events kept up a steady pressure on the work of the Cobbold Commission, which had the task of seeing this project through: in a referendum in September 1962, the electorate of Singapore decided in favour of fusion, and Lee Kuan Yew proceeded in February 1963 to have the leaders of Barisan Socialis arrested. Tunku Abdul Rahman rejected the proposal of a common market between Malaya and Singapore, and demanded that Sabah and Sarawak (in northern Borneo) be included in the future federation in order to avoid the Chinese forming the majority of its population, as would happen if it consisted of peninsular Malaya and Singapore alone.[57]

Malaysia, which came into existence on September 16, 1963, seemed to provide Singapore with the framework for a new stability, internally and externally. However, the respite did not last long: the policy of confrontation pursued by President Sukarno of Indonesia from 1963 till 1966, combined with Singapore's withdrawal from the federation when it declared its independence on August 9, 1965, intensified the problem of the emporium's survival to a degree unprecedented in its entire history.

Confrontation

In June 1963, Indonesia announced that it did not accept the 'neo-colonial' creation of Malaysia. Some months later, for reasons connected with both foreign relations and internal politics, Sukarno carried on a semi-armed confrontation consisting of regular attacks and acts of infiltration by Indonesian soldiers and agents directed against Sarawak and

56. Peter Boyce (255).
57. Dick Wilson (230), p. 9.

the west coast of the Malay peninsula. As well as providing under-cover support to the Communist opposition, and sending commandos to sabotage Singapore's harbour installations, Indonesia decreed a commercial boycott, which led to a steep decline in Singapore's entrepot activities and a noticeable falling-off of foreign investment.[58]

Although it only lasted a short time, this experience left deep scars. The leaders of the ruling PAP, led by Lee Kuan Yew, were now acutely conscious of how precarious were Singapore's traditional commercial functions, and thus of the need to diversify the economy. In the political field, they saw with stark clarity how vulnerable the island was to any hostile move by its neighbours.[59]

Separation

Lee Kuan Yew and his close collaborators, most of whom had been born in Malaya, remained convinced that the destiny of Singapore was inseparable from the economic and political life of the peninsula, after a shared colonial experience lasting more than a century. Any other solution appeared to them inconceivable.

The separation, which happened in spite of these objections in August 1964, had its origins in the many divisions which, from the very beginning, opened up between Singapore and its Malay hinterland within the federation. But transcending this dichotomy between an urban, commercial society and a rural world still largely traditional in its outlook was the irreconcilable division between Malay and Chinese, a veritable catalyst of all oppositions. This exploded in earnest when the PAP stated its intention of fielding candidates in the federal elections of 1964, standing for multiracialism and anti-Communism, throughout the peninsula against Tunku Abdul Rahman's Alliance Party. The latter was dominated by the United Malay National Association (UMNO) and supported by the minority Malayan Chinese Association (MCA).[60]

At no time did Lee Kuan Yew envisage the eventual independence of Singapore: 'It is a political, economic and geopolitical absurdity. . . . Our chances of survival are ten times higher if we form part of a Greater

---

58. M. Leifer (320), p. 81.
59. C.E. Morrison & Suhrke (335), pp. 170–91.
60. On the federation and Singapore's withdrawal, see S.S. Bedlington (251); Chan Heng Chee (419); N.M.H. Fletcher, *The separation of Singapore from Malaysia*, Ithaca: Cornell UP, 1967; W. Hanna, *The separation of Singapore from Malaysia*, New York: American Univ. Field Staff Reports, SE Asian series 13/21, vol. XIII; R.C.H. McKie, *The emergence of Malaysia*, Westport: Greenwood Press, 1973.

Malaysia than if we stay on our own.'[61] However, the communal riots which cost twenty-three lives in Singapore in June and September 1964, and the fear that they would leave a bloody trail across the whole peninsula, were a factor that served to bring about Singapore's ultimate ejection from the federation in August 1965.[62]

When this last actually occured,[63] Lee Kuan Yew — for a few hours and perhaps for the only time in his long and brilliant political career — was out of his depth: it was difficult for him seriously to imagine Singapore remaining viable if its political frontiers were to become conterminous with its geographical ones. During the night of August 9–10, 1965, he said on the radio: 'For me it is a moment of anguish because all my adult life, I have believed in the merger and unity of these two territories.'[64]

Several factors — including the continuation of the British presence in Singapore and the important role played by the economic functions of the port for the surrounding region — explain why the Indonesian confrontation campaign failed. The expulsion of Singapore from the federation did not alter the close interdependence between it and Indonesia.[65]

The small new republic now found itself called upon to take up the most formidable challenge it had ever had to face during its entire existence as a commercial entrepot, and that without delay. Now that it was politically independent but none the less inseparable from its traditional hinterland, Malaysia and Indonesia, how was its economic viability to be guaranteed? How would these neighbours be able to

61. Josey (439), pp. 159 & 189.
62. 'We dreamt of Singapore in connection with Malaysia as what New York is to America but little did we realize what the leaders of the PAP had in mind was a share in the running of Malaysia' (Tunku Abdul Rahman, *Sunday Times*, 18 Apr. 1965). 'This communal issue and the danger of widespread communal violence was apparently the chief reason why the Tengku decided on the separation' (K. Wilairat, 'Singapore's foreign policy: . . .' unpubl. Ph.D. thesis, Georgetown Univ., Washington, DC, p. 121). There is nothing in the post-independence development of the former British holdings in maritime Southeast Asia that is not ultimately related to the fears and hatreds generated by communal divisions' (Lea E. Williams (81), p. 247).
63. 'An Agreement relating to the separation of Singapore from Malaysia as an independent sovereign state', *Singapore Gazette Govt. Extraordinary*, II 66 (9 Aug. 1965).
64. Lee Kuan Yew's radio broadcast at midnight on 9–10 Aug. 1965 (Josey [439], p. 284).
65. Wilson [230], pp. 10–11.

accept, as a permanent fixture, this little Chinese enclave — and a sovereign one — in the very heart of the Malay world? This was the big question, straddling politics and economics, to which those in charge of Singapore's destiny strove tirelessly to find an answer from 9 August 1965 onwards.

Part I
THE REGIONAL FUNCTION OF THE SINGAPORE ECONOMY

1

THE TRADING CROSSROADS OF SOUTH-EAST ASIA

Singapore is a major crossroads of international trade. The figures speak for themselves: throughout the period 1965–87, its external trade has represented on average more than three times its Gross National Product (GNP).[1] This is equivalent in value to a quarter of the foreign trade of France and more than the whole for the People's Republic of China in 1984, for example.

If, as we have seen, the commercial functions of Singapore today correspond closely to its historic vocation as an emporium up to the time of its independence, they remain the area of its activity which, above all others, makes its economic role in South-East Asia truly important.

Singapore's integration in ASEAN's trade

Singapore's dominant position at the commercial heart of ASEAN is manifested in two ways. The island carries a great deal of weight in the exchanges that take place within ASEAN, but it also acts as a channel for a considerable part of the flows between ASEAN and the rest of the world; it finds itself part of an intricate network of economic relations at once intra- and extra-regional. In other words, if one is to investigate the structures and evolution of ASEAN's external commerce, it is above all necessary to analyse Singapore's position within this regional grouping.[2]

Using the statistical data of 1987 as a basis, one can observe several

---

1. Compared (in 1984) with 1.67, 0.89 and 0.67 times respectively for Hong Kong, Taiwan and South Korea.
2. R. de Koninck, 'L'accélération de l'intégration du commerce extérieur des pays de l'ASEAN au marché mondial', *Etudes Internationales*, XI, 1 (Mar. 1980), pp. 43–63.

SINGAPORE'S EXTERNAL TRADE, 1960–87 (S$ millions[1] and %)

	1960	%	1965	%	1970	%	1975	%	1980	%	1984	%	1987	%
S.E. Asia	4,044	51	2,873	42	4,096	30	8,689	25	25,324	25	36,542	29	25,909	20
ASEAN[2]	2,777	35	2,732	40	3,489	25	8,079	23	24,765	25	35,960	29	24,963	19
N.E. Asia[3]	866	11	1,077	16	2,918	21	7,329	21	21,959	22	28,375	23	37,350	29
Japan	455	6	533	8	1,820	13	4,667	13	12,501	13	16,025	13	19,479	15
Hong Kong	150	2	242	4	382	3	1,365	4	4,251	4	4,457	4	5,617	4
N. America	462	6	363	5	1,439	11	5,031	14	13,065	13	19,918	16	25,596	20
U.S.A.	398	5	318	5	1,342	10	4,799	14	12,509	13	19,215	15	24,757	19
S. Asia[4]	148	2	129	2	215	2	542	1	2,837	3	3,606	3	3,385	3
W. Europe	1,407	18	1,273	19	2,216	16	5,516	16	13,023	13	13,136	10	18,014	14
E.C.	1,215	15	1,074	16	1,946	14	4,393	13	10,648	11	11,119	9	15,591	12
W. Asia	222	3	360	5	801	6	4,841	14	14,207	14	14,622	12	10,048	8
Saudi Arabia	16	–	33	–	92	1	1,881	5	7,337	7	7,051	6	3,414	3
Oceania	320	4	339	5	614	4	1,913	6	4,635	5	4,701	4	4,097	3
Australia	241	3	260	4	501	4	1,208	3	2,833	3	3,253	3	2,963	2
Rest of the world	433	5	420	6	1,400	10	1,168	3	4,584	5	4,341	3	4,278	3
Total	7,922	100	6,834	100	13,699	100	34,628	100	99,637	100	125,242	100	128,681	100

1. In 1987, US$1 = S$2.01.
2. Includes official Indonesian statistics.
3. Comprising Hong Kong, Japan, China, Taiwan, S. Korea, N. Korea and Macau.
4. Comprising India, Pakistan, Sri Lanka, Bangladesh, Maldives, Nepal.

Source: Singapore Trade Statistics and IMF Directorate of Trade.

SINGAPORE/ASEAN TRADE, 1960–87

(S$ millions and %)

	Indonesia			Malaysia			Philippines			Thailand			Brunei			Singapore/ASEAN		
	Imp.	Exp.	Tot.	Imp.	Exp.	Tot.	Imp.	Exp.	Tot.	Imp.	Exp.	Tot.	Imp.	Exp.	Tot.	Imp.	Exp.	Tot.
1960	327	33	360	1,075	1,003	2,078	2	58	60	146	107	253	6	21	27	1,554	1,222	2,777
	(21)	(3)	(13)	(69)	(82)	(75)	(–)	(4)	(2)	(9)	(9)	(9)	(–)	(1)	(1)	(100)	(100)	(100)
1965	17	–	17	1,109	1,220	2,329	9	13	23	147	68	215	2	20	22	1,284	1,321	2,605
	(1)	–	(1)	(86)	(92)	(89)	(1)	(1)	(1)	(11)	(15)	(8)	(–)	(2)	(1)	(100)	(100)	(100)
1970	526	174	700	1,404	1,040	2,443	27	13	40	149	157	306	2	78	79	2,108	1,462	3,570
	(25)	(12)	(20)	(67)	(71)	(68)	(1)	(1)	(1)	(7)	(11)	(9)	(–)	(2)	(2)	(100)	(100)	(100)
1975	1,500	814	2,314	2,240	2,188	4,427	68	136	204	406	445	852	6	280	286	4,219	3,823	8,082
	(35)	(21)	(29)	(53)	(57)	(54)	(2)	(3)	(2)	(10)	(12)	(11)	(–)	(5)	(4)	(100)	(100)	(100)
1980	4,967	1,873	6,840	7,116	6,218	13,334	160	586	746	1,080	1,809	2,829	424	592	1,016	13,687	11,078	24,765
	(36)	(17)	(28)	(52)	(56)	(54)	(1)	(5)	(3)	(8)	(16)	(11)	(3)	(5)	(4)	(100)	(100)	(100)
1983	6,692	7,414	14,106	8,640	8,123	16,760	271	890	1,161	1,068	1,995	3,063	404	746	1,150	17,075	19,170	36,241
	(39)	(39)	(39)	(51)	(42)	(46)	(2)	(5)	(3)	(6)	(10)	(8)	(2)	(4)	(3)	(100)	(100)	(100)
1984	6,582	6,710	13,291	9,180	8,324	17,503	395	441	836	1,350	2,458	3,809	415	627	1,042	17,923	18,560	36,483
	(37)	(36)	(36)	(51)	(45)	(48)	(2)	(2)	(2)	(8)	(13)	(10)	(2)	(3)	(3)	(100)	(100)	(100)
1987	2,027	3,800	5,127	9,447	13,245	22,692	376	877	1,253	2,136	2,553	4,689	877	708	985	14,263	20,483	34,439
	(14)	(15)	(15)	(66)	(65)	(66)	(3)	(4)	(3)	(15)	(12)	(14)	(2)	(3)	(3)	(100)	(100)	(100)

Source: Singapore Trade Statistics and IMF Directorate of Trade.

INTRA-ASEAN TRADE: 1970–87
(US$ millions and %)

	Total external trade					Intra-ASEAN trade				
	1970	1975	1980	1984	1987	1970	1975	1980	1984	1987
Singapore	4,287 (100)	13,851 (100)	43,390 (100)	52,737 (100)	66,227	1,152 (27)	3,232 (23)	11,811 (27)	14,793 (30)	15,096 (29)
Indonesia	2,110 (100)	11,872 (100)	32,742 (100)	35,761 (100)	25,960	310 (15)	1,147 (10)	4,110 (13)	4,282 (12)	2,534 (10)
Malaysia	3,088 (100)	7,331 (100)	23,778 (100)	30,435 (100)	29,676	643 (21)	1,457 (20)	4,553 (19)	7,262 (24)	6,356 (21)
Philippines	2,248 (100)	5,976 (100)	14,036 (100)	11,604 (100)	12,456	75 (3)	238 (4)	866 (6)	497 (4)	1,644 (13)
Thailand	2,008 (100)	5,397 (100)	15,719 (100)	17,748 (100)	25,072	148 (7)	466 (9)	2,165 (14)	2,688 (15)	3,101 (12)
Brunei	181 (100)	1,257 (100)	5,380 (100)	3,554 (100)	2,700	105 (58)	102 (8)	749 (14)	796 (22)	563 (21)
ASEAN total	13,922 (100)	45,684 (100)	135,045 (100)	151,839 (100)	162,091 (100)	2,433 (17)	6,642 (15)	24,254 (18)	30,318 (20)	29,294 (18)

Source: International Monetary Fund Directorate of Trade Statistics (Far East and Australasia).

	Trade with Singapore				
	1970	*1975*	*1980*	*1984*	*1987*
Indonesia	229	976	3,420	3,917	2,398
	(11)	(8)	(10)	(11)	(9)
Malaysia	469	1,074	3,745	5,435	4,977
	(15)	(15)	(16)	(18)	(17)
Philippines	12	53	246	321	429
	(−)	(1)	(2)	(3)	(3)
Thailand	62	267	1,102	1,438	2,056
	(3)	(5)	(7)	(8)	(8)
Brunei	26	94	486	500	322
	(14)	(7)	(9)	(14)	(12)
ASEAN total	798	2,464	7,999	11,611	10,182
	(6)	(5)	(6)	(8)	(6)

SINGAPORE'S EXTERNAL TRADE, BY PRODUCT
(S$ millions and %)

	1975				1980			
	Imp.	Exp.	Re-exp.	Tot.	Imp.	Exp.	Re-exp.	Tot.
Food	1,654	916	628	2,570	2,915	2,008	1,359	4,923
	(64)	(36)	(24)	(100)	(59)	(41)	(28)	(100)
Beverages, tobacco	130	41	15	171	276	157	55	433
	(76)	(24)	(9)	(100)	(64)	(36)	(13)	(100)
Primary products	1,229	1,694	1,326	2,923	3,417	4,700	3,579	8,117
	(42)	(58)	(45)	(100)	(42)	(58)	(44)	(100)
Energy	4,734	3,451	208	8,185	14,889	11,966	354	26,855
	(58)	(42)	(3)	(100)	(55)	(45)	(1)	(100)
Oils, fats	242	245	188	487	1,001	1,096	695	2,097
	(50)	(50)	(37)	(100)	(48)	(52)	(33)	(100)
Chemicals	1,120	476	267	1,596	2,687	1,419	839	4,106
	(70)	(30)	(17)	(100)	(65)	(35)	(20)	(100)
Manufrd. goods	3,510	1,087	595	4,597	7,237	3,442	1,979	10,679
	(76)	(24)	(13)	(100)	(68)	(32)	(19)	(100)
Infrastructural equipment and transport	5,046	2,895	1,201	7,941	15,504	11,089	4,450	26,593
	(64)	(36)	(15)	(100)	(58)	(42)	(17)	(100)
Various manufactured items	1,331	880	211	2,211	2,951	2,572	681	5,523
	(60)	(40)	(10)	(100)	(53)	(47)	(12)	(100)
Unclassified products & transactions	273	1,073	213	1,346	667	3,004	398	3,671
	(20)	(80)	(16)	(100)	(18)	(82)	(11)	(100)

Source: Singapore Trade Statistics, Department of Statistics.

	1984				1987			
	Imp.	Exp.	Re-exp.	Tot.	Imp.	Exp.	Re-exp.	Tot.
Food	4,158 (59)	2,895 (41)	2,376 (34)	7,053 (100)	3,952 (59)	2,717 (41)	1,986 (30)	6,669 (100)
Beverages, tobacco	461 (69)	210 (31)	107 (16)	671 (100)	595 (34)	1,148 (66)	971 (56)	1,743 (100)
Primary products	2,510 (42)	3,410 (58)	2,998 (51)	5,920 (100)	2,267 (43)	3,003 (57)	2,656 (50)	5,270 (100)
Energy	16,961 (56)	13,185 (44)	435 (1)	30,146 (100)	12,526 (56)	9,747 (44)	445 (20)	22,273 (100)
Oils, fats	1,436 (48)	1,541 (52)	868 (29)	2,977 (100)	792 (50)	796 (50)	191 (12)	1,588 (100)
Chemicals	3,096 (56)	2,464 (44)	1,093 (20)	5,560 (100)	4,082 (52)	3,762 (48)	1,402 (18)	7,844 (100)
Manufrd. goods	8,045 (69)	3,625 (31)	2,424 (21)	11,670 (100)	9,537 (68)	4,523 (32)	3,195 (23)	14,060 (100)
Infrastructural equipment and transport	19,420 (54)	16,865 (46)	5,852 (16)	36,285 (100)	27,534 (51)	26,274 (49)	8,457 (16)	53,888 (100)
Various manufactured items	4,197 (55)	3,408 (45)	1,127 (15)	7,605 (100)	6,054 (52)	5,556 (48)	1,868 (16)	11,610 (100)
Unclassified products & transactions	850 (19)	3,732 (81)	520 (11)	4,582 (100)	1,077 (24)	3,501 (76)	785 (17)	4,578 (100)

SINGAPORE'S RE-EXPORT TRADE, 1970–87
(S$ millions and %)

	1970 Total Export	%	1970 Total Re-export	%	1975 Total Export	%	1975 Total Re-export	%	1980 Total Export	%	1980 Total Re-export	%
S.E. Asia	1,661	35	963	33	3,320	26	1,995	38	9,571	23	5,122	36
ASEAN (excl. Indonesia)	1,210	25	879	30	2,769	21	1,765	34	9,205	22	4,268	30
N.E. Asia (incl. China)	709	15	361	13	2,405	19	644	12	8,588	21	1,905	13
Japan	362	8	145	5	1,113	9	196	4	3,338	8	418	3
Hong Kong	194	4	71	2	937	7	185	4	3,196	8	525	4
N. America	584	12	369	13	1,901	15	657	13	5,555	13	1,337	9
U.S.A.	527	11	380	13	1,775	14	598	11	5,272	13	1,245	9
W. Europe	904	19	628	22	2,040	16	733	14	5,899	14	1,691	12
E.C.	740	16	525	18	1,709	13	621	12	5,081	12	1,337	9
W. Asia	104	2	67	2	633	5	264	5	2,476	6	968	7
Saudi Arabia	12	–	–	–	205	2	–	–	825	2	341	2
S. Asia	81	2	45	2	319	3	155	3	2,393	6	825	6
Oceania	227	5	106	4	1,163	9	272	5	3,252	8	405	3
Australia	160	3	–	–	637	5	205	4	1,671	4	298	2
Africa	137	3	68	2	433	3	180	3	1,916	5	984	7
Latin America	85	2	72	2	319	3	162	3	602	1	560	4
E. Europe and U.S.S.R.	233	5	203	7	225	2	156	3	1,241	3	447	3
Total (world)	4,756	100	2,882	100	12,758	100	5,218	100	41,493	100	14,244	100

Source: Singapore Trade Statistics.

	1984				1987			
	Total	Export %	Total	Re-export %	Total	Export %	Total	Re-export %
S.E. Asia	12,180	24	6,289	36	13,245	22	7,105	34
ASEAN (excl. Indonesia)	11,850	23	6,070	34	12,699	21	6,803	32
N.E. Asia (incl. China)	10,199	20	2,574	15	13,505	22	4,188	20
Japan	4,807	9	782	4	5,449	9	1,300	6
Hong Kong	3,176	6	863	5	3,815	6	1,274	6
N. America	10,677	21	2,446	14	15,179	25	2,589	12
U.S.A.	10,292	20	2,285	13	14,695	24	2,455	11
W. Europe	5,404	11	1,664	9	8,113	13	2,751	13
E.C.	4,980	9	1,564	9	7,353	12	2,461	12
W. Asia	3,422	7	1,738	10	1,933	3	917	4
Saudi Arabia	1,364	3	951	5	579	1	276	1
S. Asia	2,993	6	1,206	7	2,618	4	1,427	7
Oceania	2,916	6	610	3	2,525	4	700	3
Australia	1,751	3	458	3	1,650	3	1,328	6
Africa	1,500	3	482	3	–	–	–	–
Latin America	697	1	315	2	428	1	297	1
E. Europe and U.S.S.R.	875	2	307	2	613	1	359	2
Total (world)	50,863	100	17,631	100	60,268	100	21,194	100

distinct factors. First, Singapore's trade with ASEAN represents 30% of all its external trade, compared to 10–21% for each of the other member-states. Secondly, up till 1983–4 ASEAN was easily Singapore's foremost trading partner, ahead of the United States (14.5%), Japan (12.5%) and the European Community (8.6%); more recently, South-East Asia and North America have shared first place with 19% each, ahead of Japan (15%) and the EC (12%). Thirdly, 95% of Singapore's trade falls into two clearly defined compartments of about equal size: on the one hand, its trade with countries that are exporters of natural resources and/or the 'workshops' of ASEAN, North-East Asia (Hong Kong, South Korea and Taiwan), South Asia and the Middle East, and on the other hand, the industrialised countries (the United States, Japan and Western Europe).

Fourthly, of all trade among ASEAN members 79% passes through Singapore[3] and Singapore's trade with Malaysia and Indonesia accounts for 72% of its entire trade with ASEAN. And finally, of ASEAN's total external trade, Singapore accounts for 40%, Indonesia and Malaysia coming far behind with 16% and 18% respectively.

The functions of a regional entrepot: continuity and evolution

Entrepot trade — the role of commercial middleman at the heart of a Malay hinterland furnishing primary products and consuming manufactured goods — was the essential feature of Singapore's successful economic development during the colonial period. Up till 1960–5, 40% of its external commerce was still tied to Malaya and Indonesia, processing industry was still embryonic, and 70% of employment and 75% of revenue depended on the tertiary sector — linked either to the commercial and financial activities of the entrepot or to the British naval and air base which guaranteed its security.

While remaining statistically important, the entrepot function declined throughout the 1960s and '70s and, besides, underwent some radical changes.

Statistical evaluation

Because of its entrepot trade, Singapore's imports are registered either as re-exports pure and simple, or as being destined for re-exportation almost immediately. With such a definition, it should be possible to

---

3. Of the total external trade of the ASEAN countries, 21% was represented, in 1983, by intra-ASEAN trade, as against 14% in 1963.

evaluate this kind of interchange; however, a series of problems makes this exercise less straightforward than it seems.

First, imports destined for the entrepot do not always correspond, in either volume or value, with the expected re-exports; and it was only in 1976 that Singapore's official statistics began to include re-exports as a separate category among exports as a whole, whereas imports in transit only were not singled out at all.[4] Secondly, there is a moveable boundary between 'domestic exports' and 're-exports'. The latter can include simple re-exports, ingenious repacking of goods, incomplete assembly of parts, and 'paper transactions'. To this should be added a vague classification of certain kinds of transaction, such as the distinction between 'manufactured goods' and 'miscellaneous manufactured goods'.[5]

As well as these difficulties, the official figures show that re-exports, which in 1960 accounted for 43% of Singapore's external trade (and 93.7% of total exports), subsequently took a dive — to 24% (and 61%) in 1970 and 16.4% (and 35.1%) in 1987. All the same, such results show that this type of business is far from defunct: sixty warehousing companies still practise it, and numerous studies by consultants have estimated that to obtain a true picture, one should add 10–15% to the foregoing figures.[6] Furthermore, since 1983–5 the growth of Singapore's external trade has depended partly on a revival in re-exports (of food products, vegetable oils, transport equipment and machinery), while natural rubber, manufactured goods and petroleum products either stagnated or declined.

Qualitative change

A double transformation has taken place both in the geographical nature of Singapore's trade and in the types of product traded. In place of the traditional relationships with the Malay peninsula, Java, Indochina, Siam and the European colonial powers, new networks have appeared, animated by the United States,[7] Japan, West Germany, Hong Kong and Taiwan, and extending as far as East Malaysia and throughout

4. Law Kak Ew, 'Singapore revised national accounts statistics', *Singapore Statistical Bulletin*, vol. 4 (1975), pp. 1–9; Rieger (195), pp. 4–5.
5. R. Wanigatunga, 'Some developments in the foreign trade of Singapore, 1957–76', *Commerce*, 18 (76/7), pp. 31–42; Chua Joon Eng and T. Morgan, 'The accuracy and external consistency of Singapore's trade statistics', *Malaysian Econ. Rev.*, 17, 1 (Apr. 72), pp. 8–24.
6. Industrial Market Research Ltd. (139), pp. 48–9.
7. 'Decline of UK trade influence in Singapore opens way for US to improve position as a supplier', *International Commerce*, 13 May 68, pp. 16–18.

all the principal islands of the Indonesian archipelago. Singapore's colonial vocation has been metamorphosed into a kind of international launching-pad, a global city, nourished by new economic powers and centred on the needs and the natural wealth of a region registering a steep rate of economic growth. In addition, regional raw materials and energy resources already partly processed in their countries of origin, and indeed some of the early output of the new industries in these countries, distributed via Singapore to other markets throughout the world, have replaced the old trade in raw materials from these same countries which used to transit via Singapore en route for Europe. Conversely, a growing amount of durable goods and of certain manufactured products from the developing countries have found their way via this great port to the neighbouring countries.[8]

Explanatory factors
Several factors lie behind the recession and transformations undergone by Singapore's entrepot trade. The policy of industrialisation adopted in the island in 1965–70 stimulated a rapid growth in its domestic exports, which had previously been insignificant. The development of natural resources and the birth of sectoral industries in the neigbouring countries — which often had to seek assistance from Singapore before they were able to equip themselves with structures enabling them to export directly — also played an important part.

The classic relationship between colonisers and a commercial emporium on one side and colonised space on the other inspired a new kind of entrepot trade: new links were established between the major industrialised countries and Singapore, which then came to be utilised as a regional base for the re-exporting of durable goods, vehicles, special materials such as high technology and consumer goods — which today make up 60% of Singapore's re-export business.[9] At the same time, the diversification of the economic fabric of Singapore, and then of the other ASEAN countries, led to a great increase in complementarities.[10]

Finally, modern warehousing techniques and the quality of the services offered by Singapore — harbour and air terminals, speed of discharging and reexportation of cargoes, containerisation, cold storage, and mastery of the norms and procedures of marketing — all contributed to this transformation of the entrepot business.

    8. Lim Joo Jock (ed.) (164).
    9. Singapore Ministry of Trade and Industry, *Economic Survey of Singapore* (annual).
    10. Singapore International Chamber of Commerce, annual reports.

The role of middleman under fire

The functions of commercial middleman and/or financier, when exercised by a particular ethnic group or state, have been opposed or envied throughout history in South-East Asia and elsewhere. Singapore, of course, has been no exception to this rule: many regard entrepot activity as parasitic, profiting from uncomplicated movements through a port of goods produced in both neighbouring and distant countries, with a minimal input of labour.[11] The view of Singapore as the 'Jew of the Orient' is firmly established wherever, throughout the region, there is hostility to the Overseas Chinese. Without necessarily taking this radical position, numerous decision-makers in Indonesia and Malaysia seek to reduce the commercial monopoly enjoyed by Singapore and the income it derives from this false situation, which gives it the highest living standards in Asia after Japan and Brunei.[12]

Attitudes to this role of middleman fluctuate between the critical, not to say polemical reactions from its detractors who would like to reduce the objective appreciation of geo-economic realities which have never ceased to work in Singapore's favour right up to the present. The following are the weightier arguments used to defend the viability of its role as an entrepot.[13] First, Singapore has no competitor in the region as regards its geographical situation and the infrastructure and services which it offers. Secondly, the high quality of the services of reception, preparation and redistribution of goods for re-export is accompanied by advanced marketing techniques obtainable nowhere but in Singapore, affording economies of time and cost with which the neighbouring countries are in no position to compete. Thirdly, its status — unique in South-East Asia — as a free port reinforces Singapore's market competitiveness with its unbeatable prices.[14] Fourthly, Singapore's predominance is based on a 'serial' relationship

---

11. Iain Buchanan (97) proposes a Marxist critique denouncing Singapore as an instrument of the economic imperialism of the colonial powers and the contemporary neo-colonialism of the Western industrial countries.
12. E.C. Paul (355), pp. 41 & 97.
13. The following article by an Indonesian economist whom the author interviewed at Universitas Indonesia, Jakarta, in 1984 covers this question in detail: S. Reksopoetranto, *Peranan Singapura bagi perdagangan luar negeri Indonesia alternatif di masa mendatang: mem-by pass atau memanfaatkan Singapura* (The alternative concerning the future role of Singapore in the external trade of Indonesia: to by-pass Singapore or rather seek to benefit from its activities), Jakarta: Fakultas Ekonomi U.I., 1984.
14. *Pratique des marchés internationaux: Singapour* (192), pp. 88–90.

between the commercial network existing through this major port —
seen as a staging-post for international freight and medium-sized vessels
from the neighbouring countries — and complementary networks in
the ports of Malaysia, Indonesia and Thailand, which are themselves
staging-posts for intra-regional and domestic coastal traffic.

In the hypothetical situation of these countries pursuing the development of comparable infrastructures to those in Singapore, a formidable
mobilisation of the necessary capital would be required in each case, to
the prejudice of other national economic sectors which have priority,
and bringing with it an enormous rise in handling costs which would
make domestic exports even more costly than they are now. The
argument that Singapore is a parasite because of its very predominance
does not stand up to analysis.

This is far from being a reason why the governments of the region
should not feel free to plan the infrastructural development of their
ports in a manner that is appropriate to their level of economic development. The essence of the matter is not to try to outstrip Singapore
in the services it already provides — this would harm all the parties
involved — but to work towards a future in which Singapore's services
alone could no longer cope with the needs of, say, a vast partner like
Indonesia.

Anti-Singaporean feeling has certainly been confined to a minority
since 1970–5, but it has persisted none the less in the neighbouring
countries, and is potentially destructive economically. It underlines the
permanent dependence and vulnerability of the city-state in its regional
setting. Singapore is able to lessen the effect of these factors through its
control over the transit of certain goods which, taken together, are
indispensable to the neighbouring states, and by not only making its
services as competitive as possible but cultivating its image as a tiny
buffer-state between agrarian economies which are still undeveloped
(except for the west coast of the Malay peninsula) and the fierce
competition which prevails in international markets.

Singapore's two privileged trading partners

In 1960–5, Malaysia and Indonesia accounted for nearly 40% of
Singapore's total external trade, and this represented the essence of its
entrepot business. This figure (which had fallen to 25% in 1983 and as
far as 19% in 1987) made these countries the island's principal trading
partners, on a par with the United States. Malaysia on its own traditionally occupied this position, but was overtaken by the United States

in 1982 and by Japan more recently. The available official statistics, based on data provided by Jakarta, show that Indonesia had fallen to fourth place by 1983–4 with 8–9% of all Singapore's trade, but this trend was inverted in 1987–8.

The other ASEAN partners play only a small role, while that of Indochina and Burma is infinitesimal. Thailand alone, with 3%, has a not altogether negligible position, due mainly to its export of food products. Trade with the Philippines, which does not have important economic links with South-East Asia, is insignificant — less, even, than with Brunei. Its trade with the sultanate is on a small scale commensurate with the size of this new sovereign state, thinly populated but rich in resources of petroleum and natural gas.

Trade between Singapore and Malaysia
The value of available statistics

The statistics appear to be reasonably reliable, in so far as both states have inherited from the period of British colonisation a well-structured customs administration, which for a long period they shared. Five-sixths of mutual trade is concentrated in the west coast of the peninsula, and except in the case of trade with East Malaysia (Sabah and Sarawak), this lessens the temptations of large-scale smuggling. Protection of Malaysia's internal market, which is less significant than for Indonesia and Thailand, is another factor which has a similar effect.

The fact that statistics are available in these two countries should make it possible to compare and cross-check, but today the two states operate different systems of customs classification. Malaysia, whose exports to Japan are routed via Singapore, considers Japan as the final destination of these sales. On the other hand, Singapore counts them as imports from Malaysia and as exports (re-exports since 1976) to Japan. Conversely, Malaysia classes all its imports by their country of origin, whether or not they have been routed via Singapore.

The re-exports declared by Singapore included, in 1987, 60% of its total exports to Malaysia. Thus it is not surprising that Singapore's overall figures for the bilateral trade of the two countries sometimes differ from those of Kuala Lumpur by as much as 50%.

Trade flows in brief
Malaysia has always been heavily dependent on its external trade, a fact which was even more striking when Singapore belonged to the

federation. The osmosis between the two countries, after more than 140 years of shared history, could not but continue after the political separation in 1965. Malaysia represented 19% of Singapore's external trade in 1970, but ten years later in 1980 this had fallen to 13.5%,[15] rising to 16% in 1984 but then dropping back to 14% in 1987. It ceased to be Singapore's premier trading partner in 1982 when the United States overtook it. More recently, Japan has done so too.[16]

Crude oil, natural rubber, foodstuffs, clothing, vegetable oils and electrical equipment (the last two rising sharply after 1982) are Singapore's essential imports. Malaysia remains the chief market for re-exports of durable goods, transport equipment, manufactured goods and chemical products, to which domestic exports of transformed energy should be added. These bilateral exchanges show a modest deficit in Malaysia's favour.

East Malaysia (Sabah and Sarawak), which is closer physically to Singapore than the west coast of the peninsula, accounts for one-sixth of Malaysia's trade with Singapore, and continues to use the city-state as a base for its marketing (crude oil, rubber and vegetable oils for Sabah and crude oil, rubber, timber and spices for Sarawak) and for the re-routing to it of various types of equipment (65 and 72% respectively of Singapore's exports to these two eastern states of the federation).

Trade conflicts after separation

One result of the divorce of 1965 was that a project for a common market, with the rational aim of economic fusion between the island and its hinterland, was shelved. Instead a tariff war, fed by political and ethnic resentments,[17] broke out, and in the ensuing years delivered a savage blow to both entrepot trade and flows of investment. This period saw clearly emerging a certain determination on the part of the Malaysian government to use every means in its power to overtake Singapore.

But as the Rueff report of 1963[18] had emphasised, the inter-

15. Ratna Rao, 'Unity in diversity: Singapore/Malaysia economic relations', *Singapore Business*, Mar. 80, pp. 49–54.
16. In Dec. 1971, all importation of products from China, whether via Singapore or Hong Kong, was forbidden (*Straits Times* [*ST*], 23 Oct. 71).
17. 'Communalism' has become the accepted term to describe tensions – at once ethnic, socio-economic, cultural and religious – between two or more groups living together in one place, such as exist between the Malays and Chinese in the region under discussion here.
18. Jacques Rueff (198).

dependence of Singapore and Kuala Lumpur, the 'New York and Washington' of the peninsula, could not be modified, and no major obstacle to a future economic reunification has developed.[19]

Trade statistics show that Malaysia, despite official statements to the contrary over the next fifteen years, and efforts to modernise its harbour infrastructures, never lessened its ties of commerical interdependence with Singapore.[20] The reverse was also true. Complementarity became deeper: trade was increasingly diversified, and the overlapping of markets with three privileged partners — the province of Johore at the southern end of the Malay peninsula, Penang[21] and East Malaysia — became much more pronounced.

For example (and examples were to be found almost daily in the local press), Malaysia prohibited the export of timber via Singapore and urged local business circles to use the new installations at the port of Pasir Gudang in south Johore instead of Singapore.[22] There were immediate protests from the Malay Timber Industry Board in Kuala Lumpur, denouncing the lack of realism of these measures, and the government was obliged to back-track, at least in part.

Under the administration of Prime Minister Mahathir, anti-Singapore propaganda has been moderated, and relations have noticeably improved. At the beginning of 1985, the Minister of Commerce and Industry, Mr Razaleigh, actually stated that Malaysia had no intention of cutting its exports that were routed via Singapore, that it preferred to encourage direct dealings with the outside world only when it was proved to be more rational economically, and that the two states could simply be viewed as one market.[23]

Trade between Singapore and Indonesia

Statistical problems and trade conflicts

The official statistics generally used are those of the Central Statistical Bureau in Jakarta, which are based on data provided by the Indonesian customs authorities.[24]

19. Lau Teik Soon, 'Malaysia-Singapore relations: Crisis of adjustment, 1965–68', *JSAH*, 10 (Mar. 69), p. 155.
20. *Singapore Business*, July 79, pp. 13–16.
21. In 1965 Malaysia published separate statistics concerning trade between Singapore and Penang.
22. *New Straits Times (NST)*, 23 Oct. 81.
23. *Singapore Economic Bulletin*, Feb. 85, p. 40.
24. The figures produced separately by the Central Statistical Bureau, the Bank of Indonesia and the Ministry of External Trade show considerable discrepancies.

For reasons connected with Indonesia's confrontation policy in 1963–6, Singapore has not published any statistics concerning its trade with Indonesia since 1964, and contents itself with quoting Indonesian sources in all its own government publications. It has a constant anxiety on two counts: first, to avoid the distortions that would undoubtedly appear from a comparison between Indonesian and Singaporean statistics, thus fuelling the critical attitude of anti-Chinese circles in Indonesia, and secondly to save the Indonesian government from the embarrassment that would result from exposing its inability to control the two-way transactions, the level of corruption, and its collusion with Chinese businessmen both at home and in Singapore.

Faced with the Sukarno regime's denunciations of smuggling and unfair competition from Singapore, the latter proposed in 1964–5 to return to Jakarta a part of the money value of the business judged to be 'illicit'.[25] The intransigence shown on the Indonesian side led to Singapore's refusal to publish its trade statistics or communicate them in any way, and, as a systematic counter-stroke to the accusation of smuggling, to declare a free status for its port.[26] On 31 October 1976, Lee Kuan Yew and President Suharto reached agreement in principle[27] that Singapore's statistics would be made available to the highest levels of the Indonesian government. This first came into effect in 1982, and the practice was confirmed by the Singaporean ambassador in Jakarta.[28] The Indonesian authorities, for their part, have refrained — up till the present — from publishing these figures, since the facts they disclose are sensitive from the point of view of internal politics.

There are several distorting factors which explain the divergence between Indonesian statistics and the true state of bilateral trade. First, the Indonesian system of customs classification, like Malaysia's, does not include goods in transit via Singapore. Thus the imports declared as originating from the island are merely Singapore's domestic exports destined for Indonesia. These are unpublished.

Secondly, informal trade (undervaluation by customs and other forms of dissimulation) and smuggling pure and simple between Singapore and the archipelago, had existed during the period of colonial rivalry between the Dutch and the British, and continued ever since, especially with areas at no great distance from the island like the Riau archipelago,

25. A. Jørgensen-Dahl (302), pp. 106–7, and John Wong (232), pp. 20–1.
26. *ST*, 10 Nov. 73.
27. *ST*, 1 Dec. 76.
28. Lee Kuan Yew, 'Statistics given to Ministers', *ST*, 10 Sept. 82.

Sumatra and western Kalimantan. At least until 1985–6, the volume of trade which escaped all control by the Indonesian authorities amounted to hundreds of millions of US dollars.

Where trade was controlled, the pervasive corruption within the Indonesian customs services and the tariff regulations in force (which were among the most complicated in the world) resulted in only part of the true trading situation being visible. After the director-general of customs was arrested in 1984, the government at last resolved on a cleaning-up operation, seeking the customs supervising services of the Société Générale de Surveillance of Geneva and commissioning 3,000 new customs officers.[29]

Thirdly, since 1982 import substitution and barter trade have not been recorded, since they are not subject to financial regulations, but the city-state would be Indonesia's fourth- or fifth-ranking partner in this area.[30] Fourthly, there are various kinds of transaction, whether or not recorded in writing, which are handled in ways that are often employed between Singapore and its giant neighbour: a documentary transit with or without falsification of the customs declarations, the juggling of prices and packing to conceal the identity of the country of origin, and tacit agreements based on the spoken word only (within the Chinese business communities). Fifthly, the trade in pirated goods, of which Singapore is one of the world's largest centres, and which is roundly condemned by the industrialised countries, further complicates customs values. And finally, purchases in Singapore by Indonesian visitors, who spend more on average than any other nationality in this 'consumer's paradise', are not included in the trade statistics.

An assessment of trade between Singapore and Indonesia
Even if Indonesia under President Sukarno was less dependent on external trade than Malaysia, nevertheless half of its exports transited

29. *Far Eastern Economic Review (FEER)*, 25 Apr. 85. Since 1 May 1985, the SGS has been under contract with the Indonesian government to inspect all shipments into Indonesia; it is responsible above all for checking the commercial documentation accompanying the goods (invoices, customs classification, declaration etc.). The government thus collects customs revenues that genuinely correspond with the value of what is imported. The activities of SGS have made possible a reduction in the time taken in customs clearance, and an increase by as much as 50% in tax revenue over the sums budgeted by the local customs services. In this context, the government accepted in 1986 an initial average reduction of between 5 and 20% in customs dues on all existing rates.
30. *ST*, 19 Jan. 87.

via Singapore (4% of the entrepot revenues of the port in 1963–4). At times when one or other of the neighbouring states was undergoing political upheaval, like Malaysia in 1963–6, there was certainly a recession, but the business managed to reach Singapore by even more informal round-about routes than usual.[31]

With President Suharto's policies centering on the effort to develop energy resources and bring about industrial take-off, bilateral trade could only increase. Singapore was Indonesia's third- or fourth-most important trading partner, and trade increased in value, especially after the oil price rises of 1975–6, with a surplus in Indonesia's favour in every year except 1983. Official statistics show Indonesia in sixth place among Singapore's partners, behind the United States, Japan, Malaysia, the European Community and Hong Kong — and possibly behind Taiwan as well. After examining the many possibilities of distortion in the calculation of trade figures, it seems appropriate to try to come nearer to the truth, by an empirical evaluation at least, and to leave the exploration of the problem's roots to specialists in quantitative analysis.[32] In the early 1970s, for example, Buchanan and Paul in their respective works affirmed that Indonesia occupied a position parallel to that of Malaysia in Singapore's external trade.[33] Also, the International Monetary Fund and other international agencies have often indicated that trade between Singapore and Indonesia exceeded that between the island and peninsular Malaysia.[34]

For the recent period, if one admits that entrepot business rose — at least up till 1985–6 — to more than one-third of the value of bilateral trade (as in the case of Malaysia), and that contraband in both its pure and its legalised forms is still important enough to add 20–25% to the official Indonesian figures, Indonesia could well claim (before the recession of 1985–8) a position equal to Malaysia's in Singapore's external trade. Could Indonesia really be the fourth or fifth trading partner of the city-state in 1987? Some reports of the Singapore International Chamber of Commerce tend to say covertly that Indonesia comes first

31. H.V. Richter, 'Indonesia's share in the entrepot trade of Malaya and Singapore prior to confrontation', *Malayan Economic Review*, Oct. 66, pp. 28–45, and *Bull. of Indonesian Studies*, XXII, 2 (Aug. 86), pp. 103–13.
32. H.V. Richter, 'Problems of assessing unrecorded trade', *Bull. of Indonesian Econ. Studies*, 6, 1 (Mar. 70), pp. 17–44 & 45–60.
33. Approximately Sing. $2.5 billion in exchange value, of which at least $850 is accounted for by smuggling of various kinds.
34. IBRD/IDA, *Economic development of Indonesia*, Feb. 86, vol. 1, p. 18.

in the bilateral trade between Singapore and ASEAN, although the official figures invariably rank Malaysia as number one.

The debate is unresolved, but there can be no doubt that Indonesia, because of its vast population, and the extent of its present and (probably) future development efforts, is destined to overtake Malaysia as Singapore's chief economic interlocutor in the region. The ties of interdependence between Singapore and the rest of South-East Asia turn out to be even stronger than they appear: the Singaporeans themselves, moved by simultaneous feelings of fear *vis-à-vis* their immediate environment and pride in their own social and economic success, have taken their time to recognise this move towards rapprochement with their mighty Indonesian neighbour openly.

The nature of intra-regional trade and complementaries
Traditionally, Indonesia exported to Singapore raw materials for semi-processing and re-exportation. The island only sold food products and Western consumer goods.

The nature of what is traded has evolved since the mid-1970s. From being a trading entrepot, the city-state has become a magnet for industries and services, at the same time as Indonesia has started along the road of intermediate transformation of its natural resources and direct exporting.[35] Up till 1982–3, trade in the energy sector weighed heavily, with Indonesia sending crude petroleum and gas to the refineries in Singapore, and Singapore in return selling refined petrol and special petroleum derivatives. The drop of 41% in bilateral trade in 1984 (according to Indonesian sources) was due to several refineries on Indonesian territory coming into service, and this was followed, from 1985 onwards, by the worldwide fall in oil prices and economic recession in Indonesia.

Other Indonesian exports made fairly good progress: natural rubber, tin, transistors and semi-conductors, plywood, cosmetics, vegetable oils, cement, textiles, tea, spices and other food products. Singapore has achieved ever-increasing sales of durable goods, transportation equipment, civil engineering and various technical tools; also technical and management services, a sector in which it has secured its own privileged niche. Capital and technological know-how now form more than half of all Singapore's exports to Indonesia, having risen from 9% in 1961.

35. Abdullah Said, 'Low-keyed but expanding', *Singapore Business*, Aug. 84, pp. 39–43.

However, according to its available statistics Indonesia was slow to recover from the mid-1980s recession in its petroleum sales.

During the period of international recession which hit Singapore badly in 1985–6, the island authorities did not miss the chance to play the card of the decline in trade with Indonesia, and the dangers it implied, to mobilise the population for a great new wave of effort and austerity.[36]

With the signing of the first agreement on economic and political cooperation in 1974, the creation of the Indonesian Business Association in Singapore (IBAS) in 1975,[37] the institutionalisation of the regular contacts between the chambers of commerce of the two states, and Singapore making its statistics available, there was an easing of trading relations, which had been embittered by the contraband problem. Differences over trade policy and over Indonesian calls to dispense with the 'parasitic Chinese enclave' became less intense. In 1982 the Indonesian government announced a plan to export directly from the ports of Tanjung Priok (Jakarta), Tanjung Perak (West Java), Unjung Pandang (South Sulawesi) and Belawan (North Sumatra), but numerous local economists doubted whether it would be genuinely successful. The facilities offered by Singapore are such that Indonesia is quite unable to develop competing infrastructures. On the other hand, the promotion of complementarities became possible through reliance on private financial assistance from Singapore, without forgetting the vocation of the city-state as a direct supplier in cases of urgent need.[38]

Indonesia, in the same manner as Malaysia, carried on trading relations with Singapore as in the past, and, after its decline as an entrepot, actually increased them clandestinely or very discreetly owing to internal political considerations, and taking advantage of the lack of Singaporean statistics. This reality was expressed on two levels in a way that was typical of Java — favouring, in practice, a close collaboration with the city-state, while at the same time keeping up a barely concealed barrage of criticism against it. The confrontation of 1963–5 created grave problems for the Indonesian economy and was abandoned voluntarily, thus demonstrating that a boycott of Singapore could only end in failure;

---

36. *ST*, 11 May 85, and *Singapore Econ. Bull.*, June 85, pp. 24–5.
37. 5–6,000 companies established in Singapore trade with Indonesia (*Singapore Business*, Aug. 84, pp. 39–48).
38. Azhari Zahri, 'Singapore-Indonesian economic relations', and Noor Handono, 'Some salient points in Singapore-Indonesian economic relations', *IBAS Bull.*, May 80, pp. 12–18 and 29–33.

the apparent political hostility maintained by Jakarta, combining jealousy with secret admiration, was a 'cover' for a lucrative economic relationship conducted back-stage between the Indonesian regime and, especially, the Chinese business circles. This was never questioned.[39]

The trade between the two states, deeply influenced as it was by regional history and geography, multiplied the number of bridges and roads to bring about greater interdependence.

39. Williams E. James (141); C.E. Morrison & Suhrke (335), pp. 228ff.; Howard Warshawsky (399); F.B. Weinstein (400 and 401).

2

INDUSTRY AND THE REGION

Singapore as a case of accelerated industrialisation open to the regional market

For Lee Kuan Yew's government, the decline of Singapore's traditional commercial functions created an economic void at the beginning of the 1960s which threatened the city's viability, and which needed to be eliminated as quickly as possible. The development of the trading emporium had been based on mercantile transactions between the colonial powers and the South-East Asian region, transiting via Singapore. It has been on an analogous principle that investment by the industrialised countries and the countries of the region, those of North-East Asia included, have made the biggest contribution to the new industrial emporium emerging on top of the earlier one in the two decades following the late 1960s.

The economic challenges of 1965: Singapore's response and development strategy

Independence: economic viability under threat

The forced independence of Singapore in 1965 provoked intense anxiety over the outlook for economic survival. At that juncture Lee Kuan Yew did not believe that a tiny city-state faced with potentially aggressive neighbours (it had just separated from one and was subjected to 'confrontation' by the other) could be viable, and he felt great anguish at its vulnerability.[1] A Dutch economist, Winsemius, was one of the few experts prepared to wager on the success of Singapore's independence, notwithstanding all the apparent evidence to the contrary.[2]

The internal market on the island was too small, and the expulsion from Malaysia put an end to any hope of a common market that would

1. During a radio interview broadcast during the night of 9–10 Aug. 1965, Lee Kuan Yew said: 'For me it is a moment of anguish because all my adult life . . . I have believed in the merger and unity of these two territories.'
2. United Nations, *A proposed industrialization programme for the state of Singapore*, New York: UN Industrial Survey Mission, 1963 ('the Winsemius Report').

have assured Singapore of vast outlets and guaranteed the viability of its nascent industries. Its independence could hardly be taken very seriously when it still had to import part of its drinking water.

The excessive economic weight of an entrepot in decline and of Britain's air and naval base on the island created problems of reconversion and the need for a diversity of poles of activity. Finding solutions was all the more urgent in view of a high unemployment level (15.2% in 1962), chronic under-employment due to the low productivity of small-scale urban crafts, and the inevitable surge of young people progressively coming on to the labour market.

The confrontation with Indonesia and the unhappy separation from Malaysia threw Singapore's structural dependence on its immediate environment into sharp relief, and those at top government level were persuaded of the need for a massive redeployment of the island's economy to make it more compatible with the world outside. Paradoxically, these events condemned all three countries, which were strongly integrated commercially, to partition themselves on national lines and in an increasing number of ways, albeit against natural tendencies to the contrary — without being aware of where the smallest among them would be led by such developments.

Considerable material means are indispensable to achieve an effective and speedy industrial take-off. However, Singapore was a colonial city *par excellence*, and could not command sufficient capital to take up this challenge. The local market was brought to a standstill by investments from, and repatriation to, London; the capital of the Chinese diaspora was limited to local businesses and small banking houses.

Because Singaporean society was profoundly non-egalitarian, with 20% of the population in a state of poverty and a virtual absence of social service,[3] it was perpetually open to agitation and Communist subversion, which shook Singapore in 1947–50 and again in 1954–5.

Finally, all these internal and external events are always capable of endangering the very survival of an entity as small as Singapore. However, the successive political shocks to which it has been subjected in its relations with the two neighbouring countries have never sent it over the brink. A new danger alarmed Singapore's leaders after 18 July 1967, when Britain's Labour government announced that during the next decade British forces would withdraw from the base in Singapore, which not only constituted the island's only military defence, but also

3. Iain Buchanan (97), pp. 55–76.

provided a quarter of all its economic activity (20% of GNP and 40,000 jobs).

All these factors left the Singapore government with no choice but to adopt with maximum speed a policy that would guarantee economic viability, and to treat the whole matter as an emergency. From 1965 onwards, the respective modes of development of Singapore and Hong Kong diverged definitely: in a few months, the City of the Lion witnessed a transformation from colonial and liberal laissez-faire to an overwhelming interventionism by government in the newly emerging national economy.[4]

Singapore's development strategy and its regional implications, 1965–80

Confronted with this grave and urgent challenge, the team of economists working with Lee Kuan Yew's government — notably Goh Keng Swee and Winsemius — elaborated a development strategy, of which the first concrete results were already felt in 1968–70.

Singapore offers a case-study which is one of those most analysed and most often cited by Western economists as a growth model. Nothing can be gained by again discussing this subject which has given rise to such an abundant literature, and which requires the skills of a technical economist to deal with it adequately. However, it is useful for our purposes to place this development strategy in its international context and in relation to its regional implications.

Creating the preconditions for economic development, 1960–66
A certain number of conditions — all the more interesting for the way they have been lacking or only present in rudimentary form in the neighbouring countries — have helped the success of the economic strategy adopted by Singapore.[5]

In this formidable gamble on viability and development, the quality of the human resources involved played a vital role. On the top rungs of the social ladder was the government — effective (after a few troubled years between 1956 and 1963), incorrupt and single-minded in pursuit of its task; from 1965 onwards its presence ensured the political stability and the overall credibility of the vulnerable city-state. To this

4. Ong Wee Hock (459), pp. 17–23; P.S.J. Chen (ed.) (100), pp. 3–25; You Poh Seng & Lim Chong Yah (eds) (239), pp. 254–5.
5. Chen (ed.) (100), pp. 99–101.

has to be added the excellence of the ruling team activated by a leader of exceptional intelligence and undoubted charisma, who was shrewd enough to surround himself with brilliant colleagues capable of pinpointing the optimal strategy for Singapore's future and understanding what would best suit the needs of the island's own society in conjunction with the external situation.

Down at the lower levels of society, an urban population and a small territory — both of which could easily be controlled — were the only real assets the city-state had at its disposal. The culture of this population of emigrants, more than three-quarters of whom were Chinese, embraced respect for hard work, knowledge, experience, self-discipline and social success. A just appreciation of the value of the island's human resources, elevated to a systematic policy of getting the best out of a modest-sized population, and a strategy of social redistribution in tune with the development of the economy, promised good results.

At the same time as engaging in political rhetoric denouncing Western colonialism and imperialism, Lee Kuan Yew had come to the conclusion that the development of Malaysia — and even more so of Singapore now that it was independent — could only lead in one direction: towards creating a local environment which would inspire confidence in foreign investors, since they alone could provide the means to attain rapid economic growth. To the solidity of the government and the reliable mobilisation of the population the Singaporean authorities added a whole series of inducements to foreign investment: the maintenance of a free port, free convertibility, no exchange control, conversion of the entrepot, tax exemptions, export incentives, development of transport and communication infrastructures, education and training facilities – the list is extensive.

Being perhaps more dependent than any other kind of state on the interplay of its regional and world roles, Singapore also benefited from the favourable international economic situation. The 1960s saw the highest rate of growth since the Second World War in the industrialised countries, which were encouraged to invest abroad and reap the profit from advantageous local conditions. In the region, Indonesia and Malaysia in their turn chose the path of political stability and of giving priority to their economies, at the same time as the countries of North-East Asia began showing signs of an unprecedented boom. The external situation permitted Singapore, at one and the same time, to play the world card and the regional card.

The stages of Singapore's economic development and their significance for the neighbouring countries
The conversion of Singapore from a trading entrepot to a manufacturing 'workshop' dedicated to the export of transformed goods took less than fifteen years! And by the beginning of the 1980s it was already moving ahead to high technology and advanced services.

The situation at the outset. In 1965–7, the economy still rested heavily on a tertiary sector (accounting for 75% of its assets), including activities related to trade and to the military base. Singapore's only development plan (1961–5) sought to enhance several semi-processing industries already in existence with access to the raw materials of the region, and to promote an industry of import-substitution based on the internal market of Malaya. Because of the confrontation with Indonesia and the fact that the project for a common market with the peninsula proved abortive, the results were poor. As we have already seen, this provoked serious questioning as to whether the newly-independent state of Singapore would be viable.

Accelerated industrialisation, 1967–79. In the eyes of Singapore's leaders, foreign investment represented the only motor capable of transforming the national economy in record time: the Economic Development Board put into operation a plan of general liberalisation of the economy and of incentives to investors. This was inaugurated by the passing of the Industrial Expansion and Industrial Relations Acts of 1967 and 1968 respectively, which gave permanence to the new conditions of social and political stability, and increased the potential of Singapore's infra-structure, right at the heart of South-East Asia. By so doing, it allowed the city-state to become a safe haven for international investment and, within a short time, to notch up one of the highest growth-rates in the world. It became host to the regional headquarters of an impressive number of foreign enterprises, and transformed itself into a secondary workshop with both a world vocation and a regional one. The first of these was to contribute, through its subcontracting activities, to the development of keen competition between the products of the indus-trialised countries; and the second was to respond to the needs of the neighbouring countries by expanding sectoral industries and offering goods and services of high quality.[6]

6. E.K.Y. Chen (99); H. Hughes & You Poh Seng (eds) (138); Lee Soon Ann (153); Lim Joo-Jock (ed.) (164). See also Lam Khee Fui, 'The strategy of industrial

Parallel to these structural transformations of the economy, several other factors combined to make a similar contribution to this success. The Vietnam war heightened the interest of American government and business in this island base relatively close to the operational area but sufficiently far away from it, and the British withdrawal made it necessary to adopt a vigorous defensive system, and allowed the eva-cuated base to be reconverted. Furthermore, the oil crisis stimulated the valorisation of South-East Asia's energy resources.[7]

The take-off of the secondary sector in 1967–70 concentrated on labour-intensive industries which were almost entirely absent in the neighbouring countries (with the exception of the textile and wood-working sectors, where the craft tradition often still prevailed). This was to reduce unemployment. Heavy industry — limited to the naval yards, construction and petroleum — swept the whole economy along in its wake throughout the 1970s, energy products alone serving as the driving force for manufacturing industry and exports and becoming the primary focus of Singapore's activities.[8]

The city-state is thus an industrial centre in the region, adding the finishing touch to its role of commercial agent, *vis-à-vis* its neighbours, for capital goods and consumer products exported from the developed world. Despite the existence, in the other ASEAN countries, of textile industries, processing of raw materials and various subcontracting activities, Singapore still enjoyed a comfortable if not decisive lead, which had long depended, as mentioned above, on the 'three sisters': petroleum, shipbuilding related to the naval base, and construction.

The early 1980s: 'high-tech' strategy. A radical restructuring of the Singa-porean economy began in 1979–81.[9] The government defined new

development in Singapore', *Commerce*, 1973/4, pp. 47–50, and the article by Pang Eng Fong and A. Tan in R. Amjad (ed.) (88), pp. 141–74.

7. Singapore was used by the US army as a base for fuel supply and as a leave centre for its soldiers. For the British withdrawal, consult Lee Soon Ann, 'The British withdrawal and Singapore's economic future', *Solidarity*, Feb. 1969, pp. 29–35, and E. Benoit, 'Impact of the end of Vietnam hostilities and the reduction of British military presence in Malaysia and Singapore' in Asian Development Bank (ed.), *Southeast Asia's economy in the '70s*, London: Longman, 1971, pp. 581–671.

8. Amjad (ed.) (88); R. Garnaut (ed.) (122), ch. 9; Dick Wilson (230), pp. 81–9; Koh How Eng, 'The role of trade and manufacturing in the economic development of Singapore', *Commerce*, 1974/5, pp. 91–100, and Lee Soon Ann, 'Singapore as a manufacturing centre', *Trends* (Singapore), Dec. 1975, pp. 29–40.

9. Chia Siow Yue (102); A.N. Hakam (130); S.S. Hock and R.S. Bhatal (eds) (467);

priority sectors,[10] all linked to high technology and advanced services. At the same time, the National Wages Council moved towards a substantial increase in pay — of 16–20% — designed to delocalise industries that were the most labour-intensive and the weakest in value-added.[11] This policy was accompanied by various support measures: further education and training (the Skill Development Fund), the development of ultra-modern infrastructures, incentives for foreign investment including technology transfer, credits for research (the Research and Development Assistance Scheme) and the improvement of productivity (Mechanisation Scheme).[12]

Of the factors which helped to bring about this strategy in the 1980s, several reflected the evolution of Singapore's regional economic environment. The remarkable growth-rates achieved by ASEAN and North-East Asian countries show that their manufacturing industries had truly taken off. The key sectors of the Singaporean economy such as oil-refining, textiles and the processing of primary products were consequently faced with an immediate threat. The recession in the shipyards, due to competition from Japan and South Korea, was even worse. However, gaps appeared waiting to be filled, with growing demand from the region for equipment and technology.

Singapore's social costs and living standards, both of which had become exceptionally high, prevented it from competing with its neighbours in terms of manpower, of which they could offer a vast, cheap and socially unprotected reserve. On the other hand, competition among advanced industries in developed countries seeking infrastructures and employees of good quality placed Singapore in a favourable position to attract investment of this kind, and gave it the means to keep one step ahead of its ASEAN partners.

Singapore's extraordinary and universally lauded success make it easy

---

J.-R. Chaponnière, 'Singapour, l'entrepôt à l'assaut des "high tech" ', *Industries et Travaux d'Outre-Mer* (Paris), Jan. 1984, pp. 51–7; Pang Eng Fong, 'Singapore economy in the year 2000', *IBAS Annual*, 1980, pp. 59–71; Shee Poon Kim, 'Singapore 1978: Preparation for the 1980s', *Asian Survey*, 19, 12 (Feb. 79), pp. 124–30.

10. The sectors concerned are precision engineering, electronics, information technology, optics, chemicals, pharmaceuticals, aeronautics, telecommunications and biotechnology.

11. *FEER*, 6 July 79, pp. 40–1.

12. E.K.Y. Chen (99), pp. 9–10; Lim Chong Yah (158), pp. 13ff; Pang Eng Fong (182); Wong Kwei Cjeong, 'Economic growth through higher productivity', *Petir* (Singapore), 10 (1981), pp. 66–8.

to forget the actual size of the island (620 km.^{2}). In spite of having reclaimed land from the sea (in 1974 the area was no more than 587.6 km.^{2}), there is not enough space for the establishment of plants needing their own major industrial infrastructures, and the highly urbanised environment, equivalent in size to a large European city, is already suffering pollution from local oil refining. At the same time, unemployment has ceased to exist since 1972–5, to the extent that foreign labour had to be imported for the heaviest works — from Bangladesh, Pakistan, Malaysia, Indonesia and Thailand. Today it appears that, with the population density as it now is, any further recruitment from overseas will impose too great a strain, and the systematic training of the domestic human resource for the benefit of the advanced sectors of the economy, which employ relatively small numbers, seems to be the only solution available for a very young and extremely small population.[13] The city-state does not have the capacity to accommodate on its own territory a fully integrated branch of industrial activity: Lee Kuan Yew has repeatedly said that only certain carefully chosen 'niches' can ensure the continued development of Singapore in the age of modern technology. These orientations could, by the end of the century, reinforce the complementarity between Singapore offering state-of-the-art services and techniques and its neighbours — producers of energy, raw materials and manufactured goods.[14]

The international industrialisation process that began in the 1960s suggests, in South-East Asia, a 'chain-reaction' of economic development, a division of tasks and interdependences, spreading out from Japan to the developing countries of South-East Asia, stopping over in Singapore and the other newly-industrialised countries.[15]

The recession of 1985–86 and the resumption of growth

In 1985, for the first time since independence, the Singaporean economy

13. Singapore's population numbered 2,647,000 in 1984 (2,075,000 in 1970), with an annual increase of 1.5% (2.8% in 1970). Of the total, 31.5% were under 20 years old, and 72% under 40.
14. *IBAS Annual*, 'Singapore in the year 2000', 1980, pp. 65–6.
15. H.W. Arndt and R. Garnaut, 'ASEAN and the industrialization of East Asia', *J. of Common Market Studies*, XVII, 3 (Mar. 79), pp. 191–212; A. Gallez and J. Troupin (121), vol. 2; M.J. Staab, 'The production location problem and the development of industries. . .', *Developing Economies*, 18, 1 (Mar. 1980), pp. 65–95; Christian Sautter, 'Le Japon et l'Asie-Pacifique: . . .', *Economie prospective internationale*, La Documentation française, Oct. 1980.

suddenly contracted — from a growth-rate which had stood at 8.2%
in 1984 to one of − 1.8%. Had the spirit of history come to remind
the city-state of its international vulnerability after twenty years of
unclouded prosperity?

With the exception of a handful of experts, no one had foreseen the
full extent of the crisis of 1985. Within a few months, 96,000 jobs were
lost, and unemployment made a spectacular advance, reaching 4.1% of
the active population of whom 45% were under twenty-five years old.

It can also be said that scarcely anyone would have wagered on the
extraordinary recovery of the island economy in less than two years. The
growth-rate reached double figures in the first quarter of 1988 (11.2%),
and levelled off for the whole year at 10.9%, as against 8.8% in 1987.

Analysis of the 1985–86 crisis
Between April 1985 and February 1986, a committee of twelve
distinguished individuals chaired by the then Minister of Trade and
Industry Lee Hsien Loong, son of Lee Kuan Yew, was in session,
charged with examining the origins of this slowing-down of economic
activity and recommending possible remedies and new orientations for
the future to the government. The committee's final report identified
several groups of problems, both circumstantial and structural.

First, several sectors which had provided the motive force for
Singapore's development for the past two decades were now in a lasting
state of recession: principal among these were the petroleum and petrochemical industries, shipbuilding and repair, construction, and the hotel
business. *Secondly*, the policy of awarding high salaries which had held
sway since 1979–81, and the generally very high level of production
costs, had affected the international competitiveness of Singapore's
manufacturing industry (especially compared with Hong Kong, South
Korea and Taiwan); it had also reduced the attraction to potential
foreign investors, whose numbers had already declined in the period
when expansion worldwide was weak, and put the brakes on the rapid
development of sectors linked to state-of-the-art technologies. *Thirdly*,
Singapore's trade with its principal partners had declined, due to a
number of causes: the cyclical fluctuations in the electronics markets,
the high cost of the US dollar, the budget deficits and protectionist
tendencies of the United States, the fall in the price of petrol and various
raw materials adversely affecting the economic health of the neighbouring countries, and the beginning of sectoral recessions in Japan.
Fourthly, the harmful effects of maintaining high interest-rates and an
over-valued Singapore dollar were combined with a record level of

savings (41% of GNP), which were partly in the form of compulsory deductions (more than 40% of the average salary) paid into the Central Provident Fund for social needs such as housing and the payment of pensions for the ageing population. *Fifthly*, the ever-present and often exclusive interventionism of the authorities favoured the development of sectors judged to have priority, but certain recent choices were shown to have been mistaken. Government control touched every aspect of the local economy, with eighty organisations and 450 commercial enterprises being under state management. And *finally*, the spectacular bankruptcy of the Pan Electric group came on top of 400 other bankruptcies, less sensational but no less real, which occurred in 1985, causing the closure of the Kuala Lumpur and Singapore stock exchanges for several days in December of that year.

The budget in 1986 introduced a first series of tax reliefs intended to revive the economy, and these included two notable measures: company taxation was reduced from 40 to 33%, and the employers' contribution to the Central Provident Fund was reduced from 25 to 10% of employees' gross pay. The latter was to continue for at least two years, during which pay increases would also be frozen.

These measures were in keeping with the recommendations of the committee of twelve, published in February 1986, which can be summarised as follows. There should be a reduction in the costs of production and corresponding efforts to improve productivity; a greater contribution from savings to boost local investment; a lessening of the tax burden on companies and individuals; active promotion of the tertiary sector, state-of-the-art technologies and research; a partial disengagement by the authorities from their control of the national economy, giving priority instead to local businesses in private ownership, both local and foreign; and a programme of education and training for all ages and levels of ability.

The recession of 1985–6 undoubtedly resulted from a combination of external circumstances and structural changes on the world market which the Singapore government could only have foreseen in part and with considerable difficulty from more than a short time in advance. It once again underlined Singapore's extreme dependence — which to an extent it had lost sight of in the exhilaration of two decades of uninterrupted economic prosperity.

A return to growth in 1987 and future perspectives
After once again registering positive growth (1.9%) in 1986, the island economy reached its normal 'cruising speed' in 1987 with a growth rate

of 8.8%, although all the experts, including Lee Kuan Yew in his traditional speech to the nation on 9 August 1986,[16] had calculated that growth would not exceed 3–5% annually before 1990.

The explanation for this very quick recovery (confirmed in 1988 and 1989) is probably to be found not so much in the impact of the measures adopted on the basis of the committee of twelve's report of 1986, as in a certain revival of world demand and favourable factors in the exchange market (the US dollar fell and the Japanese, South Korean and Taiwanese currencies rose).

Manufacturing industry, and most of all electronics and related sectors (electrical installations, machinery, mechanical components), constituted a major driving force in spite of representing only one-third of all economic activity. For the first time in several years, the oil industry and ship-repairing showed signs of health, and construction, which had been in the worst difficulties, also seemed to be making some recovery. The other 'leg' of the Singaporean economy, that of services (62% of GNP and 64% of jobs), was developing stronger muscles than ever, even if commerce, tourism, transport and communications suffered from their close connection with the financial services which fell victim to the international stock market crash in 1987 and to increasing offshore competition, especially from Tokyo.

This great recovery was accompanied by the state revising its internal economic policy from top to bottom. The authorities concentrated on two areas in particular.

In 1986, they began a programme of privatising public enterprises, at least in part. Their choice fell upon about forty of them, which were in direct competition with the private sector and did not seem to require special support in future, in the framework of a general programme of disengagement by the state which would be accomplished over about ten years. Temasek Holdings thus sold its shares in several public companies including Singapore Airlines, Neptune Orient Lines, National Printers, National Iron and Steel Mills, and in Resources Development Corporation (a real estate company), Sembawang and Jurong Shipyard. A similar procedure would be followed as other enterprises were quoted on the stock exchange, but the government made it clear that it would retain a participation of at least 30% in every case, and a hand in their management. These first steps in disengagement by the state were largely halted by the stock market crash in October 1987, and the economic recovery in 1988 and 1989 is still too recent at the

16. National broadcast by the Prime Minister, 9 Aug. 1986.

time of writing for its long-term impact to be accurately assessed.

The authorities are trying at the same time to inspire the private sector with a new spirit of enterprise which would discourage the constant inflow of foreign investment — a factor which, from one day to the next, can make its situation very volatile and damage the health of the whole economy. Between 1965 and the middle/late 1970s, the habit of seeking foreign or state investment could doubtless be justified by the absence of local industrial entrepreneurs. With the exception of a few large transnational houses belonging to the Overseas Chinese and operating throughout the region, the overwhelming majority of local businesses, most of which were small or medium-sized, concentrated on the tertiary sector — trading, finance, real estate and transportation. However, even if, between 1970 and 1986, these local entrepreneurs did not originally receive more than 20% of preferential government investment, they none the less account for 46% of employment, 31% of total value added and 20% of direct exports, right up to the present time. The Economic Development Board is now very conscious of its former neglect of this sector, and is increasing its programmes of financial and technical support for it.

All the measures taken to deregulate and boost the Singaporean economy since 1986 have resulted in readjustments with recovery taking place within barely two years. This remarkable performance, for which the government could take most of the credit (a more favourable international situation also played its part), strongly influenced the votes of the electorate, who in September 1988 re-elected Lee Kuan Yew and his team. The recession of 1985–6 now belongs to the past, but the return to growth cannot be said to signal the arrival of Singapore at a stage of indestructible economic and social maturity. The solid health of its industry and services will depend, more perhaps than in the past, on the success with which it meets the challenge posed by the availability of new technologies in the next century and by competition from various directions. Despite its size, the city-state does not lack the wherewithal to continue its journey, but it will have to adapt itself to world and regional markets which are increasingly in a state of flux and exposed to conflicting pressures.

Singapore as a crossroads for substantial regional investment flows

Before looking at the sectors in which Singapore has come to develop a variety of complementarities with its neighbours, we should investigate the character of the investment from outside which has enabled it to meet the challenges resulting from 1965 and to pull itself up to its present position of economic influence.

Foreign investment has moved into Singapore on a massive scale due to its especially favourable socio-economic system, and the international business rivalry between industrialised states.[17] The perspectives for going on to export and invest into South-East Asia, using Singapore as a springboard, have also played a key role.

Foreign investment in Singapore and its regional impact

Statistical data

There have been many economic studies analysing with precision the mechanisms which have allowed foreign investment to be a driving force behind Singapore's economic growth. Here we should recall the global dimensions of this external contribution in order to assess to what extent the city-state succeeds in drawing in investment which is vital for itself and for the development of the whole region.

In the manufacturing sector, excluding energy, accumulated foreign investment over the years 1980–9 had reached US$7.8 billion by the end of 1989, and new commitments in 1989 amounted to $1.6 billion, more than two-thirds being from the United States, Europe and Japan. This accounted for 83% of total investment.

For the sake of comparison, this kind of investment represented in 1987 rather less than two-thirds of the total registered in Indonesia, a country with fifty times more inhabitants.[18] New outside commitments in Malaysia in 1987 were less than half those of Singapore;[19] the island was therefore second only to Indonesia, and ahead of the other ASEAN members, in its total of foreign investment of all kinds. This has been partly modified since 1989 because of a massive inflow of investment — mainly from Japan and the four Asian NIEs — to Thailand, Malaysia and Indonesia. The influx passed $500 million in

---

17. Lim Joo Jock (164, p. 89) uses the concept of west-west competition to explain the great surge of reallocation of certain manufacturing activities by the industrial countries in the Third World in 1960–75, to enable them to compete more effectively among themselves.
18. US$ 683 million as against $1.47 billion (*source*: Bank of Indonesia).
19. US$ 290 million as against $683 million (*source*: Dept. of Finance, Malaysia).

FOREIGN INVESTMENT IN SINGAPORE, 1973–87*

(S$1,000 and %)

	1973		1976		1978		1980		1982		1984		1987	
U.S.A	8,777	3	92,915	31	146,881	18	505,757	36	513,296	30	780,872	43	543,500	31
Japan	151,425	51	76,100	25	158,393	20	139,655	10	72,094	4	174,848	10	601,100	34
Europe	43,892	15	50,065	17	418,816	52	360,410	25	402,654	23	325,120	18	285,800	16
E.C.	20,892	7	45,650	15	408,106	50	268,915	19	367,722	21	318,890	18	241,000	14
Sweden	21,000	7	1,000	–	–		53,575	4	11,088	1	300	–	8,700	4
Switzerland	–		2,415	1	8,410	1	35,800	3	22,044	1	2,680	–	27,800	16
Total foreign	224,098	76	260,445	86	765,733	94	1,199,010	84	1,122,182	65	1,318,196	73	1,448,000	83
Total local	71,777	24	42,827	14	46,626	6	222,575	16	600,044	35	497,282	27	295,000	17
Grand total	295,875	100	303,272	100	812,359	100	1,421,585	100	1,722,226	100	1,815,478	100	1,743,000	100

* Excepting petrochemicals.
Source: Singapore Economic Development Board.

1978–80 (since 1976 Japan has pushed the United States into second place). More than 7,500 foreign companies — either subsidiaries or with majority shareholding (700 are in the manufacturing sector) — were recorded in 1986, against a mere 1,720 in 1970. These accounted for a third of all active companies in Singapore, 58% of employment, 68% of value added, and 87% of direct exports, mainly in the following non-tertiary sectors, ranked in order of importance: petroleum and derivatives, electronics and electricity, mechanical engineering, chemicals, transportation equipment and food products. These foreign companies included the greatest names in Western industry, which have developed a network of subsidiaries and joint ventures in the ASEAN countries, with Singapore as the regional headquarters as well as the conveyor-belt for sophisticated materials and services needed by the industrial plants in the neighbouring countries.[20]

The sum total of these data give only an incomplete picture of foreign investment in Singapore. As in Hong Kong, the detailed statistics provided by the authorities cover manufacturing industry exclusively; no official information is allowed to leak out concerning the heavy investment in the tertiary sector, which enables the city-state to fulfil its vocation as a provider of services in the region and internationally. And because only companies with foreign majority participation are accounted for, other companies in which numerous shareholders in the ASEAN countries, Hong Kong and Taiwan have interests do not appear.[21]

Investment in Singapore by countries of the region
The figures for regional investment in Singapore are divided into many separate portions. At the beginning of the 1980s, seventy-two major investments in manufacturing were listed as originating from the ASEAN countries (Malaysia: 61, Thailand: 6, Indonesia: 5), eighty from Hong Kong and seventeen from Taiwan. Totalling on average less than US$1.5 million and creating at most 50–100 jobs, these inflows went to several specific sectors — textiles, clothing, woodwork and furniture, paper, printing. But the sources of official statistics remain silent on the subject of the multiple minority shareholdings from ASEAN

20. Lists of the 100 or 200 leading companies in Singapore are regularly published in the Singapore Economic Bulletin and Singapore Business. For a complete list of foreign firms established there, see *Directories of business and firms in Singapore*, Singapore: Kompass (available for the USA, the EC, Japan, West Germany, France, Britain, Australia, Switzerland and Austria).
21. Pang Eng Fong and R.V. Komaran (186).

countries in foreign companies and above all companies owned by Singapore's Chinese diaspora: these are in the form of long-term investment in services, real estate and the hotel industry, and include inflows which have been channelled via Hong Kong or Taiwan with the sole object of changing their identity before they come to be invested in Singapore.

The initiative for these investments springs from several quite distinct motives. First, the climate for doing business in the country of origin may be unfavourable for socio-political as much as for economic reasons: limited banking facilities, the exclusion of private capital from certain sectors, the ever-present state bureaucracy and interventionism, inadequate infrastructures, low productivity. The endemic fear of political instability and of communalist movements (Malaysia operates an ethnic quota system for participation in companies) forces Overseas Chinese business circles throughout the region to regard Singapore as a refuge for their assets.

Secondly, the expansion — both economically and in quality — of the services Singapore offers is attractive to investors from the neighbouring countries, who are fascinated by this beacon of material success. Thirdly, along with Hong Kong and Taiwan, the city-state is one of the main pillars of the Chinese diaspora with links of kinship, business and clientelism extending throughout and even beyond the region. Fourthly, the internal markets of the ASEAN countries — including that of Indonesia, which is by far the biggest but also the least developed — offer only limited outlets for sophisticated products, and present some difficult problems, such as high production costs, lack of skilled labour and customs dues that penalise imports. Finally, obtaining an interest in the industrial and tertiary fabric of Singapore has allowed the neighbouring countries to have access to efficient services, various modern techniques and a more direct acquaintance with the demands of international markets.

Some members of the business community, as well as certain government circles in the neighbouring countries, have denounced — in public statements, at least — the tide of investments converging on Singapore, although there was nothing illegal in it, and Indonesia, for example, exercised no exchange controls.

Will the tendency in future be for ASEAN investment in Singapore to diminish? There is no sure answer, but Singapore's policy of discouraging local concentrations of labour-intensive industries and of encouraging investment in the ASEAN countries suggests that the answer may turn out to be positive. The high cost of setting-up in the city-state and the loss of income to the countries of the region from sales of energy and raw materials show a similar tendency. On the other hand, the uncertain economic and/or political outlook for its regional neighbours gives Singapore a privileged status in the eyes of the business circles in those countries, as a safe haven for capital and a hub of services and technologies capable of responding appropriately to their ambitions as they themselves are seeking to diversify the bases of their economies.

Investment from Malaysia
The close relationship between the Chinese business communities of, respectively, Malaysia and Singapore makes it difficult to identify investment from the peninsula — which consists of minority holdings in a large number of projects, or becomes mixed with the capital of Singaporean, Malaysian (more rarely) and 'multinational' Chinese families.

In 1982–3 the accumulated investments from Malaysia, at around US$900 million, stood in fourth place behind Britain, the United States and Hong Kong but ahead of Japan. By 1986, investment in manufacturing had risen to a value of US$65 million: there were 67 companies with a majority Malaysian shareholding, employing 1,734 people.[22] Each quarter, at least one and often several new initiatives occur, but these seldom involve more than $1 million except at times of crisis in Malaysia — for example, there was an influx in 1969–72 following ethnic disturbances.

Several Malaysian transnational companies, which traditionally dealt in raw materials and diversified their activities after 1965–70, are of special importance: Sime Darby has twenty-four companies in Singapore in insurance, real estate, cars and raw materials; Tan Chong has eight subsidiaries in mechanical engineering and the car business (it has the biggest spare parts depot in South-East Asia); Promet[23] and Dunlop (Malaysia) have each set up three companies in the areas of civil engineering and oil prospecting; and textile and clothing businesses were opened by Tai Wah, South Pacific, Lee Shing and others.

Although real estate in Singapore did not exert the same decisive attraction as a hedge against inflation as for Indonesian investors, it nevertheless played a role: here Tap Yong Seong of Duta Consolidated

---

22. Ng Kwan-Meng (176); *Singapore Business Directory*, 1982; *Report on the Census of Industrial Production*, 1986.
23. Promet founded the Asian Pacific Shipyard in Singapore in 1971. In association

and TMD Malaysia, owner of the Hyatt Regency Hotel and with a 46% share in Sealion Hotels, was the best-known operator.[24]

Even if Malaysian capital invested in Singapore did not measure up in importance to the Singaporean presence in Malaysia, the opening in 1978 of a Singapore office for the Malaysian Industrial Development Authority (MIDA) indicated a speeding-up of bilateral flows.[25]

Investment from Indonesia

The Indonesians were to figure among the first foreign investors in Singapore, with a total exceeding US$5 billion over the years 1967–80; between 20,000 and 30,000 individuals (of whom 89% were Chinese) invested the minimum required in order to obtain the status of permanent residents, and it was the resulting haemorrhage of capital from Indonesia which resulted in the identity of investors being kept secret. Here too the nature of the investments — in real estate, hotels, finance and trading — underlined the attraction of Singapore as a haven. Two names in particular illustrate the close business connections between the respective Chinese business communities of Singapore and Jakarta.[26]

The Harapan business empire, comprising around forty companies,[27] under the direction of Hendra Raharja (*alias* Tan Tjoe Hin), formed a group that included assembly plants and trading companies for cars and cycles, banks, insurance companies and real estate companies. Apart from some money-market speculations in Hong Kong, it has virtually concentrated its activities in Singapore (16 companies) with Harapan Singapore and its two offshoots: one being Harapan Import-Export (HIE) and Richland Development (RD) and the other the consortium Town City Properties, with Singaporean and Thai participation. Parallel with his commercial activities, Raharja became one of Singapore's premier hoteliers with the launching in ¹980–1 of six luxury establishments with accommodation for a total of 4,300 guests.[28]

with Intraco (Singapore) and Elf Aquitaine, its president (Tan Sri Ibrahim) and the director of APS (Brian Chiang) nurture the ambition to become the first local petroleum company in ASEAN.

24. *Malaysian Business*, May 83, pp. 17–18, and *FEER*, 2 Feb. 84, pp. 60–1.
25. *Singapore Business*, Mar. 80, pp. 49–55.
26. J.-L. Margolin (449) and Tan I. Tjhih (219).
27. *FEER*, 3 May 84, and 24 Oct. 85, with diagrams of company structures.
28. Richland Development controls the two Méridien hotels jointly with Air France and some French banks. The Glass Hotel opened in 1985. Only the planned Raharja Centre had its completion date put back to 1986–7 due to the local recession in the hotel business.

Soedono Salim, *alias* Liem Sioe Liong, is the head of an empire comprising about seventy companies, and his personal fortune is possibly among the world's top twenty; he has close relations with the family of the Indonesian President. Forty of his companies, employing a total workforce of 30,000, operate in Indonesia in a great variety of sectors, often in a near-monopolistic position relative to the internal market. The sectors include cement, timber, banking, insurance, cars, cycles, trading, real estate, hotels, textiles, cereals and spices; it is the largest private conglomerate in Indonesia.[29] Liem invests part of the profits earned by the group in foreign markets: Hong Kong, Singapore, California, the Netherlands. In Singapore he has developed a manufacturing company (Cement Grinding), real estate operations (Marine Centre) and multiple lines of collaboration with his six banks and finance companies in Hong Kong.[30]

One could name other considerable investors of Indonesian origin, such as Lim Tjoen Kong whose group Tuan Sing Holdings manufactures plastics, paper and packaging,[31] or Argus Nursalim, which is associated in Singapore with Goh Cheng Liang (T.K. Lim Properties and Mt. Elizabeth Hospital).

Behind these big names are concealed numerous more modest private investors investing their savings in Singapore, either in real estate or in deposit accounts as a 'nest egg' in case Indonesia should fall prey to instability or crisis.

Singapore's investment in the region

Its characteristics

While it has pursued, since the 1970s, a policy of mobilising foreign and local investment in the sector of advanced technology and services, Singapore has become a magnet for investment to the region as a whole, being in the leading ranks of 'developing countries', behind Hong Kong and possibly Taiwan, but ahead of the Philippines and Saudi Arabia.[32]

29. *FEER*, 7 April 83, pp. 44–56; 9 Feb. 84, p. 8, and 15 Nov. 84, pp. 148–9. Certain members of the family of President Suharto, including his son Sigit, his daughter Siti and his brother-in-law Sudwikatmono, are involved.
30. *ST*, 23 Oct. 80, and *Singapore Economic Bulletin*, Mar. 83, p. 42.
31. *FEER*, 2 Feb. 84, pp. 60–1.
32. Pang Eng Fong and Komaran (186); L.T. Wells, *Third World Multinationals*, Cambridge, Mass.: MIT Press, 1983; K. Krishna and M. McLeod (eds), *Multinationals from developing countries*, Lexington, Mass., 1981.

This situation can be explained in Southeast Asia by a 'chain' process of industrialisation, with Singapore as an intermediate link for transnational companies (including Overseas Chinese ones) eager to move into the markets of the neighbouring countries. In the latter, the emergence of a manufacturing sector has coincided with a wish on the part of Singapore to transfer certain classes of production outside the island and so circumvent local protectionism by means of direct investment. Preoccupied with the effects of the international recession on the island's economy, the government sought new guarantees for the viability of the emporium: in 1981 it set up the Government of Singapore Investment Corporation (GIC), and used part of the surpluses of public enterprises and of the state's foreign currency reserves to invest in the ASEAN countries and increase its financial assets and deposits overseas.[33]

In 1984, the estimated investment of Singapore abroad totalled US$1.6 billion, Malaysia and Indonesia being the major beneficiaries, with about 100 subsidiary enterprises. Four out of every five Singaporean companies — including such local concerns as the Overseas Chinese Banking Corporation (OCBC), Wah Chang, Jack Chia, ACMA, Intraco and Temaco — were going ahead with regional projects.[34] The Chinese diaspora was the most active element here, but its activities were the least known. The absence of exchange control and the over-valuation of investment of domestic origin reduced the statistical value of foreign investments declared by various ASEAN countries. In other cases, capital was deposited in Singapore (and Hong Kong), only to be reinjected into its country of origin to benefit from the tax advantages enjoyed locally by foreign investment.[35]

Overseas Chinese big business is represented at the top level by a club of multi-millionaires who — within the law — conduct commercial and financial (less frequently, industrial) operations throughout South-East Asia on the basis of family connections and a variety of interests in Hong Kong, Bangkok, Kuala Lumpur, Manila and Jakarta. For example, *Jack Chia*, a Chinese from Thailand, lives in Singapore where he runs the Hong Kong-based group Jack Chia Holdings (pharmaceuticals, paper manufacturing, publishing, real estate, show business). *Tan Chin Tuan*, president and patriarch of the largest Chinese bank in

33. By 1988 the official reserves had reached US$ 15.7 billion.
34. *ST*, 14 July 84, and *Singapore Econ. Bull.*, Aug. 84, p. 24.
35. *FEER*, 19 Oct. 79, pp. 81–4, and *Bull. of Indonesian Econ. Studies (BIES)*, XX, 2 (Aug. 84), pp. 96 ff.

Singapore, the Overseas Chinese Banking Corporation, cultivates banking links throughout the world. Since 1979 his son *Tony Tan Keng Yam*, who became managing director of OCBC at the age of thirty-eight, has been among the most brilliant technocrats in the Singapore government, in which he has occupied several major ministerial posts. The *Shaw* brothers control, from Singapore and Hong Kong, the world of cinema and real estate. *Wee Choo Yaw* has transformed the small family-owned United Overseas Bank (UOB) into a rival to OCBC. And finally *Robin Loh*, originally from Indonesia, and his sons have made a fortune in Singapore and Hong Kong in shipbuilding and oil installations.

Singapore's investment in Malaysia
Britain, through its Straits Settlements, initiated a policy of making investments designed to exploit the natural wealth of the Malay peninsula. Till recently Singapore has remained one of the five major foreign investors in Malaysia, and with more than US$500 million in the manufacturing sector (some 20% of all foreign investment) outstripped Taiwan, the United States, Britain and Australia; only Japan, which since 1987 has invested US$60–80 million annually, is in a stronger position. These capital flows are directed towards the states in the federation which are physically the most accessible, or which offer the most satisfactory infrastructures: Johore, Malacca, Kuala Lumpur, Penang, Sabah and Sarawak. Mostly they concern specific industries (food, basic commodities, energy, transportation) and the tertiary sector (trading, real estate, hotels, finance), of which the partnership between OCBC and Sime Darby is one of the clearest examples.[36]

The number of projects of Singaporean origin accounted for by the Malaysian Industrial Development Board (MIDA) was, for example, 531 in 1980, and had risen to 703 in 1982. Most were in the form of joint participations — only twenty were subsidiaries — and the best known among them were Fraser and Neave, Cycle and Carriage, Malaysian Breweries, Yeo Hiap Seng, and Ben and Co.[37]

---

36. For detailed figures, see M. Kulasingam and Tan Siew Ee, *Changing patterns of foreign investment in Malaysia*, Penang: Univ. Sains Malaysia, 1982; Khor Kok Peng (145); *FEER*, 12 May 78, pp. 40–3, and 19 Oct. 79, pp. 82–4; *ST*. 18 Feb. 81 and 18 May 83; *The Star*, 22 Aug. 82; *NST*, 18 Nov. 79.

37. *Singapore Business*, July 83, pp. 35–43. Among the 100 Malaysian companies analysed in 1974/5, 32% of the managerial posts were filled by Chinese, of whom 13% were Singaporeans. On this topic, see Sieh Lee Mei Ling, 'Ownership and

Since 1987–8, Singapore has been speeding up its rate of investment in Malaysia, notably in Johore, Selangor and Trengganu. This has been caused partly by circumstances (a fall in the value of the Malaysian dollar and a rise in production costs in Singapore) but above all for structural reasons (the delocalisation of Singapore's industries into Malaysia and the attraction of the production factors which Malaysia is able to offer). In 1988 new investments totalled no less than 135, with a value of more that US$70 million — an increase of more than 22% on 1987. This made Singapore the fourth-largest foreign investor after Japan, the United States and Taiwan ($147 million).[38]

The multinationals already established in Singapore, such as the British group Boustead, were partly responsible for this foreign penetration in Malaysia. Boustead controls thirteen companies in rubber, freighters, containers and insurance. The federal government has redoubled its efforts to attract investment from Singapore since the announcement that certain industries were to be delocalised, a move that was the subject of regular bilateral consultations between the Singaporean and Malaysian chambers of commerce and professional associations. In 1984–5, it put in hand a regime favouring Singaporean investors by exempting them from the rule requiring a 30% *bumiputra*[39] participation in the capital of companies registered in Malaysia, and authorising them to control 70% of the shares, even after 1990.

This legislation shows the extent to which the authorities in Kuala Lumpur see the role of the Chinese business circles as essential, communalist policies thus not preventing dialogue.[40]

Singapore's presence in Malaysia is identifiable particularly in the following sectors: foodstuffs (Central Sugars, Zuelling Feedmills, Amoy Canning, Khong Guan Flour, Lam Soon Oil and Soap, Malaysian Feedmills); textiles (South Pacific, Mahsiung, Fusan Fishing Nets); metallurgy (Rheem Hume, Joint Steel Works, Iron and Steel Mills,

---

control of Malaysian manufacturing corporations', Kuala Lumpur: UMBC, 1982.
38. *ST*, 24 Jan. and 14 Nov. 87, 27 Apr. and 20 Sept. 88, 17 Feb. and 16 Mar. 89.
39. *Bumiputra* (= 'son of the land') signifies every person who is ethnically Malay, as opposed to the Chinese and Indians who have migrated into the region at a relatively late period. As will be seen in Part II of this work, the New Economic Policy adopted in Malaysia since 1969–70 defines quotas for the participation of Malays in the national economy with a view to enlarging their role, which had previously been marginal in relation to the Chinese, Indian and/or foreign companies.
40. *Singapore Econ. Bull.*, Feb. 1985, p. 20; *Singapore Business*, Mar. 1985, p. 93.

Metal Box, Metal Containers); electrical and electronic installations (Acma Electrical, Haw Par Brothers, Pan Electrico, Wah Chang); building and real estate (Metro Holdings, Straits Trading, United Engineers, Intraco); timber, paper and publishing (SPP, Times Publishing, Veneer Products, Jack Chia), and so on. Jack Chia is the sole owner of ten companies regrouped in Jack Chia Enterprises Malaysia (various consumer goods, publishing, finance, hotels in Penang and Kuala Lumpur). Eric Chia, son of the founder of Singapore Motors, has built up in Malaysia, since creating the KK Motor Co. in 1970, an empire comprising regional distribution of agricultural, construction and transportation equipment which figures among the ten most important companies in the country.[41]

The firm rapprochement in economic relations between the two countries has come about through the development of the state of Johore, with which Singapore has always had close ties. The city-state was, in the past, crucially dependent on Johore for its water supply, but this has been successfully transformed into a form of negotiated inter-dependence.[42] The accords of 1927 and 1961–2 allowed Singapore to receive daily, through three pipelines (40 km. in length), 136 million litres of filtered water. Certainly this was dependence, with half of the island's needs being met in this way, but it was balanced by the Public Utilities Board of Singapore managing a concession of 7,195 hectares in Johore (Tebrau and Scudai, and the reservoirs of Pontian and Gunong Pulai) and producing drinking water (from five plants, including new ones at Pasir Gudang and Sungai Kahang), which it partly re-sold to the local administration of Johor Baru. To remedy the steep rise in water consumption, in both Singapore[43] and Johore, the two parties plan to harness the Johore river basin with diversions, reservoirs and pipelines over a period of twenty years at an estimated cost of US$4.2 billion.[44]

In 1988, after long and at times difficult negotiations which became very tense politically after the Israeli President's visit to Singapore in 1987, a bilateral accord on water supply was concluded: the term was to be ninety-nine years, with the possibility of revision at the end of twenty-five years.[45] Singapore, whose water consumption increases by

41. *Malaysian Business*, June 1982, pp. 6–19, and May 1983, pp. 17–18.
42. *ST*, 3 Dec. 82, 9 & 21 Feb. 83 and 29 Nov. 84.
43. The water supply problem is a regular theme for local politicians as proof of the knife-edge nature of Singapore's survival.
44. *FEER*, 3 Oct. 85, pp. 19–20.
45. *ST*, 20 July 88.

an average of 3% annually, has undertaken to buy a supplementary 2,250 million litres of water each year and to sell to Malaysia, at a concessionary price, treated water in exchange for deliveries of gas. In parallel, Johore launched a programme for building nine water treatment stations in order to be less dependent on Singapore for this service.[46]

But the trans-frontier exchanges did not end there. The central generating stations of Senoko in Singapore and Pasir Gudang in Johore were able to exchange electricity in cases of breakdown or shortage. Studies are being made of a second causeway, or at least a car ferry between Changi Point and Desaru. Johore's industrialisation benefits from Singapore's proximity: more than sixty Singaporean enterprises have already been established there, and several other projects are in course of installation, with US$200 million being invested, notably in the industrial and port zone of Pasir Gudang, which is linked to the Singapore-Johor Baru-Kuala Lumpur railway. The investments are in agricultural foodstuffs, textiles, metallurgy, electronics, petroleum installations (Promet), plastics and timber. The building of new accommodation in Johor Baru, the attraction for tourism and the creation of new free trade zones were all incentives for Singaporean financiers. With the city-state lacking space and human resources, and with its production costs becoming too high in certain sectors, the south of Johore thus provided a prolongation of its economic boom.[47]

Since 1987-8, the authorities in Johore and Singapore have assiduously intensified their mutual trade and economic cooperation. In 1988 the Singapore-Johore Trade Group was set up, and in 1989 the Johore-Singapore Joint Committee on Business Communication. The partners involved put into effect a programme of support for businesses in Singapore wishing to extend their operations to Johore. Also being developed are joint programmes for the promotion of tourism, and links by road (Singapore-Johor Baru-Malacca) and by sea (a Johore-Changi ferry) are being reinforced. The building of a second Causeway is the subject of a medium-term plan.

In short, the authorities in Johore are clearly committing themselves to a number of different forms of linkage with Singapore within the

---

46. *ST*, 7 Jan., 20 Mar. and 22 Sept. 87, 23–24 Jan., 27–28–29 June; 1 and 20 July; 2 Aug. 88.

47. Johor Baru, Investment Seminar Southern Region and Republic of Singapore, 'Economic activity and investment potentials in Johore', 28 Feb.–1 Mar. 1978 (57pp.); Univ. of Malaya Library, *Johore: A bibliography*, Kuala Lumpur: 1982.

framework of a new economic development plan for their state covering the next two decades.[48]

Singapore's investment in Indonesia

Singapore's accumulated investment in Indonesia — which, according to Indonesian sources, reached US$314 million in 1969–87 — placed the island-state in the forefront of Asian investors (with Japan and Taiwan)[49] and first among the ASEAN states, well ahead of the Philippines and Malaysia. We are talking of thirty-one projects out of a total of 844 approved by the BKPM (Indonesia's bureau for the coordination of foreign investment) in the areas where the two economies have proved to be complementary: chemicals, building, hotels, timber, textiles, foodstuffs, office equipment, metal ores and transportation.[50] In 1988 Singapore accelerated the reallocation of local industries to Indonesia, and total investment increased by 1876% compared to 1987 figures — with an amount of US$255 million against 275 million invested in Thailand.

If one compares this to the contribution of the industrialised countries, one sees that Singapore's investment has certain specific features. Its fluctuation from one year to the next depended very clearly on the evolution of socio-political stability under the regime of President Suharto. There were tangible signs of increased confidence, coinciding with the progressive consolidation of the New Order introduced immediately after the attempted coup in 1965, but the way forward remained hazardous at times, as the internal troubles of 1984–5 made clear.[51] At the same time, the Indonesian statistics (those of Singapore are lacking where bilateral trade is concerned) under-value or completely ignore the numerous transactions within (Chinese) families and those based on trust in a verbal commitment by this or that Indonesian intermediary, promising not to reveal the foreign identity of the capital provided. Each operation licenses projects of small or medium size (US$1–3 million), which are expected to return profits in the short or

48. *ST*, 10 Apr., 25 May 87; 17, 22 and 27 Apr., 21, 27 and 28–29 June, 22 July, 22 Aug., 9, 17 and 25 Sept. and 9 Oct. 88; 30 Mar. and 18 Sept. 89.
49. *ST*, 16 Aug. 87.
50. *BIES*, XX, 2 (Aug. 1984), pp. 96 ff., and XXII, 1 (Apr. 1986), pp. 34–56.
51. A violent politico-religious agitation, inspired by Muslim extremism, developed in Indonesia following the events at Tanjung Priok (Jakarta) in Sept. 1983, which resulted in several dozen deaths. Bomb attacks and criminal arson occurred in the capital and several large provincial towns, even reaching the important Borobudur temple in central Java.

medium term — in contrast to investment in infrastructures or heavy industry; limited participation is sought, and Western techniques, 'predigested' in Singapore, are adapted on the spot to local requirements.[52]

Singapore's earliest investments in Indonesia date back to the nineteenth century. The Maya group with 4,000 employees, which is among the oldest, includes six companies specialising in the export of seafood, a biscuit factory and two insecticide works; and other industries, in chemicals and plastics, may have to be transferred from Singapore. Concerns such as Prima Indonesia (agricultural products) in southern Sulawesi; United International Plastic Indonesia in western Java; and Pulo Mas Realty (a trading company), Karimun (granite) and Asia Tegoo Mining in southern Kalimantan have all been targeted by Singaporean companies (Gammon Southeast and Asia Mining Enterprises in the last two cases). Some of the companies already mentioned in connection with Malaysia such as Yeo Hiap Seng, Acma Electrical, Fraser and Neave, Intraco and United Engineers are also active in Indonesia.

The policy of industrial delocalisation adopted by Singapore affected its giant neighbour in a number of ways. Sembawang set up in west Java, jointly with PT Kusuma Wirya Perdana, a steelworks, Indo Sembawang Fabrikasi, specialising in heavy equipment for the oil industry, and Jurong Engineering plans to build a thermal power station and a petrochemical factory. But, in the same way as the development of south Johore has followed in the wake of the economic rise of Singapore, an increasing proportion of Singapore's economic relations with Indonesia are concentrated on a single island, Batam, in the Riau archipelago, a few miles south of Singapore itself.

Batam

From 1968–9 onwards, it became difficult for Jakarta to continue as the sole depot for the equipment necessary for offshore exploitation and the extraction of oil and gas in the Natuna islands and northern Sumatra. The state oil company, Pertamina, decided to sign a contract with four foreign oil companies in order to transform Batam into the new logistical base for its operations.

Taking its stand on Batam's importance in geostrategic terms, similar

52. A. Zahri, 'Singapore-Indonesia economic relations' in Wong Kum Poh and Maureen Tan (eds) (233); L.T. Wells, op. cit., note 31; *IBAS Bull.*, 1981, pp. 57–62; *BIES*, Mar. 79, pp. 69–74.

to Singapore's, Presidential Decree no. 41 of 1973 declared the island an industrial zone, under the authority of BIDA (the Batam Industrial Development Authority, with its headquarters in Jakarta) and the Batam Industrial Corporation, and raised the level of objectives fixed initially: henceforward, on the basis of a report by the consultants Bechtel (USA) and Nissho-Iwai (Japan), it was a matter of building an oil refinery, fuel storage facilities and harbour infrastructures capable of accommodating supertankers, and of attracting there a wide spectrum of industries.[53]

Although, with Javanese diplomatic finesse, the fact could not be admitted openly, Indonesia cherished the ambition to acquire an instrument capable of reducing its economic dependence on Singapore and to compete with this 'Chinese' city-state on its own terms — ever-mindful that if the Dutch had not occupied the Riau archipelago in 1819, Raffles might well have been able to land on Batam rather than stopping in the neighbouring island of Singapore.

Perhaps the means used to launch this project can be questioned: did BIDA command sufficient resources to create the necessary infrastructure and attract investment in an island almost as barren as Singapore was at the time of its first settlement? Was the government willing to devote substantial funds to the development of Batam while the needs of Indonesia as a whole, regardless of sector, remained so vast? These questions were asked by foreign observers when the giant Pertamina corruption scandal, involving the president of the company, was shaking Indonesia in 1974–6. Although a few basic projects had been put in hand on the ground, the grandiose plans for Batam were shelved.[54]

In 1978 the plan was relaunched, being entrusted by President Suharto to the powerful Minister of Research and Technology, Habibie, assisted by his brother-in-law Soedarsono, the head of BIDA, and this time it was on more solid foundations: with tax exemption for all products bonded, processed or consumed in Batam, and the opening of negotiations with Singapore regarding equipment and investment. In October 1980, agreement was reached on free movement between Singapore and Batam (but nowhere else in Indonesia) for goods, individuals and

53. *Batam Island Investment Guide*, Singapore: Delta Orient and Pertamina, May 1976 (Consultants' Paper); *New Nation* (Singapore), 13 Mar. 74; *ST*, 4 Mar. 73 and 15 Sept. 77.

54. A colossal corruption scandal, compromising the president of Pertamina, Indonesia's national petroleum company, erupted in 1974–6.

services. Furthermore, Lee Kuan Yew indicated that investment would be left — in the city-state at least — to the private sector.[55]

Among the forty foreign companies involved in Batam at the time of writing, the decisive contribution appears to come from Singapore, which has an 80% stake in the total of projects under way. One of the largest realised so far, by Tan Choon Lian in association with PT Tongkat Mas International, is Batam Island Country Club and Holiday Resort: tourism has been the first success story of Batam, bringing in more than 25,000 tourists every month in 1989 — almost all coming from Singapore on weekend package tours and allowed to buy duty-free goods, which is not allowed in Johor Baru. Other initiatives have been announced: a pig farm (delocalised from Singapore) financed by Liem Sioe Liong and the Singaporean Oei Hong Leong, a Chinese originally living in Indonesia, who owns 40% of the United Industrial Corporation; the installation of subcontracting workshops (Batam Metal Products) tied to the Singapore Metro, and the construction of a submarine pipeline allowing water to be brought to Batam.[56] Cooperation extends to the transportation sector (links by ferry-boat and hovercraft, sale of used vehicles) and labour, a commodity of which, unlike Singapore, Indonesia has no shortage. On the other hand, Singapore is able to provide trained personnel: already hundreds of specialist workers and technicians have been sent to Batam.[57] The city-state, finally, has offered several times to collaborate in an oil pipeline linking the Natuna islands to Batam, but its realisation has been constrained by the recession in the petroleum market as well as by certain feasibility problems. Since 1987, Indonesia has sought to relaunch the project in order to speed up its natural gas exports.[58]

The adoption of the second development plan (1984–9) for Batam aroused impassioned discussion, as much in Singapore as in Indonesia. On Singapore's side, even if BIDA did agree to make an unequivocal

55. Discussions on Batam recurred regularly at summit level between Lee and Suharto: *ST*, 5 Nov. 78, 19–22 Sept. 79, 1 Nov. 79, 28 Feb. 80, 5 July 80, 8 Sept. 80, 28 Dec. 83. For data on Batam see BIDA, *The Batam development program*, Jakarta: BIDA, July 1980 (see also pp. 273–5).
56. *Singapore Econ. Bull.*, Dec. 82, p. 28; *FEER*, 5 July 1984, pp. 61–2; *ST*, 23 Dec. 83, 16 Dec. 84, 27 Dec. 1984. Batam exported 75,000 pigs in 1986–7, which constituted half of Indonesia's total exports of pork to Singapore (*ST*, 7 Jan. 87).
57. *ST*, 9 Apr. 81 and 10 June 83.
58. *ST*, 10 Sept. 82, 16 Oct. 82, 6 Oct. 83; *Malaysian Business*, Sept. 1983, p. 112, and *ST*, 26 Feb. 82, 13 July 87, 3 Feb. 88. The feasibility study was carried out by the Dutch company Gasuni Amro.

budgetary effort towards providing basic infrastructures, the results nonetheless were extremely modest. An Indonesian policy aimed at building a great industrial and communications centre in Batam is still a long way in the future when the forty companies already there have to make their own arrangements to receive supplies of water and electricity. Batam is in no way a dangerous rival to the city-state, in so far as it cannot do without material contributions from there. Much of its future is linked to Singapore's economic standing.

The expansion in Singapore's activities overflowed upon its immediate environment (South Johore and Riau) on the principle of 'communicating jars', to use a metaphor of Habibie's. The whole area feels the effect of the spatial and human limits of the city-state, which is forced to delocalise certain of its industries and at the same time reinforce the complementarities which already exist with its neighbours.[59] However, the complementarity of the two islands extends to Singapore's post-industrial development in leisure activities: beyond the meagre resources of the small Singaporean island of Sentosa, Batam offers considerable potential for water sports, weekend tourism and short vacations from Singapore, and this development is proceeding apace.[60]

On the Indonesian side, the centre of power (notably President Suharto and Minister Habibie) seems convinced of the need to cooperate with Singapore, but although there is no alternative, the massive influx of 'Chinese' and transnational capital into Batam caused anxiety in some political circles. On a visit he made to Batam in 1979, Lee Kuan Yew announced the possibility of a participation of more than US$1 billion in the development of local infrastructures, on condition that investors should be able to remain the prime contractors and to repatriate an adequate part of their profits. The reaction in certain quarters, and not least that of Dr Chalik Ali of the Unified Muslim Party (PPP) and the then Minister of Information Ali Murtopo, was to accuse Singapore of wishing to turn Batam into one of its economic satellites and thus threaten Indonesian sovereignty.[61] But under the guise of a provisional

---

59. *Asian Finance*, 14, 16 (15 June 88), pp. 74–6; *FEER*, 7 Feb. 85, p. 61; Lam Kwok Weng, 'Problems of urban expansion in Singapore', *Planews* (Singapore), vol. 2, no. 4 (1973), pp. 14–17.
60. *ST*, 28 Jan. 87 and 15 July 88.
61. The accusation was immediately modified by the Vice-President, Adam Malik, and by Habibie. *FEER*, 19 Oct. 79, pp. 81–4; *ST*, 22 Sept. 79; *Asiaweek*, 14 Oct. 80, pp. 42–3.

arrangement only, the future of Batam may in fact be considered one of the best instruments for increasing the number of complementarities between the two countries.

In view of the unwieldy nature of the Indonesian administration, the international recession which affects budgets and the flow of investment from all sources, and the state of the infrastructures already laid down in Batam which remain rudimentary, the economic take-off of the island can only be expected to reach a respectable threshhold in 20–30 years.[62] Because of the vertiginous growth of the city-state since 1965, its own economic history, which began nearly 150 years earlier, tends to be forgotten. Batam cannot be built in a day.

The debate concerning the threat to Indonesian sovereignty, though dormant for the time being, is not entirely irrelevant. How does one envisage a development for Batam which is both speedy and viable if Jakarta does not define a special economic statute in its favour? This should be as much on the administrative side (as has already been done, when President Suharto, Habibie and BIDA excluded it from the local government of the Riau archipelago) as in connection with commercial and financial regulations (the adoption of a zone of free circulation between Singapore and Batam, not to be extended to relations between Batam and the rest of Indonesia).

On the hypothesis that such instruments will contribute in due course to an economic success for the Batam experiment, this could not fail to act as a challenge to the central government in Indonesia, and to provide new arguments for those who recommend a certain liberalisation of the Indonesian economic system. Singapore, which cannot be dissociated from this supposed success of Batam, would thus find its way for the first time within the frontiers of its big neighbour, there to raise — or intensify — the wind of reform.

Events towards the end of 1989 gave indications which seemed to confirm this analysis. After a meeting between President Suharto and Lee Kuan Yew on 6 October, Indonesia had become effectively convinced of the need to strengthen and/or introduce greater flexibility into the economic and financial status of Batam. For example, BIDA announced that processing industries located in Batam and exporting from there to the rest of Indonesia would not be subject to customs duties on finished products but only on imported raw materials.

---

62. For the declarations by Lee Kuan Yew and Suharto see *ST*, 28 Dec. 83. See also Singapore International Chamber of Commerce, 'Notes on the visit to Batam on 3rd March 1981 by 35 members of the Chamber', Singapore: SIIC, 1981.

Secondly, full foreign ownership of companies incorporated in Batam and which export all their production was authorised in 1989–90, with the sole proviso that 5% of the equity should have passed to an Indonesian partner within the following five years. And thirdly, private companies are now allowed (as they would be anywhere else in Indonesia) to establish industrial estates on the island and make full use of the Batam free trade zone status (US$600 million worth of goods were already shipped from Batam to the rest of Indonesia in 1989).

This new legislation is an unmistakable signal for more Singaporean investment to pour into Batam. Singapore Technologies Industrial Corporation and Jurong Engineering announced in 1989 a 40% stake in a 500-ha. industrial estate (US$214 million) in Batam. Applications for eight other industrial estates (1,800 ha. in total) were also approved in 1989/90.

After years of hesitation, these new developments indicate that Batam might become, in the long run, an alternative to Johore for the relocation of some of Singapore's labour-intensive manufacturing industry. This would also accord closely with Singapore's constant preoccupation to share its economic growth more or less equally with both its Indonesian and Malaysian neighbours.

Sectoral complementarities and rivalries originating in Singapore

Singapore's historical function as a regional entrepot engendered some traditional complementarities in its commerce with the neighbouring countries. The appearance of new complementarities since the 1960s are the result of a double evolution.

At first, manufacturing industry in Singapore underwent spectacular growth, dependent in part on a regional neighbourhood which remained an exporter of unprocessed raw materials. More recently, in a second phase, the neighbours began to exploit their vast natural resources and to industrialise. The Singaporean economy felt itself obliged to abandon, in their favour, certain key industries which had driven its expansion ten years earlier, and to establish itself in the specialised areas involving advanced technologies and the tertiary sector.

Even if complementarities were increasing in number, this evolution, seen as a whole, did not proceed from a coherent or well-oiled economic structuring of the ASEAN zone, as appeared on the surface. Competing and conflicting ambitions as between Singapore and its partners — which certainly cannot be seen purely in an economic context — became apparent on the regional scene.

Complementarities in the traditional sectors

Continuity or relative decline in some traditional sectors

Natural rubber, tin and vegetable oils were among the raw materials that were most typical of Singapore's entrepot activities from the nineteenth century onwards, and ASEAN today is still in the first rank as an exporter in this sector.

Between a quarter and a third of Malaysia's and Indonesia's sales still transit via Singapore, and thus include contraband, especially in tin. This fact allows trading companies and the city-state's raw materials market, linked to that of London, to influence the development of market prices worldwide — on which the export revenues of its neighbours depend.[63] The neighbours try to reduce this overwhelming commercial power of Singapore by improving their own infrastructures, creating their own national markets for raw materials, and fighting the contraband trade.[64]

Singapore retains an undeniable advantage in the area of marketing: the Rubber Association of Singapore (1911) handles 3–4 times the volume of business controlled by the Malaysian Rubber Exchange (1974); the rubber companies and their commercial agents are registered in both markets and, if they augment their physical purchases on the Malaysian market, most of the principal services — storage and forwarding, control of standards, documentation and financial management — remain concentrated in Singapore. As Lee Kuan Yew declared in 1980, the city-state has no wish to compete with Malaysia in the processing of its natural rubber (Singapore had less than ten rubber-processing companies in 1985, employing barely 1,000 people), but he omitted to comment on the commercial side of Malaysia's production, which passes via Singapore's services.[65] The latter consist of companies exporting throughout the world: Ann Bee, Ban Jo,

63. E.R. Grillo *et al.*, *The world rubber economy*, Baltimore: Johns Hopkins UP, 1980; Joan Wilson, *The Singapore Rubber Market*, Singapore: Eastern UP, 1958; UN/ESCAP, *Transnational corporations and distribution in the tin industry in Southeast Asia*, Bangkok, Sept. 1982; Singapore Trade and Industry, Jan. 1974, pp. 27–31; *Singapore Econ. Bull.*, Jan. 1983, p. 24; *FEER*, 24 May 84, pp. 77–8, and 5 July 84, p. 8; *Business Times* (Singapore), 6 Mar. 85.
64. *Singapore Business*, Mar. 1980, pp. 49–55; *Malaysian Business*, Nov. 1982, pp. 16–20; *FEER*, 20 Oct. 83, p. 80, and 17 Nov. 83, p. 81.
65. C. Barlow (95), pp. 309–54; Tan Eng Joo, 'The Singapore rubber market and the Indonesian producer', *IBAS Bull.*, Mar. 78, pp. 15–21; *Southeast Asian Affairs*, 1981, pp. 273–89; *Singapore Econ. Bull.*, Aug. 82, p. 17; Singapore Min. of Trade and Industry, *Economic Survey*, 1983, pp. 38–9.

Harrisons and Crossfield, Kallang, Kota Trading, Lee Latex, Pacific Resources, Tong Teik and Tropical Produce.

Renovation of other traditional sectors

Wood. The wood industry has created an interesting regional division of labour at the heart of ASEAN, notably between Singapore (with 96 companies and 2,900 employees in 1987) and Indonesia, with its 122 million hectares of forests, which is the world's foremost producer and provides Singapore with 80–85% of its purchases, the remaining 15% coming from Malaysia (Sabah).[66]

The number of industries involved in the first stage of processing is declining in Singapore, but increasing in the neighbouring countries. The thirty-four existing sawmills (there were more than 100 in 1900) came up against the prohibition by both Malaysia and Indonesia of exports of bark. In Indonesia, where the legislation affects no more than half of the local bark production, Singapore manages to obtain 40,000 m.[3] of timber per month to enable its sawmill industry to survive, but Indonesia's commercial policy in this respect could one day become more restrictive. The 350 plywood companies (making it the eighth-largest such industry in the world), which include Aeconic, Anrobois, Cominco, Far East Construction, Kranjin Plywood Industrial and Grinling, are dependent on the same sources of supply as their Indonesian counterparts, but do better because of their competitiveness in price and quality, whereas the Indonesian companies encounter serious difficulties: a low level of integration, geographical isolation, costly freight charges, an ill-qualified workforce and deforestation.[67]

For its part, the wood industry, with its high value added, is in good shape in Singapore. It specialises in the drying of extracts such as gums and resins, mouldings for parquet floors and doors, and furniture (it boasts 159 companies with 7,400 employees, and the world's largest chair factory). Meanwhile, elsewhere in the region, the industry is in an embryonic state or non-existent.

Looking to the future, the city-state holds a number of winning cards. The majority of forest concession owners in Indonesia and Malaysia are shareholders in businesses with a presence in Singapore in the form of

66. French Embassy, Singapore (Economic dept), *Les industries du bois*, 16 June 80; *Asia Research Bull.* (ARB), 11, 6 (30 Nov. 81), pp. 862–4.
67. *FEER*, 18 July 83, pp. 53–3; 6 Sept. 84, pp. 112–13, and 8 Nov. 84, p. 84; *Jakarta Post*, 11 Mar. 85.

a subsidiary or a trading office. The international companies dealing in wood products are all represented within the Singapore Timber Industry Board (seven timber yards at Sungai Kadut), and make their purchases and obtain quality control within that context. Where quality is concerned, Malaysia and Indonesia can scarcely offer resistance to the competition and the modernity of the concerns based in Singapore, which give further proof of their dynamism by investing in Sumatra and Sabah. Malaysia's efforts to achieve direct exports since 1974–6 have only shown up its limitations in the battle against Singaporean ascendancy in the marketing of wood products, in the absence of adequate infrastructures and integration in the local market.[68]

Agriculture and food. The important role of the agricultural food industry in Singapore, with 310 companies and a workforce of 12,800, is explained primarily by the extreme dependence of the emporium on outside sources of supply, with no resources of its own for feeding its population (small as that may be). Though self-sufficient in pig-meat and poultry (this is due to be delocalised in the future to the Riau archipelago and Johore), Singapore buys most of its foodstuffs from Malaysia and Thailand, and to a smaller extent from Australia and Indonesia.

The city-state also continues to profit from its vocation — inherited from colonial times — as regional distributor. This shows itself in several ways. First, re-exportation to Western countries of products from Malaysia and Indonesia (spices, coffee, vegetable oils, exotic fruits), often processed in Singapore (canned and packaged foods, fats), has been maintained and has even made advances since the early 1980s. Secondly, trade in foodstuffs places Singapore at the very centre of intra-ASEAN exchanges, with a role to play in case of emergencies, and to speed up the delivery of cereals from Thailand to Malaysia (especially its eastern parts) and Western goods to satisfy the growing demand in the urban centres of the region: the respective capitals, Penang, Johor Baru, Medan, Surabaya and so on.[69] And thirdly, Singapore's domestic exports are also making progress — notably of drinks, animal feeds, oilseeds, frozen and canned foods, and condiments. Significant examples

68. E.K. Fisk & H. Osman-Rani (eds) (118), pp. 256–7; *ARB*, 6, 8 (1977), p. 284; *Malaysian Business*, May 1978, pp. 2–10; *Business Times*, 4 Sept. 1980; *NST*, 23 Jan. 81.

69. French Embassy, Singapore (Economic dept), *Le secteur agro-alimentaire à Singapour, données actualisées*, 21 Apr. 84; *FEER*, 12 Apr. 84, pp. 51–2.

are Tai Hua Food Industries (directed by the Singaporean Peh Cheng Chuan) and the recently-created Cerebos Pacific, which manages the regional interests of the foremost British agricultural produce group, Rank Hovis McDougall.[70]

The industries instrumental to the economic growth of the 1970s: regional complementarities raise questions for the future

The petroleum industry

This sector has been the true driving force in the expansion of manufacturing industry throughout the 1970s, benefiting from the oil price rise which spurred the development of regional energy resources. It transformed Singapore, which had been a coal depot in the age of steam navigation, into Asia's leading entrepot and the third-largest worldwide, after Rotterdam and Houston, with 1.1 million barrels per day. Out of a total of some 230 oil companies existing throughout the world, 200 have invested in the local marketing of oil exploration and exploitation equipment for use in Indonesia, Malaysia, Thailand, Brunei and Burma, and in the storage and refining of crude oil imported from the Middle East and Indonesia before being sold to Japan and the ASEAN countries.[71]

Up till 1980, the oil industry contributed 60% of all imports, 45% of foreign investment and 40% of manufacturing, but subsequently it became — in part, at least — an idol with feet of clay, due both to the international recession and to structural changes in the neighbouring producer-countries. The doubts this cast on a mainstay of the economy — which some considered to have played an excessive role, in view of the inherent dependence of all emporia — have been behind the whole range of factors which have persuaded the governments of the region to orient themselves towards more diversified activities.

Singapore, regional centre of refining: some uncertainties. With its geographical situation on the route for oil exports from the Middle East and South-East Asia, the city-state, anxious to take advantage of its special position as a middleman, offers an annual refining capacity of 50

70. *Singapore Econ. Bull.*, June 1982, p. 21.
71. *Singapore Trade/Industry Yearbook*, 1974, pp. 23–33; *Financial Times (FT), Singapore Survey*, 1 Oct. 73, 29 Sept. 75, 22 Nov. 82.

million tonnes.[72] However, from 1983–4 onwards, this was only used to 60–70% of its capacity, and Shell had to close down one of its four plants.[73] How did this come about?

Even more than the drop in demand for petroleum resulting from the world recession and the emergence of new energy sources, it was above all the excess capacity existing internationally to which the refineries in Singapore fell victim. Deliveries of crude from the Middle East (55% of the total) and Indonesia (30%) dropped in tandem with the entry into service, in 1984–7, of new refineries in the suppliers' own countries. Supplies from Indonesia fell by a half in 1982–5, as the three refineries of Balikpapan, Cilacap and Dumai acquired sufficient capacity to process the entire output of the archipelago (above 800,000 barrels a day since 1986–7), and as direct purchases from the Middle East of the types of petroleum which Indonesia cannot produce increased. Thus the old rivalry in petroleum-related services between Singapore and Indonesia – which assumed concrete form with the ambitious projects of Pertamina's president, General Ibnu Sutowo, in Batam — has returned.

However, there are a number of reasons for thinking that in the name of what has become their classic policy of mobilisation for the survival of the emporium, the authorities in the city-state may have taken to using more alarmist language than the situation warrants. First the initially poor performance of the new Indonesian refineries gave Singapore a respite in which it could seek other markets and re-convert certain installations. In addition, some categories of Indonesian petroleum (notably those with low sulphur content) can only be processed in Singapore, at Pulau Bukom and Jurong. The delivery of Indonesian natural gas from the Arjuna fields will also gradually replace oil trading.[74] Secondly, purchases of crude oil from Malaysia (already 23% of the total in 1983), Brunei[75] and Thailand will keep Singapore's petroleum industry going. Petronas, the national petroleum company of Malaysia, sells it 80,000 barrels a day at a high price, which it accepts in order to keep its refineries busy. The laying-down of new refineries at Trengganu and Malacca in Malaysia does not seem to have jeopardised

72. Five refineries: Shell (460,000 barrels per day); Esso (231,000); Singapore Refining (170,000), grouping Caltex-Singapore Petroleum-BP; BP (27,000).
73. *ST*, 3 July 85.
74. *ST*, 25 Feb. 1 Mar. and 14 May 83; *FEER*, 19 July 84, pp. 90–2; 8 Nov. 84, p. 98; 15 Nov. 84, p. 116; 22 Nov. 84, pp. 91–2.
75. Brunei Shell Petroleum: *FEER*, 15 Mar. 84, pp. 57–60, and 4 Oct. 84, pp. 68–9.

the project for a gas pipeline from Trengganu to Singapore to feed Singapore's central storage plant and its chemical industry, whose needs it is expected to supply increasingly.[76] Confronted by a world surplus of refining capacity, Bangkok, like Kuala Lumpur, is hesitant about making significant investments in this area. In 1987, Malaysia renewed its contracts to supply 60–70,000 barrels of crude oil daily to the refineries in Singapore, which in 1988 were once again working at 90% of capacity. In due course, these deliveries are certain to become less when the refinery at Malacca comes into service.[77] As mentioned above, a new bilateral accord on water supplies signed in 1988 committed Malaysia at the same time to supply Singapore with gas on preferential terms for fifteen years from 1990–1.[78]

Thirdly, the exploration carried out in China jointly by Shell of Singapore and Sino Chemicals of China has resulted since 1983 in China supplying 80,000 barrels a day.[79] Finally, the worldwide fall in prices and petroleum consumption was not altogether of disservice to Singapore with its exceptionally competitive infrastructures.

In 1986–8 the favourable development of the international situation enabled Singapore (which exports two-thirds of its production of refined petroleum, also equalling 25–30% of its total of domestic exports) to bring the utilisation of its refineries above 80% of their capacity.[80] On the other hand, medium-term projections (for 1990) were less optimistic, anticipating a drop to 70% or below, actual capacity being 850,000 barrels a day.

Regional competition continues to increase: Indonesia has become more or less independent in the treatment of its crude, and Malaysia could be in the same situation in 1991–2 when its second refinery is expected to go into service.[81] With the deregulation of the petroleum markets in Australia and Japan, meaning new forms of competition but

76. *ST*, 24 July 82, 18 Mar. 83, 5 July 83, 8 Sept. 83, 22 Oct. 83, 14 Jan. 84, 4 Mar. 84; *Malaysian Business*, Feb. 82, pp. 28–33; *FEER*, 2 July 82, pp. 82–6; 31 May 84, pp. 56–8; and 18 Oct. 84, pp. 80, 81. The gas-pipeline project has been somewhat delayed: *FEER*, 9 Feb. 89.

77. *ST*, 29 May 87.

78. *ST*, 1 July 88.

79. The contract had to be extended to 1988–90.

80. Development Bank of Singapore, *The Singapore petroleum industry*, Dec. 1987.

81. Malaysia still buys 60,000 barrels a day — there is only a single refinery at Trengganu up till the present. Petronas is building a second refinery at Malacca, which should enter into service in Jan. 1991, with a capacity of 100,000 barrels a day. See also *ST*, 6 Feb. 1988.

also new business opportunities for Singapore, the local companies are undertaking investments aimed at creating production of a more specialised nature and with higher value added.[82] In short, the local oil industry seems doomed to have to adapt itself to external fluctuations, whether over new foreign competition, international deregulation of markets, exports and world prices that become ever more volatile. Still, the economic dynamism of the Asia-Pacific region augurs well for the health of Singapore's petroleum industry.[83]

Singapore as a centre of petroleum trading. Singapore remains the most important centre for this trade in the Asia-Pacific region, and in this it has the edge over Tokyo. The core activity is in the free market, where more than fifty professionals trade daily, and Japanese trading houses have established themselves to a remarkable extent since the Japanese industry was deregulated in 1986.[84] Since 1984, Singapore has thrown itself into dealings in forward contracts in conjunction with SIMEX (Singapore International Monetary Exchange) and NYMEX (New York Mercantile Exchange), and in 1987 transactions of this type exceeded US$7 million.

Singapore as a regional base for offshore exploration and exploitation.[85] To cover an area of ocean in South-East Asia that extends for 3 million km.[2] and coordinate numerous concessions to a variety of companies requires a regional base capable of offering the necessary logistical services, qualified technicians, and infrastructures which reduce the interruption of production to the minimum.

Singapore, with all these conditions to hand, has 350 companies dealing in equipment for the petroleum industry, either connected with the oilwells themselves or with secondary storage centres spread throughout the region. Their activities have developed mostly in the direction of Indonesia, 60% of whose deposits are not yet explored, but also Burma, Thailand and Brunei. Concentrated at Jurong (Marine Base)

82. Between 1980 and 1986, the Singaporean refining companies raised US$ 848 million in new investment, supplemented by a further $490m. in 1987–8.
83. Doshi Tilak, *The Singapore petroleum industry*, Singapore: ISEAS, and Honolulu: East-West Center, 1989.
84. *FEER*, 28 May 88, pp. 86–8.
85. French embassy, Singapore (Economic dept), *Circuits d'achats pétroliers*, 14 Apr. 81; Economic Development Board, *Singapore serving the region's offshore oil industry*, Singapore, Feb. 76; Rashim Ishak, 'Singapore's role in regional offshore oil industry', *Speeches*, 3, 1, July 79; Lim Joo-Jock (ed.) (164), pp. 5–93.

and the former British military base of Loyang (Singapore Offshore Petroleum Services), their volume of business lessened during the period 1983–7, but prospecting for oil and, above all, for gas is likely to remain in full vigour, with consequent benefits for Singapore, through which 80% of the equipment transits.

Singapore as a regional centre for petrochemicals. Drawing inspiration from optimistic forecasts of worldwide petrol consumption made in the 1970s the idea of creating a new type of complementarity between Singapore, which is highly specialised in petrochemicals, and the regional producers of crude and/or refined petroleum is the origin of the Petrochem complex of Pulau Ayer Merbau, set up in 1982 by the Petrochemical Co. of Singapore and the Japanese Sumitomo group, with a capital of US$2 billion. This project includes a steam cracking unit for ethylene and prophylene, with an annual output of 465,000 tonnes, situated up the line from industrial plants producing artificial resins, plastics, synthetic fibres, chemicals and pharmaceuticals. The reduction in world consumption during the 1980s and projects for creating rival industries in Indonesia and Malaysia hindered the expected take-off of the Singaporean complex, which numerous commentators have described as a 'jumbo-sized' mistake. Rather than utilising 70% of the naphtha produced by the local refineries, as originally planned, Petrochem has turned to external supplies, on a much more substantial scale than originally planned, of liquid gas from Japan, Indonesia, Malaysia and Saudi Arabia, in order to cut the costs of production.[86] For the time being, there are no indications that it will become the regional centre for petrochemicals, as anticipated.

Efforts to develop a centre for storage of fuels, chemical products, fertilisers and synthetics appear to have a much greater chance of success. Shell and Mobil are putting into operation programmes for energy conservation and for developing a specialised workforce, while the Dutch companies Van Ommeren and Paktank have built storage terminals on the islands of Sebarok and Busing.

Shipbuilding
Another mainstay of the economy, the shipyards were bequeathed by the departing British on closing down their naval base, and by Singapore's vocation as a port. Four groups are dominant in this sector:

86. *ST*, 4 Oct. 83; *FEER*, 22 Nov. 84, pp. 91–2; *Business Times*, 26 Mar. 85.

Keppel, Jurong and Sembawang Shipyards and Mitsubishi Industries.[87]

Shipbuilding is carried on by around a dozen companies (as against thirty in 1984–5). The whole industry, including ship-repairing and offshore services, has to cope with a depressed international market, but is doing well in the region (21% growth in 1988). Before it encountered strong competition from Japan, South Korea and Taiwan and a net fall in demand for large tankers due to the oil recession, it set out to specialise in small vessels with specific functions (such as drilling, carrying cement, and other cargoes) and designed for the regional market. This is an area in which, since 1984, Indonesia has announced its intention to compete, though without any significant result so far.[88] Shipbuilding in Singapore remains, up to the time of writing, the only industry of this type in South East Asia. It has weathered the international storm without potential newcomers (if there are any such in the region) being able to enter the market and operate profitably.

The 200 companies engaged in ship-repair and refitting handle each year an average of 4,000 vessels, of which two-thirds are under foreign flags — thus making Singapore the world's third-largest centre of this activity. Accounting for 40% of the city-state's entire revenue related to shipping, they take in hand Middle Eastern and Japanese tankers which discharge there. They also take advantage of the regional market, offering their services to the tankers of the oil companies operating in South East Asia and to the hundreds of commercial coasters which come to Singapore from Malaysia and Indonesia. On the whole, ship-repairing appears to have weathered the international crisis better than shipbuilding.[89]

During the 1970s, the oil companies of the Gulf of Mexico, drawn by the proximity of Singapore to the offshore exploration and exploitation zones of South East Asia, have invested in the building of platforms. Foreign companies like Baker, Bethlehem, Robin Shipyard, Far East Levingstone, Marathon and Le Tourneau, and local ones like Promet,

87. *Singapore Shipbuilding and Repairing Directory*, 1984/5; UN/ESCAP, *Review of development in shipping, ports and inland waterways in the ESCAP region*, Bangkok: ESCAP, 1980.
88. Announcement by the Ministry of Research and Technology (BPPT) and by Pt Pal to replace 300 obsolete coasters. *FEER*, 8 Nov. 84, pp. 66–70. For the Malaysian shipping industry, see V. Ganapathy, 'The shipping industry of Malaysia', *UMBC Economic Review*, 13 Jan. 77, pp. 5–25, and *Maritime Asia*, 10 (1981), pp. 31–7.
89. *Maritime Asia*, 10 (1981), pp. 43–7; *FT*, 29 May 75 and 22 Nov. 82; *Singapore Econ. Bull.*, May 1983, p. 22; *Singapore Business*, Feb. 85, pp. 4–6.

have raised Singapore to the position of the world's second largest concentration, with a quarter of all production and 15–20 orders annually. During the years 1982–6 demand suddenly slowed down, with a sharp fall in revenue from more than US$600 million in 1981 to less than $10 million in 1986. The outlook in this sector has been much brighter again since 1987–8.[90]

Equipment and services for shipping constitute an industry with forty-five companies involved, and is the most recent and the smallest infrastructurally. However, it also appears to have the most dynamic future, with engines, propellers, offshore equipment, anti-corrosives, spare parts, direction-finding equipment and so on. It is attentive to local needs, as has been shown by recent bilateral cooperation (e.g. Keppel with Sobrin and Setama of Malaysia), and benefits from the efforts at diversification of the traditional shipyards now wishing to invest in the carrying trade. Other activities, related to the tertiary sector, have been developed successfully: maritime travel agencies, freight management and surveillance, control and maintenance of vessels (Veritas, Lloyds), and geophysical and applied scientific services (Det Norske, Veritec Marine Technology Consultants).[91]

Textiles

Without having played such a crucial role as the two sectors we have been considering above, or as has been played by its counterpart in Hong Kong, Singapore's textile industry, which employs 31,000 people, is nevertheless interesting as having both anticipated and evolved from the economies of the neighbouring countries.

The textile mills, owned by seventy-two companies, are due to disappear progressively as part of the process of delocalisation into Malaysia and Thailand, and at the same time as other countries – ASEAN, China and Hong Kong (which has invested heavily in Singapore) – are exporting in less significant quantities to the world market; in Indonesia's case the goods exported are often of poor quality.[92] The vacated plants are being converted to activities at the top of the quality range – the making-up of garments from ready-made pieces, ready-made clothes, higher-quality clothes and *haute couture*,

90. *Maritime Asia*, 11 (1980), pp. 12–30, and 3 (1981), p. 17; *Shipper's Times*, 5 (1981), pp. 3–5; *Singapore Econ. Bull.*, May 1982, p. 28; *AWSJ* (weekly), 21 Sept. 87.
91. *Singapore Econ. Bull.*, Sept. 1981, pp. 30–1; May 1982, p. 28; Oct. 1984, p. 15; *Business Times*, 26 Mar. 85.
92. *Singapore Econ. Survey*, 1983, p. 26; *FEER*, 18 July 83, pp. 43–5.

spinning looms and after-sales service: this activity, involving 330 companies, accounts for the greater part of the value added for the textile industry. Sensitive to the urban bourgeoisie in the capitals of the neighbouring states, to the buying habits of its own population and the many tourists,[93] and to the current fashions in Western countries (especially the United States), Singapore relies on the advice of the great couturiers and foreign consultants, and is alone in South East Asia in occupying a respected place in international fashion. Its first exhibition — 'Singapore Apparel, 1985', held in Tokyo — was a convincing demonstration of this.[94]

Specialisation in advanced technology for the year 2000

Aeronautics, biotechnology, electronics and information technology, chemicals and pharmacology, optics and telecommunications: these are some of the priority sectors identified since 1979–80 in the strategy of the desired 'second industrial revolution'. It is a matter of introducing new solutions to cope with the decline in certain traditional activities and the recession in the industries which had been vitally important in the previous decade: in this process ASEAN is the beneficiary. Under the assault of advanced technologies, of which two examples are discussed below, Singapore seeks to keep a step ahead of its regional environment, and to do so through the mastery of new instruments that bring possible complementarities with them.

Electronics

The electronics industry — which numbered only two local companies, Roxy and Setron, in 1968 — took the place of energy and shipbuilding as the engine of growth in manufacturing production, and now accounts for one-third of the total value added in manufacturing.[95] Accumulated investment in this branch had risen above US$2 billion by 1987 involving several hundred companies, as against $120 million and about forty companies in 1973. The inspiration came from the expansion of the American market. Singapore's electronics exports grew ten times over in the ten years up to 1983, and in 1982 the United States overtook

93. Singapore as a crossroads for tourism (see following chapter).
94. *ST*, 22 Oct. 83; *Singapore Econ. Bull.*, Mar. 82, p. 22.
95. Pang Eng Fong and Linda Lim (183); Banque Nationale de Paris (Singapore), *The electronics industry in Singapore*, Apr. 1984; Chapponière, op. cit., pp. 51–7; *FEER*, 14 Mar. 85, pp. 68–70.

Malaysia as its chief trading partner. With sales at this level, the city-state now assumed fourth place on the world scale, and made three particular areas its own: components (the most important), consumer goods (television, radio, videos) and industrial goods (computers, office equipment, telecommunications).

The lightning development of electronics in Singapore resulted from the development of markets in the industrialised countries and from a strategy in the United States to compete with Japanese production outside its own frontiers.[96] If the whole South East Asian market is of insufficient scope for a vertically integrated electronics industry to exist there, the regional dimension is nonetheless present in this evolution. In climbing, step by step, up the electronics ladder to productions of the top level (industrial electronics), Singapore has begun to lay off the fabrication of simple components in favour of Malaysia, which has become one of Asia's leading exporters in this sector. Except for this complementarity between the 'two sisters' of the peninsula, the virtual absence of electronics in the other ASEAN countries works to the advantage of the city-state, which is able to extend its functions as a regional distributor (hence a re-exporter) of components and low-priced consumer goods (radio-cassette players, TV videos, personal calculators) for which its neighbours are eager customers. It invests in Malaysia, but also more recently in Indonesia (Sampoerna and Servio Logic) and Thailand (Singapore Computer System Advisers), countries where industrial ambitions often follow in Singapore's footsteps in order to acquire advanced goods. The electronics industry provides a good example of the regional division of labour between Singapore and its neighbours, which has accelerated in the late 1980s.[97]

Aeronautics

To be at one of the major meeting-points of the world's air routes, to possess one of the world's most modern airports, to acquire the leading air force and civil airline in ASEAN, to have on its territory a concentration of electronic and precision mechanical industries — as well as building up an aeronautics industry oriented towards the triangle India-

---

96. Tsang San Yin, 'Links with international companies crucial (electronics industries in Singapore)', *Singapore Trade and Industry*, Jan. 1976, pp. 8–13.
97. N. Akrasanee & V. Vichit-Vadakan (eds) (244); Linda Lim, & Yuen Chinh, *Multinational firms and manufacturing for export in LDCs*: . . ., Ann Arbor: Univ. of Michigan Press, 1978, 2 vols; Tony Tan (Minister of Commerce & Industry), 'Developing Singapore as a software centre', *Singapore Econ. Bull.*, June 1983, pp. 17–18.

Hong Kong-Australia, with ASEAN at the centre: this is Singapore's aim.[98]

Local companies like Saeol (Singapore Aero Overhaul), Samco (Singapore Aerospace Maintenance Co.), Samaero (Saeol and Samco), Heli-Orient, SGAS (Singapore General Aviation Services) and SIA (Singapore International Airlines) offer the air operators of the whole region a complete spread of maintenance and repair facilities which alone is capable of carrying out detailed overhauls for the leading carriers or the remaking of mechanical equipment, thus obviating the need to rely on the United States or Europe for these services. MAS (Malaysia Air System), Thai Airways, Garuda and many private (mainly Indonesian) fleets — Airtrust, Air Fast, Satas, King Airs — use them regularly.

The fabrication of components 'made in Singapore' has been a more recent development, and has benefited from American approval on the international market. Sunstrand (the world leader for speed regulators), Garett (gearing), Fas Orient (hydraulic systems, ground equipment), Aero Plane Refurnishing and Heli Orient (seating), Vac Hyd Processing (jet engines, turbines, combustion chambers, compressors), SIA, Samco, Aerosystems and International Aeradio (electronics, communications) supply local aviation (SIA and the Singapore Air Force) and the companies of South and South East Asia. Small aircraft manufactured abroad for agricultural or industrial use (oil exploration, forest exploitation) and helicopters (Dornier, Bell, Evergreen, Bristow, Okanagan) are traded.

Singapore's aeronautics industry, which in 1981 hosted the first aerospace exhibition in Asia, made an appearance at the 35th *Salon International* at Le Bourget, France, in 1984 under the colours of SAI (Singapore Aircraft Industries), and in the 1990s it could undertake the assembly of existing models. It is not affected by the modest presence of AIM in Malaysia (repairs, helicopters) or Nurtanio in Indonesia (assembly under license).[99]

The second industrial revolution in the 1980s: challenges and perspectives

Singapore, a small emporium without a large population or natural

98. French Embassy, Singapore (Economic dept), *Industries aéronautiques*, 12 June 1980; *The Mirror*, 'Priority for aerospace industry', 8 (1981), p. 5.
99. *Singapore Investment News*, Oct. 81, pp. 1–2; *Singapore Econ. Bull.*, Oct. 1981, p. 21, & Mar. 1982, p. 18; *ST*, 12 Mar. 84; *Singapore Business Yearbk*, 1984, pp. 103–5; *FEER*, 12 July 84, pp. 54–5.

resources of its own, hit in 1985–6 by a recession that affected both traditional and newer economic sectors and by a sluggish international
market, finds itself once again facing challenges in which both structural
and cyclical variables are combined.

In opting for delocalisation of the most labour-intensive and least
remunerative sectors, and for the development of advanced industries
and services, it has scarcely any choice but to try to infiltrate certain
specialised areas and to make those compatible with external investment.

The gamble of high technologies: winning cards and limitations

Winning cards

Putting into operation a 'planned' policy of transforming the economic
fabric of the city-state can rely on a fund of high-quality experience
embracing infrastructure and existing manufacturing industries. On the
other hand, nothing is possible in such a tiny country without the
maximum mobilisation of intelligence and talent, an extreme rationalisation of the society's productive activities, and major financial and technological contributions from abroad.

As regards human resources, the level of education of Singaporeans
has reached a satisfactory stage of evolution, but the introduction of
advanced technologies requires today an improvement in local productivity, i.e. training of technicians and highly-qualified employees,
and measures of increased rationalisation of the economic apparatus.

Since 1979, the government has launched a programme to strengthen
the channels of technical education of the Singapore Polytechnic,
Nanyang Technological Institute (1981), Ngee Ann Polytechnic and the
National University. Each year the state has added 20–30% to its
educational budget, and has financed several training plans (Vocational
and Industrial Training Board, Skills Development Fund, Training
Grant Scheme). In 1982–3, 'Basic Education for Skills Training' was set
up to provide genuine qualifications for 320,000 adults who have never
passed beyond primary school. The aim of all these schemes was to
produce each year, from 1985 onwards, 1,000 new engineers, 5,000
technicians and 10,000 qualified employees. The measures have been
clarified in political and publicity campaigns advocating gains in
productivity and the adaptation of existing mental outlooks and social
structures.[100]

In the area of foreign investment, purely as a means of securing

100. Lim Chong Yah (159) and (160), pp. 75–81; Pang Eng Fong (182); Seah Chee
    Meow (469); G. Shantakumar in You Poh Seng & Lim Chong Yah (eds) (239),

substantial transfers of capital and know-how, tax exemption has been decreed by the Economic Development Board, which is responsible for selecting and then supervising projects, for periods up to ten years. Plans to provide support for bringing in new companies and for innovation in priority technologies have come into being in the form of the Product Development Assistance Scheme and the Research and Development Assistance Scheme. A science and technology park has been created in which projects are going forward involving dozens of companies with 1,000 employees: *inter alia*, the National Computer Board, the Marine Technology Centre, the Institute of Standards and Industrial Research, and an institute of molecular biology, without counting the great international names like Silicon Graphics, Exxon or Polysar.[101] This strategy oriented towards highly sophisticated industries seems to have met with initial success, with investment being channelled mainly into electronics and information technology.[102]

Limitations

Even if the first indications are encouraging, the fact of urging the development of advanced technologies cannot be enough in itself. In a period when activity is slowing down worldwide, and when technological restructuring (at first in the industrial countries) is in an evolutionary process, Western companies have little inclination to make vast transfers of advanced technology and are thus especially sensitive regarding cities like Hong Kong and Singapore, which were seen till very recently, as the homes par excellence of counterfeiting and piracy. With the exception of certain markets tightly linked to the countries of the region, which makes the transfer of sophisticated know-how to Singapore unavoidable, research and development in the city-state remain at a low level — there are only a limited number of engineers working in this area — and the parent-companies limit themselves to transferring very specific segments of their sophisticated production, notably components.[103]

pp. 165–88; *SE Asian Affairs*, 1984, pp. 287–8; *Singapore Business Yearbk*, 1984, p. 100.

101. *FEER*, 14 Mar. 85, pp. 68–71; *Asian Finance*, 15 Apr. 88.
102. Tan Boon Wan & Han Chun Kwong, *The sophistication of information systems in the electronics industry of Singapore*, Singapore: NUS, Oct. 1982; *Singapore Business*, Oct. 84, p. 107, and Apr. 1985, pp. 20–5; *Singapore Econ. Bull.*, Feb. 81, pp. 19–21; June 1983, pp. 17–18; Nov. 1983, p. 21.
103. Pang Eng Fong, 'Technology transfer and Singapore's restructuring strategy', *ASEAN Business Qly*, 2 (1980), pp. 26–32, and 'Technology transfer: The

The inadequate number of engineers and experienced technicians constitutes another obstacle, which the policy of limiting the recruitment of foreign staff, adopted in 1983–4, temporarily accentuated. In a speech broadcast nationally in 1985, the Prime Minister himself recognised the error and declared that it was impossible to attract investments in technology unless they were managed on the spot by a minimum number of competent expatriates. However, the small number of qualified Singaporeans is not the only problem. Even if the socio-cultural environment, which is hierarchical and dirigiste, produces some excellent executive-level personnel, the foreign companies established in Singapore complain that it does not encourage intellectual creativity or a spirit of initiative — a serious drawback which could well make the second revolution of industry and services which is under way less deep than it might be.[104]

Another handicap is that the pay increases of 1979–85 were not as effective, in terms of gains in industrial productivity and rationalisation, as expected. This policy could only sharpen the perception by the potential foreign investor that economic and social costs have become high in Singapore compared with the other newly industrialised countries in Asia.[105]

Globally, numerous observers are asking whether Singapore's future does indeed lie (with the exception of certain possible niches) in the local development of advanced industrial technologies, or whether services with high value added might not promise better results and be more easily realisable.[106]

It seems that advanced industries have a number of obstacles to surmount: the absence or insufficiency of the required personnel, the insignificant size of the internal market, the weakness of the structures for research, the physical limitations of space for industry, and the long-term ambitions of the neighbouring countries .... On the other hand, the rise of the tertiary sector, an observable tendency in most industrial countries, corresponds most exactly with the trump-cards which the city-state holds: the tertiary vocation of the emporium, the dynamism of the services which already exist, the unimportant role which small

Singapore experience', *Singapore Business Yearbk*, 1981, pp. 70–89; A.N. Hakam (130).

104. Pang Eng Fong & Linda Lim, 'Restructuring in Singapore', *Singapore Banking & Finance*, 1981/2, pp. 58–62.

105. See also *ST*, 16 Aug. 88: 'PM warns against pushing wage increases to the limit'.

106. Chow Kit Boey (103); *Singapore Business Yearbk*, 1982, pp. 7–33.

physical size and a small population actually play, its modest infra-structural and manpower needs, minimal dependence on outside supplies, more lasting regional complementarities. . . .

Singapore at the heart of a regional division of labour

In the endless debate on competition versus complementarity between the countries of the region and Singapore, complementarities clearly outweigh competition flows if one looks closely at the external trade and industrial fabric of the city-state in a regional perspective.

The competitiveness of Singapore's manufacturing industry working to the detriment of the other ASEAN countries shows clearly in a few rare instances (oil refining, bark and plywood, textiles) which have been flourishing at the very time when they are being delocalised or converted to more modern techniques. Even if the picture of a Chinese city, accumulating wealth due to its privileged links with transnational companies and thanks to the work done by others, still thrives in the ideology of certain *pribumi*[107] politico-religious circles in Indonesia and Malaysia, the lack of industrial competitiveness in these countries (especially Indonesia) during the 1960s and '70s had its origin more in their unadapted socio-economic structures than in competition from Singapore. International circumstances make it highly unlikely for the time being that the ASEAN countries would succeed in launching themselves into advanced manufacturing on a serious scale, which would face Singapore and other newly industrialised countries either with bitter competition or a structural recession.[108]

However, potential NICs like Malaysia and Thailand and even relative newcomers like Indonesia have benefited from the new international division of labour since the second oil crisis of 1979. Some huge amounts of foreign investment have been poured into ASEAN labour-intensive manufacturing, especially in 1986–90, pushing these economies upwards, even in highly specialised production like automobiles (Malaysia) or aeronautics (Indonesia). Such changes in the region have reinforced Singapore's strategy of rapid industrial delocalisation to its neighbours, and the future niches of the city-state will be concentrated more and more in services rather than pure manufacturing.

---

107. *Pribumi* = indigenous/autochthonous person. See definition of *bumiputra* (p. 71, n. 39, above).
108. *FEER*, 12 July 84.

New ties of complementarity are to be found everywhere in the primary and secondary sectors, as in the service sector. Singapore functions today as a regional pole for development, distributing to its neighbours low-priced equipment, products and services and, in addition, transfers of finance and know-how which thus multiply intra-regional and external interdependence.[109] This division of labour, of which the industrialisation of Johore and Batam are good examples, is not unilateral. Due to its size and limited resources, Singapore has neither the capacity nor the ambition to develop on its territory the complete network of modern industry. Its neighbours are not restricted to second-rate production. Reciprocally, these countries, which command only limited industrial and financial capital, cannot fail to benefit from the presence on their doorstep of a concentration of industrial and technical facilities to be used for their own efforts at economic diversification.[110]

The survival and viability of the emporium can only be guaranteed by means of a judicious choice between several areas of specialisation which — as has often been said — do not imply a superiority, a leading position or even cutting itself off from the neighbouring countries. It is a question of defining those areas in the necessary process of constant adaptation to international market conditions, and to the foreseeable evolution of the regional environment in the next two to three decades. Constant adaptation has to be the major preoccupation of the island society. The local Overseas Chinese, who have enjoyed the comforts of material success and have adopted a somewhat condescending attitude towards the poorer populations of the neighbouring countries, need to make more effort to know these populations better in order to identify local demand. Indonesia, vast and proud as it is, will not seek a relationship with them if they do not, on their own, make very clear their interest in contributing to its development.

It is also imperative for the city-state never to forget that every break in relations with the regional environment, whether brought about by its own action or by one of its neighbours, could spoil the geopolitical conditions which have governed its brilliant development, based at one and the same time on regional and worldwide links. The damage,

---

109. For the economic theory of poles of development and growth, the work of François Perroux (incl. *L'économie du XXème siècle*, Paris: PUF, 1961) may be consulted. See also J.-C. Perrin, *Le développement régional*, Paris: PUF, 1974.
110. *IBAS BULL.*, May 1980, pp. 41–3, and *IBAS Annual*, 1980, pp. 59–71.

however, would probably not be fatal because of the close ties it has established with the industrial countries.

In short, looking at Singapore's difficulties with a rising tide of protectionism penalising its exports, and at the sometimes uncertain mobilisation of the foreign investments which are indispensable for the successful realisation of its technological ambitions, the industrial and financial expansion of Singapore outside its frontiers (in ASEAN and its periphery, South Asia, China, Australia and California) represents a third possible way forward, giving offence to none and allowing it to transcend the narrowness of its geographical and human limitations.[111] It is all too clear why Lee Hsien Loong and many other Singaporean leaders have been insisting so much in recent years on its future 'golden triangle' of Johore/Singapore/Batam and the Riau islands.

111. *FEER*, 12 May 78, pp. 40–3.

3

INFRASTRUCTURE AND SERVICES
FOR THE REGION

Following on from trade in the colonial period and manufacturing industry in the 1960s and 1970s, the tertiary sector as a whole has become the transmission-belt for the Singaporean economy.

Closely tied to the emporium's vocation as a regional middle-man (and long ignored by researchers), this sector has played an essential role in the economic history of Singapore, which has differed in its evolution from the classic model of industrial countries where the primary and secondary sectors lead towards the service sector. Analysis of the period 1921–57 shows that Singapore has always been a society providing services — which have, on average, employed 60% of the active population and accounted for two-thirds of GNP, a figure not even attained by Hong Kong.[1]

Around the end of the nineteenth century, various services already existed in the form of commercial agencies, harbour facilities, shipping companies and branches of banks controlled by the City of London. In 1921–57, nearly 70% of employment depended on the entrepot trade, on its infrastructural framework (communications and transport) and on other services (the British base, banking and insurance, and social services). Industrialisation in the 1960s caused a relative and temporary reduction of this proportion (to 60% in 1980), but by becoming mixed with the commercial functions and services that were already established, created a demand for new benefits, both within the region and outside it, in tune with the remarkable development of Singapore's economy following independence.

The era of tertiary economies and of post-industrial societies was born in most Western countries at the beginning of the 1980s, with the buying and selling of services representing more than one-fifth of all international business flows. Singapore, with its long experience in this field, has set up several records: it is one of a group of four or five countries in the world where the tertiary sector accounts for an exceptionally high proportion of GNP (70% in 1988) and of employment (63.5%); it is among the fifteen chief exporters of services and ranks third after

1. Greg H.F. Seow (206), and in *Malayan Econ. Review*, 24 (Oct. 1979), pp. 46–73.

Norway and Switzerland for the ratio of invisible exports to the number of inhabitants. Its economy is heavily dependent on invisible earnings, which compensates for the deteriorating trade balance, and contributes regularly to the balance of payments; year by year, net receipts from services exceed the net contribution from capital by between two and four times.[2]

The tertiary sector — 787,000 employees in 1988 against 436,000 for manufacturing industry and construction — registered the highest rate of growth and produced the highest level of value added. Services of a commercial nature retained their lead, with 284,000 employees and generating about one-fifth of the total tertiary revenue, followed by various services (272,000), communications and transport (120,000) and financial and business services (111,000).

One could ask whether Singapore, by emphasising the increasing role played by services of control and distribution of knowledge (education, research, communications and media, information science and its derivatives, advice and consultancy), is not in the process of becoming a 'brain centre' or an 'information society'. The importance of the tertiary sector is tied to the comparative advantage which the city-state possesses in offering and exporting services in the direction of its immediate environment; from this one can assume that the island has a vocation, at least up till the end of the century, to develop as a regional centre of sophisticated services and brainpower.[3]

A developed system of transport and communications

Whether one is considering the most ancient functions of this emporium, namely those connected with trade, or its most recent ones with the take-off of advanced tertiary services, it could never have achieved such a wide spread for its activities without a remarkable system of international communications.

Port services — bringing together the region and the world

Singapore, the world's second- or third-largest port

Singapore's entire history has been, before all else, that of a colonial,

2. Source: *Yearbooks of Statistics, Balance of Payments, Singapore* (annual).
3. R. Badham, 'The sociology of industrial and post-industrial societies', *Current Sociology*, 32 (1984), pp. 1–141; M. Jussawalla & Cheah Chee-Wah, 'Towards an information economy: The case of Singapore', *Information Economics and Policy*, 1 (1983), pp. 161–76; Marc Porat, 'Global implications of the information society', *J. of Communication*, 28, 1 (1978), pp. 70–80.

commercial and military port, its development depending on its geo-strategic position at a meeting-place of sea-routes which are as vital for various great powers outside the region as they are for the countries of South East Asia. This vocation, consolidated since 1965 by the implantation of shipping and oil industries, has allowed the city-state to take its place among the world's leading ports along with Rotterdam, New York, Kobe and Houston.[4] As a major staging-post for more than 700 shipping lines throughout the world linking 500 different ports, accepting all types of vessel (including military ones) and all flags, Singapore asserts its position as a discharging point for shipping of high tonnage, and as a centre for collection or redistribution of products regionally, by coasters or freighters of small capacity. Its harbour traffic has doubled in ten years, registering in 1988 69,000 movements of vessels and 248 million tonnes of freight (petroleum accounting for 64%). South East Asia is the second-ranking maritime partner of the city-state after North East Asia, including Japan: in the former, of course, one has to include freighter traffic with Indonesia, although Singapore does not publish the relevant statistics.[5]

Combined with industrial capacities designed to receive custom from outside, such as the terminals of oil refineries and ship repair yards, the port of Singapore offers infrastructures which are on a vast scale: five docks; 15 km. of quays, some with specialised functions; 2,000 hectares of covered warehouses, and 10,000 employees working round the clock for 365 days of each year. Keppel Wharves alone can receive 30 vessels at one time and complete the necessary work in record time. From 1973–4 onwards, the Port of Singapore Authority launched a programme to modernise its installations and improve productivity in terms of speed of forwarding freight and maintaining the moderate prices charged for services rendered. The movement of goods is now computerised, and container transport is increasing steeply in volume with nine new working terminals in Tanjong Pajar (35 million tonnes of freight were handled in 1987) and the laying-down of five other terminals in one of Singapore's small islands, due to become operational in 1992.[6]

The scope of Singapore's maritime strength also takes in a merchant

---

4. Celine Kiew-ting Teo (74); Wee Siew-Run (80).
5. Source: *Singapore Yearbk of Statistics* (annual), Marine Dept, Primary Production Division and Port of Singapore Authority.
6. Port of Singapore Authority, *The port of Singapore* (annual); Singapore Shipping Agencies, *Guide to Singapore port facilities* (annual).

fleet which, with 1,230 vessels and 725 million gross tonnes, ranks fifteenth in size in the world; it is bigger, for example, than India's, double the size of Hong Kong's, and represents half of ASEAN's total tonnage. One-fifth of the fleet is managed by the national enterprise, Neptune Orient Lines. Finally, Singapore stands third in the world league, behind Liberia and Panama, for the number of vessels and the gross tonnage of foreign vessels flying its flag, most notably West Germany and Japan.[7]

The effort undertaken by the neighbouring countries to develop direct trade, by-passing Singapore, has as its corollary the building up and efficient functioning of their own port infrastructures. Malaysia and, more recently, Indonesia are attempting to go down this path, but come up against the multiple problems which make it difficult for them to compete with the services offered by Singapore,[8] without forgetting the highly competitive performance of the East Asian countries (Japan, South Korea, Taiwan).

Port relations with Malaysia

Singapore continues to carry out functions which are vital for Malaysia, not only as regards international freight but also as a pivot between the two coasts of the peninsula, and between the peninsula as a whole and East Malaysia. Even if the frequency with which the Malaysian ports are used and the total freight registered in Malaysia were to rise to more than a third of the corresponding figures for Singapore, Port Klang (the port of Kuala Lumpur) and Johore Port (Johor Baru and Pasir Gudang) would not, individually, be able to compare with the city-state as regards facilities. They are limited to despatching and receiving goods respectively before and after they pass through Singapore — the essential activity taking place between them and the other ports of Malaysia such as Penang and Sabah.[9]

Costs in Malaysia are inflated by customs and port dues; they are 15% higher than in Singapore, and neither Port Klang nor Pasir Gudang

7. UN/ESCAP, *Review of developments in shipping, ports and water ways in the ESCAP region*, Bangkok, 1980; OECD, *Maritime transport 1982*, Paris, 1983; UNCTAD, *Review of maritime transport 1981 and 1982*, Geneva, TD/B/C.4/251 & 258. FEER, *Shipping Annual*, 10 Feb. 83 & 16 Feb. 84.

8. 'Indonesia and Malaysia continue their uneconomic effort to enlarge the number of ships under their respective control that call at their respective ports . . .' in Jaafar Abu Bakar (140).

9. *Malaysian Yearbk of Transport Statistics* (annual); *Malaysian Business*, Dec. 75, pp. 47–9; *Maritime Asia*, 2 (1981): 'The shipping of Malaysian exports', pp. 40–3.

(14 m. deep as against Singapore's 20 m.) are able to accommodate tankers of more than 80,000 tonnes. More than 80% of exports destined for Singapore are carried by rail or road at prices which are increasingly competitive compared with those of coastal shipping.[10]

Parallel to modernising and relieving congestion at Port Klang with improved access routes and telecommunications, and container terminals, Malaysia wished to create in the port of Johore, from 1974, infrastructures which would enable it to divert some of Singapore's maritime traffic. Pasir Gudang was built in spite of the fact that no very precise feasibility study had been carried out in advance, and it was discovered subsequently that the approach to this new port across the straits of Johore was long and difficult: large vessels require the services of a pilot boat, and have to pass through Singapore's territorial waters to the north-east of the island, and have reason to fear that the authorities there might consider, as a possible lever for applying pressure, the imposition of payments for using this route and of strict controls over flags of convenience with a view to preventing pollution. Here again, the interdependence of Johore and its 'little' neighbour seems to have become an established fact, confirming largely identical observations in the area of investment and industrial delocalisation.[11]

The weakness of port infrastructures in Indonesia
Although no reliable statistics are available for bilateral maritime trade, Singapore, also through Penang and Port Klang, continues to draw off a substantial proportion of Indonesia's trade with the rest of the world. The country's merchant fleet consists of numerous small and aged craft which are specialised as carriers of raw materials and passenger traffic within the archipelago. At the same time, the two national companies which show the severest losses — Jakarta Lloyd and Pelni — carry international freight.[12] In general, the infrastructure of ports is outdated, and suffers from numerous disadvantages: the scattered

10. The transporting of rubber to Singapore from Kelantan, even though it is the state at the northern extremity of the peninsula, is 10% cheaper by road or rail than by sea from Port Klang. G.K. Iyer, *A study of the railway services to Singapore in relation to greater utilization of ports in Peninsular Malaysia*, Kuala Lumpur: Prime Minister's Dept, Govt Press, 1981.

11. Johore Port Authority, *A glimpse of Johore Port project*, 16 July 77; Christiani and Nielsen Consultants, *Johore Port: Economic and Technical Study*, Copenhagen, 1971; *NST*, 27 Mar. & 4 Apr. 75; 15 Jan. & 4 May 76; 23 Jan. 81; *Malaysian Business*, Mar. 75, pp. 16–21.

12. *FEER*, 16 Feb. 84, pp. 50–1.

territory, the isolation of the ports themselves, the slowness of voyages within the archipelago, congestion in the larger ports, an inefficient workforce, insufficient or superannuated equipment, a heavy-handed bureaucracy, very high harbour dues, and corruption.

A presidential decree of April 1982 submitted Indonesian companies handling internal maritime traffic to obligatory control, and required international trade to be handled solely through the large ports: Tanjung Priok (Jakarta), Tanjung Perak (Surabaya), Ujung Pandang (Sulawesi) and Belawan (North Sumatra). Several World Bank loans have made possible their modernisation and rationalisation, and the nourishing of an ambition to reduce the current harbour dues in order to be able to compete with Singapore. As well as these projects, the creation of a shipbuilding industry was mooted by Minister Habibie in 1984.

Most foreign and even Indonesian analyses express the strongest reservations over the viability of all these proposals, with a wide gap remaining between the identification of the objective and its real feasibility. While it is possible to discern a beginning of complementarity in the seaborne trade of the Malay peninsula, relations between the Indonesian ports and Singapore can more aptly be described as dependent, with Singapore acting on an almost regular basis as the staging-point for the archipelago's external commerce.[13]

Singapore and free circulation at sea in the Straits of Malacca
In 1970–3, Singapore and the two neighbouring states were at odds over the legal regime governing the Straits of Malacca. Singapore played the role of firm defender of its international status, guaranteeing free navigation as inseparable from its economic viability, whereas Indonesia and Malaysia were looking for the greatest possible extension of their exclusive economic zones, and contro', for security reasons, of the passage of the 150 vessels which on average pass through this seaway every day. The control would have extended to military vessels and to preventing pollution from wrecks that results from the shallowness of the Straits. Indonesia and Malaysia pursued a double objective: to increase their pressure on Japan, which receives most of its energy supplies via the Straits, in order to obtain important economic concessions in return; and to lessen their dependence on Singapore by threatening one of the basic preconditions of its viability.[14]

13. Reksopoetranto, op. cit.; chapter 2.
14. J.M. Cain (98); Chia Lien Sien in C. McAndrews (ed.) *Southeast Asian frontiers for development*, Singapore: McGraw-Hill, pp. 239–66; M. Liefer (156); Yaacov

At the heart of ASEAN yet sustained by the United States, the Soviet Union, Japan and Thailand, Singapore has reached the point of deflecting the original political intentions of its ASEAN partners and transforming them into technical problems for regulation by international maritime law. Among the world's 121 major straits, how could an exception be made in the future convention on the law of the sea guaranteeing to Singapore, as an enclave, the permanent internationalisation of the Straits of Malacca and access to the economic zones of the riparian states?[15]

On 16 November 1971, a tripartite 'non-accord' came into being, with Singapore cannily playing the card of moderation in taking note of the position of its two neighbours, inviting the fleets of all nations to continue the free use of its port, and accepting the idea of formal cooperation between the riparian states in ensuring the security of navigation in the Straits. In April 1973, Singapore proposed the setting-up of a tripartite system to prevent accidents to supertankers and warships. The wreck of the oil tanker *Showa Maru* in January 1975 8 km. south of Singapore reinforced the credibility of this project; the 'Traffic Separation Scheme', adopted in February 1977, came into force on 1 May 1981 without any other modification to the international status of the Straits, to which the Singapore government has regularly reiterated its attachment.[16]

Thailand's project to cut a canal in the region of Kra to link the Bay of Bengal with the South China Sea and remove the need to circumnavigate the Malay peninsula was taken out of cold storage in 1973–5; this is another scheme that would affect the almost exclusive control of the principal sea-route between East Asia and points west, from which Singapore benefits.[17] This project did not seem likely to take shape in

---

Vertzberger, 'The Malacca-Singapore Straits: the Suez of Southeast Asia', *Conflict Studies* (London), 140 (1982).

15. C.V. Das and V.P. Pradhan, *Some international law problems regarding the straits of Malacca*, Singapore: ISEAS, 1973; K.E. Shaw, 'Juridical status of the Malacca Straits and its relations to Indonesia and Malaysia', *Nanyang Univ. J.*, 3 (1969), pp. 284–320.

16. *Basic Agreement between Indonesia and Singapore in the Strait of Singapore*, Jakarta, 25 May 73; *ST*, 1 May 85.

17. The idea of this canal was launched in the 19th century by Ferdinand de Lesseps and revived several times but never realised. Patrick Low, 'To cut or not to cut (Kra Canal Project)', *Singapore Trade and Industry*, Sept. 1973, pp. 21–5; *ARB*, 4, 30 Nov. 74, and 31 Dec. 84, pp. 32–3; Y. Yeung, *The proposed Kra Canal*, Singapore: ISEAS, 1973.

the short term, but in 1989 it was reactivated following the mounting pressure to deconcentrate activity out of Bangkok to new industrial and trading areas. In any case, the project clearly illustrates, like the crisis over the status of the Straits, the extent to which the city-state would be affected by any change or rupture suddenly introduced in the region.

A crossroads for air routes in South-East Asia

A world-renowned airport

In order to make the attractions of its geographical position, the dynamism of its economy and the quality of its services felt far beyond its territorial boundaries, Singapore needs to be equipped with an outstandingly effective aerial infrastructure. As a gateway to the Asia-Pacific region along with Bangkok and Tokyo, and the pivot of intra-ASEAN traffic, the ultra-modern and luxurious Changi airport, opened in 1981 and costing US$800 million, is classed among the world's top ten.[18] Served by forty-seven foreign carriers, Changi handles 620 movements a day and can receive twenty at one time. In 1987 it received more than 11 million passengers, of whom 4.7 million were travelling within the South East Asian region, and handled 418,000 tonnes of freight, respectively four and twenty times more than the airport at Kuala Lumpur. The ASEAN countries and East Asia are its two principal users, accounting for 47% of passenger traffic and 22% of freight (85% of intra-ASEAN air freight is channelled through Singapore).

Despite having two runways and excellent organisation, saturation point has been reached, and the building of a second airport and extra runways at Changi are planned in order to double possible capacity to 20 million passengers a year and sixty-six movements in one hour by the year 2000. The two airports would be linked by a high-speed automatic train, the first system of this kind to be installed outside the United States and Britain. Already in 1984, the Singapore Civil Aviation Authority was classed as in the first bank worldwide as regards the quality of its installations for traffic control and management, on a par with London, Amsterdam and Frankfurt.[19]

The regional preponderance of Singapore International Airlines

The national airline, SIA, which employs 10,000 people and has been

18. Peter Hutton, *Wings over Singapore: The story of Changi airport*, Singapore: Dept. Civil Aviation, 1981; Changi Airport Dept., *Changi Airport Data*, Singapore, 1980; *Singapore Business Year*, 1981, pp. 16–23.
19. *Singapore Econ. Bull.*, May 84, p. 31; June 84, p. 35, and Oct. 84, p. 39.

in the process of being partly privatised since 1985, contributes to this enviable position in the prize-list. Serving fifty-four cities in thirty-seven countries, it ranks in the bracket sixth to eight in international civil aviation, and ranks third for productivity (tonne/km./employee).[20]

SIA weighs heavily among the airlines of the region, and for that reason is resented by the others. Even if MAS (Malaysian Air System) carries more passengers than SIA (6.2 against 5.8 million in 1986–7, including those carried on Malaysia's internal routes), all other indicators show SIA as being ahead. With a strong presence on long-haul journeys (it has twenty-two Boeing 747s) and in the region (with nineteen A310 Airbuses), SIA has the most modern and high-quality fleet, though as regards quality Thai Airways comes a close second, being very active on the routes of South and North East Asia.[21]

Between Singapore and Kuala Lumpur SIA and MAS have organised an equitable system of alternate flights, which have been extended since 1983 to Penang, Pulau Tioman and Langkawi (the last-named for tourism); SIA alone carries 20% of passengers and cargo handled by the airport at Kuala Lumpur. Indonesia, with its airline Garuda, has consented to a similar shared exploitation on the two routes Singapore-Jakarta and Singapore-Medan, offering 2,000 seats daily, but has conceded SIA no other routes except to Bali. Since 1987 Garuda has linked Singapore to a sixth Indonesian town, Padang in Sumatra.[22]

In 1981 there was a difference of opinion between Malaysia and Singapore: Kuala Lumpur wanted to reduce by two-thirds the length of the two approach corridors to Changi, fixed at 90 nautical miles and covering the south of Johore. And pilots' organisations have opposed any extension of the South Johore Flight Information Region, maintaining their preference for a single and unique network of air traffic information controlled, as in the past, by Singapore.[23]

There are certain groups in Malaysia, hostile to the economic strength of the Singapore Chinese, who from time to time denounce the international predominance of SIA, which, they claim, has a detrimental effect on MAS. Thus in 1987 these groups, which often collaborate

20. Peter Hutton, *The pursuit of excellence: An island and its airline*, Singapore Airlines, 1979; D. Sikorski, *Singapore Airlines: Case study. . .*, Singapore, Dept of Business Admin., NUS, Mar. 83; *Business Times*, 8 Feb. 85.

21. *Malaysian Yearbk of Transport Statistics* (annual); *FEER*, 17 Oct. 85, pp. 96–7; 'SIA's ascendancy in the 70s', *Singapore Statistical News*, 3 (1981), p. 164.

22. *ST*, 2 Apr. 80 & 27 June 87.

23. *ST*, 19 Dec. 84.

closely with Malay nationalist and Islamic youth (the UNMO Youth Organisation), were largely responsible for a press campaign denouncing the agreements on aviation between the two countries. This was in protest at a visit to Singapore by President Herzog of Israel.[24]

ASEAN's pro-Singapore solidarity in aviation

In 1979 Singapore's partners gave clear evidence of the importance they attach to the functions of Changi as a hub of regional air transport. Australia had announced unilaterally a promotion of Qantas flights to Europe without a stop-over in Singapore. Furthermore, in an effort to sow dissension in ASEAN, additional flights to Sydney were authorised for other ASEAN but non-Singaporean carriers. Singapore, controlling 30% of traffic between Europe and Australia, found itself the target of these discrimination measures, Canberra presumably calculating that this blow struck at its aerial supremacy would not be unwelcome in the other ASEAN capitals.

However, an ASEAN ministerial meeting on 22 February 1979 manifested a remarkable unity by rejecting any external discrimination against one of the five regional airlines and threatening Australia with collective retaliation. Canberra finally withdrew its decision.

Because of their fear of any reduction of flights transiting via Singapore, which would have penalised the regional tourist market, the five demonstrated an economic solidarity which coincided in that particular year with a common political will: Vietnam had just invaded Cambodia and it was the eve of the fifth UNCTAD congress opening in Manila. Singaporean diplomacy manoeuvred neatly on this territory, emerging from the ASEAN-Australian battle of wills with advantage to itself by exploiting to the utmost the politico-economic circumstances in the terms perceived by its partners.[25]

Singapore, regional crossroads of business and leisure travel

Being at the point where the tourist routes of South East Asia meet, Singapore, of all the ASEAN countries, welcomes the most foreign visitors (3.7 million in 1987, even more than Thailand) and obtains the largest revenue from them. The traveller is attracted not by the Chinese city — China Town — which the builders of high-rise blocks in the city have all but obliterated, but by the excellence of its hotels (22,000

24. *ST*, 3 Jan., 15 Feb. 21 Mar., 10 Sept. 13 Sept. 87.
25. A. Broinowski (ed.) (259); R. Garnaut (ed.) (122), ch. 9; *FEER*, 18 May 79, pp. 87–8, and 25 Sept. 79, p. 79; *NST* (Kuala Lumpur), 7 Mar. 79.

rooms of international standard) and its business infrastructures, which are typical of a highly westernised urban society, and complement the more traditional environment of its neighbours. In the context of economic cooperation within the region, the ASEAN countries see Singapore as the point of departure for numerous organised tours and one of the major centres for exploiting the tourist market in that part of the world.[26]

Among the flood of visitors, the ASEAN nationalities represent 52% of the total: Malaysians come well ahead of the Japanese or the Australians, who account for 8% each. Malaysians, Indonesians and Thais stay, on average, for 4–5 days and profit from the choice — and the prices — of a variety of consumer goods of far greater appeal than what is available in their own countries. They thus create a flow of informal 'touristic' business between Singapore and its neighbours in photographic and optical equipment, micro-computers and luxury goods. Many of them (the offspring of Chinese families) also come on visits to their parents, to put their affairs in order, to reside briefly in local apartments bought at astronomical prices, or to travel on to other destinations after making a few purchases.[27]

So as to limit the foreign travel of its nationals and the continuous financial haemorrhage that has resulted from it, Indonesia has levied since November 1982 a departure tax of US$150 per person. However, this measure does not prevent wealthy Indonesians from travelling frequently and in increasing numbers, and the 30% fall in Indonesian visitors to Singapore in 1983 seems only to have resulted in a devaluation of the rupiah in March that year.[28] Similarly, the Malaysian customs have taken a tougher attitude towards traffic using the Singapore-Johor Baru Causeway, but any policy that contemplated genuinely closing it would come up against the economic interdependence of the two sides of the Strait of Johore, where thousands of workers cross from one side to the other, in both directions, every day.

If the business of leisure tourism has proved remunerative, business travel (630,000 people in 1987), based on the reality that all the foreign

26. Singapore Tourist Promotion Board, *Tourist Statistical Report* (annual); *ARB*, 31 July 80, pp. 702–3, and 31 Jan. 82, pp. 882–4; *Singapore Business*, Apr. 78, pp. 8–13, and July 83, p. 35.

27. Singapore Tourist Promotion Board, *Survey of overseas visitors*, 1983; Seetoh Oi Moon, *Patterns of Tourism in Asean*, Singapore: NUS, Geography Dept., 1977–8; Chow Kit Boey, *External linkages and economic development: The Singapore experience*, op. cit., pp. 22–3.

28. *Southeast Asian Affairs*, 1984, p. 287; *ST*, 11 May 85.

companies active in the region are concentrated in Singapore, is no less so. In the expectation of profiting from the island's privileged position as the meeting-point of international lines of communication, the real-estate and hotel sectors have created a new vocation for the city-state: to assert itself as an 'Asian Geneva' by providing — with the Convention Centre, Science Park etc. — headquarters facilities and meeting halls for international conferences, socio-professional seminars, and international fairs and exhibitions. The 75-storey complex alongside the old Raffles Hotel is the most spectacular — and challenging — achievement in this area so far.[29]

A regional capital for the dissemination of knowledge and know-how

The development of advanced tertiary services, with their origin in Singapore and relaying technological change as it occurs in the industrial countries, creates an ever more dynamic image of a city-state containing a high concentration of brainpower and know-how. For more than a decade, Singapore has wished to be seen as a centre of expertise in a number of leading branches of technology — one that the outside world cannot afford to ignore.

A crossroads of international communications

Singapore is one of the great meeting-points of international tele-communications — it ranks first in the region and sixteenth worldwide for communication by satellite. The Telecommunication Authority assures a range of non-stop services for air and sea traffic and business relations, all of which are of high density at this point on the globe.

The island is linked by telephone and telex to 207 territories and by a direct automatic link to more than 150. Of its inhabitants 45% have telephones (in Hong Kong the proportion is even higher). In 1987, 16 million phone calls, 15 million telex messages, 270,000 overseas telegrams and 685 million postal despatches to all destinations were recorded.

The two stations of Sentosa are linked to the Intelsat and Immarsat (International Maritime Organization) systems covering the Indian and Pacific oceans, and the Yio Chu Kang base is in permanent contact with aerial and sea navigation for telecommunications, meteorology, rescue

29. Tan It Koon, 'Motivations, reasons and mechanics of hosting a conference', *Singapore Professionals*, 1 (1980), pp. 27–31.

services and medical assistance. In collaboration with Britain and Norway, the Telecoms company is putting into service in 1990 the world's first integrated aeronautical telecommunication service by satellite covering the Atlantic as well as the Indian and Pacific oceans. Other sophisticated services available are Telefax, Telexmail (with subscription to a public telex service), Telepac (access to databases in twenty countries), Prisnet (a private communications network), Flight Information Distribution Service (air travel and hotel reservations, Travelnet (a computerised tourist reservation service) and Credit Card Authorisation Telephone for international verification. In 1986–8, French and American companies equipped Singapore's twenty-six telephone exchanges with optical fibres, and launched the creation of integrated circuits on the spot.[30]

A communications network by submarine cable links all the ASEAN countries except Brunei, which — for the first time in the region — will be linked by an optical fibre cable. This cable will be part of the ASEAN-Pacific Optical Fibre Submarine Cable Network linking Singapore and the rest of South East Asia with the Middle East and Western Europe, Hong Kong with Taiwan, and Australia with Indonesia. Also, since 1988 Singapore has installed the first regional system of automatic communication of databases.

Leaving aside the close collaboration between Singapore, Malaysia and Brunei, motivated by reasons of geographical proximity, cooperation is being developed with Indonesia, notably with its dynamic national telecommunications company Perumtel: two new cables have been laid, via Singapore, between Medan in Sumatra, the Middle East and Europe, and between Indonesia and Australia. Jakarta has invited Singapore to participate in its satellite programme 'Palapa', with the island-state playing the role of relay-transmitter of satellite communications towards the neighbouring Riau archipelago, Sumatra and Kalimantan. It is worth noting that as early as 1982 the two states were considering the possibility of an audiographic teleconference system, but the project was abandoned because businessmen prefer meeting face to face. Jakarta and Singapore, after all, are only an hour's flying time apart.[31]

30. P. Guevara, *ASEAN transport and communication equipment manufacturing industries*, Conference on ASEAN-EEC industrial cooperation, Jakarta, 26–28 Feb. 1979; *Singapore Business*, Mar. 85, p. 69.

31. Dept. of Transport, Communications and Tourism, Directorate of Posts and Telecommunications, *ASEAN Indonesia-Singapore submarine cable*, Jakarta, 1980; *Antara* (Jakarta), 28 Aug. 84; *Singapore Econ. Bull.*, May 72, p. 40; Sept. 82, p. 44; Oct. 82, p. 52; *Singapore Business*, Aug. 84, p. 48.

A regional centre of education and training

Singapore was already outstanding during the colonial period for the quality of its private secondary schools and the close links with the University of Malaya in Kuala Lumpur. These two urban poles of the peninsula have long offered a network of higher education unique in South East Asia.

Since 1959–60, Lee Kuan Yew's government has given priority to education: in 1959–78 it attracted 10% of the annual budget and in 1980–7, 15–20%. As the only instrument which can realise the potential of the city-state's small human capital (the only resource to which it can lay claim), this educational mission inevitably began a great movement towards social cohesion, of receptivity to international constraints, and familiarisation with modern techniques.[32] The disciplined and rigorous educational system that has grown up is famed throughout the region. Between 4,000 and 6,000 Malaysian children and a considerable number from Indonesia and Thailand are sent to the 425 primary and secondary schools in Singapore, which had 534,000 pupils in 1987. From there they emerge with solid training and mastery of the English language – something which is far from being the case elsewhere, above all in Indonesia.[33] The same phenomenon occurs in higher and technical education as well (45,000 students and 5,648 instructors): those who make up the regional élite, especially in business, have studied at the National University of Singapore (in commerce, management, economic sciences, and specialised engineering), the high quality of which is recognised worldwide and where foreign specialists make significant contributions. Among the students from ASEAN countries, those of Chinese origin, who find themselves subject to discrimination as regards entry to university in Indonesia and Malaysia, form the majority. Their families will have links with some close or distant family member, who is already established in Singapore, and thus in some way is faithful to the old tradition of sending at least one son to study at the fountainhead of Chinese culture. With China itself having become Communist, the 'cultural transfer' and point of attraction became focused on 'little Chinas' like Singapore, Hong Kong and Taiwan.

Likewise, Singapore attracts numerous researchers and senior officials

32. On Singapore's educational system, see the concluding part of this book. Also, Seah Chee Meow in P.S.J. Chen (100), pp. 240–67; G. Shantakumar in You Poh Seng & Lim Chong Yah (eds) (239), pp. 165–79; Singapore Min. of Educn, *Annual Report* (since 1959).

33. *ST*, 19 Apr. 84.

of ASEAN, who are interested by the rich collections and excellent organisation of the local national and university libraries, by its language training centres for perfecting knowledge of English, and by two specific institutions related to the creation of ASEAN: the National Public Service Institute and the Institute of South East Asia Studies.

The picture would be incomplete if one passed over the role of industry and the tertiary sector in professional training: banks and transnational companies offer the local personnel of their South East Asian branches some specialised on-the-job training in their regional headquarters.[34] In-service training has become a new 'product' offered to satisfy the demand for trained skilled labour from Singapore's large neighbours in the area, even though Singapore's training facilities do not have unlimited capacity.

The Singaporean educational system is often held up as a criterion of excellence. For example, it inspired the former Indonesian minister of education Nugroho, who died suddenly in 1985, to reform the secondary school system in his own country.

A regional printing and publishing industry[35]
Singapore during the colonial period was home to a printing and reprinting industry and, from the 1950s onwards, to several publishing companies — Donald Moore, Eastern Universities Press, Marican and Sons — and is today trying to compete with Hong Kong, which is better established in the regional markets. To this end it organised the first world printing congress in 1978. With 395 separate enterprises employing a workforce of 15,400, it stands third in importance among Asia's centres for printing, after Japan and Hong Kong, and is dominated by four principal companies — Tien Wah Press, Singapore News and Publications, Times Printers, and Singapore National Printers — and eight distribution centres.[36]

The packing and forwarding industries — which are dominated by such major investments as Lamipark and Panthers, Tetra Park, Metal Box, Polarpark, Fraser and Neave, City Carton, Union Containers and

34. *Vocational and technical training in Singapore: The potential of a regional training centre*, Singapore: NUS, Economic Research Centre, Mar. 81, 2 vols.

35. Lee Hsien Loong (Min. of State for Trade, Industry and Defence, 'Singapore as the regional printing and publishing centre' (speech), *Singapore Econ. Bull.*, Mar. 85, pp. 18–19.

36. *Singapore Econ. Bull.*, Aug. 84, p. 8, and *Singapore Business*, Sept. 84, pp. 8–13. For Hong Kong, see J. Woronoff (235).

Win Box — cater for the greater part of regional demand, with the flow of merchandise among the ASEAN countries transiting via Singapore in considerable quantity. They have expanded by a factor of six since 1970.

The third component of this group of industries is publishing. The companies that existed in the immediate post-war era have been joined by 600 others, including (in the 1960s) Federal Publications and Far Eastern Publications, and (in the 1970s) Pan Pacific, Times Educational, Pan Asia, World Book and Chopmen Publishers. As a relay-point in South East Asia for the big American, Australian and British publishers, Singapore distributes about 100 foreign newspapers and periodicals (forty-seven in 1979) and scientific and university textbooks which would otherwise be unobtainable in the region. Copy for certain dailies and weeklies such as *The Economist*, the *International Herald Tribune* and *Time* magazine is transmitted by fax. For other periodicals Hong Kong uses the city-state — or has done so till recently — as a post-box and centre for re-transmission owing to the more advantageous postal charges.[37]

Singapore is also used as a centre for the distribution of publications with an international readership in the direction of the ASEAN capitals — except Manila, which is nearer to Hong Kong. The concentration and modernisation of this activity led to the emergence in 1984 of Singapore Press Holdings, an amalgamation of Times Publishing, Straits Times Press and Singapore News and Publication. Because Malaysia has a cultural orientation towards English-language publications, several of the Singapore companies already mentioned have local marketing branches there. Towards Jakarta, Medan and Kuala Lumpur, the city-state also actively pursues its traditional function of redistributing works of a religious (Islamic) nature — an activity which, like that of staging-post for aircraft carrying Indonesian pilgrims on their way to Mecca, is an inheritance from the colonial past.

A centre for medical care in South-East Asia
Between 60 and 70% of pharmaceuticals imported into Burma, Brunei, Malaysia, Thailand and Indonesia come from warehouses in Singapore and, in the case of penicillin, for example, from its own laboratories. The setting-up in Singapore of an ASEAN project for the production of the American vaccine for hepatitis B is only the latest evidence that

37. *Singapore Business*, Dec. 83, pp. 25–9.

the city-state has a dominant position as a centre for medical care and related manufacturing.[38]

Several dozen pharmaceutical companies, 80% foreign-owned, are present in Singapore. Of these the British Beecham group made its third successive investment there in 1982, and Glaxo had decided to start a US$100 million pharmaceutical process development before 1993. If the production of equipment in this sector remains modest, the state authorities and various companies (e.g. Temasek, Travenol Laboratories, Biotech and Karnegafuchi) are oriented towards advanced technologies: molecular biology, antibiotics, biotechnologies, electro-medical instruments.[39]

In the matter of medical care, there are ten public hospitals and twelve private clinics (with, between them, 12,000 beds and 224,000 admissions annually), twenty-three maternity and paediatric units, and a wide range of specialised services. These attract numerous patients from elsewhere in the region, both citizens and expatriates. They are cared for by a body of 3,000 doctors, often trained in the best American and British medical schools, and 8,700 nurses.

Chinese medicine also continues to have a great influence in Singapore and Malaysia, with 12% of pharmaceutical imports emanating from Hong Kong and China.

Concentration of brainpower and knowledge

Analysis of the tertiary sector in Singapore reveals the existence of at least 5,000 companies, with 50,000 staff, engaged in legal and tax consultancy, engineering, business forecasting, publicity, marketing, personnel recruitment and socio-medical services. There are some hundred of concerns specialising exclusively in consultancy, mostly in the fields of company management, and others in real estate, aviation and shipping, pre-shipment certification, insurance, security and detective work, public relations, and so on.[40]

Along with banks and embassies, these firms are the first recourse for

38. French Embassy, Singapore (Economic dept), *Industrie et circuits d'achats pharmaceutiques*, Singapore, 21 Sept. 81; C. Sepulveda & E. Meneses (eds), *The pharmaceutical industry in ASEAN countries*, Bangkok: UN Asian & Pacific Devel. Inst. and UNIDO, 1980.
39. *ST*, 12 Sept. & 21 Nov. 84, 19 Jan. 85; *FEER*, 14 Mar. 85, pp. 68–71; *Singapore Business*, July 80, pp. 49–53; *Singapore Econ. Bull.*, July 82, p. 33, & Nov. 83, p. 20.
40. Dept. of Statistics, *Report on the survey of services* (various years); Min. of Labour, Research and Statistics Dept., *Report on the labour force survey of Singapore* (various years); *Times Business Directory*, Singapore (various years).

businessmen seeking information on the markets of ASEAN and on local procedures for negotiation, marketing or investment, and their advice is often indispensable for understanding the weight of bureaucracy, corruption and the complexity of legislation in the ASEAN member-countries.

For example, civil engineering accounts for some 120 companies in Singapore, of which 30% have parent organisations in the United Kingdom. It began to enlarge its reputation in Singapore and South East Asia from 1960–5 onwards, basing itself on networks of local clientalism (the Chinese diaspora), but its precise geographical extent is today difficult to ascertain because of the reluctance of interested parties to reveal much about their business in view of tax laws and competition. Probably at least 10–15% of the total volume of contracts negotiated in the region are controlled entirely by drawing-offices in Singapore, which export all their work. One could name private offices: Anderson Connell Consultants in Sabah (real estate) and in Johore (the aluminium industry), Chan Consulting Engineers in Brunei (the airport), Chan Chee Wah Mansell in Malaysia and Thailand (real estate and new towns), and Dames and Moore in Malaysia (geology and geophysics). Other companies have a presence in all the ASEAN countries: port projects (Sir Bruce White and Wolfe Barry), soil research (Fugro), industrial and residential zones (Engineering Associates), and engineering, airports and irrigation (Sir William Halcrow).

Inspired by their local experience of small- and large-scale construction, the Singapore government's own drawing-offices are also active in the region as a whole (the Ministry of Public Works, the Housing Development Board, the Port Authority, the Public Utilities Board and Jurong Town Corporation). In the field of electrical engineering there are dynamic firms like Monenco Asia, Bassett Shipp, Sing Chow, Lim Kim Hai, Lindeteves Jacoberg Far East and Sinhim Electric.

Should one follow Lee Kuan Yew[41] in concluding that Singapore's future lies in having a bias towards specialised services tied to information technology and scientific knowledge, which will consolidate and guarantee its range of already well-established commercial and financial activities? This strategy appears attractive, even if it requires at least the tacit agreement of the neighbouring consumer countries with their own national ambitions in science and technology and of the industrial countries as well (especially in the case of technology transfer). On the

41. *FEER*, 31 July 81, pp. 48–50.

other hand, the accumulation within the city-state of a certain technical knowledge, designed to produce material profits under all circumstances, should not create feelings of superiority among the Singaporeans towards the more traditional cultures which predominate in the neighbouring countries: this was unfortunately quite often the case during the first twenty years of rapid growth in Singapore, and encourages conflicts and misunderstandings with the neighbours which could be avoided in the future.

A regional and international financial centre

Singapore's privileged geographical position, strengthened by the development of communication infrastructures, has favoured, ever since the inter-war period, the emergence of dynamic financial activities linked to entrepot trade and quickened by the local branches of London-based banks. Out of Singapore the colonial power created a network that extended throughout the hinterland — Kuala Lumpur, Penang, Malacca, North Borneo — thanks to the installation in 1899 of a common currency, the Straits dollar, and the establishment in the island of an exchange for basic commodities such as rubber, tin and spices.

Immediately after independence, the expansion of trade and international investment, with Singapore as the particular beneficiary, was accompanied in 1972–80 by a spectacular diversification of financial services.[42] The economic take-off of the North East Asian countries, of Singapore and then more recently of the whole of ASEAN created an enormous need for financing on the capital markets of London and New York, via Hong Kong. Basing itself on the experience bequeathed by Britain, the city-state — the Bahrain or Luxembourg of South East Asia — became the relay-station of the international financial market: a regional centre for the supply and demand in capital for the ASEAN countries, where the local markets still have little substance; and a place for the exchange of American, Arab, Asian and European capital seeking investment in a zone outstandingly rich in natural resources.[43]

42. The principal financial institutions of Singapore made their appearance in 1968–73: the Asian Dollar Market (1968), the Monetary Authority of Singapore (1970) and the Post Office Savings Bank (1971).
43. 'Singapore as the financial centre of ASEAN', *ASEAN Review*, Oct. 77, pp. 18–19; R. Cottrell, 'Singapore: Home of the Asia and regional treasury', *FT, Singapore Survey*, 21 Nov. 82; B. Bonness, 'Bahrain: The financial centre of the Middle East', *Singapore Banking and Finance*, 82–3, pp. 79–80.

The dimensions of Singapore's financial activities

Conditions favouring the expansion of its financial market

Several fundamental factors have contributed to the rapid success of the financial market of Singapore, and enumerating them will clarify the characteristics which distinguish the city-state from the markets in the other ASEAN member-countries. Singapore is the only town in this region of the world answering to the description of a financial centre, that is to say a place endowed with a network of financial institutions and markets, offering a range of services, facilitating the domestic, regional and international flows of investment, and involved in the economic growth of its neighbours. By this definition, one could add several other conditions which Singapore fulfills:[44]

— a regional environment where important informal or underground financial surpluses exist, that are seeking investment opportunities beyond the national frontiers and constraints and often even outside the region;

— a solid domestic economy (except briefly in 1984–6), a strong national currency, minimal inflation and a favourable balance of trade;

— a panoply of means of promoting investment and foreign capital deposits;

— the presence of diversified and successful financial institutions which are capable of recruiting well-trained staff locally;

— the existence of solid stock and foreign exchange markets, relayed by secondary markets facilitating transactions, especially between banks;

— the functioning of instantaneous and uninterrupted communications with other financial centres all over the world, Singapore being in a time-zone that enables it to work with both Asia and Europe.

The government has made this scenario yet more attractive with various incentives:

— judicial and fiscal legislation encouraging the installation of foreign banks (with both full and restricted licenses up to 1969–72, with offshore licences subsequently — see below);

— the abolition of exchange control, which has been complete since 1 June 1978;

— freedom for banks to fix their own interest rates (since 1975);

— the easy financial conditions for obtaining the status of a permanent

---

44. Tan Chwee Huat (216); *Financial Markets and Institutions of Singapore*, Singapore UP, 5th edn, 1987.

resident in Singapore (investments or deposits amounting to *c.*
US$500,000);
— flexibility and limitation on taxability of the bank accounts of both
residents and non-residents (since 1969);
— the guarantee of secrecy of banking transactions, reinforced since
1983[45] — this is of special value to private clients from certain
countries in the region.

The preponderance of Singapore in figures
In 1987, there were 350–400 commercial banks operating in London and
New York (a quarter of the world market), 154 in Hong Kong and 137
in Singapore. In the 1980s Singapore ranked seventh in the world for
international banking activity (with 4.5% of the total), behind the four
largest (Britain, the United States, Japan and France) and immediately
following Switzerland and the Bahamas, but ahead of the Netherlands,
Canada, West Germany, Hong Kong and Bahrain (2.31–2.6%
each).[46] Among the 137 banks in Singapore, thirty-seven possess a full
licence (twenty-four of them foreign ones and the remaining thirteen
the only banks of purely local origin), fourteen a restricted licence
(deposits and loans for residents above a defined threshhold), and eighty-
one an offshore licence (non-residents and the inter-bank market). Fifty-
four are the local representative offices of foreign banks. The list
continues with sixty-three merchant banks (in 1970 there was only one),
thirty-one finance companies, ninety-nine insurance companies and a
few brokers.[47]

The entire history of foreign banking in South East and East Asia has
consisted of banks being established in Hong Kong and Singapore, and
those two cities becoming entrepots of capital to finance loans in their
respective areas of influence. Most foreign banks of international repute
have an affiliate or agency office covering the whole of South East Asia
and often beyond. Since the 1970s, Singapore has developed as a regional
centre for the collection of funds and booking of credits, mostly
offshore. A kind of division of tasks has taken shape between the city-
state and Hong Kong, in the form of international banking syndications.
The banks which have chosen to establish their regional headquarters

---

45. *FEER*, 5 May 83, pp. 93–5.
46. Source: *Bk of England Qly Bull.*, 1983–4.
47. Michael Skully, *Merchant Banking in ASEAN*, Kuala Lumpur: OUP, 1983;
    Singapore Banking and Finance, 1981–82, pp. 46–7; *FEER*, 12 Mar. 83, pp. 41–68,
    & 11 Sept. 83, pp. 73–4.

in Singapore are linked by branches and representative offices to the other ASEAN capitals, taking advantage of the laws currently in force; they channel information on development and financing needs, and in return they release loans and services after due consultation with their head offices in London, New York, Tokyo or Paris. Most South East Asian countries have been important clients for deposits and loans in response to their quite rapid economic take-off in the 1980s, when fluctuations on the world commodity markets and in the rates of exchange have particularly affected their development programmes (Indonesia is a notable example).

All the world's major banks have a presence in Singapore, including Asian ones (Hong Kong and Shanghai, Mitsui, Bank of China, Indian Bank) and several of the most important in ASEAN (Bangkok Bank, Malayan Banking, Philippine National Bank). Foreign banks control about 70% of the total banking assets in Singapore.[48]

Ten of Singapore's thirteen banks are among the fifty major banks of ASEAN, and belong to Chinese families such as the Tans (Industrial and Commercial Bank) and the Ngs (Far East Bank). Two of the 'Big Four' — Development Bank of Singapore (DBS) and United Overseas Bank (UOB) — rank second to none but the Bangkok Bank.

— DBS is the only one of the Four in which public authorities own a majority of the shares. Closely linked to the Economic Development Board, it lends to foreign investors approved by the state, supports various government programmes, and participates in bank syndications.[49]

— Its rival in the private sector, UOB, was founded in 1949 by Wee Kheng Chiang with the name of United Chinese Bank. It controls three other local banks: Chung Kiaw Bank and Lee Wah Bank since 1971–3 and Far East Bank since 1984. Its president Wee Cho Yaw, one of Singapore's richest men with a fortune of some US$380 million, is behind some of the most important bank syndications in Asia.[50]

48. Lee Sheng Yi (150).
49. Lee Sheng Yi, 'Ownership and control of local banks', *Singapore Banking and Finance, 1980–81*, pp. 109–17; *FEER*, 'The rise of the Big Four', 20 Aug. 82, p. 61; 'The long arm of DBS', *Decision* (Singapore), 7 July 75, pp. 8–20; Tan Gim Wah, 'Taking risk for development's sake (DBS)', *Singapore Trade and Industry*, Aug. 74, pp. 49–52; Tan Nee, 'DBS fights its way to the top', *Asian Finance*, 15 Sept. 82, pp. 62–4.
50. *FEER*, 20 Aug. 82, pp. 52–8, and 16 Aug. 84, pp. 68–9; 'UOB: Largest of the Big Four', *Malaysian Business*, Nov. 79, pp. 44–9.

— The Overseas Chinese Banking Co. (OCBC), till 1972–3 the principal local bank, forms a conglomerate of fifty-five companies active throughout the peninsula, and is controlled by the Tan family (Tan Chin Tuan is reputed to have a fortune of US$335 million) and the family of Lee Keng Wee. Although it acquired the Four Seas Communication Bank and the Bank of Singapore, its international ramifications and the degree of modernisation of its services are less dynamic than those of DBS and UOB.[51]

— Overseas Union Bank (OUB) belongs to the Lien family, whose fortune is estimated at US$240 million. It is only one-third the size of the other banks mentioned.

Since 1989–90 there have been growing rumours of a further concentration or merger of the Big Four.

Among other structures contributing to the financial influence of Singapore is its stock exchange, which came into existence in 1973 when the exchange of Malaysia and Singapore was divided, and quotes over 300 firms (a few dozen for the Jakarta exchange) with a capitalisation of US$40 billion (still behind Hong Kong's $54 billion). Its transaction in 1987 amounted to $17 billion. The foreign exchange market transacts daily some $33 billion of business, compared with $12.5 billion in 1985 and only $369 million in 1974. Its dealings are principally in US dollars (15% of transactions are between US and Singapore dollars), Yen, Deutschmarks, British pounds and Australian dollars.

The Asian dollar market (ADM)

The ADM was founded in 1968 and constitutes one of the mightiest limbs of the financial infrastructure of Singapore. This is an international 'offshore' market in which all currencies other than local ones are exchanged mainly between banks and financial institutions, which must maintain their accounts separately from those accessible to residents and non-residents alike.[52] The establishment of this market, which today accounts for one-tenth of all the offshore currency movements throughout the world, resulted from an initiative of the Bank of America which hoped to profit from the abolition of all taxes on deposits

51. Dick Wilson, *Solid as a rock: The first 40 years of OCBC*, Singapore: OCBC, 1972; 'UOB: largest of the Big Four', loc. cit.
52. Lee Sheng Yi, *Recent development in Asian Currency and Asian Bond Market*, Singapore: Nanyang Univ., Inst. of Econ. and Business Studies, Apr. 79; Tan Chwee Huat (217), pp. 51–72; Tay Tuan, 'The prospects of the Asian Market', *Singapore Banking and Finance*, 1978, pp. 163–73.

by non-residents — a factor which made Singapore more attractive than Hong Kong, with its 15% tax, and Tokyo with its exchange control. The object was to create a funding centre in Singapore, as a link between the floating capital markets of London and New York and the countries of Asia and the Middle East (Bahrain), capable of tapping various sources of finance to underwrite the economic development of the region.

The growth surpluses of the Western world, which have been doubled since 1973–5 by the revenues of the oil-producing countries invested worldwide, have contributed to the spectacular expansion of the ADM — US$130 billion in 1984 (down to $116 billion in 1987 after the world crash in the autumn of that year), as against $55 billion in 1980 and $400 million in 1970. Four-fifths of transactions are between banks, but the Monetary Authority of Singapore does not publish any price indications as to their identity or where they are ultimately put to use.

It seems that at least half of deposits and loans, in the framework of the ADM, involve the Asian region, with ASEAN accounting for 20% of that.[53] Deposits not made by banks are savings in currencies transferred directly to Singapore by regional businesses, while much of the borrowing is destined for large-scale industrial or infrastructural projects in the countries of the region. Hong Kong is the principal client of Singapore's 'financial supermarket', redistributing in the form of financing arrangements in North East and South East Asia. Indonesia and Malaysia are the second-largest borrowers on the ADM, followed by the Philippines, China, South Korea, Thailand, Australia, Japan and Taiwan. The banks of these countries have recourse to the ADM as to one instrument among others, capable of supplying their need for liquid funds. They can obtain dollars and resell them to the central banks, or to other banks in their countries, and borrow on the internal market the relative value in local currency. Sometimes they can sell dollars directly, or they can take part in a syndication.

Despite the preponderance of London and Hong Kong in the area of syndications, those originating from Singapore have multiplied through the initiative of foreign groups, and also of local banks such as DBS, UOB and the Post Office Savings Bank. While there are dense flows

53. Zoran Hodjera, *The Asian Currency Market: Singapore as a regional financing centre*, Washington, DC: IMS Staff Papers, 25, 2 (June 78), pp. 221–53; Lee Sheng Yi, *The role of Singapore as a financial centre*, Singapore: NUS, Development Business Admin., Jan. 83.

of business linking Singapore with London and New York, the regional character of the ADM is constantly developing.[54]

Singapore and the gradual integration of the financial markets of ASEAN

Singapore's regional supremacy

Singapore's financial assets are half those of ASEAN as a whole, excluding Brunei; four times those of Indonesia, Thailand and the Philippines; and three times those of Malaysia (1987).[55] From the colonial past has come a very close financial integration with Malaysia and Brunei. Relations with Indonesia are measured according to the extent of bilateral exchanges and of interpenetration by Overseas Chinese business; it is suggested that in the closing years of the century Indonesia will represent the prime market for Singapore's financiers. Thailand and especially the Philippines are more closely linked to Hong Kong and remain relatively detached from this process. The city-state is alone in having welcomed representation by banks from all its ASEAN partners.

This supremacy has its origin as much in the strength of Singapore's financial system as in a certain structural weakness in the banking systems of the neighbouring capitals. As regards the latter, most banks in these countries are oriented primarily towards the domestic market only with gradual diversification overseas. Access for foreign banks — with the granting of restricted or offshore licenses — is kept low in order to maintain restrictive legislation (only the Philippines is more liberal in this respect). This allows for the opening of no more than agency offices, at the most. Of the thirty most important foreign banks active in the ASEAN region, all have their principal agency and 80% of their regional assets in the island (with 10% in Malaysia). In Singapore 73% of financial assets are controlled by foreign banks, against 6% in Thailand. Inversely, the local ASEAN banks have no foreign network except, for the most important ones, in Singapore and Hong Kong. The dirigisme of the local authorities subjects banks to onerous procedures for the authorisation of credits and the freeing of capital: 56% of the capital of the ASEAN commercial banks (except Singapore) is controlled by public funds, as against 26% in the case of

---

54. N. Suwidjana (215); Ernest Wong, 'Singapore: International capital market of the 80s', *Singapore Banking and Finance*, 1980–1, pp. 29–32.
55. Lee Sheng Yi & Y.C. Jao (152); Lin See Ann, 'ASEAN financial growth and interdependence', *Singapore Business*, July 84, pp. 47–64.

THE BANKING MARKET, SINGAPORE, 1974–87
(S$ millions)

	1974	1977	1980	1984	1987
Total Assets	12,405	18,238	33,316	65,707	86,484
Cash:	97	115	272	291	328
Amounts due from banks	2,666	3,713	6,880	17,088	33,853
Balances with MAS	445	546	923	1,742	2,153
Investments in securities & equities	1,241	1,911	2,604	4,379	8,525
Loans and advances	6,930	10,183	20,207	36,868	37,869
All other assets	633	1,041	1,418	2,819	3,620
Total Liabilities	12,405	18,238	33,316	65,707	86,484
Deposits of non-bank customers	6,585	8,970	16,035	28,026	39,393
Amounts due to banks	3,475	5,044	9,243	25,404	36,398
NCDs issued (S$)		513	334	301	897
All other liabilities	2,343	3,711	7,007	11,976	6,384

Source: Monetary Authority of Singapore.

THE ASIAN DOLLAR MARKET, SINGAPORE, 1974–87
(US$ millions)

	1974	1977	1980	1984	1987
Total Assets	10,357	21,018	54,393	128,058	244,869
Loans to non-banks	2,697	5,281	12,402	33,769	55,011
Inter-bank funds	7,460	12,253	39,552	85,329	171,093
Other assets	120	485	2,438	8,960	18,765
Total Liabilities	10,357	21,018	54,393	128,058	244,869
Deposits of non-banks	1,614	2,255	9,251	21,526	41,576
Inter-bank funds	8,531	18,350	40,880	100,187	192,485
Other liabilities	212	413	4,262	6,345	10,807

Source: Monetary Authority of Singapore.

Singapore. If to all this one adds the obvious political and economic difficulties, it becomes clear why the level of deposits is so weak: less than 10% of the GNP, compared with 30% in Singapore. Interest rates, which are tied to unstable currencies liable to devaluation and to an often high level of inflation, remain prohibitive in some cases. Business circles prefer to seek out the most advantageous conditions for financing, i.e. on the Western markets; these are relayed by Singapore, which offers a wide range of possible loans, medium- and long-term.[56]

56. N.L. Sirisena (210).

The integration of the financial markets of Singapore and Kuala Lumpur
Up till 1966–7 a common currency and free movement of capital were
maintained between Singapore, Malaysia and Brunei. The failure of
negotiations on a common project in August 1966 resulted, in June
1967, in the dissolution of the Currency Board and the creation of three
separate currencies; in May 1973 these ceased to be convertible, except
between Singapore and Brunei, and their respective commodity markets
were also separated. The sharp decline in the quality of financial
integration which had existed previously was accompanied by deep
political divisions (see Part II).[57]

This separation, like Indonesia's recourse to confrontation in 1963–6,
arose from internal national politics, and could not conceal a web of
economic interdependence which continued after the years 1967 and
1973, with the respective financial markets compelled to work in
harmony, as previously. The appearance of the banknotes certainly
changed, but legislation deriving from British law remained largely
intact on both sides; the free circulation of capital was maintained with
a simple declaration being lodged with the Central Bank of Malaysia
when major transfers of funds were being made to Singapore, and the
London markets for basic commodities and European currencies
remained the common point of reference for both sides. The enormous
influx of capital, due to the perception of Singapore as a haven where
it would maintain its value (notably during the international monetary
crises of 1971–3 and the ethnic conflicts in Malaysia), only reinforced
these close links almost immediately after the separation. Almost two-
thirds of the companies quoted on the Singapore stock exchange have
interests in Malaysia, and virtually all Kuala Lumpur's state loans
launched in the financial markets of ASEAN are launched on the
Singapore market too. The separation between the two national
currencies has had little effect, since their respective supports – basic
commodities in one case and services in the other – appear more
complementary than mutually competitive.

The stock exchanges of Kuala Lumpur (KLSE) and Singapore (SES).   Of
the companies quoted on the SES, 180 have their headquarters in

---

57. J. Purcal (ed.), *The monetary system of Singapore and Malaysia*, Singapore: BUS,
    Dept. of Extra Mural Studies, 1967; Bank Negara Malaysia, *Money and Banking
    in Malaysia*, Kuala Lumpur, 1984 (2nd edn); *ARB*, 3, 1 (June 73), pp. 1819–22
    & 1828–30, and no. 4 (Sept. 73), pp. 2062–3; *FEER*, 1 Sept. 66, 'Death of a
    dollar', pp. 410–12.

Malaysia and represent 40% of the total capitalisation. Thirty-three companies quoted on the KLSE were, till late in 1989, incorporated in Singapore (30% of the total capitalisation). As a commentator has put it, 'The stock exchanges of Singapore and Kuala Lumpur are as closely tied as runners in a relay race. Singapore and Kuala Lumpur constituted in effect a single market with a double identity.'[58] Nevertheless, the Malaysian government decided late in 1989, mainly for political reasons, to separate the two. Jointly the two occupy second place after Tokyo, ahead of Hong Kong. It is trading and banking groups like OCBC, DBS, UOB, Sime Darby, Promet, Faber Merlin, Taiping, Consplant, KL Kepong and Maybank that are responsible for keeping up this connection between the two markets.

The creation of two distinct stock exchanges did not present problems for most businessmen with lines of credit, agents and family connections on both sides of the Causeway, but the impact of the total separation of the two stock exchanges in 1989 remains to be seen. The volume of shares traded was up till then largely in the SES's favour, a fact for which there were several causes. First, Singapore offers a much wider range of contracts and services; the extent of the funds in circulation makes all share dealings more important than in Kuala Lumpur; the financial rules governing the professionals who operate on the exchange are more flexible than elsewhere; the SES is relatively independent of world commodity prices; and since 1979–80 sophisticated high-tech communications systems and data processing have been in use.

The KLSE, which performs less successfully, suffers from rigidities due to the New Federal Economic Policy (requiring increased participation by Malays in the capital of companies), the shackles of clientelism, the fixed limits for the repatriation of dividends abroad, and political uncertainties arising from chronic communal tension.[59] Meanwhile, the recession which struck .he KLSE in 1982–3, causing a 20% fall in turnover, led the authorities to turn to the stock exchange rules prevailing in Singapore to reform the relevant legislation at home, which was in many ways ill-adapted to its purpose (for socio-political

---

58. *FEER*, 12 Apr. 84, p. 57. This was re-affirmed at the end of 1985 with the spectacular collapse of the Pan Electric group, which caused the simultaneous closure of two stock exchanges.

59. Steve Danson, 'A test of stock recommendations and market efficiency for the KLSE', *Singapore Management Review*, 1981, 2, pp. 69–72; S. Menyanathan, 'Futures trading in the KLSE', *ASEAN Business Qly*, 1981, 2, pp. 28–31; *FEER*, 24 Sept. 82, pp. 84–7; 12 Mar. 83, pp. 60–2; 12 Apr. 84, pp. 57–64.

reasons), and thus give itself the means of attracting a similarly high level
of business to that handled in Singapore. Several observers have asked
whether this would lead to a return of the situation before the break
in 1967–73.[60] Did not the simultaneous closing of the two stock
markets at the time of the Pan Electric crisis in December 1986 and the
international crash in October 1987 demonstrate once again their close
interdependence? Beyond the pure logic of hard facts, only politics and
renewed bilateral tension can explain the decision of Kuala Lumpur in
1989 to disconnect the stock exchanges of Malaysia and Singapore.

The financial markets of the two countries. After Singapore, the financial
market of Kuala Lumpur is clearly the most substantial in ASEAN, and
the most closely comparable to that of Singapore itself. The importance
of the economic exchanges between the two countries results in a certain
convergence of their rhythms of inflation and of their exports, investments and savings. Of Malaysia's receipts and payments 45–55% transit
via Singapore, and Kuala Lumpur stands fifth as a borrower on the Asian
Dollar Market. The tendency for government measures in the peninsula
to be similar to, and sometimes even to imitate, those of Singapore (it
is rarely the other way round) encourages Kuala Lumpur, for example,
progressively to liberalise its financial markets.

Of the five Malaysian commercial banks with operations in Singapore
(they represent 80% of domestic deposits in Malaysia) four enjoy a full
licence: Malaysian Banking Co. (since 1960), which has twenty-two
branches and, in Malayan Finance, one finance company; the Sarawak-
based Kwong Lee Bank (since 1926); Ban Hin Lee of Penang (since
1936); and United Malayan (1961). Bank Bumiputra has been granted
offshore status, but has registered the best results.

The Singapore banks established in Malaysia (OCBC, UOB, OUB)
embrace about 10% of credits, deposits and loans in the country. OCBC
and Sime Darby Holdings, which are often thought of as local versions
of Morgan and Rockefeller, control, in part at least, thirty-eight of the
country's 100 leading companies and fifty-five lesser enterprises working
in the most varied fields. OCBC has four Malaysian branches and is the
third largest foreign bank after Chartered and Hong Kong & Shanghai.
Four insurance companies are active in the peninsula. In merchant
banking, several second-generation members of the Chinese Kwek
family are active in both Singapore and Malaysia in dozens of finance

---

60. *Asian Wall St. J.*, 28 Nov. 84, and *ST*, 29 Nov. 84.

and industrial companies of the Hong Leung group. The latter is also active in Hong Kong, where it took over Dao Heng Bank in 1982.[61]

The new economic policy, and notably its system of quotas for the participation of the constituent ethnic groups in the economy, does not apply to Singaporean companies! If it were otherwise, similar discrimination towards Malaysia's banks in Singapore would swiftly follow. The sheer volume of interests involved is far too great for anyone to venture along this path.[62]

Singapore and Brunei, two financial poles predestined for a close mutual understanding

With several billions of US dollars of reserves and a population of 300,000, Brunei, South East Asia's oil-rich 'emirate', is one of the world's wealthiest states. The family of the Sultan, whose new palace cost US$200–300 million to build, invests its revenues from the export of oil and gas (US$3.7 billion annually) to Japan, Europe and the United States, but very little in the region. Indonesia and the Philippines did not even appear for a long time in the overall external statistics published by this country. Traffic with Singapore alone is intense; the city-state is Brunei's second-most important partner after Japan, with energy sales and purchases of foodstuffs and equipment, and the common monetary history of the two tiny territories has followed a course analogous to that of Belgium and Luxembourg. The ending of the agreement on interchangeability with Malaysia in 1973 was never applied to their bilateral relations: the currencies of Singapore and Brunei are accepted everywhere in each other's territories.[63]

The quantity of funds deposited by Brunei in Singapore increased considerably along with successive rises in the price of oil, and have reached US$50–100 million in certain months, but the exact figures remain secret, including those linked to real estate and hotel operations.[64] In 1980–4, the local Chinese in Brunei, anxious about

61. *FEER*, 5 Dec. 85, pp. 81–6.
62. Lee Sheng Yi, 'Some aspects of banking and finance in ASEAN countries', *Singapore Banking and Finance, 1982–82*, pp. 130–3; Lim Lin Leans & Cheng Peng Lim, *The Malaysian economy at the crossroads*, Kuala Lumpur: Malaysia Econ. Assoc., 1984, pp. 195–213; *Singapore Business*, July 83, pp. 35–42.
63. 'Brunei-Malaysia & Split', *New Nation* (Singapore), 23 May 73; *FEER*, 15 Mar. 84, pp. 58–61.
64. 'High cash flow from Brunei', *New Nation*, 6 Nov. 76.

their status after independence (only 6,000 out of the total of 54,000 were granted citizenship), placed all their assets in Singapore!

The banks of the city-state are involved in several projects in Brunei, such as a plant for the liquification of natural gas. Conversely, Qaf Holdings has made its debut on the Singapore stock exchange by acquiring control of Ben and Co. (the Straits Steamship group of Singapore). Qaf, which is managed by the Sultan's brother and advised by the Rothschild merchant bank, is a conglomerate — comprising real estate, trading, services and oil subcontracting — which aims to transform Ben and Co. into a quasi-bank with the participation of all sectors of the Brunei economy; by being quoted on the stock exchange, it would be open to foreign investment in the form of joint ventures.[65] On the other hand, drawing inspiration partly from Singapore's example, the local authorities have sought since 1986 to strengthen state control in the financial affairs of the country. This tendency was reinforced following the bankruptcy of the National Bank of Brunei.[66]

In 1987–9, in many areas, new links were forged between the two tiny states and existing ones were strengthened. As regards communications, SIA and Royal Brunei Airlines (RBA) signed a particularly liberal agreement providing for one flight by SIA and two by RBA per day,[67] and the telephone link was modernised with the installation of an optical fibre cable at a cost of more than US$50 million. While Brunei decided to coordinate the command of its coastguard launches with Singapore, the city-state began to invest in several new building and town-planning projects and to increase its involvement in technical cooperation.[68]

The Sultan, a close friend of Lee Kuan Yew and his family, has become aware of the need to diversify Brunei's economy in anticipation of the eventual end of the oil boom. Faced with a partner not lacking in financial wherewithal, Singaporean enterprises have entered the Sultanate to provide equipment, technologies and engineers — all of which need to be imported. Exchanges between Singapore and Brunei owe more to the need for technology transfer and the training of personnel than through oil sales, which are destined to remain at a more

---

65. *FEER*, 26 Jan. 84, pp. 28–34, and 2 Aug. 84, pp. 80–1.
66. *AWSJ* (weekly), 30 Nov. 87; *FEER*, 5 Nov. 87, p. 82, and 22 Nov. 87, p. 115.
67. *ST*, 23 Apr. 88. According to 1987–8 statistics, at least 200,000 passengers would be carried annually.
68. *ST*, 21 Apr. 87, 22 Sept. 87, 22 Sept. 87.

or less constant level, but at the mercy of fluctuations in the US dollar and the world market.[69]

Financial relations between Singapore and Indonesia
Before the recession hit Indonesia, bank assets there had risen to US$20 billion in 1983–4 (compared to $31 billion in Singapore's banks). Only five local banks figure among ASEAN's fifty-five largest, and the stock exchange remains embryonic, with twenty-four companies quoted in 1988 and transactions totalling US$6.8 billion (85% in bonds). The dollar market in Jakarta exercises no function between borrowers and lenders in third countries, as does that of Singapore. Involved solely with the national banking system and responding to the currency require-ments of the internal market, it accepts deposits of US$1,000 upwards (the minimum in Singapore is $25,000) and grants short-term loans.[70] Of course, some of these comments will be made obsolete in the 1990s if the current deregulation of the Indonesian financial market is successful.

BNI 1946 has a branch in Singapore, while Bank Indonesia (the country's central bank) and Bank Bumi Daya content themselves with agencies. There are numerous finance companies in the city-state dealing with deposits and portfolio management for rich Indonesians, but if the country's banks on the whole wish to establish a higher profile for them-selves in Singapore, Indonesia will have to act reciprocally, which would call in question its own restrictive policy on the installation of foreign banks: BNI 1946 has operated in Singapore since 1967–8 without a licence and without any corresponding favours being granted to any Singaporean bank in Jakarta. This anachronism is the result of the policy of appeasement followed by Lee Kuan Yew after the hanging in 1968 of two Indonesian servicemen found guilty of terrorist acts on the island during the confrontation.[71]

OCBC has been established in Indonesia since 1933, with four branches, but in common with all foreign banks it was expropriated in 1963–6. Up till the present, and in spite of the volume of bilateral

69. B.A. Hamzah (131); Bernard Long, 'Brunei seeks to diversify its economy', *Singapore Trade and Industry*, Dec. 74, pp. 35–42; Lim Pasty, 'Brunei in ASEAN: Implications for us', *Singapore Business*, Jan. 84, pp. 3–7.
70. Sritua Arief (90); H.W. Arndt & N. Suwisjana, 'The Jakarta Dollar Market', *BIES*, July 82, pp. 35–64.
71. *FEER*, 20 Dec. 84, pp. 116–17; *Singapore Banking and Finance, 1981–82*, pp. 109–17.

exchange, no licence has been granted to the three agency offices of the International Bank of Singapore (OCBC-DBS-OUB-UOB), of Tat Lee Bank (the Goh Tjoei Kok family, originally Indonesian) and of the Asia Commercial Banking Co., all of which have been established there since 1976–7. With the exception of short-term deposits by the Chinese business community and foreigners active in the country, capital has shown a preference for moving outside the frontiers, and Singapore is one of the destinations offering the best guarantees of stability and anonymity. Within the Indonesian Chinese minority there is a latent but never-absent feeling of insecurity, with memories of the murderous Tanjung Priok riots and arson as recently as 1984; this is partly responsible for the flight of private capital unfettered by exchange control. The repeated threats of devaluation are another factor, but the fundamental economic reason is the excessive power and interference of Indonesian state organs.

Up till the end of the 1980s, five state commercial banks, under the close supervision of the central bank, accounted for 75% of all deposits and loans. The seventy private banks (eleven of them foreign), which transacted the remaining 25% of business,[72] were not authorised to work with public enterprises, and were compelled to refuse free access to credit, which was channelled as a priority towards industrial sectors administered by the state. They were short of capital and of liquid assets in the form of currency allocations from the central government, and they suffered from the extremely high cost of borrowing. Foreign banks were not authorised to establish themselves outside Jakarta. There have been attempts to bring about a modest liberalisation of the system; nevertheless, offshore operations conducted from Jakarta were heavily taxed, and as the result the private sector had turned its attention abroad.[73]

Faced by an all-powerful administration, informal mechanisms of power and clientelism (a route along which the Chinese move with particular ease) have multiplied, and Singapore has its own means of penetrating them. Borrowing in Singapore (and in Hong Kong) in all its forms — via London, Sydney or Tokyo, when needed, to benefit from double taxation exemption agreements — reduces the fiscal

---

72. M. Skully, 'Commercial banking in Indonesia', *Asian Survey*, Sept. 82, pp. 875–93. The article examines the five state commercial banks (BNI 1946, Dagang Negara, Bumi Daya, Rakyat Indonesia, Expor-Impor) and four private banks (Central Asia, Pan Indonesia, Duta Ekonomi, Niaga).

73. *FEER*, 26 Apr. 84, pp. 96–8; 11 Oct. 84, pp. 113–14; 15 Nov. 84, pp. 91–5.

pressure of the Indonesian state, circumvents its policy of restricting credit, and provides the means for foreign banks to participate in big projects throughout the vast archipelago without taking the forbidden step of extending its direct presence outside Jakarta.[74]

Faced with recession and with the country's considerable debt, the Ministry of Finance and Bapepam undertook from 1987 a vast programme of reforms and deregulation in order to ease the mobilisation of capital without having to resort to systematic borrowing. The measures announced in 1987 and October 1988 — such as the creation of provincial stock markets, the opening of the exchanges to foreign investors and the granting of licences to the major international banks — seemed to signal a genuine response to the needs of business after ten years of immobility. But even from the point of view of Singapore, it is still too early to judge the actual impact of these measures in the medium term.[75]

The financial functions of Singapore in the region: future perspectives

Competition and complementarity of Hong Kong and Singapore on the ASEAN financial markets

Up till 1960, Hong Kong, the Singapore of North East Asia,[76] and Singapore itself manifested a similar historical development and thus a potential rivalry in external financial markets, even if the success each of them has achieved is seen detached from their respective hinterlands.

In reality the commercial and financial activities of the Chinese diaspora links the destinies of the two cities both officially and, in particular, unofficially, on the markets of ASEAN — with Hong Kong having the edge in the Philippines and Thailand and Singapore in Malaysia, Indonesia and Brunei. This complementarity between the two emporia occurs in their economic approach, the one motivated by private business and laissez-faire, and thus open to various resounding scandals, the other hedged about and also promoted by an often inflexible governmental will.

Singapore has established itself as a regional booking and syndication

---

74. *FEER*, 19 Apr. 84, pp. 74–7.
75. *FEER*, 20 Aug. 87, pp. 66–7; 22 Dec. 88, p. 48; 29 Dec. 88, p. 58; 23 Feb. 89, pp. 63–4.
76. On Hong Kong and Singapore, see Th. Geiger (123); M. Hermann (133); Leung Chui-Keng (ed.) (157); Woronoff (235).

centre. All the banks with a presence in one city are also to be found in the other, and Singapore, ahead of the United States and Britain, is the source of the greatest quantity of deposits effected in Hong Kong. These deposits are recycled in the form of international loans, with Hong Kong coordinating three to four times more syndications than Singapore. This kind of activity greatly declined in the later 1980s.[77]

The city-state suffers from several handicaps compared to Hong Kong: the often excessive dirigisme of the Monetary Authority, over-valuation of its currency, higher production costs, the absence of one single market in the immediate vicinity as vast as China, and a lack of well-qualified and experienced banking personnel. On the other hand, the expiration of its present political status in 1997 hangs over Hong Kong like a heavy cloud and erodes its credibility. Even if the Sino-British accord of 1984 looks forward to the existing financial system being respected, political uncertainty remains — deepened by the events of June 1989 in Peking. This uncertainty is expressed in the flight or enhanced fluidity of capital, as has been illustrated by the departure of the Millie and General Oriental groups and the transfer to Bermuda of the headquarters of the celebrated British company Jardine Matheson, which had been established in the colony since 1841.[78] Up to the present, these withdrawals have not benefited Singapore, but the city-state is nonetheless seeking to attract technologies and skilled brain-power from the British enclave. China's policy of economic liberalisation was leading Singapore, like its ASEAN partners, to use Hong Kong as a window on the Chinese market: in the autumn of 1985, Lee Kuan Yew and Mahathir visited Beijing within a few weeks of each other, and Lee made subsequent visits. Investments such as those of Singapore United Industrial Co. (Oei Hong Leong, of an Indonesian Chinese family, and Dennis Lee are the main shareholders) and of Ng Teng Fong have targeted the areas of the Hong Kong economy — real estate, commerce and industry — which are potentially less susceptible to the uncertainties of 1997 than those of finance and services. Reciprocally, China, which was becoming a direct competitor of Indonesia and other countries of the region on the regional market, was

77. Lee Sheng Yi & Y.C. Yao (152); Wu Yuan-li (236); D. Blye, 'Banks prefer Hong Kong', *Asian Business*, Aug. 80, pp. 31–3; *Asiaweek*, 7 Sept. 84, pp. 36–8; *Singapore Banking and Finance, 1980–1*, pp. 19–21.
78. *Asiabanking*, Oct. 1 84, pp. 41–2 & 66; *FEER*, 17 Feb. 82, pp. 22–8; 5 May 83, pp. 12–14; on the withdrawal of companies from Hong Kong: *Newsweek*, 9 Apr. 84, pp. 34–5; *Le Monde*, 5 July 84; *FEER*, 11 July 84; 13 Dec. 84, p. 10.

able, via Hong Kong and Singapore, to have access to the Overseas Chinese network to promote its exports and its 'new' economic image — although the latter is difficult to determine in view of the difficulties which the Chinese reforms have run into since 1988, and particularly after June 1989.[79]

What does the future have in store? Hong Kong and Singapore have succeeded in maintaining the vitality of their economic activities even during the most severe internal or external crises that have affected their respective giant neighbours — e.g. the Cultural Revolution in China and the confrontation with Indonesia in the 1960s. Certainly, 1997 casts a deep shadow over the future prosperity of Hong Kong, which has depended hitherto on a series of historical accidents, but is not the situation with Singapore similar? The city-state certainly differs from Hong Kong in enjoying a political independence and a sovereignty which are not contested,[80] but this factor does not, for all that, confer a decisive advantage. Singapore remains as dependent on the internal evolution of Indonesia and Malaysia in the social and political spheres as Hong Kong does on the orientation and changes that emerge in China.

The difficulty of betting on the future
As has been noted in connection with the process of industrialisation in the region, Singapore, like Hong Kong, has adopted a hierarchical financial system consisting of major banking centres (London, New York, Tokyo) and of links with the ASEAN countries. In a tense international monetary situation, and faced with the serious indebtedness of numerous states and a recession which affected Singapore in 1985–6, the neighbouring countries and the world economy since the early 1980s, the authorities in the city-state have striven to give a new impulse to its financial activities with an eye to the future.

The major question is whether, like Hong Kong, it will give preference to free initiative, or whether it will preserve a policy of intervention. The Monetary Authority of Singapore (MAS) has opted for the second course, which is relatively unpopular with business circles, but is judged to be indispensable for weathering any future phase of international crisis. Torn between its determination to protect the viability of the city-state as a banking centre and to create sufficiently flexible conditions to attract further financial activity, the MAS has reinforced

79. *FEER*, 17 Dec. 82, p. 68; 5 July 84, pp. 61–2.
80. Dick Wilson (230), pp. 109–10.

its control over the transactions of foreign banks, discouraging for a time new implantations and expelling certain foreign financial houses which have contributed to disorder and fraud. At the same time, various taxes penalise offshore syndications, and operations on the Asian dollar market were suppressed from 1983 onwards.[81]

A second question is whether the use of the Singapore dollar should be internationalised. Since exchange control ended in 1978, deposits and loans contracted in Singapore in this currency by non-residents, including those from the neighbouring countries, have increased four-fold, profiting from an uninterrupted appreciation over a period of a decade and a half, from its role in inter-ASEAN trade, and from the expansion of Singapore's investments abroad. Representing today more than 15% of all financial transactions in ASEAN, the Singapore dollar could quickly become a kind of unit of account, thus extending the island's regional vocation. On the other hand, the authorities refuse any 'regionalisation' of the national currency, giving preference, for the sake of stability, to the balance of the national economy by keeping a close watch over currency transactions.[82]

In the inauguration of a second phase in the financial development of Singapore, innovation has not been neglected, as recent innovations bear witness:

SIMEX (Singapore International Monetary Exchange). Founded in 1984, SIMEX is a market for futures contracts in gold and currencies linked to the Chicago Mercantile Exchange (CME) and operating for twenty-four hours in every twenty-four between Chicago and Singapore. It is the first such link to be established anywhere. A dozen or so different types of contracts are exchanged, and the volume of business rose from an average of 1,600 contracts per day in 1984 to 8,500 in 1987. Different tax exemption measures have contributed to the sustained development of SIMEX, which already consists of more than 300 members, of which 236 act in an individual capacity.

81. *ST*, 12 Oct. 84; *Singapore Banking and Finance, 1980–81*, pp. 80–1 & 102–5, *Southeast Asia Affairs*, 1984, pp. 302–4; *FEER*, 9 Feb. 84, pp. 56–8; 25 Apr. 84, pp. 110–13; 18 Oct. 84, pp. 94–9; 15 Nov. 84, pp. 88–90.
82. Saw Swee Hock & Lim Choo Peng (eds) (201), pp. 154–63; *ST*, 12 Oct. 84; *Mirror*, 1980, 4, p. 6; *FEER*, 9 Feb. 84, pp. 58–60, and 19 July 84, p. 95; *Moniteur du Commerce International*, July 83, pp. 30–1; *Singapore Business Yearbk, 1984*, pp. 26–7.

The development of new financial activities. In response to worldwide movements towards deregulation of financial markets (notably in South East Asia, Australia and Japan), and to the recommendations in the report of the 'Committee of Twelve' in February 1986.[83] Singapore is seeking to develop new forms of activity in several areas. These include: risk management, i.e. the management of funds for foreign companies active in the region; fund management, with the object of attracting to Singapore the financial surpluses of South-East and East Asian business circles, and so becoming an 'Asian Switzerland'; a more dynamic capital market by developing obligatory bond issues by the state and by public corporations to create a wider spread of financial investments that would be negotiable on the spot; a secondary market for unlisted companies — this was created in February 1987, and numbers about ten at the time of writing; and a futures market in commodities and foreign stocks.

Human resources and the need for banking skills. The first phase in the financial development of the city-state took a dozen years (1968–80) to be able to attract more than 125 banks and 275 other institutions and to offer a wide range of services. The second phase consisted in setting up specialised activities, of which some are of particular value to the countries of the region, and requires financial experts of high calibre to be available locally. Unlike in Hong Kong, the local banking personnel in Singapore have not yet fully accumulated sufficient experience, or a capacity for innovation in the matter of new 'products' of the banking system. The evolution which the authorities hope for is to retain the foreign specialists already employed in the profession there, with others possibly being recruited in addition (from Hong Kong). The organisation of training programmes by the leading banks is also promoted.[84]

The success of the financial market in Singapore depends, now as in the past, on stability both in the region and on the wider international scene — something without which no emporium is able to function. On the local chessboard, a single crisis can destroy everything. The uncertainties hanging over the future of Hong Kong emphasise the

83. *The Singapore economy: New directions*, Report of the Economic Committee, Feb. 86, pp. 169–76.
84. Tan Choon Tee, 'Banking education in Singapore', *Singapore Banking and Finance*, 1978, pp. 75–82; *Singapore Banking and Finance, 1980–81*, pp. 24–6 & 118–22; *1981–82*, pp. 66–9 (Peng Por Seng, 'Training bank staff for the year 2000'); *ST*, 20 Nov. 84; *FEER*, 9 July 82, pp. 74–5, and 25 Apr. 84, pp. 110–13.

fragility of the colony, especially in an area as sensitive to circumstances as that of financial operations. In analogous terms, the prosperity of Singapore is inseparable from the political stability of Malaysia and Indonesia. Any change there can deliver a violent or even fatal blow to what has been laboriously built up over the years.[85]

Success depends as much on this stability as on the stability of the international financial situation. In 1984–7 the Asian dollar market ran out of steam as the result of world recession: the volume of debt and monetary tensions weighed heavily on the good health of the international banking system, and Singapore does not exercise such power that it can hope to influence the course of events in any significant way.

The preceding chapters attempt to show how Singapore plays a role, out of all proportion to its geographical size, as an economic magnet in the heart of ASEAN. While the dimensions of its commercial, industrial and tertiary activities make it incontestably an economic leader, its regional functions cannot be limited to those of a political midget. The international stature of the Prime Minister, Lee Kuan Yew, who has gained great prestige from the extraordinary economic success of the little republic and is received throughout the world as a leading statesman, has already influenced, in a very exact way, the shape of Singapore's original contribution in regional diplomacy and political cooperation.

85. *FT*, 22 Nov. 82.

Part II
SINGAPORE AND REGIONAL
POLITICAL COOPERATION

4
THE REGIONAL ENVIRONMENT IN
SINGAPORE'S FOREIGN POLICY

Although Singapore is populated mainly by Chinese, the fact that it is at the heart of the Malay world makes it both an actor and a victim of contradictory influences — consisting of economic complementarity versus ethno-political tension within the region.[1] The city state has not only to take up the challenge of achieving economic viability, which it has done with great success; it also has to achieve a political presence in an environment where mistrust, rivalry and rampant jealousy have long divided the region's peoples and cultures. Therefore Singapore's economic achievements have to be followed up by active diplomatic efforts to establish means of cooperation with its neighbours, and at the same time to reduce its own vulnerability to external influences.

The diplomatic instruments used by Singapore are based on certain basic principles which define its foreign policy and its membership of ASEAN.

The basic principles of Singapore's foreign policy and membership of ASEAN

Life in the emporium is played out against the ever-present backdrop of external dependence. Thus Singapore's expulsion from the Malaysian Federation in 1965 and the confrontation declared by Indonesia (1963–5) posed the urgent problem, of ensuring its viability, and have encouraged ever since the collective sense of being an island under siege in order to mobilise every resource to guarantee its survival — completely and permanently.[2] Among all the means which could serve to attain this

1. 'Even secession from Malaysia cannot eliminate the fact that 1.5 million Chinese (Singapore) are surrounded by over 100 million people of the Malay race.' Malaysian minister Tan Siew Sin, *ST*, 23 May 65.
2. Chang Heng Chee (419); P.C.N. Hardstone (132); Morrison & Suhrke (335);

primary objective, the affirmation of a policy of regional cooperation goes hand in hand with the consolidation of the national economy: since the very moment of independence, the governing team has been resolutely engaged in this twofold task.

This almost obsessional notion of a struggle to survive is reflected in Singapore's external trade policy, which rests on several guiding principles, above all on the acceptance and reinforcement of its interdependence with the region's milieu.

The basic principles of 1965–67

The vulnerability of a mini-state, the dominant theme in the thinking of Lee Kuan Yew and his collaborators, has been a spur to seek knowledge of, and friendship with, as large a number of states as possible, and to establish with them, whatever the nature of their political and social regimes, commercial relations at the very least, and more if circumstances permit.[3]

In developing the image of a global city at the service of the rest of the world, Lee wishes to convince all countries of their interest in guaranteeing the island's continued independence and development. By inviting all the powers, including China and the Soviet Union, to use Singapore as an international platform, he is making known his judgement that neither security nor stability can be lasting in South-East Asia if they do not have a presence in the region (what he calls 'multiple involvement'). He thus demonstrates to Indonesia at the same time that Singapore is not an outpost for any particular large state — either China or the former colonial master, Britain.[4]

Singapore first applied the principle of friendship with all by diversifying its trade relations. The traditional functions of an entrepot economy implied an excessive dependence on the London/Kuala Lumpur/Jakarta triangle. Strongly opposed by its neighbours and in decline since the late 1950s, they did not release sufficient resources to allow the city-state to increase its chances of viability quickly. On the other hand, the opening up in the direction of commerce and investment

E.C. Paul (355); Seah Chee Meow, 'Singapore's foreign policy in Southeast Asia: . . .', *Pacific Community*, July 73, pp. 535–51.
3. 'Half the problems of international survival is to win friends who understand and sympathize with us.' Lee Kuan Yew, *ST*, 20 Jan. 64.
4. *ST*, 5 & 27 May 66, 8 & 15 Oct. 69. *The Mirror* (Singapore), 7 Nov. 66, p. 5.

from industrial countries represented a potential contribution to meeting the challenges of independence adequately.

Politically, the establishment of commercial relations offered the advantage of lessening the importance of ideological affinity between Singapore and any one of its partners: the city-state could profit from several worlds simultaneously without compromising itself with any of them. This is one condition of its autonomy, if not of its independence, which the neighbouring countries are able to accept.

As a second logical application of the above-stated principle, it is required that this mercantile strategy should be clothed in a political garb of attentiveness to the world's developing countries and thus to its neighbours. Even before independence, Lee Kuan Yew began to cultivate his popularity on the world stage by meeting the star performers in the non-aligned movement (Nasser, Sihanouk, Chou En-lai, Tito), a task which he pursued in tandem with his friend and foreign affairs minister, Rajaratnam.[5] In the immediate aftermath of August 9, 1965, he adopted a tough style of speaking, often anti-Western, but with the opportunistic intention of being not merely accepted as a new member of the Afro-Asian club but even recognised as one of its leading protagonists — and thus appeasing the hostility of Indonesia in 1963–5.[6] Moscow, like Peking, welcomed the independence of Singapore, and many associated Lee Kuan Yew's stance with that of his friend Prince Sihanouk.

As the third application of the principle, the non-alignment policy seems to have been an expedient aimed at obtaining the recognition of the island's sovereignty by the international community. The radical talk of Lee Kuan Yew quickly dried up, and gave way to what one might term a positive neutrality; with its membership of the Commonwealth, the continued presence of British air and naval forces (till 1971), the provision of logistical support for the American forces engaged in Vietnam (from 1966) and adherence (in April 1971) to the ANZUK collective security pact, involving Australia, New Zealand and Britain, Singapore showed a certain *de facto* involvement with the West, even though Soviet vessels were still free to call there.[7] The beginning of an

---

5. *ST*, 27 Sept. 65 & 27 May 66; Chan Heng Chee, 'Singapore's foreign policy, 1965–68', *J. of SE Asian Hist.*, X, 1 (1969), pp. 117–91.
6. *ST*, 11 & 19 Aug. 65. Tunku Abdul Rahman asked for the support of the Afro-Asian countries in obtaining Singapore's entry to the United Nations.
7. In the spring of 1966, the first American soldiers came to Singapore on leave, *ST*, 6 Apr. 66. In 1967, Singapore's supplies to the US army amounted to S$ 300 m.

uninterrupted flow of American, European and Japanese investment, the undoubted lever of the city-state's economic rise, made it clear that ever since the earliest years of independence the balance was decisively tilted in favour of the West.

Keeping up a large number of international friendships, forging commercial links with all comers, encouraging the presence of the major powers in the region, advertising its non-alignment while at the same time showing special favour to large holders of capital with the inclination to invest, expressing views on international affairs only when the interests of the city-state were directly affected — all these principles gave Lee Kuan Yew a free hand to pursue an absolute pragmatism, an art in which his Chinese heritage and the influence of his studies in England have made him a past master. This flexibility is merely a response to the specific situation of the emporium as a state which is condemned to adapt itself endlessly to external events strictly in the order in which they occur. It also produces the diplomacy needed in relations with the neighbouring states, which are the most delicate ones that the city-state has to cope with since they provide the only guarantee of Singapore's continued development.

Recognition of a 'limited' independence in relation to Malaysia

The autonomy in foreign policy of an emporium, even one that is sovereign, is limited by definition. The Singapore government, which neither desired nor asked for independence for the island in 1965, admits to interdependences with the peninsula in most economic and political matters — even, as we have seen, for its water supply. If it does not admit it to the same extent, Malaysia none the less adopts a similar attitude.

The peninsula's foreign policy has never completely coincided with that of Singapore — their status as colonies was not the same, and after the fusion between them in 1963, Lee Kuan Yew spoke in the name of Malaysia on his overseas travels, yet the two countries are welded together by culture, history and their economies. When the Federation lost Singapore in 1965, there was once again a constitutional division, but the actual interdependence of the two was expressly recognised in the agreement regulating the modalities of their separation: articles V

(see Goh Keng Swee, *Singapore Parliamentary Debates*, 26, 8 [17 Dec. 67], cols 287–8).

and VI, dealing with questions of defence and economic cooperation, stipulated that a close collaboration would be pursued regarding security, and that neither state could formally ally itself with a third state without first consulting the other.[8]

The Japanese invasion in 1942, the anti-Communist emergency in 1948–60, and the uncontrolled outbursts of communal tensions in 1964 and 1969 demonstrated that even in political matters the state of interdependence was such that either of the two partners could cause injury to the other by any action that did not take the other's interest into account. On December 17, 1965, Rajaratnam declared in the Singapore parliament: 'The most important aspect of our foreign policy resides in our relations with Malaysia. Constitutional status is one thing, and historical, geographical, economic and demographic realities are another. I have my parents and a brother in Malaysia, and I cannot force myself to regard them as foreigners. The survival and development of Malaysia are essential for Singapore's survival.'[9]

This analysis can, on the whole, be extended to the relations between Singapore and Indonesia. As a general rule, the city-state's freedom of initiative in foreign policy, before finding expression, must anticipate the possible reactions of the two neighbours and engage in self-censorship in consequence. Singapore wants to tone down the image of itself as a colonial middleman and of the Overseas Chinese exploiting the resources of the region for their own profit, and therefore it does its utmost to avoid provoking serious discontent in Malaysia or Indonesia. It does not wish to play the role of a kill-joy in its relations with the immediate environment, even if its remarkable economic successes in the 1970s increased its sense of confidence on the international scene.

Interdependence joins together here factors of economic complementarity and elements of political conflict which are still potential rather than actual. The ethnic tensions, the break-up of the fusion with Malaysia, the confrontation with Indonesia, the covetousness to which it is subject — all these have revived resentment and mistrust which can only be removed, on either side, very slowly. The city-state has not yet

8. 'Agreement relating to the separation from Malaysia of Singapore as an independent and sovereign state', *Singapore Gazette Govt. Extraordinary*, vol. II, 9 Aug. 65, art. V, al. 4: 'Each party will undertake not to enter into any treaty or agreement with a foreign country which may be detrimental to the independence and defence of the territory of the other party.'
9. Parliamentary Debates, Singapore, 24, 17 Dec. 65, cols 192–295. Rajaratnam, *The Mirror*, 28 Feb. 66, pp. 1–7; *ST*, 2 & 12 Sept. 65, where Tun Abdul Razak compares the separation to a surgical operation on Siamese twins.

altogether forgotten them, in spite of the strengthening of economic complementarity: its long-lasting perception of the regional environment as essentially hostile is the result of its miniscule physical size and its very distinct identity in relation to its two neighbours. When the British announced the withdrawal of their forces (taking effect in 1971),[10] the little republic was seized with an anguished fear that it would fall victim to a pirate attack or an insidious undeclared war with the peninsula or the archipelago. Singapore dreads the possibility of Indonesian territorial expansionism resulting from domestic political instability, from visions of regional domination, or from the exploitation of resentment against the Overseas Chinese scapegoat due to internal difficulties. There is no lack of precedents: in Brunei, Sarawak and Irian Jaya (the western part of New Guinea, ruled by the Dutch till 1962).[11]

Singapore has made the choice of giving special privileged status, even within its boundaries, to the major powers of South East Asia, and has done so in response to its simultaneous concern for economic development and security: these elements can neutralise eachother through ASEAN and Indochina and at the same time hinder any individual regional ambitions on the part of either Indonesia or Vietnam, the two large states in the region.[12]

Economic and political interdependence between the emporium and its vicinity, evolving by means of overlapping factors of cooperation and conflict — such is the analytical framework which marks out the field of manoeuvre for Singapore's external policy.

Singapore's accession to ASEAN, 8 August 1967

Only two years elapsed between Singapore's expulsion from Malaysia and the end of Indonesia's active confrontation (1965) and the creation of ASEAN. Thus the adherence of Singapore may seem paradoxical in view of such recent manifestations of open hostility from its immediate

10. S. Rajaratnam, 'A time of perils and hopes for Singapore', lecture at Nanyang Univ., Singapore Govt Press Statement, 10 July 69.
11. A. Jørgensen-Dahl, (302), p. 79; M. Leifer (320), pp. 124–77; J.A.C. Mackie (325).
12. 'Indonesia is recognised as having the right and a primary responsibility to guard security and peace in the region together with its neighbouring states the Philippines and Malaysia.' Sukarno, Independence Day speech, in Leifer (320), p. 89.

vicinity. In reality, the island-state took account of events which had occurred during those two years which actually narrowed the political gap between them.

The attempted coup in Jakarta on 30 September 1965 ended the political era of President Sukarno and the period of confrontation against Malaysia and Singapore. President Suharto and his foreign minister Adam Malik proclaimed their desire to relax tensions and cooperate with Indonesia's neighbours. For Malaysia the withdrawal of Singapore did not mean a cutting of the umbilical cord joining the two states, even if the injuries each had inflicted on the other during their open opposition in 1964–5 were deeply resented. The two prime ministers met in Kuala Lumpur in June 1966, and both of them individually, unable to regard themselves as 'foreigners', believed that Singapore would soon be re-integrated in the Federation. Embarrassment reached its peak when Lee Kuan Yew published a note from Tunku Abdul Rahman pointing out that, due to bad health, he was not in actual control of government affairs at the time of the separation.[13] When Britain's impending military withdrawal was announced in January 1968, the shared nature of their security concerns was re-emphasised.

Finally, in the Philippines the elections of November 1965 brought to power Ferdinand Marcos, who did not share the negative attitude of his predecessor President Magapagal towards the Malaysian Federation. The quarrels over sovereignty in East Malaysia (Sabah), which halted the first ventures into regional grouping (ASA in 1961 and Maphilindo in 1963), also quietened down, although the dispute has not been formally abandoned even today.

In April 1966, Indonesia made a proposal to recognise Singapore and establish diplomatic relations, even before the end of confrontation was officially announced in Jakarta.[14] In accordance with Article V of the agreement on their separation, the city-state consulted Malaysia, which might have felt anxiety over such a rapprochement. But Singapore did not take long to discover that secret negotiations had taken place without its knowledge from October 1965 to May 1966 between Kuala Lumpur and Jakarta to bring about an end to confrontation and recognition of Malaysia (diplomatic relations were established in August 1967). Astonished at this behaviour, which was so clearly out of keeping

13. *ST* and *New York Times*, 11 Aug. 65; *ST*, 19 Sept. & 6 Nov. 65.
14. *ST*, 10, 11, 13, 14, 23 & 26 Apr. 66; 'Indonesian recognition', *The Mirror*, 13 June 66, p. 1.

with their accord of 1965, Lee Kuan Yew sought reassurance from Tunku Abdul Rahman in June 1966 that what he was witnessing was not a bilateral alliance between fellow-Malays turning against the Chinese island enclave in their midst. The Tunku, as a pledge of his good intentions, then proposed that the Association of South East Asia (ASA), founded in 1961, be revitalised, and enlarged to include Indonesia and Singapore.[15] The initiative to create a new association, ASEAN, was expressed officially by Indonesia shortly afterwards, and the Declaration of Bangkok (8 August 1967) was drawn up, to which Singapore subscribed.

The accession of Singapore to ASEAN, a grouping which differed from ASA and Maphilindo in not expiring at birth, represented a gain in weight for the city-state despite the apparent slackness of the association, especially in the early years of its existence. The first reason for this was that Indonesia and Malaysia, jointly with their two partners (though the latter were less concerned), recognised the independence of Singapore, whose position in ASEAN was that of a full member-state. Secondly, the intangible sovereignty and thus the territorial integrity of the city-state were formally respected by these same two countries since they were committed to rectify any future differences strictly within the ASEAN framework and by peaceful means. This principle was put to the test, but not in fact seriously questioned, in 1968 when Malaysia and the Philippines took opposed positions over the status of Sabah. Thirdly, the participation of Thailand and the Philippines offered Singapore an increased guarantee and room for manoeuvre in the possible event of tensions with its neighbours, and a useful counterweight against the anti-Chinese feelings of the latter. And finally, because it carries as much formal weight as each of its four partners in the institutional system of ASEAN (the prevailing principle is one of unanimity, not consensus), Singapore transcends politically the small size of its territory and population. Because it associates its voice with the voices of its partners, its influence on the international scene is enhanced.[16]

In short, the dreaded scenario of a new 'confrontation', which could destroy the prosperity and even the very existence of Singapore, is

---

15. *ST*, 9 June 66. Malaysia did not propose a revitalisation of Maphilindo in 1963, since this regional project insisted on a regional association having an exclusively Malay approach.
16. P.S.J. Chen (ed.) (100), p. 297; G.G. Thompson (ed.) (395), p. 82.

receding. ASEAN symbolises a new instrument allowing the city-state to increase its chances of survival.[17]

After an interval of ten years, the sultanate of Brunei, which became independent in 1984, joined ASEAN, thus producing a crucial test of the reactions of Malaysia and Indonesia. Singapore for its part, recalling the attempts at internal subversion in Brunei in 1962 when it was still a British territory, observed these reactions with close attention.[18] Because of the cultural and religious identity of Brunei — and its enormous wealth controlled by the family of the Sultan in association with the Shell Company — Kuala Lumpur and Jakarta unanimously welcomed the sultanate into ASEAN. Those two capitals confirmed on the same occasion their respect for the sovereignty of the small states of the region, a fact which Singapore could only perceive as being of benefit to itself.

Brunei's geographical situation compelled its adherence to ASEAN, but it is not certain that its contribution has developed entirely in the way desired by its two large Malay neighbours. A variety of factors drew Brunei and Singapore together: the geopolitical factor of two small states within the same regional space, their proximity, their national wealth, the complementary character of the two economies (exploited in Brunei's case by a small and highly active local Chinese minority), and the personal ties between the Sultan and the family of Lee Kuan Yew.[19]

The institutional equilibrium of ASEAN would necessarily be modified. Singapore, from this time onwards, felt less isolated than

17. M. Leifer (319), p. 146. 'Singapore's involvement in ASEAN stems basically from the desire to maximise options for survival' (Seah Chee Meow [203], p. 18).
18. In 1966, Zaini, who had collaborated with Azahri in the attempt to destabilise Brunei in 1962 and been in prison ever since, escaped. Malaysia offered him asylum, and allowed him to open a representative office of the Parti Rakyat Brunei. Malaysia supported the PRB in the sultanate. Brunei responded by laying claim to the district of Limbang, which had been annexed to Sarawak in 1890. This confrontation, during which Brunei put down a coup organised from outside (in Malaysia?), came to an end when Datuk Hussein Onn became Prime Minister of Malaysia. *ST*, 25 Mar. 67; *Asiaweek*, 12 Aug. 77; T. Bhagwan Singh, 'Concept of "Malaysian Malaysia" ', *J. of the Hist. Soc.*, Kuala Lumpur, 6, 1967–8, pp. 41–50.
19. Lee Kuan Yew became the first ASEAN leader to visit Brunei in March 1979, which the Sultan reciprocated in Jan. 1980. The latter, after having visited Jakarta, made his first official visit to Singapore as head of state in Sept. 1984. *ST*, 29–30 Mar. 79; *FEER*, 13 Sept. 84, p. 13.

before, and has been able to seek the support of the second small member-state, which has shown skill in playing on its socio-cultural image to bring it into a close relationship with its two big neighbours. Reciprocally, Brunei has oriented itself towards Singapore in economic affairs; several of its diplomats have been trained there, and the city-state often represents the interests of the sultanate abroad.[20]

The evolution of Singapore's regional policy

In a relatively short period, the quasi-emotional tensions inherited by Singapore from its separation from Malaysia and confrontation with Indonesia have been gradually absorbed. Singapore's regional policy has gone through three phases which have followed eachother in a logical succession: in the first period (1965–71) the inherited traumas exerted their maximum influence on intra-regional relations; a transitional time (1971–7) marked the reopening of Singapore towards its neighbours due to geopolitical developments that affected the stability of South East Asia and made a greater cohesiveness among the ASEAN countries indispensable; and finally normalisation and a multiplication of the ties linking the city-state to the development of Malaysia and Indonesia, which continues up to the present.

The weight of the traumas of 1965 (1965–71)

During the years immediately after independence, Singapore's foreign policy was oriented resolutely outside the region. The separation of Malaysia, the hostility of Sukarno's Indonesia and the heightened nationalism prevailing in all the South East Asian countries drove Singapore to look to more distant places for means of guaranteeing its economic and political independence with as little loss of time as possible. The British military presence and, above all, the commercial and financial support of the industrial countries facilitated the quick consolidation of the island which had become a state. It was immediately accused of giving priority to cooperation with the outside and having closer relations with the rest of the world than with its local partners. However, apart from its colonial inheritance, Singapore's external involvement was no more marked than that of its neighbours; it was merely content to opt for a policy of general openness to Western investment at a time when all the other countries — including Indonesia,

20. D. Mauzy (ed.) (330), pp. 294–305.

with a start of several years — were taking similar steps to ensure their own economic take-off. The impact of this strategy is naturally more densely visible, and excites greater envy, in a tiny territory of 620 sq. km. than in the peninsula or the vast Indonesian archipelago.[21] In cooperating with outside powers and distancing itself from a regional environment which was markedly hostile at least till 1965–6, the city-state simply sought the greatest security and stability at the best price.

The traumas of 1965 nourished a way of talking in Singapore that was frankly bitter and critical towards the neighbouring countries, which they in turn interpreted as arrogant, condescending and contemptuous. The preoccupations of national survival, inward-looking but necessary, and then the first indications of economic success largely account for the behaviour that was manifested at first in an insistence on the disparities between Singapore and the rest of the region, and on the inferiority of the traditional societies surrounding it, combined with the corruption of their ruling cliques. Lee Kuan Yew described the city-state as 'like Venice in the Middle Ages', an 'Israel in a Malay-Muslim sea', and 'an oasis in a desert'.[22] He travelled the world, but did not visit Kuala Lumpur throughout the whole of 1966 and grandly ignored Jakarta altogether.

Some sociologists maintain that this attitude results from a logic in which the urban milieu and the countryside tend to be in opposition, where the financial and mercantile abilities of the Singapore Chinese encourage a materialistic character which is often abrasive and unsociable, and where the overt élitism practised in the city-state is at odds with the value systems of the neighbouring countries, which encourage humility, modesty, an indirect manner of speech, and the need for face-saving.[23] All the same, the unflattering comparisons between the latter qualities and the achievements of Singapore, which Lee Kuan Yew and his followers enjoyed exploiting in those early years of nation-building, seemed aimed less at provoking the countries concerned than at mobilising the population of Singapore itself on a grand scale.

If the creation of ASEAN has reinforced respect for the sovereignty and security of the city-state, the latter has shown, beyond that particular

21. *The Mirror*, 24 Apr. 72, pp. 1–5; K. Wilairat (402).
22. Alex Josey (439). 'Singapore's urgent nationalism had stressed her individuality, her separateness from her immediate neighbours. The need for survival engendered a self-centered outlook, while success bred arrogance' (Mary Turnbull [78], p. 328).
23. Lam Pu Trang, 'The ties that blind', *Malaysian Business*, June 81, p. 9.

concern, much less zeal for the building up of regional cooperation. The failure of the common market with Malaysia and then the separation could hardly leave it with much hope of using the excessively loose structure of ASEAN as one of the motors of its national development.

The Singapore government is aware of the numerous obstacles in the way of extended regional cooperation, believing that all groupings of developing countries result in only very slender gains, which it is then required to share out for the benefit of the poorest member-states (in the case of ASEAN, it is the most populous state, Indonesia, which would be favoured). The exercise ends in a stalemate: the small states, Singapore and Brunei, are afraid of economic and/or political absorption by the big ones (Indonesia and Malaysia), and these in their turn show little inclination to cooperate with the small which, as the most developed in the group, are likely to reap most of the resulting benefits.

At the present time, regionalism interests the five ASEAN partners, not for itself but for the contributions it can make to the realisation of national objectives. In order not to discourage the involvement of the big powers in its development and its security, the little republic rejects the idea of a special comradeship among the South East Asian countries, with some of which it still finds itself in open conflict, and which must show reciprocal and long-lasting good intentions.[24]

Singapore and Malaysia: consequences of separation
The contentious matter of Singapore's expulsion from the Federation of Malaysia weighed on the future application of the 1965 separation agreement, and several events served to deepen the division between the two countries.

First, in the autumn of 1965, when diplomatic relations had barely been established, the accumulated resentments on both sides set off a crisis. Kuala Lumpur addressed two protests to Singapore, in September and October respectively, and the respective high commissioners were recalled. Lee Kuan Yew had in effect delivered an attack on the Malaysian Chinese Association (MCA), a member of the tripartite

---

24. 'First of all let us demonstrate to each other that we mean well to each other . . .', Lee Kuan Yew in ASEAN Bangkok Declaration, Aug. 69, Proceedings Doc. 3, cited in Jørgensen-Dahl, *Regional organisation and order in Southeast Asia*, op. cit., p. 106. Lee Kuan Yew, *The Mirror*, 26 Feb. 68; S. Rajaratnam, *Singapore Parliamentary Debates*, 26, 3, 8 Sept. 67, pp. 183–6, and *The Mirror*, 25 Mar. and 12 July 68, 16 Dec. 69, 22 Mar. 71, 24 Apr. 72; Goh Keng Swee, *Singapore Newsletter*, 1 Feb. 70, pp. 1–6; Tommy Koh, *ST*, 25 Apr. 70.

governing alliance in Malaysia — the other members being the United Malay National Organisation (UMNO) and the Malaysian Indian Congress (MIC). He reproached it for being the 'eunuch' of the majority UMNO and for having dug the grave of the union between the two countries. More generally, he attacked the 'feudalism' of Malay society.[25] Parallel to this was a 'war' of restrictions over work permits and permission to travel between the countries, which was to continue till 1967. Immigration controls were greatly tightened up at Johor Baru, it became necessary to show a passport, and tens of thousands of work permits actually in force were rescinded.[26]

In April 1966, Malaysia, using its dissatisfaction at Indonesia's recognition of Singapore as a pretext, subjected Singaporeans crossing the Causeway to customs measures, and increased certain import taxes for reasons of protectionism. Singapore immediately decreed retaliatory measures (the chicken and vegetable 'war' of 1966–7).[27] In June 1967 the differences extended to monetary policy and, as an emergency remedy, an agreement on the interchangeability of the two national currencies was negotiated, which ended five years later.[28] In 1969, the possibility of a Chinese electoral campaign, escaping from the control of the MCA and the ruling alliance, provoked murderous riots in Kuala Lumpur and elsewhere. Singapore, which had anticipated a similar development by decreeing a curfew and making numerous preventive arrests, was powerless to do more than deplore the violent riots in Malaysia.

In 1971, as a result of the desire of Malaysian politicians to boycott the city-state in order to encourage direct foreign trade, all imports from the People's Republic of China which had passed through either Singapore or Hong Kong were prohibited. Also in 1971, the jointly-operated Malaysian Singapore Airline (MSA) was divided into two distinct national airlines, MAS and SIA.

Meanwhile, even if any project of reunification seemed highly unlikely to succeed, there were other signs that the interests of the two countries remained indivisible. The predominant atmosphere of political hostility did not prevent a meeting in June 1966 between Lee Kuan Yew and Tunku Abdul Rahman, of which the most direct consequence was the proposal to revive the ASA founded in 1961, accepting Singapore

25. *ST*, 18 Sept. and 20 Oct. 65, 13 Apr. and 10 May 66.
26. *ST*, 4 and 18 Nov. and 22 Dec. 65, 19 Mar. and 4–5 Apr. 67, 28 Mar. 68.
27. *ST*, 17 Apr. and 27 July 66.
28. *ST*, 20 Aug. 67, and *FEER*, 1 Sept. 66, p. 410, and 8 Sept. 66, p. 449.

in its midst, and an agreement on double taxation exemption.[29] When Malaysia and the Philippines were in conflict over Sabah in 1969, and thus ASEAN's viability was endangered soon after it had been founded, Singapore offered Kuala Lumpur the assistance of volunteers![30]

The coming to office of a new Malaysian prime minister, Tun Razak, in 1970 marked the start of an improvement in bilateral relations, which in any case Kuala Lumpur regarded as essential. Maurice Baker, Singapore's high commissioner in Malaysia, suggested the building of a second Causeway, and the two national trading companies, Pernas and Intraco, decided in 1971 to collaborate both in their respective internal markets and with outside markets.

Singapore and Indonesia: the difficult aftermath of confrontation

Relations between Singapore and Jakarta had reached such a pass in 1966–7 that they could only be relaunched on an entirely new basis. So deeply rooted were the fears and suspicions engendered by the conflict in the minds of the governing circles in the city-state that they expected at any moment to find Indonesia reaffirming its expansionist ambitions and its aspirations to regional leadership. The vast and bloody repression that followed the *coup d'état* of 30 September 1965, which claimed tens of thousands of victims including numerous Chinese, profoundly shocked the Singaporeans. To them Jakarta seemed the chaotic capital of a state which was economically irresponsible, socially troubled, politically explosive and suffering acutely from maladministration — even if this situation, combined with the considerable resources of the archipelago, meant that opportunities existed for very lucrative business. In 1966, reversing the previous national order of priorities, and ending a chapter of Indonesian history where politics had prevailed over economics, General Suharto declared in favour of regional cooperation and the period of confrontation being forgotten as quickly as possible.[31] Communications with Singapore were re-established on 9 September and diplomatic relations came into effect a year later (7 September 1966) soon after the birth of ASEAN, with Indonesia as a participant.

In the economic area, the decision by Singapore to refrain from

29. *Agreement between the Government of Malaysia and the Government of the Republic of Singapore for avoidance of double taxation and the prevention of fiscal evasion with respect to tax on income*, Kuala Lumpur: Govt. Press, 1966; *ST*, 17 Aug. 66.

30. *ST*, 16 Feb. 69; Tommy Koh, 'The Future of Malaysian/Singapore relations', *Speech, United Nations*, New York, 27 Jan. 71.

31. 'The creation of regional stability and cooperation in Southeast Asia will get first priority', Suharto, *New Year Message*, 31 Dec. 66.

publishing the statistics for its trade with Indonesia increased differences over 'contraband', which Indonesia regarded as illicit. Even though the first discussions on this topic did not take place till August 1971, a trade promotion agreement came into being as early as 1968: both sides had learned the lesson of the disastrous suspension of a great part of their economic relations in 1963–5.[32]

Politically, the legacy of confrontation was long-lasting, and on several later occasions poisoned bilateral relations. In 1968, despite pleas for mercy from both President Suharto and Tunku Abdul Rahman, Singapore executed two Indonesian sailors who had been condemned to death for a terrorist attack perpetrated in the island during the confrontation in 1964, causing the deaths of three bank employees. The following day, murderous anti-Chinese riots broke out in Surabaya and Jakarta, where the Singapore embassy was ransacked, but Suharto rejected the urging of several senior military figures to respond strongly without delay. In this way the city-state dared for the first time to brave the displeasure of its big neighbour. Perhaps it was a calculated risk? This retrospective punishment for the infiltration of Indonesian agents into Singapore in 1963–5, symbolised by two capital sentences, could not weaken the ineluctable movement towards détente between the two countries. It served as a reminder to President Suharto of his country's wild actions during the previous three years, which had been damaging to the neighbours. It is also possible that in this crisis Singapore wished to test just how far its Malay partners in ASEAN, and Indonesia in particular, were prepared to respect the fledgling sovereignty of the little republic with its Chinese majority.[33] In view of the evidence of Indonesia's pacific intentions, Singapore did not hesitate in 1969 to endorse, in return, the annexation of Irian Jaya to Indonesia's national territory.

None the less, the city-state's mistrust of Indonesian foreign policy extended to its regional aspirations, which were partly an inheritance from Sukarno, even if the declaration of a New Order was able to give

---

32. Singapore Ministry of Foreign Affairs, List of trade agreements between Singapore and other countries, 1968, *ARB*, 1, 3, Aug. 71, p. 195; *FEER*, 10 Apr. 69, p. 80; *ST*, 5 May 72.

33. '. . . Acute sense of vulnerability exhibited by the government of Singapore as the government of a conspicuously Chinese republic, which was alarmed by the effusive expression of Malay blood-brotherhood which had attended the end of the confrontation. In consequence, it felt obliged to inject an abrasive element into close relationships in an attempt to ensure that its recently sovereign status would be accorded due respect'. Leifer (320), p. 123.

the illusion of a break in continuity. The crisis in 1971 over the status of the Strait of Malacca revealed Indonesia as wishing to see itself recognised in the role of 'first among equals' inside ASEAN. But the other member-states, and Singapore most of all, were unwilling to concede such a role to Jakarta, although they would not over-react to the familiar Javanese type of declaratory diplomacy — something its fellow-members, with Singapore at their head, were unwilling to concede — beyond a formal recognition of the declaratory diplomacy which is a characteristic of the Javanese.

The opening of Singapore's foreign policy to the region, 1971–77

During the six years between the departure of the British and the first ASEAN summit conference, some important changes occurred on the regional chessboard, with new threats to the security and viability of Singapore, obliging the city-state to adapt to them rapidly.

The military withdrawal of Britain in 1971, already announced in 1968 but which Lee Kuan Yew had hoped to delay at least till 1975–6, posed the urgent problem of converting the air and naval base to economic use and at the same time the formidable task of organising a credible defence for an island which had never before had to worry about its security.

Then the disengagement of the United States from Vietnam demonstrated how uncertain the guarantees provided by the great powers can be. The external danger of Vietnamese Communism on the very doorstep of ASEAN, confirmed by the fall of Saigon in 1975, disturbed Singapore and its partners, which were particularly concerned at its links with the activism of Communist movements within their own borders. This new Indochinese crisis was the motive force behind the political revival of ASEAN within the Bali (1976) and Kuala Lumpur (1977) summit meetings, at which the heads of state and government of the five member-states met for the first time.

International monetary instability, the fresh outbreak of inflation and the oil crisis set off the first stages of recession together with protectionist tendencies in the industrial countries which could affect an economy as outward-looking as Singapore's. These potential pressures from the world market pushed the newly-industrialising city-state into paying more attention to its neighbours, and starting to explore the possibilities of the regional market.

This evolution in Singapore's environment contributed to a new balance being struck between its intra-regional and regional interests. In 1972, as we mentioned above, the Foreign Minister, Rajaratnam, coined the slogan 'global city'.[34] Singapore now referred to ASEAN in more favourable terms than before, and thus avoided irritating its neighbours. In 1972–4 Lee Kuan Yew undertook his first series of official visits to the ASEAN capitals, where he affirmed that the regional association would have to form a counterweight to the expansion of Communism in Indochina, and that the economic development of Indonesia and Malaysia could only be advantageous in guaranteeing the stability of the ASEAN zone and the take-off of the city-state itself.[35] Jakarta and Kuala Lumpur were aware that the gut anti-Communism of the People's Action Party (PAP) parallelled their own; conversely, Singapore profited through its two neighbours from the good relations that subsisted between ASEAN and the countries of the Middle East, and thus escaped the oil boycott of 1973. Except over the East Timor affair,[36] the city-state has sided with its partners at the United Nations, and has taken an active part in the relaunching of ASEAN in 1976–7. Anxious to have access to a vast regional hinterland as a substitute for its tiny internal market, its opening up towards the neighbouring countries minimised its role, which was not easily accepted in any case, and brought new lines of activity into prominence — services and technologies — which could contribute usefully to the development of Indonesia and Malaysia.[37]

'Normalisation' of relations between Singapore and Malaysia
Several chronic differences and obstacles remained in the relations between the two countries, but these improved in the early 1970s, helped by the stability and good management of the government of Tun Razak, which had had no direct responsibility for the traumatic events of 1965.

34. *ST*, 14 and 23 Aug. 73; *FT*, 30 Sept. 74; Wilairat (402).
35. 'My government regards ASEAN as a more and more necessary and important factor in the determination of national policy . . .' ASEAN is increasingly important for us, especially for economic development and protection in the years ahead.' Rajaratnam, ASEAN ministerial meeting, May 1974, in *ARB*, Aug. 74, p. 2973.
36. Namely, Indonesia's forcible occupation of this former Portuguese colony situated in the midst of the archipelago, and its attempt to subdue the Fretelin independence movement.
37. *ST*, 15 Aug. 73; *FEER*, 5 Aug. 72, p. 9; K. Wilairat (402).

The British withdrawal made it imperative that, with due allowance for the separation agreement, there should be cooperation between them over security. This included working within the framework of the five-power arrangement (ANZUK), in which Britain still maintained a commitment concerning the defence of the region.

Kuala Lumpur's policy of proclaiming the neutralisation of South East Asia (the Zopfan declaration of 1971) is supported by Singapore, which cannot criticise this utopian pipe-dream for fear of seeing Malaysia adopt a more realistic stance and once again draw close to Indonesia.[38] Lee Kuan Yew contents himself with preferring a balanced presence of all the powers in the region, and he regrets Kuala Lumpur's rejection of a request to authorise the Singaporean army to train in the Johore jungle.

Even if every new Malaysian head of government always makes Jakarta his first call, Lee singled out Kuala Lumpur for his first official visit to an ASEAN capital in March 1972. Tun Razak's visit to Singapore in 1973 was the first by a leader of his country, and came seven years after the island became independent.[39] This initiative towards warmer relations made it possible for drama to be largely avoided when Malaysia unilaterally announced the separation of the two national currencies on 8 May 1971, thus ending the 1967 agreement on interchangeability, and the creation of separate stock exchanges. The break of 1965 and the economic break which subsequently opened up between the two states thus received its definitive ratification.[40]

When Tun Razak died on 14 January 1976, his successor Datuk Hussein Onn hoped to pursue the work of reconciliation thus begun.

Rapprochement between Singapore and Indonesia, 1972–76
The repercussions of the execution of the two Indonesian sailors soon evaporated, and the talented personality of the Singaporean ambassador in Jakarta, Lee Khoon Choy, created a more relaxed atmosphere. In 1972, the Indonesian Minister of Defence, General Panggabean, made an official visit to the island republic and in the same year five Indonesian warships went there on a friendly mission. Singapore also received

---

38. A. Jørgensen-Dahl (302), p. 150; Morrison and Suhrke (335), pp. 167 ff.; T.B. Millar, 'The Five-Power Defence Agreement and Southeast Asia security', *Pacific Community*, Jan. 72, pp. 344–60.

39. *ST*, 23–4 Mar. 72, and *ARB*, Mar. 72, pp. 778–9, for Lee's visit; *ST*, 13–14 Nov. 73, for that of Tun Razak.

40. *ST*, 4 and 9 May 73, 20 Aug. and 4 Sept. 73; *FEER*, 13 Aug. 73, p. 9, and 9 Aug. 74, pp. 40–3; Ilsa Sharp, 'A time to end comparisons', *Singapore Trade and Industry*, July 73, pp. 65–75.

authorisation to open, in Medan, its first consulate abroad.[41]

The warming of relations made further progress with Lee Kuan Yew's first journey to Jakarta in 1973, during which, in a symbolic gesture, he visited the memorial to the two sailors hanged in Singapore in May 1968 and bowed his head before it. Conversations on the status of the Strait of Malacca and of the archipelago took place in complete privacy between Suharto and Lee, who speaks Malay fluently. From these contacts and those of May 1974, when Suharto visited Singapore, the two men discovered a mutual sympathy, of which the immediate applications were the adoption of a framework for economic and technical cooperation, a frontier treaty, the launching of the Batam project, and the realisation in September the same year of a first joint exercise involving the navies of both countries.[42]

In spite of Singapore's repeated abstentions on the Timor question and its reticence in face of the establishment of diplomatic ties between Indonesia and the Communist regime in Vietnam, active collaboration continued. Lee and Suharto met in Bali in September 1975 and in Singapore in November 1976, the agenda for these two meetings being the preparation for ASEAN summits, cooperation on the development of Batam, the difficult negotiation of an extradition agreement which stumbled on the question of the legal status of smugglers, and the provision by Singapore of its trade figures to Indonesia.[43]

When Malaysia, the Philippines and Thailand recognised the People's Republic of China, Singapore undertook not to establish diplomatic relations with Peking before Jakarta did so. The situation came to an end in 1990 when Indonesia and then Singapore established full diplomatic relations with China.

Singapore's regional policy in the 1980s

During the later 1970s, Singapore felt concerned about is own security and that of the whole region in opposition to Indochina, and it showed redoubled interest in regional matters in three principal areas. The city-state could only congratulate itself on the reinforced political cohesion of ASEAN brought about with the summit meetings in 1976 and 1977.

41. *ST*, 7 Apr., 7 and 10 June.
42. *ST*, 25–6 May and 11 June 73 for Lee's visit; *ST*, 2 June and 29 Aug.–1 Sept. 74 for Suharto's trip to Singapore; *FEER*, 'Singapore-Indonesia: The ice melts', 13 Aug. 73, pp. 13–20 and 35–6.
43. *ST*, 2–4 Sept. 75, 28 June and 29–30 Nov. 76.

It hailed the double success of the association in the peaceful solution of all the intra-regional differences which had occurred hitherto, and the long way they had come since 1965 in the whittling away of mutual mistrust and misunderstanding. Even if the cohesion of ASEAN was manifested chiefly in response to external challenges, this approach expressed Singapore's preoccupations, among which the security of the region took precedence over all others.

Secondly the relaunching of ASEAN, which introduced as its primary objective regional economic cooperation as a guarantee of the development and the stability of the member-states, corresponded to the interests of the island-state and its new strategy of growth in the tertiary sector and technologies, taking on a more extended complementarity with the economies of the neighbouring countries.

Finally, the invasion of Cambodia, which confirmed Singapore's apprehension over the dangers of Vietnamese expansionism, and directly threatened Thailand, also provided it with the justification for embracing a forward policy on the regional scene and for seeking to rally the other members of ASEAN for an anti-Communist policy directed primarily against Indochina.

Singapore and Malaysia: the 'Lee–Mahathir era'
The journey to Singapore which Prime Minister Datuk Hussein Onn made in May 1980 already constituted a decisive stage in the rapprochement between the two countries: on this occasion an intergovernmental committee, attached to the offices of the two Prime Ministers and meeting at regular intervals, was created.[44]

The coming to power of Mahathir as the new Prime Minister in 1981 — he visited Singapore in December — opened a period of genuine reconciliation, and a new dynamism appeared in bilateral relations. Relatively young, very attentive to economic problems and anxious to bring about a certain liberalisation in his country, Mahathir made this renewed move towards Lee Kuan Yew despite their earlier conflicts over the question of multiracial policy, and the two men and their respective teams thereafter consulted together frequently.[45]

44. Dhanabalan, speech at the first meeting of the Intergovernmental Committee, Kuala Lumpur, 2 Dec. 80, in *Singapore Econ. Bull.*, Jan. 81, pp. 26–7; *FEER*, 30 May 80, p. 24.
45. Victor J. Morais, *Mahathir: A profile in courage*, Singapore: Eastern UP, 1982; *ST*, 16–19 Dec. 81 (on the 19th it carried the headline 'Mahathir's Singapore visit great success: settled all major issues'); *The Star*, 22–26 Aug. 82.

An agreement was reached on the division of the territorial waters in the Straits of Johore (governing access to the port of Pasir Gudang and on the Malaysian army's evacuation of the Woodlands naval base on the north shore of Singapore island.[46] For the first time in fifteen years, a head of the federal government praised Singapore's economic success in terms specifically related to its contribution to Malaysia's own economic take-off: 'Singapore's history of success in the economic and social fields can only be a model for Malaysians and not an object of envy. What each of us does within our respective countries contributes to, and completes, the progress of the other . . . I see no reason why we in Malaysia should nurture mistrust and suspicion of Singapore and vice versa.'[47]

The much-publicised visit of Vice-Premier Datuk Musa Hitam to Singapore in February 1983 set the seal on several cooperative projects regarding the development of Johore, air travel and touristic links, the migration of workers, oil deliveries and the Trengganu–Johore–Singapore pipeline, water supply, electricity and professional training.[48] Only the possible construction of a second Causeway seemed to make Kuala Lumpur hesitant. The excellent relations between Lee and Mahathir were given an additional dimension in 1984 when the Sultan of Johore, a personal friend of Lee, was elected as constitutional monarch of Malaysia.[49]

As already mentioned, one can observe a more and more frequent interdependence between the respective policies pursued in Kuala Lumpur and Singapore, most notably over economic matters. This seems most marked in times of recession; at the end of 1985 the two national stock exchanges were closed simultaneously following on the failure of the Pan Electric industrial group, which had ramifications in both countries.[50]

The years 1986–7 were marked by several diplomatic 'incidents' which, in appearance at least, caused a certain cooling in bilateral relations. The visit to Singapore — the first such — of the President of Israel, Chaim Herzog, in November 1986 aroused strong protests in Malaysia, especially among the youth of the Malay party, UMNO, belonging to the ruling coalition and in orthodox Muslim circles, and

46. *ST*, 5 Aug. and 10 Sept. 83.
47. Mahathir, *ST*, 18 Dec. 81.
48. *ST*, 11 and 19 Feb., 4 Mar. 83; *The Monitor*, 12 Feb. 83; *NST*, 12 Feb. 83.
49. *ST*, 27 Nov. 84.
50. *FEER*, 12 Dec. 85, pp. 87–91, and 19 Dec. 85, pp. 86–7.

the government in Kuala Lumpur also showed signs of irritation.[51]

In 1987 Lee Kuan Yew's son Brigadier-General Lee Hsien Loong, Minister of Commerce and second Minister of Defence, questioned publicly the loyalty and patriotism of Malays in Singapore's army (they form 15% of the population in the city-state),[52] and a little later Malaysia complained of Singaporean military personnel engaging in espionage in Johore.

Such incidents, occurring two decades after the Malaysia–Singapore divorce in 1965, clearly demonstrated how sensitive are collective perceptions and memories on both sides of the Causeway, and from time to time set the limits within which the Singapore authorities can act autonomously.

All the same, at a deeper level the improvement of bilateral relations reached an important new stage in 1988/9, first with the renewal of agreements on the supply of water and natural gas by Malaysia, and then, much more spectacularly, with the military training exercises on land (in Sabah and in Singapore itself) at the end of 1989.[53] These were the first to be held since 1965.

There can be no doubt that the political involvement of the two Prime Ministers has had a deep influence on the various ways in which the close interdependence of the two states has been reaffirmed. The similarity in the political style of the two men has even extended, in recent years, to a kind of convergence in their respective strategies on domestic policy, particularly in the struggle against signs of political opposition, both real and imaginary. The two regimes had no hesitation, in 1987–8, in having recourse once again to the Internal Security Act.

Meanwhile, certain new anxieties have come to preoccupy the two capitals as they seek to guarantee an unflagging pursuit of good bilateral relations. It is clear that on both sides of the frontier new men, progressively but unavoidably, must succeed to the positions of power, but both Lee Kuan Yew and Mahathir sense a certain worrying lack of political maturity in the young generation who will soon be called upon to succeed them. For one thing, Kuala Lumpur has complained bitterly of the increasingly noticeable technocratic nationalism shown by the PAP's young ministers and senior officials who, in the name of Singapore's absolute sovereignty and independence, have had no qualms about taking initiatives in interior and foreign policy without consulting their

51. *FEER*, 25 Dec. 86, p. 20, and 19 Feb. 87, p. 42. *ST*, 10 Jan. and 4 Mar. 87.
52. *FEER*, 2 Apr. 87, pp. 30–2; *ST*, 3 and 28 Feb., 7–10 and 25 Mar., and 8 Apr. 87.
53. *FEER*, 23 Feb. 89, p. 27; *ST*, 27–9 June, 1 and 5 July 88.

counterparts in neighbouring Malaysia, either officially or informally.[54] A second factor is that Singapore deplores the absence of close personal relations between colleagues of the younger generation who, unlike the old leaders, did not have the shared experience of the colonial period and of Greater Malaysia.[55] For the sake of interdependence, and because of the often sensitive nature of relations between the two states, the two governments are making contacts and meetings between the new younger governing echelons as numerous as possible so as to lay a solid foundation for the future.[56]

Singapore and Indonesia: the 'Lee–Suharto era'
The Lee–Suharto meeting in Bali in June 1978, which took place only a few hours after the accidental disappearance of the Indonesian ambassador in Singapore, H. Tasling, while on his way to join them, marked the beginning of a period in which bilateral consultations became so frequent as to be unremarkable.[57] In 1979, Lee and the Indonesian Minister of Science and Technology, Habibie, met twice to prepare an agreement covering the development of Batam (ratified in June 1980). In 1980–2, cooperation was established in the fields of communications (overflying rights and a second submarine cable between Singapore and Medan) and trade (the provision of Singapore's statistics; trade in petroleum and natural gas). President Suharto's visit to Singapore in 1983 occurred only two months after that of the army chief General Murdani, and caused astonishment in the city-state, which had had little experience of hearing Indonesians speak so favourably of economic cooperation in the private sector. The first meeting of the respective chambers of commerce was held in Jakarta in November 1984.[58]

For more than one reason, 1985 represented a symbolic culmination of the efforts towards cooperation. The opening of a new Indonesian embassy building in Singapore, the most modern and spacious which Indonesia possesses in any country, gave the lie to those who still felt suspicious and wished to boycott the regional functions of the

54. *ST*, 8–9–10, 18 and 29 Mar., 17 and 30 Dec. 87.
55. 'Unlike their older leaders who, having grown up in one milieu and gone through crises together, have got the measure of each other, the younger ones of both sides differ in political exposure, style and tone.' Lee Hsien Loong, *ST*, 21 July 88.
56. 'Neighbourly ties now depend on the successors,' *ST*, 22 Mar. 88. See also *ST*, 17 Dec. 87, 8 Nov. and 5 Dec. 88, 21 Jan., 17 Feb. and 2 Sept. 89.
57. *ST*, 26–7 June 78.
58. *ST*, 29 Nov. 84.

Singaporean economy.[59] The friendship between Lee and Suharto was never demonstrated more clearly than on the occasion of the summit at Jakarta and Ujung Pandang in April 1985. For the first time, in the absence of any differences, bilateral questions were treated as secondary. Even in relation to Batam, Suharto did not voice his idea that Singapore was in a sense 'morally obliged' to participate in the development of that island. Instead he gave precedence to private sector initiatives in conformity with the beginning of a more general liberalisation in Indonesia of administrative and economic mechanisms.[60] Repeating his assurance that he cherished no territorial ambitions, he devoted his energy to discussing the political stability of the region, which he knew to be as vital for the future of Singapore as for the success of the New Economic Order in Indonesia. The two leaders broached subjects which were politically sensitive, but which none the less were at the very heart of their joint concerns: the recession in the oil industry and its repercussions on the socio-economic balance of Indonesia, the terrorist agitation and atrocities by extremists which were shaking Jakarta and other Javanese towns at that time,[61] succession problems in the ruling élites, and anxieties over the future of the Philippines. In all this the two men showed a remarkable spirit of mutual confidence, in which the armed confrontation of twenty years earlier and the all too obvious disparities between the city-state and the archipelago seemed to be forgotten.

Bilateral visits multiplied in the late 1980s, in the military sector among others, and the happy picture was not overshadowed either by certain differences of opinion over how to control the crisis in Indochina and over the visit of the Israeli President to Singapore in 1986 — to which there was only a slight reaction in Indonesia. Further, after having established direct commercial relations with China in 1985, Jakarta announced in February 1989 its hope of having diplomatic relations with Beijing as well (it became a reality in 1990). This development tended to take the sting out of Indonesia's anti-Chinese attitude, which, by extension, included the Overseas Chinese in Singapore, at least up to the end of the 1970s.

59. *Jakarta Post*, 9 and 11 Mar. 85.
60. *ST*, 4–6 Apr. 85, and *Jakarta Post*, 3–4 Apr. 85.
61. The sensational arrest of Gen. Dharsono, former Secretary-General of ASEAN, and the bloody riot at Tanjung Priok (Jakarta) in Sept. 1984 followed by a series of explosions and arson attacks. In particular, a large ammunition depot south of Jakarta was blown up and in Jan. 1985 the famous temple of Borobudur in central Java was damaged by a bomb. Dharsono was amnestied in 1990.

In 1987 bilateral relations — which were judged to be excellent — were relegated to second place in the agendas for the meetings of Lee and Suharto in Singapore (February) and Batam (November): the two men set themselves the task, above all, of preparing for the Second Summit of ASEAN Heads of State and Government, which was to be held at Manila in December.[62]

However, bilateral relations were by no means uninteresting in so far as, since 1967, a process of political opening-up by Indonesia towards Singapore has been occurring in a number of subtle ways — in this the excellent relations between the families of Lee Kuan Yew and Suharto have been of decisive importance, even in economic affairs. There is every indication that President Suharto is seeking to play a mediatory role, either directly or indirectly, in the more delicate areas of bilateral relations between Singapore and Malaysia and of trilateral ones between those two countries and his own. Hence,

– In February 1987, Suharto went to Johor Baru — for the first time during a state visit to Singapore — via the Causeway that links Singapore to Malaysia (Johore). The main reason for this initiative was to appease the anti-Chinese reactions which had been aroused in Malaysia by the Israeli President's visit to Singapore not long before. A further reason was to reaffirm the unavoidable interdependence of the two states.

– The year 1987 also saw the inauguration of new premises for the Singaporean embassy in Jakarta and, above all, a much-publicised visit by Lee Kuan Yew's son, the Minister of Trade and Industry. It could not have escaped the notice of Kuala Lumpur that several sensitive subjects of common concern to all the three neighbouring states were among the principal matters discussed (e.g. the transition to a new top political leadership, the change-over from the old to the new generation in power, the promotion of Malay culture and language).[63]

— Reciprocal visits by the highest-ranking military leaders have multiplied since 1987. General Murdani was awarded the highest decoration of the Singaporean army, and in 1988 — in the first act of its kind — Indonesia granted military facilities for Singaporean aviation in Central Sumatra.[64]

— Of even greater symbolic significance was the beginning of

62. *ST*, 6, 7 and 8 Feb. and 29 Nov. 87.
63. *ST*, 21, 22 and 23 July and 11 Oct. 87.
64. *ST*, 30 June and 1 July 87, and 16 Sept. 88.

intergovernmental consultations between the two states on religious questions, especially the theme of Islam and the religious minorities in the region.[65]

— In the summer of 1989, Indonesia — and President Suharto in particular — reacted in much more moderate terms than Malaysia to a unilateral proposal by Singapore to offer the United States certain military facilities in the city-state, notably in the event of an American withdrawal from the Philippines.

Beyond the complementary aspects of their economies, Singapore and Jakarta still have much to learn from eachother in the political domain — on the one side the cultural and intangible values of an Indonesian society that still has a largely traditional form, and on the other the primacy in Singapore of action and firm commitment over mere talk. The only imbalance here is that whereas good relations with Indonesia appear indispensable to Singapore, it is less obvious that the reverse is true. Thus the burden is on the Singaporeans to be aware of this fact and to learn to adapt themselves to their neighbour's situation.

65. *ST*, 27 Sept. 87 and 11 Feb. 88.

5

SINGAPORE AND ASEAN
ECONOMIC COOPERATION

Compared to the tightly-knit fabric of commercial, industrial and financial relations which Singapore has developed with its neighbours, its contributions to institutionalised economic cooperation in the region remains limited, not to say peripheral. If the city-state has an unchallenged position as one of the principal channels for business contacts in South East Asia, its role in bringing the institutions of ASEAN into play seems to have been obliterated. We should try to identify the reasons for this.

The city-state has attempted several times over to convince its partners of the need to elaborate effective regional economic cooperation, but ASEAN's initial achievements fell far short of those original attempts, and aroused no interest on Singapore's side. Singapore, more perhaps than any other member-state, found the advantages of its membership of ASEAN to be essentially political. The relaunching of the association in 1976-7 was in response to needs and in anticipation of advantages of just that nature: to compensate for the very slender negotiating strength of each member-state individually on the international scene by the cohesion of the five speaking with one voice, as much to the industrial countries as to Communist Indochina. At the intra-regional level, cooperation has been extended to the peaceful settlement of existing bi- or trilateral conflicts, but little progress has been made on the economic front.

There have been some signs that a change is beginning, but it is far from certain that in its present form the institutional machinery of ASEAN finds favour with the island-state, which gives preference to flexibility over rigidity and to the role of private initiative over the omnipresence of state power.

Singapore's contributions to relaunching ASEAN through economic cooperation

Singapore was not backward in insisting, in 1967, on the economic dimension of the proposed ASEAN cooperation being established, and the specific character of its interests did not appear to present an obstacle to this being inscribed in the basic documents of ASEAN. The explanation for this situation was the seeming convergence of the economic development policies which the member-states aspired to put into operation. The content of ASEAN declarations reflects this community of ideals, even if the instruments envisaged for their realisation are not specified at any given moment.

Economic cooperation in ASEAN's basic documents and the position of Singapore

When the preparatory negotiations were under way in 1966-7, Singapore proved to be the most fervent advocate of regional economic cooperation. Deprived of any prospect of fusion with Malaysia, and dreaming of a regional common market of more than 250 million people, it was in this area that it had most to offer to its partners.[1] On the other hand, in the immediate aftermath of the events of 1965 its freedom of diplomatic initiative became entangled in its very delicate relations with Malaysia and Indonesia. Furthermore, the adoption of economic and social recommendations with regional scope was used to mask political differences which still persisted among almost all the member-states; paradoxically, it is here that ASEAN deserves congratulation on having carried off an unquestionable political success.

Singapore was one of the principal framers of the passages in the Declaration of Bangkok (8 June 1967) which envisaged regional economic cooperation as one of the determining factors for the peace and security of South East Asia. This fundamental idea, taken up by Malaysia in the Declaration on a Zone of Peace, Freedom and Neutrality (27 November 1971), also identified some of the economic and social objectives common to all the ASEAN countries like trade and exports, opening up to foreign investment, welcoming transnational companies, the framing of civil and social liberties. . . . ASEAN is a rare example among regional groupings of developing countries in showing no inclination for regional import substitution or control of foreign investments.[2]

This convergence of objectives is all the more significant for the city-

1. Lau Teik Soon, 'Singapore and ASEAN' in Chen (ed.) (100), pp. 285–300.
2. Ho Kwok Ping in Broinowski (ed.) (259), pp. 196 ff. Of Indonesia, this writer says that the country, 'under the leadership of General Suharto, had joined an informal network of like-minded states spanning Southeast Asia and beyond, of which Thailand, Malaysia, Singapore and the Philippines were already members.' Leifer (320), p. 120.

state; its size and the necessary conditions for its viability require it to show itself to be in prudent harmony with its neighbours and partners. By playing the card of the permanent struggle to ensure its national survival, the small republic is able to play down its economic power and to cultivate some kind of diplomatic and political autonomy on the regional scene.

Singapore is wagering on a rapid development of regional economic cooperation through sectoral negotiations, and in 1967–8 it made concrete propositions regarding trade, industry, navigation, tourism etc. This functional approach to regionalism, which was included in the Declaration of Bangkok, was taken up again with the firm support of the city-state, in the Treaty of Friendship and Cooperation in South East Asia (articles IV, VI and VII) and the Declaration of ASEAN Concord of 24 February 1976, which began the structural transformation of the grouping finalised in the summits of 1976 and 1977.[3]

In reaction to the growing pressure of both international economic problems and the Vietnamese Communist threat, Singapore believed that its partners explicitly recognised the necessity for genuine economic cooperation to assist in their growth and hence reduce the risks of political destabilisation or internal subversion.[4] The Singaporean authorities expected, according to the Declaration of Concord, some rapid benefits from the opening up of regional markets, the permanent guarantee of food and energy supplies, and the cohesion of the Five in major external economic negotiations.

It was not long before hope turned to disillusionment.

Singapore's liberalism and pragmatism over regional economic cooperation

Singapore's position within ASEAN reflects its national economic and political structures; the city-state mainly pleads for the adoption of the same kind of instruments as those that have governed the efficient development of its own society and its remarkable economic success.[5] Liberalism combined with regulatory supervision by the state, clear and

3. Brigid Burns, 'The Association of Southeast Nations' in J. Jamar (ed.) (299), pp. 1–52.
4. 'Indo-China and ASEAN were in direct competition as the showcases of economic and social development for their respective ideologies' (Broinowski, op. cit., p. 41).
5. H. Crouch (278).

firm long-term objectives as well as adaptability, disciplined commitments combined with flexible and pragmatic reactions – these are some of the characteristics of Singapore's regional policy, which rests on three major principles.

1. The predilection for concrete action corresponds to the materialism and practical sense of the island's population and government. This is translated into a mistrust of any insensitive and unhelpful institutionalisation, which normally produces unrealistic projects dreamed up by diplomats and politicians, with little regard to feasibility. Thus, at ASEAN's fifth ministerial meeting in April 1972, Singapore drew attention to how few of the resolutions adopted by ASEAN since 1967 had been followed by action.

The various constraints weighing down upon Singapore's survival and viability do not allow the governing élite to waste money, time and energy in frequent meetings which do not produce concrete results: likewise, the island's civil service, whose numbers are limited, cannot dwell on the numerous papers which are produced on regional cooperation if nothing valuable can be expected from them.

During the Bali and Kuala Lumpur summits, Singapore, supported by Malaysia, opposed the creation of a heavily institutionalised ASEAN secretariat in which Indonesia would be able to play an important role. In June 1982, so as to make clear its hostility to any administrative centralisation of ASEAN, Singapore made clear that it was in no position to nominate one of its few most senior diplomats to the post of ASEAN secretary-general, even when for the first time it was the turn of a Singaporean national to occupy it. Finally, Chan Kai Yau, director at the Ministry of Education, a man without international experience, was sent to Jakarta, the seat of the secretariat.[6]

2. The second rule of conduct observed by Singapore is to reject economic dogmatism, embracing free enterprise and free exchange but not laissez-faire; competent and effective public administration but no state dirigisme and muscle-bound bureaucracy; denunciation of all forms of protectionism and acceptance of only transitory measures. Dismissing the European integration model, when applied to ASEAN, as unrealistic, Singapore envisages gradual regional cooperation when directed towards precise and realisable objectives. In the same line of thinking, it is out of the question that the close links between Singapore and the

6. Hans Indorf, 'Some speculations on a second blueprint for ASEAN', *Contemporary Southeast Asia*, Sept. 81, pp. 140–59.

industrial countries should be sacrificed on the altar of regional cooperation — a demand which, in ASEAN's case, has not yet been made.[7]
3. As a third priority, preference for flexible and pragmatic instruments
of cooperation gives an advantage to Singapore's capacity for self-
adaptation to an outside world, which never sleeps, and to its harmo-
nious relations with the business community, which far transcends the
island's national territory. Rather than intergovernmental meetings at
ASEAN headquarters, regional white-elephant industrial projects and
sectoral planning, the city-state's diplomacy prefers clubs of indus-
trialists and financiers acting as expert representatives for a single area
of activity, chambers of commerce and federations of industry, in which
Singaporeans and the Chinese diaspora are represented very much
according to their key role in the economic development of the region.

Frustrated by the slow pace of regional cooperation within ASEAN,
Singapore has, for example, criticised the rigidity of the intra-regional
negotiation process which has taken place since 1980 and which
systematically seeks consensus;[8] this is ill-adapted to the very different
economic interests of individual member-states. It is the view of Lee
Kuan Yew that any member-state should be allowed to dissociate itself
from this or that decision without paralysing regional construction
which is too much built on the lowest common denominator by the
member-states.[9] By virtue of its small size, at least in political terms,
and its high economic performance, Singapore's principal aim is to
preserve its freedom of decision whether or not to participate in ASEAN
projects.[10] Such arguments as these were repeated in the ASEAN Study
Group's report of 1983 and then by the ASEAN Chamber of Commerce

7. 'The economic aspects of cooperation provide the greatest lure as far as the
importance of ASEAN to Singapore in concerned . . . To Singapore, ASEAN
supplements rather than dictates the pace of economic development' (Seah Chew
Meow [373], pp. 22–3).

8. This is diplomacy according to *musyawarah* and *mufakat*, which reproduces a
political tradition suited to rural life and the village community in Indonesia, and
to some extent in Malaysia and the Philippines. See Crouch, op. cit., pp. 10–15,
and Jørgensen-Dahl (302), p. 166.

9. S. Drummond, '15 Years of ASEAN', *J. of Common Market Studies*, 20, 4, June
82, pp. 301–9; *FEER*, 10 Dec. 82, pp. 70–2.

10. 'ASEAN has been used by member nations as a device for promoting national
rather than regional interest . . . National interests exist . . . Regional interests
are abstract concepts which ASEAN members cannot as yet clearly define or reach
agreement on.' Rajaratnam, speech at 4th ASEAN ministerial meeting, Manila,
12 Mar. 71.

and Industry's report of 1987, both of which have remained largely a
dead letter up to the present.[11]

Singapore and the principal areas of regional economic cooperation: participation and frustrations

Taking up proposals made by the United Nations in 1972,[12] the Treaty
of Friendship and the ASEAN Declaration announced three areas of
possible cooperation: a progressive liberalisation of trade, a strategy for
regional industrial projects and the identification of potential package
deals based on complementarity of the national economies. The confirmation of these objectives by the two ASEAN summits of 1976 and
1977 coincided with a policy on Singapore's part more open to regional
affairs than before. The city-state displayed a cautious but none the
less genuine enthusiasm for ASEAN cooperation in the three ways
announced. However, ten years later Singapore could only deplore the
slender results achieved.

Cooperation versus conflicts over commercial policy

The cleft within ASEAN over commercial policy follows the dividing-
line between Singapore and Indonesia — the pair of countries which
stood for many years in diametrical opposition to eachother in most
negotiations within the group. This opposition — between a city-state
dedicated to free trade[13] and a vast archipelago which till recently has
been highly protectionist — is merely a prolongation of the old trade
rivalry between the British colonies on the Straits and the exclusive
Dutch monopoly based in Java.

Between these almost irreconcilable positions, the other ASEAN
members impose tariffs which are often high in the cases of Thailand
and the Philippines, though more moderate in that of Malaysia.[14] The

---

11. *AWSJ*, 6 July 87, and *FEER*, 9 July 87, pp. 54–5.
12. United Nations, *Economic Cooperation for ASEAN*, report of a UN team, New York, 1972.
13. Rep. of Singapore, *Trade Classification and Customs Tariff 1968*, Govt Printing Office, 1968; Trade Development Board, *Singapore Trade Classification and Customs Duties*, Singapore, 1983. At the beginning of the 1980s, 92% of Singapore's tariffs actually corresponded to 'zero ratings'. *Ad valorem* taxes of 10–20% existed in the case of about 40 items, including alcohol and tobacco.
14. In 1981–2, more than half of Indonesia's tariffs, one-third of those of the Philippines and a quarter of Thailand's were above 30%, and some exceeded 70%.

leading commercial role of Singapore in the region is seen by other member-states, Indonesia especially, as a major competitor to their own infant national industries and manufacture of exports, and thus any intra-regional concession on tariffs is thought likely to be to the advantage of Singapore's exports of manufactured goods. In their dealings with Singapore, Indonesia and in varying degrees the other member-states show the classic attitude of the least economically developed countries in fearing that a significant liberalisation of regional markets would essentially benefit the most developed member-states like Singapore.[15]

Intra-regional trade: Singapore and the inadequacies of ASEAN's agreement on trade preferences

Since October 1968, the Philippines, quite protectionist in fact but subject to American liberal influence, proposed the creation of a regional free trade zone to lead ultimately to a common market. Meanwhile, one had to wait for the Declaration of Concord in order for ASEAN to pronounce in favour of an agreement on trade liberalisation, but without stipulating detailed terms and conditions, due to the profound differences between member-states.[16]

Trade agreements between Singapore and, respectively, Manila and Bangkok envisaged an overall tariff reduction of 10% and this came into being in the early 1970s. But the refusal of Jakarta and Kuala Lumpur to be associated with them, which lasted up till the Bali summit in 1976, obliged Singapore, supported by the Philippines, to withdraw its twin proposal for an ASEAN tariff rise moratorium and the launching of a regional free trade zone.

An alternative solution, more modest in scale, was envisaged at the Lee–Suharto meeting in November 1976 and following a second dismantling of tariffs between Singapore and Bangkok in January 1977. Indonesia recommended the negotiation of trade preferences, product

See Tumbocon Haresco in *ASEAN Econ. Bull.*, Singapore: ISEAS, July 84, pp. 47–8.

15. A.W. Axline, 'Underdevelopment, dependence and integration' *International Organization*, 31, 1 (1977), pp. 85–105; *FEER*, 18 Mar. 83, p. 39, and 10 May 84, pp. 72–3.

16. ' "Agreement in principle" was the lowest common denominator; it was the distance the most reluctant member, Indonesia, was prepared to go to meet the expectations of the most "activist" members, Singapore and the Philippines' (Jørgensen-Dahl, op. cit., p. 55). See also *FEER*, 23 Jan. 76, pp. 47–52.

by product, on the basis of lists of unilateral concessions submitted by the respective governments. An agreement was finally signed at Manila on 24 February 1977; it was ratified by the second ASEAN summit in August that year, and named the 'Preferential Trading Agreement' (PTA).[17] At first, seventy-one concessions were covered, but by 1987 negotiations held at regular intervals had raised this number to 20,000 and were leading to a limited multilateralisation. In April 1980, a general reduction of 20% was adopted for any national import flow of any one product of ASEAN origin not exceeding a total annual value of US$ 50,000; in 1984 this ceiling was raised to $10 million, and virtually automatic concessions were applied to certain categories of products (textiles, chemicals, rubber, cement). As regards the origin of goods, there were rules defining the applicability of the PTA: these distinguished goods produced and exported directly by ASEAN from those in which the element of foreign processing did not exceed 40–50% of the final value.[18]

The agreement on the PTA did not compensate for the stalling of the project for a free trade zone, and Singapore did regret that regional cooperation had to evolve at the pace of minimum concessions from the least developed member-states. The Singaporean director-general for ASEAN affairs declared in August 1977: 'Although we would be prepared to accept any compromise, we also have the feeling that because of the pace at which ASEAN is disposed to evolve, we would rather rely on our own arrangement.'[19] For the city-state, as for numerous foreign economists, the theory of the beneficial effects of the PTA — that it will create new flows of trade between member-states and provide substitutes for some imports from outside — has hardly been proved in view of the extremely modest scale of the arrangement:

— The concessions exchanged remain insignificant despite their large number. For political more often than economic reasons, the obligation on the governments to present several hundred concession offers each year leads them to choose tariff reductions on products which are of only

17. For a detailed technical presentation of the PTA, see Ooi Guat Tin (349) and Gerald Tan (391).
18. Singapore Dept of Trade, *ASEAN preferential tariffs*, 24 Jan. 81; *FEER*, 13 Aug. 82, pp. 46–8, and 8 Mar. 84; and *Singapore Business*, July 84, pp. 66–7; Tom Jackson, 'The "Game" of ASEAN trade preferences', *ASEAN Econ. Bull.*, Nov. 86, pp. 255–67.
19. Quoted in Chia Siow Yue, *Singapore and ASEAN economic cooperation*, Bangkok: Asian and Pacific Devel. Inst., 1978, p. 19.

very minor importance in their foreign trade, or which have never been traded before with their ASEAN partners. For example, in 1981 Thailand included certain kinds of wood which it had never imported and which are not produced in the region; Indonesia proposed some components of nuclear reactors, and the Philippines equipment for dealing with snowy weather.[20]

— Except for the respective national lists of unilateral concessions of Malaysia and the Philippines, and of Malaysia and Singapore, there are too few similarities between the national lists generally, thus making it impossible to promote intra-regional trade more effectively.

— A reduction of 10–20% in import taxes turned out to be of only limited effect, because the tariffs in question were prohibitive. In the hypothetical case of existing tariffs being dropped altogether by the Philippines on all imports with an annual value below US\$ 500,000, it was calculated in 1984 that the total increase in import purchases would have increased by only 2%.[21]

— In Singapore and even in Malaysia, numerous concessions have included goods which were already free of duty; of 147 offers made voluntarily by Singapore in May 1981, fifty-three were already in this situation. Inversely, some other ASEAN countries have presented goods also bearing low tariffs but they have excluded 'sensitive' products which could foster import creation to their disadvantage.[22]

— Negotiations on the basis of unilateral concessions, product by product, are long and subject to lobbying from pressure groups, especially those very closely linked to the governments of the three most protectionist ASEAN countries. Manufactured goods, which are precisely the major productions of Singapore and Malaysia, are also a constant source of conflict and disagreement among member-states.

— Various products exported by Singapore are not eligible according to the PTA rules of origin (concerning re-exports and manufactured goods containing too large a proportion of foreign components).

20. See the country-by-country tables in Tan, op. cit., pp. 14–41. 'It will be useful if future PTA negotiations could be directed not only at expanding the number of preferences exchanged, but also at exchanging preferences on items with real trade potential' (Goh Chok Tong, Singapore Minister of Trade and Industry, *ASEAN Information*, Dec. 80).

21. W. Lütkenhorst, 'Import restrictions and export promotion measures in Southeast Asian countries', *ASEAN Econ. Bull.*, Singapore: ISEAS, 1, July 84, pp. 43–69.

22. ASEAN General Secretariat, *ASEAN trade preferences*, Jakarta, 1981 (ASEAN Documentation Services); Singapore Dept of Trade, *ASEAN preferential tariffs*, 1981.

— Finally, it should be noted that ASEAN has not started any serious negotiation on non-tariff barriers among member-states.[23]

No one should expect from the PTA a substantial increase in intra-ASEAN trade. Even if PTA marks a first step, it plays down the comparative advantage of some member-states for manufactured exports, and of others for exports of raw materials or semi-processed goods. Facing considerable political resistance within ASEAN, PTA gives little benefit to either Singapore or Malaysia, which however offer a wide range of products in demand from their partners, but which cannot absorb much of the primary exports of the latter. For its part, Singapore is afraid that the PTA will favour and protect ASEAN's least efficient entrepreneurs but also contribute to the decline in competitiveness of certain branches of regional or national economic activity because of excessive isolation from world markets. Because of its competitive and privileged relations with the industrial world, Singapore is naturally unwilling to scuttle itself.

Despite several attempts and advance declarations, the third summit of ASEAN heads of state and government in Manila in December 1987 did not allow any decisive step forward to be taken in the area of trade.[24] Meanwhile, the member-states are formally committed to make effective before 1992 half of the intra-ASEAN concessions exchanged within the PTA framework and progressively to dismantle their non-tariff barriers. It has to be said that this is an ambitious agreement in view of the fact that Thailand excludes more than 1,600 products, accounting for 63% of its foreign trade, from the lists of concessions to be negotiated between member-states. All ASEAN states also continue to reserve their right to implement safeguarding measures at any time, and the excessively rigid rules of origin of merchandise have not been relaxed up to the present. Some representatives of Singapore to the Manila summit asked once again whether the Six were really prepared to put into operation a genuine multilateralism within the ASEAN region.

The establishment of a free trade zone — rather than a customs union which would oblige free trader Singapore to raise its customs protection in conformity with a common ASEAN external tariff — is what the city-state aspires to. It would not only stimulate the growth of its

23. Aurora Sanchez, 'Non-tariff barriers and trade in ASEAN', *ASEAN Econ. Bull.*, 4, 1, July 87.
24. *ASEAN Information*, nos 11 & 12/87 and no. 1/88; *FEER*, 3 Dec. 87, pp. 22, 24–5, 104–10, and 24 Dec. 87, pp. 8–10; *FT*, 11 Dec. 87.

industry and services, but it would also enable products from the outside world to enter the ASEAN market via Singapore on a massive scale, at the risk of obstructing or delaying the industrial take-off of ASEAN's most backward countries. This solution is not viable politically: Indonesia and indeed other countries are not willing to sacrifice their own development for the benefit of Singapore and Malaysia, or to enable a process of regional industrialisation with little benefit or spill-over effect for themselves.[25]

The perspective of a common market remains, even more so, in the realm of fiction. The possible combination of a free trade zone and a customs union, which would preserve Singapore's special position, has not yet been shown convincingly to be feasible.[26]

Relative cohesion in external economic relations

ASEAN's external trade policy. Oriented pre-eminently towards the Western economies, the ASEAN countries have shown the same cohesion in relation to the industrial countries as they have politically towards Indochina. ASEAN's unity is a response to a shared perception of external challenges and potential threats, from which Singapore would be the last to dissociate itself. The city-state's close co-operation with the OECD countries determines the intrinsic viability of this small emporium, but its insertion in a regional grouping like ASEAN increases its negotiating capacity and weight.

The close complementarity of its economy with the region gives authority to the reciprocal allocation of interests between member-states in a community-based approach to external relations. The city-state stands close to its partners wherever trade and the marketing of basic commodities, energy products or semi-manufactured goods are in question since Singapore is both a consumer of all these items and, for the most part, a middleman distribution agent for them. In return it receives ASEAN support in the denunciation of protectionist measures adopted by the industrial countries, which may badly hit ASEAN's

25. 'As long as Indonesia is not willing to accept that it is its fate to play the role of Portugal (in the model of Ricardo) to Singapore's England, an ASEAN free trade area cannot come into being' (Crouch, op. cit., pp. 55–6).
26. See H.C. Rieger, 'Towards an ASEAN common market: a concrete proposal' in Sopiee, 1988, pp. 71–80; *ASEAN Information*, Aug. 83; *FEER*, 1 May 86, pp. 58–60; H.C. Rieger (195); Sopiee, op. cit.

efforts to promote manufactured exports from the region.[27] In the case of trade tensions among ASEAN states, Lee Kuan Yew is shrewdly aware of how to play diplomatically on Malaysia's pivotal position as an exporter of both primary products, like Indonesia, and of industrial goods, like Singapore. The city-state occasionally seeks the support of the Philippines, which, like itself, depends heavily on the American market for exports, and which is much influenced by the American concepts of free trade and a liberal economy.

Within ASEAN's institutional framework, Singapore has been designated to be the country leader responsible for official relations between ASEAN and New Zealand but with no other major economic power! But in reality, Singapore's economic performance and its broad exposure to world markets allow it to play a far from insignificant role in most of ASEAN's external economic negotiations, even if it is more appropriate in most negotiations to cede formal precedence to Indonesia or Malaysia. This role is facilitated by several factors. First, the Singaporean representatives have a total command of the English language and an intimate knowledge both of the Anglo-Saxon culture and of their Indonesian and (mainly) Malaysian colleagues. Secondly, the island's administration, in spite of being numerically small, is efficient and highly qualified when it comes to intervening in the most technical cases and coordinating, indirectly if necessary, the positions of its ASEAN partners.[28] Thirdly, it has a competent and pragmatic ruling team who are listened to with respect in influential world economic forums like the World Bank, the International Monetary Fund and GATT. Finally, Singapore has the capacity to express at least a 'verbal' solidarity with its ASEAN partners in the great debate on a new international order taking place in Geneva, New York and around the world (the Group of 77, the Non-Aligned Movement, the Commonwealth conferences) in order to gain political advantages, even if the concrete results of these dicussions cannot be easily forecast.

27. As a member of ASEAN, Singapore has long resisted the tendency of the industrial world to class it among the newly industrialised countries and not to concede it trading preferences. Since January 1989, the United States has ceased to grant Singapore systematic general trade preferences.
28. For example, within the committees of ASEAN ambassadors at the EC in Brussels and at the UN in Geneva and New York. In 1972, it was through the mediation of Singapore and Malaysia that the EC first entered into dialogue with ASEAN. This resulted, in 1980, in the signing of an agreement on cooperation between ASEAN and the EC, the first of its kind between two regional groupings.

The opening of ASEAN to foreign investors. Each national policy regulating foreign investment has developed a kind of competitive convergence among ASEAN member-states, with each country seeking to obtain the maximum of foreign investment flows into the region. In the case of Singapore, foreign investment has been closely associated with the concept of the economic viability of the island, and to the priority guarantee of its permanent existence as a political entity and sovereign state. In the other ASEAN countries, excepting Brunei whose situation is quite similar to that of Singapore, the annual amount of foreign investment is also very important but not so closely related to national survival: these states are cushioned by large rural societies and by a diversity of natural resources; the role of foreign investment in these economies is mainly to bring about the speedy realisation of certain development projects in the fields of infrastructure or industry. ASEAN has never been hostile to transnational companies, unlike some other regional groupings such as the Andean Pact; it has adopted, and only in the form of a resolution, a code of conduct for multinationals.[29] The welcome given to foreign investment is more or less determined by the degree of economic and cultural nationalism and the level of development of each member-state: Indonesia and Singapore were for a long time at the two extremes, with semi-liberal or semi-restrictive regulations on foreign investment in place in Malaysia, Thailand and the Philippines. Since the 1987 summit in Manila, the six member-states have been engaged in promoting intra-ASEAN investment and the harmonisation of their national systems of guarantees offered to foreign investors.

The city-state constantly works its hardest to damp down the potential jealousy of its neighbours looking at the considerable flow of foreign investments that pour into Singapore every year. This area of potential tension has eased somewhat over recent years with increasing investment flows into Indonesia, Malaysia and Thailand; Singapore is able to emphasise the diversity of services it can offer for the benefit of the neighbours' economies, and its investment in Indonesia and Malaysia (including relocation of labour-intensive industries) became highly significant in the 1980s.

Singapore also knows well how to exploit diplomatically the very specific conditions of its national survival and viability: in allowing the

29. Chia Siow Yue, 'Codes of conduct for MNCs and governments in ASEAN', *Contemporary Southeast Asia*, Sept. 83, pp. 219–36.

greatest possible number of foreign investments into the island, it tries to compensate for the limits imposed by its small area and population and the absence of natural resources. The major challenge is not to depend on any specific source or type of foreign investment in order to be able to forge the instruments of a relative national autonomy (but such an autonomy must be analysed and measured in relation to the tiny size of the island city-state with a wide international economy).[30]

Singapore and the difficulties of ASEAN industrial cooperation

Singapore's particular position with regard to intra-ASEAN trade can also be observed in the industrial sphere. As the only economy showing a true complementarity with its partners, it instinctively distrusts regional industrial cooperation attempts that result from pure inter-governmental negotiations. Based, most often, on superficial economic analyses, such initiatives result from political motives without enough prior consideration for the rigid economic interests of each ASEAN country involved. As the promoter of a fabric of effective intra-regional ties which derive from the play of market forces and the direct involvement of local and international business circles, Singapore sees no valid argument that could support an administrative and institutional approach to cooperation between ASEAN industries. For these industrial branches which can only attain viability through vast economies of scale, a highly unified ASEAN market would not even bring enough economic incentive: the regional market would remain too small considering the current level of development of the ASEAN economies.

It is now easier to understand why Singapore shows so little interest in the three types of industrial cooperation proposed so far by ASEAN inter-governmental meetings.

The near-failure of ASEAN's industrial projects

Initiated in haste because of the climate of political revival prevailing at the Bali summit of 1976, the six ASEAN industrial projects did not owe their inspiration to any coherent feasibility study and were immediately criticised by Singapore for their gigantic scale. Each project was estimated to cost around US$ 250 million, and a 40% financial participation by the member-states was programmed without knowing the possible source of the remaining 60%, which in principle was to be the res-

30. Thakur Phanit (359), pp. 162ff.

ponsibility of the country receiving the project; nobody could tell either if the regional market could absorb the future production.[31] None the less, Japan offered a US$ 1 billion line of credit.

The planning of two industrial complexes for production of urea-based fertilisers (each with a capacity of 500,000 tonnes), to be built in Indonesia and Malaysia, envisaged output in excess of the most optimistic forecasts of regional demand. Only one of the two was finally realised, in northern Sumatra: officially inaugurated in 1984, it is mainly an Indonesian plant serving national interests.

Thailand was to build a soda ash factory, but its competitiveness by world price standards was nullified by the fact that unrefined salt had to be transported over a distance of 430 km. from the north of the country to the coast. The Philippines presented a project for exploiting copper, then phosphate-based fertilisers, and then timber, without ever choosing one project which was economically realisable.[32]

The case of Singapore set off a crisis within ASEAN. With its proposal for creating a petrochemical complex, for which the financial support had already been obtained (from Sumitomo in Japan), the city-state met with a refusal from Indonesia, which wanted to develop its own refineries. When the manufacture of diesel engines was considered by Singapore, Jakarta renewed its obstruction in order to protect its own embryonic national industry (PT Boma Bisma in Surabaya).[33] Singapore withdrew from the regional negotiations concerned and pursued this second project with United States cooperation (the Cummins Engine Co.), reduced its financial contribution to the other ASEAN projects by 99%, and refused all preferential customs arrangements in favour of their future productions.[34]

Only in 1984, Indonesia, embarrassed by the inauguration of its fertiliser plant in Acheh in the presence of ASEAN delegations, allowed — just a few days beforehand — the adoption of a centre for producing the American hepatitis B vaccine in Singapore as an ASEAN project. Estimated to cost US$ 4 million, ASEAN financing would be limited to 1% of the total (like the amount of Singapore's financing of

31. *FEER*, 13 Aug. 82, pp. 39–84. Japan (following the Fukuda Doctrine) decided to back these projects to the amount of US$ 1 billion, and paid over a first tranche of $90–147 m. for Indonesia and Malaysia.
32. Broinowski, op. cit., chapter X.
33. 'Feasible diesels?', *ASEAN Business Qly*, 3rd q. 77, pp. 34–5.
34. 'The Singapore decision to move ahead with Cummins on its diesel project clearly begs the question of its commitment to the entire concept of ASEAN industrial cooperation.' *FEER*, 20 Oct. 78, pp. 61–2.

the four other ASEAN projects); however, Brunei announced, with calculated publicity, its support for the project.[35]

The agreements on industrial complementarity (1978–9): absence of concrete developments?
The objective of these ASEAN agreements was to implement a division of labour among member-states for some sophisticated manufacturing productions which were well beyond the individual capacity of any one of the countries on its own. Singapore immediately expressed its opposition to any attempt at regional industrial planning imposed by ASEAN governments and to any exclusivity clause binding member-states to buy the final products resulting from such agreements. In 1979, however, certain national chambers of commerce launched the idea of a first complementarity agreement in the automobile industry, with each country specialising in the supply of particular components and agreeing to sell the ASEAN cars on its domestic market with a 50% tariff exemption. Jakarta and Kuala Lumpur also proposed that any production resulting from a complementarity agreement should be at least 51% controlled by ASEAN investors.[36] The principle of a general agreement on intra-ASEAN industrial complementarity was signed much later in October 1986.

Singapore disapproved of the possible development of protected industrial monopolies, which would kill free competition in the region and favour many inefficient firms. Therefore, it further reduced its import taxes, increased those on components and parts, and declared that it would not implement the proposed complementarity arrangements. It also heavily questioned the ASEAN decision-making based on unanimity and consensus: any member-state should be permitted not to participate in certain regional projects without preventing them from being activated between other member-states. Finally, no ASEAN government wished to see Singapore isolate itself as it did from the ASEAN industrial projects of 1977. A compromise was found, which almost entirely eliminated the initial plans for state intervention: no ASEAN production of a similar nature would be discriminated against

35. *FEER*, 15 Mar. 84, pp. 80–2, and *ASEAN Information*, May 84.
36. *FEER*, 27 July 79, p. 101; 2 May 80, pp. 54–5; 13 Aug. 82, pp. 46–8. The division of tasks in this automobile project (it was not envisaged that a complete vehicle would be built) was as follows: Indonesia – diesel engines; the Philippines – transmission gear, car-body shells, axles; Malaysia – cables, cycles, computers; Thailand – shells of utility vehicles.

by another member-state specialising in any type of component; the commercial preferences granted to the goods as the result of complementarity agreements would be left to the discretion of each country; and they would not be allowed to exceed the concession rate granted in the framework of the ASEAN PTA.

Singapore has succeeded in holding in check the idea of a planned division of industrial labour within ASEAN. The entry of South Korea on to the world automobile market has not convinced business circles of the potential for an ASEAN car to be developed. When the production of a regional motor-cycle was suggested in 1984, Malaysia was quick to indicate that it wished (on its own) to produce a prototype![37]

Joint industrial enterprises: modest hopes
Conceived as a more flexible instrument, better adapted to the demands and needs of the private sector, the basic agreement on ASEAN industrial joint ventures (signed in December 1982) stipulated that if two or more ASEAN entrepreneurs of different nationalities decide to collaborate, their final production would benefit from a reciprocal tariff concession of 50% in their respective countries. In addition, eighteen sectors were initially identified — like ferrous alloys, mini-tractors, special paper, textile machinery, chemicals. . . .[38]

Singapore reacted positively as the one member-state which has already invested most through joint ventures in the region, and well before any regional agreement of that kind existed. The city-state judged the basic agreement to be incomplete, and made it clear that it would not participate if it did not obtain satisfaction. Clarification was forthcoming in 1984 on the two following points.[39] First, the preferential treatment applied between the countries of the participating entrepreneurs was to be extended, after a lapse of four years, to other ASEAN member-states according to the trade agreements already in force (and not by the application of a 50% tariff exemption as stipulated by the 1982 agreement). Secondly, a foreign company established in one of the member-countries could control up to 49% of the joint venture or of some of the companies involved in the deal — a principle which certain ASEAN delegates had rejected in 1982. The first of these two points was adopted at the Manila summit in December 1987, and indeed

37. *FEER*, 25 Aug. 82, pp. 80–1; 15 Sept. 83, pp. 86–7; 3 Nov. 83, pp. 76–7; Lee Sheng Yi, *ASEAN's AIJVs in the private sector*, Vienna: UNIDO, 21 Apr. 82.
38. *FEER*, 8 Dec. 83, pp. 82–3, and 5 Nov. 84, pp. 113–14.
39. H.W. Indorf (298).

without such a provision the actual impact of the ASEAN industrial joint venture could not be gauged.

In 1981, the ASEAN Economics Ministers had recommended feasibility studies in several sectors: industrial treatment of magnesium, mechanised farming and paper mills. Other projects have been envisaged since then (such as car components, ferrous alloys, acetylene, freon), but in most cases the deliberations within ASEAN have not led to concerted actions of any substance.

In Manila in 1987, the Japanese Prime Minister Takeshita reactivated ASEAN-Japanese cooperation when he proposed a new ASEAN development fund of US$ 2 billion for the promotion of industrial joint ventures, at least between two member-states. The first such fund, set up during the premierships of Fukuda and Suzuki, had very meagre results in practice. At the time of writing it was still too soon, although Malaysia began to submit draft projects in 1988–9, to measure whether this new Japanese fund would prove to be more than an additional vehicle for sustaining Japanese investment and a Japanese presence in South East Asia.

Singapore as promoter of financial cooperation in the region

Banking and financial activities constitute one of the few business sectors where the influence of the Singapore market has been translated into a determined effort at regional coordination by the city-state. It is doubtful whether its approach, which is more institutional in this area compared to other fields of economic cooperation, is pure chance; Singapore seeks to profit from the relative weakness of the other ASEAN national markets in order to extend its predominance as the major financier of the region, a position from which it can extract durable economic and even political power in relation to other member-states.[40]

The beginnings of financial cooperation in the region go back to 1975, when Singapore and the Philippines decided to start a working group within ASEAN's International Chamber of Commerce (ASEAN CCI). The two Singaporean delegates — Wee Cho Yaw, president of the Overseas Union Bank, who was already in charge of ASEAN's working committee on industrial cooperation and was to become president of ASEAN CCI in 1979; and his deputy Lim Kee Ming, also a banker –

40. Hua Pak Cheong (137); M.T. Skully (211).

made a strong impression on that occasion. March 1976 saw the creation of COFAB — the ASEAN Committee of Finance and Banking — and the association of ASEAN banks, which chose the city-state as its headquarters and Tony Tan, formerly managing director of the Overseas Chinese Banking Co. and then minister of state in Singapore, as its first president.[41] In 1977–8, liquid assets of US$ 200 million were made available to support any member-state suffering from balance of payments problems.[42] Finally, a committee of insurance experts, mainly from Singapore, was convened: Singapore, Manila and Bangkok proposed the creation of a regional reinsurance company, but came up against opposition from Jakarta and Kuala Lumpur.

For Singapore the underpinning of regional financial cooperation, modest in scale but none the less concrete and flexible, is already in place as part of the overall design. Several other instruments came into being in 1980–2 to provide the finishing touches.[43] First, the ASEAN Finance Corporation, set up in 1981 with an initial capital of US$ 10 million, contributed by the (then) five member-states in equal shares, was destined to play the part of a sort of regional investment bank. It forged financial links with similar institutions in the industrial countries, and has succeeded in developing: at the end of 1985, its capital and its assets had already respectively exceeded US$ 50 and 60 million.[44] Secondly, the ASEAN Trading and Investment Corporation, planned in 1981, was destined to become the great trading house of ASEAN on the pattern of its Japanese, South Korean and Taiwanese counterparts, but this idea remained a dead letter after 1982, since the ASEAN Chamber of Commerce was unable to raise sufficient starting capital.

For the time being, the city-state seems disinclined to formulate more ambitious regional objectives.[45] One can cite several examples. First, the creation of a regional centre for the issuing of trading bills, would reduce ASEAN's dependence on the major world financial centres but it presupposes sophisticated banking services which the region's own institutions cannot offer so far, and Singapore itself is only beginning

41. B. Rojanasatien, 'The ASEAN Bankers Association: . . .', *Singapore Business and Finance*, 1982–3, pp. 115–16.
42. ASEAN, *Memorandum of Understanding on ASEAN Swap Arrangement*, 1977.
43. *ASEAN Information*, Apr. 81 and Oct. 82; see also A. Sheng, 'ASEAN cooperation in money and banking', in Sopiee, 1988, pp. 139–60.
44. ASEAN Finance Corporation Ltd., Singapore, annual reports., 1988, pp. 139–60.
45. N.L. Sirisena, *Problems and prospects of cooperation in banking, finance and monetary policy in ASEAN*, Singapore: Nanyang Univ. Inst. of Economics and Business Studies, Mar. 77; Tan Fuh Gih (392).

to familiarise itself with them. It also implies a hypothetical harmonisation by ASEAN of exchange controls — something abrogated by Singapore since 1978. Secondly, the launching of a regional payment union,[46] or in other words the annual negotiations of compensatory credits to face any serious balance of trade deficit in a member-state, has not been approved by Singapore; this system is rejected because of the need for a common currency and the likely internationalisation of the Singapore dollar as a result. Besides, no one has yet been able to say how ASEAN's banks, with their limited resources, would be able to underwrite on their own the risk of fluctuations in regional trade. Thirdly, it seems premature to set up a common network of export credit guarantees, since this instrument has only just been introduced in each of the national markets. And fourthly, the idea of creating an ASEAN regional development bank, proposed by Indonesia in 1981 for reasons which owed more to chance circumstances (the visit of the Japanese Premier Suzuki) than to careful thinking, was met with a general reluctance. The ties between ASEAN's financial markets seem too small, apart from those between Singapore and Kuala Lumpur, to assure the viability of such an initiative.

The totality of these future projects calls for the fulfilment of several preconditions: first, a substantial development of intra-ASEAN trade and industrial cooperation to generate a genuine need for a financial network to serve the whole region; secondly, the harmonisation of national banking and financial policies; and thirdly, a strengthening – not a questioning — of the cooperative links with banks and finance companies in the industrial countries.

Singapore and ASEAN: recent evolution and perspectives

Stronger consensus in favour of flexible instruments of regional cooperation.
During the recession of the mid-1980s, contrasting with the rapid growth of the previous decade, and considering the proximity of ASEAN's twentieth anniversary, the member-states all denounced — to varying degrees — the failure, paralysis or lack of adaptability of the existing instruments of regional cooperation and the absence of any firm commitment to genuine economic cooperation. Meanwhile, the report of the 'twelve', published after the fifteenth meeting of ASEAN foreign ministers in order to diagnose ASEAN's inadequacies and what reforms

46. *FEER*, 8 Mar. 85. This project was supported notably by Thailand.

should be introduced, produced no significant reaction.[47] The results of the Manila summit in December 1987 were, in their turn, somewhat deceptive.[48]

Criticisms and new proposals, like a multi-tier ASEAN grouping, have proliferated, especially from Singapore since the beginning of the 1980s — a situation directly related to the economic recession of 1984–6 which prompted the island's authorities to give renewed attention to making the most of the regional market. Certainly, Singapore does not have the power to initiate political moves in the region, but the neighbouring capitals have encouraged step-by-step, economic liberalisation measures at home (even in Indonesia), and a regional cooperation that is more business- and market-oriented than before — this was probably due to the international economic recession of the mid-1980s and its aftermath. The example of Singapore, where the business community circles and the governmental administration are two separate entities even if often working in close collaboration, has an influence on other ASEAN states whose domestic economies were often suffocated by bureaucratic and/or very corrupt public interventionism.[49]

The Six are giving increasing attention to more flexible instruments of cooperation like the chambers of commerce (federated in the ASEAN CCI), clubs of manufacturers and business associations of the tertiary sector, which have the greatest economic credibility: it is unnecessary to add that Singapore plays a more influential role here than anywhere else. Information and ideas have begun to circulate and help to break down barriers among the most nationalist countries in ASEAN — the very ones which continued up till recently to be mistrustful or hostile to the commercial and financial predominance of the city-state.[50] For the first time since 1967, the private sector in ASEAN is exerting increasing pressure on the six governments to make appreciable progress in mobilising the real forces of the regional market. Singapore is much less isolated than before, and probably even better integrated in the ASEAN forum.

47. *ASEAN Information*, Sept. 84; *FEER*, 10 Dec. 82, pp. 70–2; 8 Mar. 84, pp. 78–89, and 5 Sept. 85, pp. 53–4 (for Kukrit's appeal in Bangkok).
48. *FEER*, 24 Dec. 87, pp. 8–10.
49. J. Behrman, 'Cooperation in removal of constraints on ASEAN industrialization', *UMBC Econ. Rev.*, XVI (1980), pp. 26–30.
50. R.H. Fifield (281).

Singapore and Indonesia: a key pair of member-states for the future development of ASEAN

The radical differences in their geography and demography, in their natural resources and wealth, and in their historical heritage place Singapore and Indonesia in most situations at the two extremities of ASEAN negotiations.[51] One of the two favours the promotion of very concrete economic cooperation, while the other remains rather cautious on most occasions. The two countries have expressed for many years opposed concepts of regionalism — this is probably a function, as was mentioned in the first chapter, of the difficult relationship, at once complementary and competitive, between an island emporium and a vast neighbouring agrarian archipelago. The burden of two different but also rival colonial systems which radiated from Singapore and Batavia respectively has to be remembered in the study of those contrasted relations between the state organisations of a commercial emporium and a vast agrarian archipelago. Still today, these major differences determine the character of the respective external policies of Singapore and Indonesia — and of many of the main tensions or potential areas of agreement within ASEAN.

If ASEAN's evolution depended on the individual will of Jakarta, regional institutionalisation, interventionism, economic protectionism and a certain defiance of the outside world would probably be more accentuated. However, the ASEAN consensus diplomacy has safe-guarded the interests of the smallest states,[52] and allowed Singapore to cultivate its special position by providing the function of a critical intelligence at the heart of the ASEAN decision-making process even if, as Lee Kuan Yew contends, this diplomacy seems less and less adapted to tackling economic and social problems at the regional level. This strategy has been proved all the easier since the Indonesian government — while seldom admitting as much publicly — is no more comfortable than its partners with the poor performance of ASEAN economic cooperation so far, and since Indonesia benefits as much, if not more, from the effective complementarities developed by the island economy within the region.[53]

51. Broinowski, op. cit., p. 243, and Tony Eng Wah Seah (374). 'These differences between Singapore and Indonesia are not based merely on economic technicalities but more fundamentally on perceptions which owe much to historical experiences and the geographical and physical composition of the two countries . . .' (Jørgensen-Dahl, op. cit., p. 138).
52. Jørgensen-Dahl, ibid., p. 209 ('The tyranny of small membership').
53. N. Akransee, 'ASEAN: Economic trends and potential', *Contemporary Southeast*

Being very much integrated with the regional and international economies, Singapore is a crossroads, and acts as a middleman, for the dynamic development of intra- and extra-ASEAN economic flows. As such, it counterweighs any tendency on the part of Indonesia, the most nationalistic member-state, to isolate itself from its partners, and the positions of the other ASEAN states fluctuate between these two extremes according to their sectoral interests. Singapore's freedom of regional manoeuvre is delicate and narrow, but it is none the less real. Because of its standards of living and level of development surpassing those of all the other member-states, the city-state regards as part of its regional mission constantly to question and to remind its colleagues of the principles of 'rationality' for the sake of regional economic growth and social stability. Being heavily dependent on its neighbours for safeguarding and promoting its most vital interests, Singapore has no choice but to come to terms with the domestic economic and social situation of its less developed ASEAN partners.

The 'competitive complementarity' between Singapore and Indonesia does not appear explosive. Strengthened by its economic power, the city-state aspires to transcend its geopolitical insignificance, while Indonesia aspires to be recognised as the leader of ASEAN and would like to be able to overcome its physical size and numerous social and economic handicaps.[54] Indonesia can play the double role of a regional spectator and an actor. It leaves ASEAN cooperation with little choice but to evolve according to the pace set by Jakarta. Singapore and Kuala Lumpur always keep a sharp watch on the expressed or unexpressed mood in Jakarta, but there is also some kind of reciprocity, since Jakarta is aware of the chronic anxiety of its neighbours over any new attempt to revitalise the idea of a 'Great Indonesia'.[55]

Asia, Sept. 83, pp. 205–18; R.L. Lau, 'The role of Singapore in ASEAN', *Contemporary Southeast Asia*, Sept. 81, p. 99.

54. Lee Kuan Yew in Josey (439), 1st edn, p. 370: 'Until its massive problems of poverty and development are solved, Indonesia will find it difficult to claim its rightful position in the world community.' Broinowski, op. cit., p. 232. 'Indonesia does not possess the resources and capability to assert a regional dominance . . . The conspicuous disjunction between declaratory policy and its actual practice will remain' (Leifer [320], pp. 170–1). See also Leifer, 'Indonesia's regional vision', *World Today*, Oct. 74, pp. 418–25.

55. Leifer (320), op. cit., p. 124. 'Indonesia's action over Timor has stirred fears about what some "adventurist" generals would do if the restraining influence of President Suharto was not available' (*FEER*, 6 Feb. 76), p. 19. Other analyses of Indonesia's foreign policy include H. Warshawski (399) and F.B. Weinstein (400, 401).

Singapore has opted for the strategy of an 'involved' actor on the regional scene: its ASEAN policy is generally based on a high sense of political will, at home and externally, and it can even be quite vocal sometimes in government statements. Such an attitude is intended to play down a kind of 'spectator complex': beyond pure economic performance, the city-state is well aware of its excessive dependence on regional affairs and especially on its immediate neighbours, with very little power of its own to exert any decisive influence.

In both the economic and political construction of ASEAN, most influx of cooperation or conflict inevitably passes through Indonesia. Jakarta seems somehow to lead ASEAN from behind, yet Singapore is not fully able to pull the association along from the front.

6

ANTI-CHINESE COMMUNALISM AND ANTI-COMMUNISM IN ASEAN

What political answer from Singapore?

The mercantile beginnings of the emporium were transcended as soon as its external economic influence had ceased to be proportionate with the smallness of its geographical area and population. This phenomenon had a political influence on the neighbouring countries: they profited from well-established sectoral complementarities originating from this prosperous emporium, but they were opposed to any state of dependence which would acknowledge Singapore as having a certain domination or power over them.

Because of the extent of its regional influence, Singapore cannot remain a political pawn on the ASEAN chessboard, but it must take account of the unstable ambivalence of relations with its external environment that are made up of both regional cooperation and conflict, at the heart of which lies the problem of the island's Chinese identity in the very midst of the Malay world. The wide spectrum of its political role and the quality of its ties with the two other hard-core members of ASEAN have long fallen foul of communalism and anti-Communism.[1] Both issues are historically rooted in the mentalities of the regimes of Indonesia and Malaysia, and their common denominator is some kind of defiance and mistrust of China in the political sphere and the Overseas Chinese in the economic sphere.

Anxious to ensure its political independence and the viability of the economy it has built up since 1965, the city-state seeks to work these two levers: the anti-Chinese communalism and anti-Communism shared by most ASEAN regimes.

Singapore, a fourth China? Its response to anti-Chinese communalism in the ASEAN countries

The distinction between communalism and anti-Communism, both of which were expressed, up till the 1960s, in terms of hostility towards the Chinese minorities in the region, should be related to the double perception of Singapore by its neighbours in both ethnic and political terms. The freedom of action of the city-state is limited for as long as

1. See page 42, above, note 17.

there continues to lurk, behind the image of a Chinese island emporium, the political shadow of China itself (which was regarded as subversive up till the 1970s) and the envied economic success of the Chinese in Hong Kong and Taiwan. For Indonesia and Malaysia, Singapore still represents a kind of "fourth China", which they cannot ignore, but whose existence muddies the waters of a regional sea which they would prefer to be uniformly Malay.

Historical continuity and change

Ethnic tensions seem to be of very ancient origin in South-East Asia, and it is often difficult for a foreign observer completely to grasp, let alone describe, their internal and external dimensions in the societies of the region. They are confused in any case, but are further enmeshed with psychological and emotional elements which elude easy quantification.

One can distinguish four types of conflict, which are closely complementary to each other, and which have been accentuated in the collective consciousness of South-East Asians in different places at different times.[2] First, there is an ethno-racial communalism which has pitted the indigenous populations of Malay origin (Pribumi or Bumiputra), in the case of Malaysia and Indonesia, against the Chinese immigrants who arrived first in small groups from the 9th–10th centuries onwards and then in great waves during the time of British and Dutch colonialism. Then there is a socio-cultural communalism which has accused these Chinese of forming — linguistically, socially and culturally (which includes religion) — a state within the state, and of being unwilling to assimilate fully with the local South-East Asian society, which they deem to be less 'civilised' and sophisticated than themselves. Thirdly, a kind of socio-economic communalism denounces the commercial and financial middleman role adopted by rich Overseas Chinese who exploit the indigenous local labour, control the economies of the great urban centres and sometimes (as in Malaysia) of the rural milieu as well, and make sure that they obtain a share of political power — if not by official participation, then by collusion with certain corrupt government circles. Finally, there is a communalism of a geostrategic nature based on the

---

2. C.P. Fitzgerald (282); Guy Hunter (297); P. Kunstadter (ed.), *Southeast Asian tribes, minorities and nations*, Princeton UP, 2 vols, 1967; Gosling and Lim (290); Shee Poon Kim (375); M. Talabot (390); A.R. Walker (ed.), *Studies of ethnic minority people*, Singapore: Bd of Editors, Contributions to SE Asian Ethnography, 1982.

centuries-old fear of China, which has extended its hegemony to South-East Asia several times, both by military incursions and through a trade system of suzerainty. This, in the eyes of the local populations, makes the Overseas Chinese objects of suspicion; indeed, these Chinese immigrants are named Overseas Chinese precisely because of the links which they actually or supposedly maintain with their country of origin.

Anti-Communist sentiment mainly directed against the People's Republic of China and its human ramifications overseas is a factor of change within the historical continuity of the communalist phenomenon, and since 1949 it has merely become superimposed on the pre-existing anti-Chinese sentiment. Tarnthong Thonswadi has written about this that it is very difficult for the ASEAN countries to distinguish between the Overseas Chinese, Chinese Communists, and people from mainland China itself.[3]

The awakening of national independence movements in South-East Asia coincided with the progressive reconstruction of a 'Greater China', first by the Kuomintang which had close links with the Overseas Chinese, and then by the Chinese Communist Party. The latter put pressure on local Chinese, either simple labourers or intellectuals, who had become hardened in the resistance to Japan, and who showed themselves remarkably well organised when it came to denouncing rural poverty in Malaysia and Indonesia or poor working conditions in manufacturing in Singapore, which in both cases affected many Chinese families. In 1945–65 this pressure became transformed into defiance of the existing political regimes and sometimes into guerrilla operations, which still remain quite active in the Philippines and Thailand today.

Centre of a transnational Overseas Chinese business network

The Overseas Chinese in Singapore and the region: agents of economic integration in ASEAN
The transnational network formed by the Overseas Chinese consists of several geographical spheres of business influence: the triangle Taiwan-Hong Kong-Singapore is the very centre with dense ramifications in all the ASEAN countries and the whole Pacific Basin: North East Asia, North America, Australia and the South Pacific.

Based historically on family, cultural and language ties according to the geographical origin in China of the immigrants (Hokkien,

3. T. Tarnthong (393), p. 161.

Cantonese, Fukien, Hakka. . . .) and supported by local Chinese secret societies and chambers of commerce, various networks of Overseas Chinese quickly transcended national and even regional boundaries.[4] Scarcely concerned with the formal divisions between national states or with their respective political systems at home, such networks symbolise one of the most tangible dimensions of ASEAN's integration and internationalisation in the economic sphere, along with the role played by the mighty transnational foreign companies which have implanted themselves throughout the zone.[5] This phenomenon illustrates the economic power that a single ethnic minority whose vocation is trade can command in South-East Asia. This phenomenon can be seen in some other parts of the world with other groups of ethnic minorities,[6] but the Chinese dimension of the ASEAN economies is a unique feature among all regional groupings in the world so far: Overseas Chinese business can rapidly adapt to the rather flexible ASEAN mould, thus making possible a relaxation of the vociferous nationalisms of some member-states and the development of a vision of a larger and more coherent regional market.

Without a realistic appraisal of the transregional functions performed by Overseas Chinese capital and entrepreneurs, whose exact identity is often unclear because of various socio-cultural barriers and the virtual absence of written data, potential Western investors cannot grasp every feature of the ASEAN business world.

The big Chinese families and transnational firms have chosen to make their headquarters in Singapore, Hong Kong or Taipei so as to develop profitable commercial and financial activities both on the spot and throughout the region. By becoming entrepreneurs, merchants, technicians, administrators and members of the liberal professions, this Chinese business élite has come to control 80% of all economic flows between Singapore and its neighbours,[7] 25–30% of the domestic economy of Malaysia, very significant business interests in all other ASEAN countries (with strong ramifications in Singapore, Hong Kong and

4. S.A. Carstens (263); Mark Lau Fong (327); Lee Poh Ping (314).
5. W. Moese (ed.) (332); Wee Mon Cheng (228); Wu Yuan Li (408).
6. As is, or was formerly, the case for the Jews, Arabs, Lebanese and Indians. 'A certain similarity between the position of Jews in medieval Europe and the condition of Chinese in colonial Southeast Asia, of Indians in colonial East Africa and Burma, Armenians and Greeks in feudal Turkey, Syrians in West Africa . . .' W.F. Wertheim, *East-West parallels: Sociological approaches to modern Asia*, Chicago: Quadrangle, 1965, p. 75.

Taiwan), and dozens of local banking groups in the region.[8] Never revealing the true origin or the exact nature of their transactions, they manage to adapt to any political and social regime and even to periods of instability and conflict.[9]

However, their power should not be exaggerated, contrary to ideas put forth by some indigenous politico-religious groups or in Marxist slogans.[10] Their activities are only important in trade and certain services, and less so in manufacturing (with a few exceptions like textiles and the agro-food industry). Their individual investments seldom reach the scale of those made by foreign multinationals or even by the public sector, whose financial capacity can only be compared with the very richest Chinese businessmen in the region — a small number. Their direct involvement in the political sphere remains very limited, even in Singapore where Chinese businessmen occupy less than 10% of parliamentary seats. This could change in the future, considering the current movement of general deregulation and privatisation taking place in Singapore since the mid-1980s and, more recently, elsewhere in the region.

The Chinese business élite tend to form a regional network, but they should not be thought of as one unified entity within each country or in ASEAN as a whole. These Chinese immigrants are divided into family groups and clans, even among the richest.[11] Distinctions and divisions exist according to the length of local residence and the degree to which, socially and culturally, they have taken root in the host-country. The Chinese are not socially homogeneous: low-income and average middle-class groups form the majority in Singapore, but in Malaysia, for example, very wealthy Chinese cohabit with the urban and rural poor. Fortune has smiled not only on the Overseas Chinese but also on some Indians and indigenous interest groups engaged in both the public and the private sectors; some are self-employed, while others are sub-contractors or work for foreign companies.

---

7. Lee Sheng Yi, 'Business elites in Singapore' in K.E. Shaw (ed.) (471), pp. 13–27.
8. At the beginning of the 1980s the numbers were: Indonesia, *ca*. 45, Hong Kong 25, Singapore 15, and Thailand 11.
9. Seah Chee Meow (373), p. 29.
10. I.B.A. Buchanan (97).
11. For example, relations between Chinese business circles in Jakarta and Surabaya (east Java) are rather competitive.

The struggle for power: the ASEAN and Singaporean Chinese at the centre of domestic and regional tensions

The remarkable economic success of the predominantly Chinese city-state, combined with the very efficient regional network of the Overseas Chinese business circles, has made it an object not only of admiration but also of envy and political mistrust. This is part of a historical legacy of age-old communal tensions. The indigenous populations fear that the economic supremacy of the local Chinese might shift to direct control of political and social decision-making. None of them, and the Malays in particular, are prepared to share political power with the local Chinese whom they think of as the 'Jews of the Orient'. Furthermore, many locals would like to supplant the Chinese, and thus increase their chances of securing their own control over economic power.[12]

Most ASEAN governments have adopted or at least tolerated an anti-Chinese attitude at home, resulting in various incidents of physical violence. Some of the pretexts on which this position has been based are that the Chinese have founded their wealth on the exploitation of the local population and resources; have close links with foreign powers such as mainland China, the old colonial masters and the new multi-nationals; and form a separate socio-cultural entity playing against national cohesion. Anti-Chinese communalism has too often repre-sented a brutal expedient of internal or foreign policy in response to particular situations and short-term crises — a fact well known to Singapore and the Chinese minorities in ASEAN. The socio-ethnic balance is still very fragile in several member-states, and the problem also has a spill-over effect on intra-regional relations; it is now easier to understand why ASEAN — and Indonesia and Malaysia in particular — does not always follow Singapore's prescription for more rapid progress in economic cooperation.[13]

Anti-Chinese sentiment is hardly of any significance in the city-state's relations with Thailand and the Philippines, in so far as it does not seem to be a hot issue within those two countries. The assimilation of the

12. Mary Heidhues (295); Gosling & Lim (290); Victor Purcell (363); Wang Gungwu (398). 'It is not cultural divergence which is at the root of the tensions . . . Lack of assimilation is not the real motive . . . It provides an excuse to select a special group of "foreigners" as the target' (Wertheim, op. cit., p. 76).
13. 'Free and informal discussions among the heads of government have made us realise why the present objectives of ASEAN cannot be achieved as quickly as some of us would have wished them to be. There are difficulties which, for a variety of reasons, cannot be overcome as simply as we would wish' (Lee Kuan Yew, 5 Aug. 77, quoted in Morrison [334], p. 190).

Chinese minority has progressed a long way there, helped by tolerance and the acceptance of mixed marriages in societies dominated respectively by Buddhism and Christianity.[14] The situation is different in societies influenced by Islam, where discrimination against minorities is much more at the heart of nation-building. While of different weight demographically in Indonesia and Malaysia, their local Chinese minorities have been segregated in similar ways, such as by selective admission to and exercise of nationality, indigenisation of capital and management of firms, and by restricted access to education and to employment in the public service. [15] Under strong pressure from Malay nationalist-religious groups, the local Chinese have been a sort of 'second-class' citizenry, in marked contrast to their outstanding role in the economic and scientific development of these two countries. In Indonesia and Malaysia, the government and certain pressure groups have created a very tense situation in the political sphere, which actually erupted in bloody rioting in Singapore (1964) and Malaysia (1967 and 1969) and huge massacres in Indonesia (1966). These recent events keep alive in Singapore and among all Chinese minorities in ASEAN a latent psychosis of insecurity, which is passed on from one generation to the next.

, The problem of internal communalism spills across the frontiers of each of ASEAN's plural societies, the quality of relations between Singapore and its neighbours being partly determined by the social treatment of the Chinese minority in Indonesia and Malaysia, and for Jakarta and Kuala Lumpur by the fate of the Malays in Chinese Singapore (15% of the island population).[16]

The governments have obviously learned some lessons from the dramatic traumas of the 1960s. They have progressively admitted the need for economic collaboration with the local Chinese and have acknowledged the very indifferent success of their measures taken to encourage greater indigenous economic initiative. Paradoxically, anti-Chinese communalism has been replaced in the forefront in recent years

14. S.W. Skinner, *Chinese society in Thailand*, Ithaca: Cornell UP, 1962.
15. In Indonesia, most of the Chinese entrepreneurs are placed under the formal protection of a senior army officer (*cukong*); in Malaysia, the heads of companies are often 'figureheads' who are ethnically Malay: and in Thailand a representative of the state authorities has a seat on the board of every local Chinese company.
16. The concept of a 'plural society' in relation to Southeast Asia was introduced in the 1940s by J.A. Furnivall: see *J. of the Roy. Cent. Asian Soc.*, 29 (1942), and *Netherlands India: A study of plural economy*, CUP, 1944.

by a new form of activism from those who were precisely the most anti-Chinese. Jakarta and Kuala Lumpur have had to deal with the rising politico-religious communalism of Muslim fundamentalist movements which could threaten the governments and regimes currently in power.[17]

Singapore and Malaysia: communalism and conflicts
Being centred on a deep division between the Malay and Chinese communities, *multiracialism* is an extremely acute problem in Malaysia. It is also one of the most highly sensitive issues among the six ASEAN countries, and has the greatest influence over Singapore's relations with its immediate neighbours and even over the island's internal ethno-social equilibrium.[18]

The Chinese in Malaysia, about 35% of the total population, form an ethnic minority which is a *de facto* majority in the economic life of the country. They concentrate in urban centres such as Kuala Lumpur, Penang, Malacca and Johor Baru and in most areas of life (except the senior civil service, higher education and politics); the Malaysian Chinese Association (MCA) forms part of the ruling coalition that has been in power since independence.[19] This major area of potential conflict could endanger the political stability of the entire peninsula, including independent Singapore. The Malays, who are in a majority in the interior of the Federation and particularly in the northern states, believe that since colonial rule and the increase in Chinese immigration they have not received a just and proportional share of the national product and of their contribution to the country's prosperity. They feel excluded from the most important mechanisms of economic life in favour of both the local and Singaporean Chinese, and denounce their

17. M.A. Bakar, 'Islamic revivalism and the political progress in Malaysia', *Asian Survey*, Oct. 81, pp. 1040–59; B.J. Boland (253); P. Fistie & P. Sockeel-Richarte, 'L'Islam et la politique en Malaysia', *Projet* (Paris), Dec. 79, pp. 1287–93; J. Nagara, 'Ethnic and political aspects of Malay religious revitalization', *Southeast Asia Ethnicity and Development Newsletter* (Singapore), Sept. 78, pp. 28–33; J.L. Peacock (356); S. Siddique, 'Contemporary Islamic development in ASEAN', *Southeast Asian Affairs*, 1980, pp. 78–90.
18. 'Communalism is not an internal event. However well the Malays may behave in Singapore, their welfare depends upon how well the minority Chinese are treated in Malaya' (P.D. Beaulieu [250], p. 273).
19. MCA, *The Malaysian Chinese: Towards national unity*, Kuala Lumpur: MCA Research and Service Centre, 1982; N.J. Funston (286); M.S. Sidhu, 'Chinese dominance of West Malaysian Towns', *Geography*, 61, 1 (1976), pp. 21–2.

indirect but strong hand in local politics. The goodwill of the federal authorities always oscillates between the indispensable political support of the majority Malays and the indispensable economic contribution of the Chinese and, to a smaller extent, of the Indians.[20]

The electoral and political representation of the Chinese, which had already caused many difficulties in the constitutional lead-up to independence (1945–55), became a burning problem after the fusion of Singapore with Greater Malaysia (1963), which made the Malays and Chinese demographically almost equal. The electoral reverses of the Alliance Party — which comprised the United Malaysian National Organisation as the dominant partner (the UMNO also provided support for the Malay National Action Committee in Singapore) as well as the Malaysian Chinese Association (MCA) and the Malaysian Indian Congress (MIC) — and the rise of Lee Kuan Yew's People's Action Party (PAP) in Singapore and its decision to take part in the federal elections were directly responsible for the bloody racial riots in Singapore in September 1964.[21] The number of deaths that resulted did not prevent these riots from continuing into the following year. Bitter tensions between the PAP and UMNO leaders and confused fears among the Malays at the prospect of Lee Kuan Yew eventually becoming Prime Minister of Malaysia were the origin of the separation of Singapore in August 1965.[22] Despite all this, the communalist trouble was far from over: the electoral reverse suffered by the MCA and the development of a Chinese opposition not controlled by the UMNO-MCA-MIC Alliance caused a new outbreak of violence in May 1969, killing more than 1,000 people in Kuala Lumpur.[23] The Malaysian Vice Premier, Tun Razak, said on this occasion: 'The 13th May 1969 should be marked

---

20. Goh Cheng Teik (289); W. Hashim (294); Marvin Rogers, 'Malaysia/Singapore: . . .', *Asian Survey*, Feb. 71, pp. 121–30.
21. The total was 33 dead and some 600 injured. *ST*, 21 July 64; R.L. Clutterbuck (274), pp. 319–20; M. Leifer, 'Communal violence in Singapore', *Asian Survey*, Oct. 64, pp. 1115–22.
22. P. Fistie, 'La rupture entre Singapour et la Malaysia', *Rev. fr. sc. pol.*, Apr. 67, pp. 237–62; M.S. Noordie (346).
23. Malaysian National Operations Council, *The May 13 Tragedy*, Kuala Lumpur, 1969; F. Gagliano, *Communal violence in Malaysia, 1969: The political aftermath*, Athens, Ohio: Ohio UP, 1971; R.S. Milne, 'The 1969 parliamentary election in West Malaysia', *Pacific Affairs*, 4, 1970, pp. 203–26; N.L. Snyder, 'Race, leitmotiv of the Malaysian election drama', *Asian Survey*, Dec. 70, pp. 1070–80; Tunku A. Rahman, *May 13 – before and after*, Kuala Lumpur: Ulusan Melayu Press, 1969.

by a black stone in our history — it is a day of national tragedy. On that day, the deepest foundations of our nation were shaken by racial conflicts of a violence exceeding all that have previously been known.'

The state of emergency decreed on the day after the riots was not lifted till the beginning of 1971. Rajaratnam's statement, made in 1966, that the two countries could inflict mortal wounds on each other had quickly become a reality: at the moment when rioting broke out again in Kuala Lumpur, communalist agitation reached Singapore; four people were killed and 700 arrested.[24] To re-establish civil peace and stability, the Alliance government initiated an economic and social 'bumiputrisation' policy (named after Bumiputra, son of the land), i.e. participation of the Malays in the control of the national economy.

The New Economic Policy (NEP), dating from July 1971, is based on several constitutional provisions reserving economic and social privileges to the Malays,[25] and it was no accident that the NEP was launched when Kuala Lumpur was deepening Malaysia's economic separation from Singapore. Access to recruitment into the administration or the university favours Malays, who for example enjoy a fixed quota of 70% of all university admissions except in the University of Malaysia in Kuala Lumpur. Bumiputra economic organisations were created to promote more Malay participation in the economy. Here an ambitious objective was envisaged: by 1990, 30% of the capital of companies was to be held by Malays, 40% by non-Bumiputra Malaysians (mainly Chinese), and 30% by foreigners.[26]

The NEP encountered harsh criticism for these discriminatory measures from the Chinese business community in both the peninsula and Singapore. However, the third economic plan of 1976–80 declared that development should be for all Malaysians, and the policy of excluding the local Chinese began to be modified. The government authorities realised that they were imposing too heavy constraints on those in actual control of a large part of the country's economic activities and that they had much to lose in their attempt to by-pass the services offered by Singapore. In the early 1980s, foreign investors still owned

24. Rajaratnam, *Singapore Mirror*, 28 Feb. 66, pp. 1–7.
25. Art. 71: Rights and Prerogatives of the Malay rulers; Art. 152: Malay as the National Language; Art. 153: Malay Special Privileges.
26. E.E. Fisk and H. Osman-Rani (eds) (118), pp. 105–24; Khor Kok Peng (145); R.S. Milne and D.K. Mauzy (331); R.S. Milne, 'National ideology and national building in Malaysia', *Asian Survey*, July 70, pp. 563–73; 'The politics of Malaysia's New Economic Policy', *Pacific Affairs*, 49, 2, 1976, pp. 235–62.

48% of Malaysian private companies; the Malays (who make up half the population) controlled only 15%, as against at least 37% for the Chinese and Indians. The latter belonged to dynasties of entrepreneurs in both Malaysia and Singapore, and were able to make the Malaysian laws on foreign investment and national shareholding conform to their own interests.[27]

The argument that Malays are poor is less and less sustainable in the face of progressive social diversification and mobility, and the emergence of a large middle class, which identifies itself with its Chinese counterpart in the cities of Malaysia and in Singapore. If the majority of Malays still live in very modest circumstances, less prosperous and even poor people also exist among the Chinese; no ethnic group can be classified socially in a stereotyped way as it was in the past.[28]

The international recession of the early and mid-1980s, which hit Malaysia's commodity exports and its rapid industrialisation process, and the rise of extremist and sometimes violent Muslim agitation, which caused considerable anxiety domestically and overseas, highlighted the gap between declaratory policies like the NEP and the concrete forces available to be utilised for real economic achievement.

The future of the NEP after its deadline, 1990, remains open and uncertain. A consultative economic committee was created to give urgent attention to this thorny problem; its membership of 150, half Bumiputra and half from the other ethnic groups, consists of businessmen, politicians, farmers, academics and even clerics. Analysts of the results of the NEP are divided: according to some of them, Malays today own less than 20% of the capital of the country's companies, as against the 30% recommended by the NEP, and this figure would stand no higher than 12% if one omitted the many cases of semi-public economic activity — other analysts place little confidence in the origin and the quality of statistical data provided on such a sensitive issue. Some are convinced that the NEP has not only sustained but actually increased inter-racial divisions, while others give positive emphasis to the emerence of a Malay urban middle class and the Malays' entry into the industrial and service sectors. There is no doubt at all that the debate

27. See the profiles of leading businessmen in the peninsula, such as Tun Tan Siew Sin (Sime Darby), in *Malaysian Business*, Jan. 77, pp. 2–4; D Nai-Wai Lee (Bousteads), ibid., July 79, pp. 47–9; Tan Sri Ibrahim Mohamed and Brian Chiang (Promet), ibid., Apr. 82, pp. 45–8; and Eric Chia (Jack Chia), ibid., June 82, pp. 6–19.
28. *FEER*, 5 May 83, pp. 25–6; 12 Apr. 84, pp. 70–3; 26 July 84, pp. 22–31.

remains polarised between partisans of the consultative committee president (also one of the original architects of the NEP in the 1960s), former Foreign Affairs Minister Tan Sri Ghazali Shafie, and the NEP's opponents, notably the opposition Democratic Action Party which decided to boycott the committee for as long as its former secretary-general, Lim Kit Siang, remains in prison. It is also clear that the inter-ethnic tensions which have again shaken Malaysia since the autumn of 1987 make a just evaluation of the NEP impossible.[29]

Singapore and Indonesia's anti-Chinese communalism
There are about 3.5 million Chinese in Indonesia — or about 2.5% of the total population — concentrated in the major industrial centres and ports such as Jakarta, Medan, Surabaya and Bandung. Thus they are demographically less important than the Chinese in Malaysia, and has no decisive influence on the essential balance of forces in the life of the country. None the less, they are often mistrusted and discriminated against by the Pribumi for economic and political reasons very similar to those which operate in Malaysia.[30] In 1985 the congress of the Muhammadiyah, the most moderate Muslim-inspired political movement in the country (in contrast to the conservative Ulamas), reaffirmed its strategy to fight against all forms of economic dominance by the local Chinese![31]

The correlation between the local status of the Chinese minority, who have very close business and family ties with the city-state, and the nature of official relations between Indonesia and Singapore is clear. Any episode of communal agitation in the big neighbour automatically alarms the island authorities, who examine the possible consequences in both economic and security terms. 'Chinese' Singapore is well aware of the conditions for its existence as an independent and sovereign state within the Malay neighbourhood, and any potential expansionist tendency from across the Malacca Straits always inspires fear; this could take the form of some aggressive action against the city-state as a diversion from some sudden internal crisis within Indonesia, as occurred on the eve of the confrontation in 1963–5.

29. *AWSJ*, 30 Nov. 87; *FEER*, 9 July 87, pp. 13–14; 12 Nov. 87, pp. 21–3; 1 Dec. 88, p. 31; 2 Feb. 89, p. 30.
30. C.A. Coppel (277); Kwee Tek Hoay, *The origins of the modern Chinese movement in Indonesia*, Ithaca: Cornell UP, 1969; L. Suryadinata, *Pribumi Indonesians, the Chinese minority and China*, Kuala Lumpur: Heinemann, 1978.
31. *FEER*, 26 Dec. 85, pp. 34–5.

The permanent anxiety of the Chinese in Singapore and throughout the region is the dramatic outcome of a whole series of traumatic events in their history which are still very much alive in their collective memory. Racial riots, massacres and destruction of Chinese property have taken place periodically in Indonesia at least since the 18th century (1727–40) and up till recently (1963, 1965, 1973–4, 1981). Even the young local Chinese are made continuously aware of this reality. The tragedy of 1965–6 forms the background to Indonesian political life right up to the present day. The repression which followed the abortive coup d'état against President Sukarno cost the lives of several hundred thousand people, many of them innocent Chinese who, in the name of the fight against Communism, were victims of all kinds of discrimination and jealousy.[32] The confrontation with Indonesia was not yet over, the separation from Malaysia was only a few months old, and Singapore could do little except passively witness the tragedy. The later decisions to suspend publications of its official statistics for Indonesia-Singapore bilateral trade and to execute (in 1968) two Indonesian servicemen found guilty of a terrorist action in Singapore during the confrontation were the only two reactions of the island city which had turned into a sovereign state in the midst of this dark period for the region.

Sukarno's policy had swung between the wish to assimilate the Chinese and bring them into the mainstream of political life (through Baperki, the consultative committee for Indonesian citizenship), which was found to be difficult because of the rapprochement between certain Chinese and the local Communist party, and the adoption of discriminatory measures such as excluding the Chinese from business and from owning land in the rural areas and imposing restrictive import quotas on them in port and trading cities. In 1959–61 such a policy caused the voluntary emigration of about 100,000 Chinese who refused to adopt Indonesian nationality. But after 1968, General (later President) Suharto let it be widely known that the New Order regime would regard economic development as its priority, and that part of its success would depend on the participation of Overseas Chinese business, both in Indonesia and from Hong Kong and Singapore. The 1972 policy of Indonesianisation for all firms in the country was intended, of course, to benefit Pribumi interests, but it coincided with a relaxation of the restrictive conditions whereby local Chinese could acquire Indonesian nationality and Indonesianise their names at the same time. This period

32. A.C. Brackman (257); John Hughes (296), pp. 119–299.

also saw the beginnings of a political rapprochement between Singapore and Jakarta. Were all these changes a mere chance of timing?[33]

In its process of consolidation, the Suharto regime has enjoyed a close and unconcealed collaboration with local Chinese business circles — the Harapan and Liem Sioe Liong groups being among the best-known examples.[34] This policy of course fuelled criticism from certain intellectual and (mainly Muslim) religious circles, which preach a lessening of economic materialism and corruption in the country (like, for instance, the Petition of the Fifty in 1980). This has also found expression in the press (the journals *Merdeka*, *Indonesian Observer* and *Matahari* were banned in 1979 precisely for their open criticism of the regime's collusion with the Chinese). For as long as such movements are able to exploit the popular mood of frustration over various questions of socio-economic justice, over the strategy of national development which is perceived to benefit mainly the regime leaders and the rich Chinese business families, and over the lack of opportunity for popular participation in politics and the implementation of a certain standard of political morality, the danger of further communalist clashes — even violent ones — will persist.

The promulgation in 1980 of two new presidential decrees authorising one million local Chinese to take Indonesian citizenship (with the obligation of giving up their existing nationality at the same time) gave proof of the determination of the regime, in association with the business community, to pursue a policy of ethnic integration and pacification. This had, in turn, an important psychological influence on the development of good relations between Indonesia and Singapore — and especially between Suharto and Lee Kuan Yew.[35]

One should finally consider whether in the most recent years the complexity of Indonesian political life has not relegated the problem of anti-Chinese communalism, which was so sensitive up till the 1970s, to the level of all the other problems of national cohesion and unity. The Overseas Chinese issue has been partly displaced by anti-Javanese communalism, which is far from having disappeared in many islands and regions of Indonesia, and above all by a revitalisation of Islam, in Sumatra and elsewhere, which flies in the face of the non-sectarian ideology of the New Order.[36]

33. A.C. Brackman (258).
34. *FEER*, 7 Apr. 83, pp. 44–56, and 26 Apr. 84, pp. 188–9.
35. *Kompass* (Jakarta), 29 Feb. 80; *FEER*, 21 Sept. 79, p. 9, and 22 Mar. 84, pp. 40–1.
36. Boland (253); M. Leifer (319); W.F. Wertheim, *Moslems in Indonesia*: . . ., Univ. of North Queensland, 1980.

Singapore and ASEAN in the struggle against Communism

In South-East Asia, the aftermath of the Second World War and the Chinese revolution of 1949 gave impetus not only to the rise of local Communist movements but also to strong anti-Communist reactions, especially in what became the ASEAN countries. This anti-Communism was essentially directed against the People's Republic of China and its potential secular arm, the Overseas Chinese, not only because of the PRC's obvious subversive activism in the region, but also because it closely matched the locally prevalent anti-Chinese sentiment that included the Overseas Chinese among its targets.

After an interval of eighteen years, first Malaysia and then Indonesia (not to mention Thailand, which recently faced localised guerrilla insurrections by the Communists, and the Philippines, which still does) threw themselves into a campaign to eradicate Communism internally and to denounce its direct support from Peking aimed at destabilising the whole region.[37] The state of emergency in Malaya (1948–60) made possible the dispersal of the Malayan Communist Party, which was composed largely of Chinese and was rampant throughout the peninsula.[38] In Indonesia, the attempted coup in September 1965 was followed by a complete break with Peking and the bloody elimination of the Indonesian Communist Party (PKI) which, in alliance with Sukarno for fifteen years, and supported by China and certain local Chinese groups (Baperki), had succeeded in building itself up into the world's third largest Communist party.[39]

Kuala Lumpur and the newly-established regime in Indonesia were worried about the social and political complexion of Lee Kuan Yew's People's Action Party in Singapore, which was now in control of an independent Chinese island enclave, and they had some doubts about the nature of the PAP's ties with China. For the two capitals it seemed out of the question to accept a Chinese enclave linked to Peking right at the very heart of the Malay world and within a few miles of their respective borders. Like a poisonous canker festering within a fruit, a pure and hard socialist regime in Singapore (a wing of the PAP was actively

37. Central Committee of the Chinese Communist Party, 'Resolute support for armed struggle led by the Communist Party of Thailand', *Peking Review*, X, 8 Dec. 87.

38. R.L. Clutterbuck (273 and 274); J.M. van der Kroef (310); Lim Joo Jock and S. Vani (323); E. O'Ballance (347); L. Pye, *Guerilla communism in Malaya*, Princeton UP, 1956; A. Short (377).

39. Brackman (257); F. Cayrac-Blanchard (265); F. Corsino, *A communist revolutionary movement as an international state factor: The case of the PKI-Aidit*, Singapore: Maruzen Asia, 1982; R. Mortimer (336).

pro-Communist up till the early 1960s) could not have been tolerated by its two big neighbours.[40]

In reality, Lee Kuan Yew opted for an open battle against Communism from the late 1950s onwards, both in Singapore/Malaya and in the region, but without sharing the systematic mistrust of the People's Republic felt in Jakarta and Kuala Lumpur. Seeking to minimise Singapore's image as the fourth China in the region, Lee succeeded in eliminating subversive internal Communist agitation and he proved, through the rapid rise to economic prosperity of independent Singapore, that Overseas Chinese colonies are not condemned to the same economic and political destiny as China itself. In the field of external affairs, he used the lever of the Indochinese crises, with the constant pressure they placed on Thailand, to pinpoint Vietnam and not China as the principal danger most directly threatening ASEAN.

Communism in Singapore and its elimination

The omnipresent Communist danger; emergence of the PAP (1948–59)
A few films and archive photographs are enough to show convincingly that Singapore has not always had the image of prosperity and high living standards which is today conveyed throughout the world.

Between 1948, when the state of emergency was declared in Malaya, and the end of the 1950s, Communism steadily gained ground in Singapore, benefiting from the prestige which the Malayan Communist Party (MCP) had earned through its resistance to the Japanese in the peninsula. But it rallied support mainly from the existence of a genuine proletariat (consisting largely of the workforce in the naval dockyards and local transport), from widespread urban poverty, and from a young student population open to ideological influence.[41] In 1946–7, the General Labour Union, reorganised by Soon Khwong within the Pan Malayan Federation of Trade Unions, could count more than 70,000 members who were sympathetic to the MCP. The Communist control of trade unionism led to strikes in 1948.[42] Between 1948 and 1953, some 12,000 Singaporeans were arrested under the emergency measures.

---

40. Jakarta later made official use of this argument to justify its intervention in Timor, fearing that this small island would be impelled by Fretelin to become a miniature Cuba in the very heart of the archipelago.
41. Cheah Boon Kheng (267); Clutterbuck (274); J. Drysdale (279); J.M. van der Kroef (309); Lee Ting Hui (317); M. Turnbull (78), ch. 7.
42. Singapore Labour Dept., *Annual Report 1948*.

In 1954–8 there was increased agitation among local labour, due to poor working conditions and the halting of democratic trade unionism initiated by the British, and among non-anglophone Chinese students (the Singapore Chinese Middle School Students' Union and Nanyang University, opened in 1956).[43] Lim Chin Siong's Singapore Factory and Shop Workers' Union, with 30,000 workers in 1955, and the Singapore Bus Workers' Union caused a series of strikes and outbreaks of violence. The strikes of May 1955 led to the resignation of Chief Minister David Marshall,[44] and further demonstrations between September and November 1956, resulting in fifteen deaths, sparked off a wave of repression launched by the new Chief Minister Lim Yew Hock: several trade unions were disbanded, and Lim Chin Siong and numerous other Communist leaders, some close to the PAP, were arrested.

From the time of its foundation in 1954,[45] the PAP, chaired by Toh Chin Chye, was divided into a left-leaning majority made up of Communists and Communist sympathisers educated in the Chinese language, and a more moderate anglophone wing, anti-colonial but in favour of dialogue with London. This was led by Lee Kuan Yew, the party's secretary-general, and friends who had studied with him in Britain. The unity of the party was achieved through Malaya's necessary independence and preparation for the elections of 1955, which finally opened the road to self-government. In 1956–7, the PAP's image could be mistaken for that of the MCP or any other very leftist workers' party; Lee Kuan Yew understood that he had to travel along the same political road as the PAP's left wing, at least for a while, until an opportunity presented itself to break free from the Communists.[46] Such an opportunity came in 1957 when Chief Minister Lim Yew Hock imprisoned thirty-five Communist leaders, of whom five were on the ruling committee of the PAP; this decision was probably taken in order to prevent the island, and the PAP, from falling further under Communist control.

43. 'Any man in Singapore who wants to carry the Chinese-speaking people with him cannot afford to be anti-communist. The Chinese are very proud of China' (*ST*, 5 May 55).
44. Chang Heng Chee, *A sensation of independence: A political biography of David Marshall*, Singapore: OUP, 1984; A. Josey, *David Marshall's political interlude*, Singapore: Eastern UP, 1982.
45. *ST*, 24 Oct. & 19 Nov. 54.
46. Drysdale (279); Lee Ting Hui, 'The communist open united front in Singapore, 1954–66' in Lim Joo Jock (322); J.-L. Margolin (449); Pang Chong Lian (460).

Thus, before he gave up power, and perhaps encouraged from London, Lim Yew Hock had given a fair wind to the career of Lee Kuan Yew: the extremist wing of the PAP was decapitated, and Lee was now in a position to take over the direction of the party.[47]

The PAP comes to power: Kuala Lumpur's anxieties (1959–61)
It appears that Lee Kuan Yew would have assured the British government of his moderate political views in case of his election in Singapore. However, he was very careful not to reveal in public his anti-Communism and his personal strategy for the future as long as the anti-colonial support of the PAP leftists was needed. He proved himself a remarkable tactician, and his pragmatism allowed him to adapt to Singapore's rapid and turbulent internal evolution in the late 1950s.

Because of Lee's total silence concerning his true political intentions, the PAP's electoral victory in May 1959 — winning 43 out of 51 parliamentary seats — caused some panic among the foreign and local business community. During their campaign, Lee and his colleagues had adopted a strongly anti-Western tone (on the subject of decolonisation), the gaoled Communist PAP members had been freed, and Lim Chin Siong was even appointed as political secretary of the Finance Ministry! Few had envisaged the possible fusion of Singapore into Malaysia as a means of isolating the Communists, who had just suffered failure in 1960 due to the victorious ending of the state of emergency.

In 1959–61, the rivalry between Lee, who had become Chief Minister, and the PAP's left wing burst into public view as an open battle. Lee and Ong Eng Guan, who had been the first (and only) mayor of Singapore and had just become Minister of National Development, opposed Lee Kuan Yew on the question of a big Federation of Malaysia, of which both the MCP in Malaya and the PKI in Indonesia also disapproved. Tunku Abdul Rahman was well aware that the Communists could possibly oblige Lee to resign, and he was afraid that a mini-Cuba might be set up virtually on his doorstep. He therefore gave his approval in May 1961 to the creation of a Federation of Malaysia, to include Singapore.[48] Although he was excluded from the PAP in 1960, Ong was however re-elected to the Legislative Assembly in July

47. Legislative Assembly, *The Communist Threat in Singapore*, Singapore, 1957 (Sess. Paper no. 33). See also Turnbull (78), pp. 253 & 266.
48. 'We must prevent a situation in which an independent Singapore will go one way and the Federation the other' (Tunku A. Rahman, *Parl. Debates*, Kuala Lumpur, 3, 16, 16 Oct. 61, cols 1590–1613).

1961, and Kuala Lumpur expected the worst.[49] Lee finally asked for a vote of confidence on the unification issue: the voting was 27–24 in favour, and of those twenty-four against, thirteen PAP members of parliament founded a new party close to the Communists, the Barisan Socialis, on 26 July 1961.

The long-term elimination of subversive Communism in Singapore

Lee Kuan Yew wanted to settle the unification debate once and for all with a referendum, and in September 1962 the PAP won a great victory with a 71% 'yes'.[50] But the sudden and unexpected disappearance of three of the PAP MPs ruled out the possibility of a comfortable majority supporting the local government, and its stability was once again threatened.

In February 1963, Lee invoked the Internal Security Ordinance against the opposition, which was accused of having supported an abortive Communist upheaval in Brunei, and he then initiated the 'Cold Store' operation by the police, in which about 100 Communist leaders or activists and half the leaders of the Barisan Socialis were arrested.

It seemed for a while as if the Communist threat had been warded off, but after the birth of the big Federation of Malaysia, the Barisan Socialis captured 46.9% of the vote in the elections of September 1963 (and 13 out of the 51 parliamentary seats, with 37 going to the PAP). More arrests followed, and some of those imprisoned were only given a conditional release at the beginning of the 1980s.[51]

The violent communalist agitation which occurred in Malaysia in 1964–5, and led to the withdrawal of Singapore from the 'big Federation', also eliminated most of the previous Communist activism and preoccupations. Faced with the PAP's rapid consolidation in power, and decapitated and battered by internal crises, the Barisan Socialis could not even use the failure of the big Federation of Malaysia to try and discredit Lee Kuan Yew.

The political stabilisation of Singapore after 1965 was greeted with much relief in Kuala Lumpur and Jakarta. Was it mere coincidence that the final elimination of the Barisan Socialis occurred at the same time as the PKI was being destroyed in Indonesia? In December 1965 three Barisan Socialis MPs resigned. The last five followed in October 1966, preferring to carry on with an underground struggle. The violent riots

49. *ST*, 16 Apr. 59 and 19 Aug. 60; Chang Heng Chee (419).
50. Singapore Govt White Paper no. 33, 1961.
51. *ST*, 23 Sept. 63.

of 23 October 1966 in support of North Vietnam provided the occasion for arresting the last known Barisan Socialis leaders.[52] In the elections of 1968 and 1972, the PAP made a clean sweep of all the parliamentary seats against an opposition which, in spite of having the real support of about one-third of the electorate, was disorganised and had no means of seriously challenging the PAP's supremacy. The PAP government was afraid of the rise of clandestine and subversive groups which might pose a sufficient challenge to public order and stability to threaten the economic and political viability of a small city-state. Such stability and viability had yet to become well established.

The offensive against the left and its sympathisers continued till 1969–70 from internal motives, also to let both the neighbouring countries as well as potential Western investors become fully convinced of the anti-Communism of Lee Kuan Yew's regime.[53] Numerous students at Ngee Ann College and Nanyang University were expelled, and the authorities began to exert a strict control over the whole world of higher education. In the administration of justice, the jury system was abandoned in favour of verdicts given jointly by two magistrates for all categories of cases. In the political sphere itself, the Socialist Club of the University of Singapore, which had been linked to the Barisan Socialis, was banned and replaced by the Democratic Socialist Club, an organ of the PAP. At the same time, the National Trade Union Congress (NTUC) was transformed, under the leadership of Devan Nair, into a mere channel of communication between government and organised labour.

By the beginning of the 1970s, Lee Kuan Yew and his colleagues had largely accomplished their 'clean-up' operation, and they were later able to exploit politically a series of opposition episodes, which enabled them to reaffirm their anti-Communist principles, both for the purpose of internal cohesion and for the sake of making their foreign policy coherent. In 1971 two newspapers, the *Eastern Sun* and the *Singapore Herald*, disappeared after being accused of having too close contacts with Peking, and four editors of the *Nanyang Siang Pau*, a local Chinese newspaper, were arrested for similar reasons.[54] In 1974 the authorities revealed the existence in Singapore of an 'army of liberation' and imprisoned thirty sympathisers of the MCP, several of whom were

52. *ST*, 8–9 Jan. and 8 & 24 Oct. 66.
53. Kroef (310), pp. 102–6.
54. *The Herald Affair*, May 1971, Univ. of Singapore, Library Reference Dept. Lau Teik Soon (311).

members of the Barisan Socialis. Unable to produce any tangible proof of an actual Communist danger at home, they denounced the subversive re-emergence of the left.[55] In the autumn of 1976, when some similar arrests of journalists (on the *New Straits Times* and *Berita Harian*) and politicians (the Vice-Minister of Science and Technology) were made in Kuala Lumpur, the Singapore government announced that it too had just uncovered a plot.[56] The imprisonment of a pro-Communist lawyer, G. Rahman, established the existence of a secret leftist intelligence network and provided the British Labour Party with enough material to exclude the PAP from the Socialist International movement and to launch an international campaign against Lee Kuan Yew's regime. Several arrests, including those of well-regarded journalists like Arun Senkuttuvan and Ho Kwon Ping, started a trial that led to the secretary-general of the People's Front of Singapore, Leong Mun Kwai, who subsequently admitted the existence of 'black operations', as for example some campaigns of defamation aimed at discrediting the regime abroad and destabilising it. The exclusion (or 'withdrawal', according to how one interprets it) of the PAP from the Socialist International at the end of 1976 was the object of vigorous controversy. Lee Kuan Yew declared that the party had withdrawn in protest at obvious support from abroad for the pro-Communist left in Singapore, especially from the foreign press. But the Socialist International in its turn denounced the PAP as too authoritarian, and criticised it for leaving dozens of political opponents in prison year after year.[57]

In the spring of 1987 the Singapore government claimed to have discovered a new 'Marxist plot', and used the Internal Security Act to arrest twenty-two individuals, some of whom were deeply involved in the various activities and social work of the Christian churches in Singapore. This was the start of a series of court actions against certain small groups of citizens alleged to be opposed to the rule of Lee Kuan Yew. All the actions took place against the backdrop of the campaign

55. *ARB*, 31 Dec. 74, p. 38, and *Yearbk on International Communist Affairs*, 1976–76, Stanford: Hoover Inst. Press, 1976.
56. *ST*, 2 Sept. 76; Lee Boon Hiok, 'Singapore: Reconciling the survival ideology with the achievement concept', *Southeast Asian Affairs*, 1978, pp. 229–44.
57. In 1977 Lee Kuan Yew declared that there were 61 political detainees who could be freed if they renounced Communism in writing (*Amnesty International Report*, 1977, pp. 211–17); T.J.S. George (432), pp. 110–31; A. Josey (439), 1980 edn, pp. 143–6; Lee Ting Hui (317), pp. 1–36 and 124–39, where one can consult a list of detainees, the dates of their detention and their renunciations.

preceding the general elections of September 1988: eight of the twenty-two people arrested the previous year and then conditionally released were re-arrested in April 1988; the circulation of certain foreign newspapers accused of direct interference in Singapore's internal affairs was restricted; the well-known lawyer Francis Seow, a former president of the Law Society of Singapore, was detained for several weeks and the first secretary for political affairs at the United States embassy was expelled in May 1988.

At the beginning of 1989, Chng Suan Tze, Kevin de Souza and Wong Souk Yee were freed, but the well-known British human rights lawyer Anthony Lester was banned from practising in the Singapore courts, and two of those arrested in May 1987 remained in prison till 1989–90: the lawyer Teo Soh Lung and the Catholic social worker Vincent Cheng. The Singapore parliament abolished *habeas corpus* and the right of appeal to the Privy Council in London for detainees under the Internal Security Act and for all local lawyers.[58]

Singapore and ASEAN facing a Communist threat from their neighbours: China and Vietnam

Which is the greatest external Communist threat faced by ASEAN? On the one hand there was anti-Chinese communalism and anti-Communism directed against the People's Republic of China, and on the other hand there was the expansion of Vietnamese Communism and Soviet influence throughout Indochina. The different perceptions of these two dangers by the various ASEAN member-states enable Singapore to have a narrow but more the less real freedom of manoeuvre to establish its own finely-tuned foreign policy *vis-à-vis* China and Vietnam. The city-state makes every effort to play down its 'Chinese image' in the eyes of its two closest neighbours;[59] it had no diplomatic relations with Peking till 1990. It has supported Thailand and the resistance against the Vietnamese and the regime of Heng Samrin in Kampuchea, and it seized on every opportunity to reassert its own independent identity.

58. *AWSJ*, 16 May 88, p. 14; *FEER*, 17 Dec. 87, p. 28; 10 Mar. 88, pp. 24–5; 28 Apr. 88, pp. 15–16 & 28–30; 12 May 88, pp. 13–14; 29 Dec. 88, pp. 11–12; 26 Jan. 89, p. 12, and 23 Mar. 89, pp. 31–2.
59. 'The many efforts of the Singapore government to change the image of the island state has yet to remove the stigma of being an "outpost" of China in the region' (Jørgensen-Dahl [302], p. 230).

Singapore and Peking: the absence of diplomatic relations
For Malaysia and Indonesia China has remained the greatest peril, threatening both their internal stability and the security of the whole region. Singapore also had to cope with major Communist upheavals in 1948–65, partly inspired from China, and it had no possible choice, wedged in between its two anti-Chinese neighbours, but to adopt a low profile in its relations with Peking.

The concept of Singapore being a 'third' or 'fourth' China (enunciated by Lee himself in 1965), an outpost or fifth column of China in the heart of South-East Asia, refers — in the perception of its neighbours, especially the Malays — to the Overseas Chinese and their main business centre in the region, Singapore. The Overseas Chinese had cultivated close links in the past with the Kuomintang, and benefited from the legal protection of the Canton government and the opening of Nationalist Chinese consulates in Singapore and elsewhere. Peking continued after 1949 to maintain a link between them and their ancestral home, mainly because of their cultural isolation in their South-East Asian countries of adoption. Peking also played on their pride in helping in the restoration of a 'great China'. With the prevalence of pro-Communist convictions, especially among Overseas Chinese close to the MCP or the PKI, Peking no longer needed local consulates and the conservation of Chinese citizenship among the local Chinese because it could now rely on local Communist parties, which were especially strong in Indonesia and Malaysia.

Influenced by this historical heritage, Kuala Lumpur and Jakarta have cultivated till quite recently a stereotyped image of their own local Chinese communities and those of Singapore as very active agents of China's ambitions in the region. Up till 1963–5, the steady progress of the PAP pro-Communists in Singapore could only give support to such an analysis.

In Malaysia the liquidation of the internal Communist upheaval after 10–12 years of emergency rule (1948–60), and the establishment of diplomatic relations with Peking in 1974 left unresolved the problem of China's role in relation to the Overseas Chinese community living in the peninsula, and thus the social and political equilibrium of the whole country.[60] Kuala Lumpur could not tolerate any interference of this kind by the PRC, nor could it tolerate any pro-Peking orientation in Singapore, as was feared in the late 1950s and early 1960s. The fear

60. C.P. Fitzgerald (282) and S. Fitzgerald (284); Shee Poon Kim (375).

of the city-state possibly playing a role of political middleman between China and the Malaysian Chinese, was far from baseless, especially when one considers that Singapore, like Hong Kong, was already an important economic agent for China in its dealings with the region and the rest of the world.

In Indonesia the suppression of the coup in 1965 and the destruction of the PKI was followed by the suspension of all direct relations with China till 1985. General Suharto officially accused Peking of assisting the PKI in its alleged attempt to seize power, and of giving political asylum to some of its leaders when they fled the country.[61] For reasons quite similar to those advanced in the case of Malaysia, Singapore always refused to establish diplomatic relations with China until Indonesia took that step (which it did only in 1980). Jakarta was inclined to delay normalisation with Peking: the danger of Communist subversion was used by the new regime of Suharto for its own legitimacy, based on its own official interpretation of the events of 1965. This aversion to Communism, and to China in particular, was one of the cornerstones of the New Order ideology of Suharto's Golkar party and of the new type of national political stability that had been established. Like Adam Malik in 1972–3, Mochtar, the Indonesian Foreign Minister, stated in 1978–80 that the Indonesian Chinese would have to become completely assimilated before a rapprochement with China could be envisaged![62] On the eve of the thirtieth anniversary commemoration of the Bandung conference of independent Afro-Asian nations in 1985, the Indonesian government declared that it was still expecting formal recognition and an apology from Peking for China's part in the tragic events of September 1965.

However, much has changed since then. President Suharto has consolidated his regime and also the economic and social take-off of his country, and China and Indonesia have become competitors in Third World markets. For these reasons among others, direct commercial relations were re-established in 1985 between Jakarta and Peking, and

61. *Antara Daily News Bull.*, 'Address of the Acting President General Suharto before the Gotong Royong House of Representatives', Jakarta, 16 Aug. 67; A.C. Brackman (257); Kroef (310), pp. 217–60; R.P. Howie, *China and the Gestapu affair in Indonesia*, Canberra: Australian Political Studies, 1970; R. Mortimer (336); J. Taylor (394).
62. *New Nation* (Singapore), 10 Jun. 74; *Indonesia Times*, 9 June 78; *FEER*, 16 June 78; R.L. Rau, 'Normalization with PRC with emphasis on ASEAN states', *Pacific Community*, Jan. 76, pp. 230–47; L. Suryadinata, 'The Chinese minority and Sino-Indonesian diplomatic normalization', *JSEAS*, 1, 1981, pp. 197–206.

this was a clear diplomatic signal announcing a progressive improvement in bilateral relations. There is no doubt that this major change in Indonesian-Chinese relations made Singapore's position in the region *vis-à-vis* its two large Malay neighbours much easier than in the past. As had been expected, Singapore established diplomatic relations with Peking in 1990 only a few days after a similar move by Indonesia.

A short account of relations between Singapore and China
The absence of official diplomatic contact between Singapore and Peking did not mean, as in the case of Indonesia, that there were no direct bilateral relations. On the contrary, a certain dynamism was to be seen in bilateral trade activity, and in the development of the regional political crisis in Kampuchea and Indochina as a whole. The history of these relations can be divided into five periods.[63]

Phase 1 (1965–8).   Despite the character of its regime, and its supportive role up till the 1960s in relation to the MCP in Malaysia and the Barisan Socialis in Singapore, China was accorded an instinctive respect by Singapore's PAP leaders because of the common Chinese cultural and historical heritage, the greatness of the Chinese nation and civilization, and China's renaissance since 1949, after long decades of decline and civil war. Singapore has always made clear its desire to forge business links with as many countries as possible, and it began to do business with Taiwan as well as with Peking; by abstaining in the vote at the United Nations on the People's Republic's application to join the world organisation, it showed its lack of opposition to this development.[64] When the local branches of the Bank of China and the Kwangtung Provincial Bank were closed down in Kuala Lumpur and Penang, they were authorised to continue business in Singapore provided they employed only local personnel.

The Cultural Revolution, of which Hong Kong and Macau felt the full impact, had less effect on Singapore, being at a safe geographic distance. However, China did accuse the city-state of acting as a rear base for the United States forces fighting in the Vietnam war, and it criticised the imprisonment of several members of the local opposition (the Barisan Socialis) and the participation of Singapore in ASEAN (1967), whose regional *raison d'être* was precisely derived from anti-Communism and anti-Chinese communalism.

63. Lee Lai-to (313); T. Tajima (389); R.O. Tilman (396).
64. *ST*, 29 Nov. 67.

Phase 2 (1969–71). Singapore's political relationship with China remained hostile up till the beginning of the 1970s, with Peking intensifying its support for the Viet Minh and continuing its strategy of internal subversion in the ASEAN states, including Singapore. Lee Kuan Yew appealed to the small countries of South-East Asia to mobilise themselves against the slightest whiff of Chinese hegemony and chauvinism.[65] The crisis over the Singapore branch of the Bank of China coincided with another crisis over the local pro-Chinese press. The branch of the bank was accused of failing to maintain liquid assets to the minimum level imposed by the Monetary Authority of Singapore, and of using its assets to finance Communist agitation inside the city-state. Fully aware of the business middleman's role played by Singapore, from which it benifited, Peking hastened to re-establish the *status quo* to avoid the bank being closed and thus jeopardising fruitful bilateral trading relations with the city-state.

Phase 3 (1971–7). Singapore drew rapid and practical conclusions from the early signs of American withdrawal from Vietnam and the rapprochement between Peking and Washington.

In the absence of diplomatic ties between the ASEAN states and China, and after five successive years of abstention, Singapore voted with Malaysia in favour of China's entry to the UN, with Indonesia abstaining.[66] The first official contacts were made between the respective chambers of commerce of the two countries, and bilateral sporting competitions were organised. The visit to Singapore of the Chinese table-tennis team in July 1972 was a good opportunity for Lee Kuan Yew, in spite of an incident when pro-Communist slogans were shouted by some Singaporean spectators during the tournament, to promote bilateral relations on a more official footing and to welcome the Chinese team personally.

In 1974 it was already possible to think in terms of *de facto* mutual recognition, and this evolution was encouraged by the establishment of diplomatic relations with Malaysia the same year (Thailand followed in 1975) and by Peking's declaration abandoning all forms of dual nationality or citizenship for the Overseas Chinese.

Phase 4 (1975–8). The unification of Vietnam under the red banner led to the relaunching of ASEAN as a political entity and to the attempts

65. Wu Yuan Li, *Strategic significance of Singapore*, Washington DC: American Enterprise Institute, 1972.
66. *ST*, 12 Oct. 71.

by China to improve its relations with the regional group. For Thailand and Singapore, Vietnam became the greatest danger in South East Asia; for China, because of Vietnam's alliance with the Soviet Union, it became a second front on its southern flank threatening national security, and Peking sought to respond with an anti-Vietnamese pincer strategy supported by both ASEAN and the Kampuchean resistance.[67]

This conjunction of geostrategic interests heralded the first official visits to China by Singapore's leaders: Rajaratnam, the Minister of Foreign Affairs, in 1975 and Lee Kuan Yew himself in 1976. China welcomed these guests with the highest state-visit protocol, declared full support for greater cohesion in ASEAN and full respect for Singapore's sovereignty (including citizenship), and announced that it would establish diplomatic relations as soon as Singapore was ready to do so. This new Chinese attitude was obviously directed through these first contacts with Singapore, to the other ASEAN governments and especially to those hitherto very hostile to Peking. The message was clear: Peking was giving exaggerated emphasis to Singapore's independence to minimise the ASEAN perception of China's influence on the Overseas Chinese and the local Communist parties of South-East Asia. Its anxiety to be able to launch official relations with the city-state was also a message to Jakarta, since China was well aware that Singapore would never respond to this invitation until Indonesia had first agreed to re-establish political dialogue with Peking.

Singapore's direct responsibility for the somewhat cold and rigid atmosphere during Deng Xiao-ping's visit to the city-state late in 1978 proceeded from the same logic. Lee Kuan Yew insisted that China should end all assistance to South-East Asian Communist movements. He also laid great stress on China's respect for Singapore's independence, an indirect yet clear message to Indonesia and Malaysia, both of which watched Deng Xiao-ping's visit to Singapore with close attention.[69]

Phase 5 (the 1980s). Lee is well aware, like his ASEAN partners, that South-East Asia historically came within the Chinese sphere of influence, and Chinese power could again play an important role in regional geopolitics. However, he does not believe that China will be expansionist and threatening in the coming decades, due to its colossal domestic tasks of development and modernisation — in the military

---

67. J. Camilleri (262).
68. Khaw Guat Hoon (306); Shee Poon Kim, 'Will China continue to smile on ASEAN?', *Trends Jnl*, Singapore, Mar. 77, pp. 36–46.
69. *FEER*, 24 Nov. 78, p. 33; E.W. Martin (328).

sphere among others.[70] This is probably why China was so reluctant to teach Vietnam a second 'lesson' across its southern frontier after the invasion of Kampuchea.

The identity of interests between China and Thailand, a country strongly supported by Singapore in order to balance and oppose the Vietnamese occupation of Kampuchea, has contributed to a climate of broad understanding between Peking and the island-state. However, their true bilateral rapprochement lies in the economic field, and goes far beyond the basic opposition of their respective systems. The multiplication of trade and economic contacts at the highest level matched Deng Xiao-ping's new policy of 'economic liberalisation' in the late 1970s and early '80s; a tiny proportion of the Chinese market would reinforce Singapore's economic viability, especially when the city-state had to face a world market recession in the mid-1980s. Singapore can use either direct trading channels or those previously established with Hong Kong and Taiwan, and the Overseas Chinese business networks have an intimate knowledge of the Chinese economy and its local working mentalities. Several contracts, covering oil production, construction and civil engineering *inter alia*, and an agreement between China Airlines and Singapore International Airlines were initially signed as a starting-point.

Today more than ever, even after the Peking student massacres in 1989, economic factors and profit carry most weight between China and the Overseas Chinese, and it is not necessary to play them down so much for political reasons as it was from the 1950s up till the 1970s. The strong networks in ASEAN and the rest of the Asia-Pacific region have strengthened their key position as privileged business middlemen promoting China's economic interests worldwide. The collaboration between Singaporean businessmen and their counterparts in Canton, Hong Kong, Shanghai and Taipei can evolve without criticism from the most anti-Chinese of the ASEAN governments. Peking and Singapore showed that they had understood this remarkably well when, in 1985, the former Singaporean Vice Premier Goh Keng Swee, one of the major architects of the development strategy of the 1960s and '70s, was

70. 'I don't think there is going to be a sizeable Chinese presence elsewhere in Southeast Asia for a long while' (Lee Kuan Yew, *ST*, 4 June 71). 'China today is in no position to support a major military presence outside its near environment . . . but may at some stage see that environment as including Singapore' (T.B. Millar, *Geopolitics and the military-strategy potential*, CSIS Georgetown Univ., Indian Ocean conference paper, Mar. 71).

appointed as a special counsellor to China for the promotion of the Chinese special economic zones!

Also hit by the economic recession of the mid-1980s, the Malaysian authorities have become aware of the urgent need for more cooperation with the local Chinese business community as much for the sake of healthier national development as to gain access to the Chinese market. At the end of 1985, visits to Peking by Lee Kuan Yew and Mahathir took place within two weeks of each other.

Jakarta has followed a similar route: the Indonesian and Chinese chambers of commerce established direct official contact in 1985, and the Chinese Foreign Minister was invited to Bandung to commemorate the historic non-aligned conference held there thirty years earlier.[71] Indonesia no longer expressed its view of China only in ideological and political terms, and started to realise that it would increasingly have to cope with Chinese competition in Asian and Third World markets.

Following the re-establishment of direct trading relations between Jakarta and Peking in 1988, bilateral contacts have entered a new stage: in February 1989 the two governments announced that they would open negotiations to prepare mutual diplomatic recognition (achieved in 1990). The positive reaction of Singapore was clear from the start, because in the previous month Vice Premier Goh Chok Tong declared that the island-state would establish diplomatic relations with China as soon as agreement had been reached between China and Indonesia. It was not merely by chance that this declaration also coincided with the first official visit to Singapore of a major Taiwanese political figure, President Lee Teng-hui, on 6–9 March 1989. Leaving aside the very substantial economic and military affinities between the two island regimes, which they have no choice but to continue and even reinforce, the timing alone of this presidential visit was significant, coming as it did at the possible beginning of a vast readjustment in the regional affairs of South-East Asia. The rapprochement between Indonesia and China and the relaxation of the fraught relations between Peking and Taipei are two new elements from which Singapore will know how to derive the maximum profit. Although full diplomatic relations were resumed between China and Indonesia, then between China and Singapore, in 1990, it seems so far that the city-state is able to maintain a very close relation with Taiwan and to increase its cooperation with Peking at the same time.

71. *FEER*, 2 May 85, p. 12, and 9 May 85, pp. 18–19.

*The Indochinese crisis and the strengthening of Singapore's regional
diplomacy after 1975-8*

At the time when the Philippines and Thailand were normalising their
relations with Peking, China ceased to be seen automatically by ASEAN
as the most immediate Communist danger. The fall of Saigon in 1975
and of Phnom Penh in 1978 propelled the Vietnamese peril into the forefront of ASEAN preoccupations concerning regional security and
stability.[72]

Singapore worked hard during the first decade of its existence as a
sovereign state to create the key internal conditions for its concrete
independence. It would then engage in a more active foreign policy, and
use the new crises in Indochina as a lever to overcome its small
geographical size, not only through its regional economic performance
but also through new and well-defined goals of regional diplomacy. The
chosen instrument was to channel ASEAN's anti-Communism primarily into an anti-Vietnamese and anti-Soviet direction, and at the same
time to regard China as only a minor danger to the region compared
to Vietnam and the Soviet Union. Singapore's regional policy thus
aimed at a significant lessening of sinophobia and of the perception of
itself among its ASEAN neighbours as the 'fourth China'. At the same
time, Vietnam was obviously conducting a diplomatic 'charm offensive',
seeking a benevolent or neutral attitude from those countries traditionally most opposed to China, namely Indonesia and Malaysia.

ASEAN and the Vietnamese crisis in 1975. With the exception of
Singapore and Thailand, the ASEAN countries, before 1975, preached
co-existence with Vietnam. Malaysia, by virtue of its declaration on the
neutralisation of South-East Asia in 1971, hoped to welcome the three
states of Indochina as observers within ASEAN, with a view to eventual
full membership in the future. Kuala Lumpur and Manila went even
further and proposed their cooperation in the post-war reconstruction
of Vietnam. Indonesia was always attentive to any sign of internal
agitation, and would ascribe it instinctively to Communist subversion
and the hidden hand of Peking; it therefore viewed Vietnam with some
sympathy. There are several factors which help to explain this attitude:
the physical and maritime distance between the two countries, their
shared experience of anti-colonial wars, and the similar ambition of each
to be recognised as the dominant power in its own region (Vietnam in

---

72. Pfennig & Suh (eds) (358); Shee Poon Kim (376); Suh (ed.) (386); T. Tarnthong
(393); D.S. Zagoria (412).

Indochina, Indonesia within ASEAN) compared to the more specific vocations of smaller states in the region.[73]

Singapore has learned the lessons from the dark years of internal troubles at home in the early 1960s, and it has remained detached from this relatively benevolent attitude to Vietnam, and has continued to be firmly opposed to any form of conciliation with the Communists. Its support of the US forces fighting in South Vietnam was just one expression of its concern not to see Communist influence sap the stability of ASEAN, which was also so important for the island's own prosperity. The neutralisation of ASEAN was seen as a utopian dream, and only firm commitments by all major powers in South-East Asia could offer guarantees of peace and security for the region.[74]

Bangkok took a position close to that of Singapore in opposing Vietnam, its long-standing enemy which, in the course of such a new period of expansionism directed towards neighbouring Kampuchea, could establish direct links with the Communist party of north-east Thailand and thus begin a new job of domestic destabilisation within ASEAN territory! The security of its eastern borders and the preservation of Kampuchea as a buffer-state became an obsession with the authorities in Bangkok.[75]

With the fall of Saigon and above all the Vietnamese invasion of Kampuchea three years later, the earlier predictions and suspicions of Singapore and Thailand were becoming a reality and assumed a new regional meaning.

The critical years (1975–8): the gap between words and deeds. The fall of Saigon fuelled a collective fear within ASEAN similar to Malaysia's fear of a possible Communist coup in Singapore in 1961–3. As the Singaporean authorities had always claimed, the common fear of an external Communist threat was the only thing that could give a new political stimulus to regional cohesion among ASEAN members.[76] The guarantee of regional stability, manifested in the Declaration of Concord and the ASEAN Treaty of 1976, pointed to Vietnam as an expansionist and subversive country in close alliance with a great power outside the

---

73. Leifer (320) and *FEER*, 16 July 76, p. 13.
74. 'Singapore was regarded as controversial by its partners' (H.H. Indorf [298], p. 35).
75. *ST*, 16 June 78.
76. 'The only interest which appears to have a regional character is fear of communism' (Rajaratnam, *ST*, 19 Dec. 69).

region. As an ASEAN response, the member-states did not however envisage a coordination of their military forces, and their political unanimity went little further than declarations of intent. Indonesia and Malaysia cherished the hope that Vietnam, now united, rid of foreign occupations at last, and exhausted after three decades of war, would opt for a policy of co-existence with ASEAN.[77] Singapore and Thailand remained deeply sceptical of any apparent change in Vietnam's attitude. Lee Kuan Yew, with his acute perception of long-term historical trends, had no doubt that the Vietnamese war machine was to be linked with old dreams of Vietnamese domination over the whole of Indochina and would soon spread beyond Vietnam's national frontiers.

The visits in 1976 by the Vietnamese Vice Minister of Foreign Affairs, Phan Hien, to all the ASEAN capitals except Bangkok seemed to provide early confirmation of this analysis. Up till 1978, Hanoi and Moscow kept up a very hostile attitude towards ASEAN; Vietnam declared that it would establish diplomatic relations with each member-state individually, but refused any collective negotiations between Hanoi and ASEAN. The Vietnamese critics of ASEAN focused on some sensitive issues of intra-ASEAN cooperation like the relations between Singapore and China, the existence of United States military bases in the Philippines and Thailand, and the bilateral naval exercises between some ASEAN countries as a first attempt at launching a military pact among the five member states.

In 1978, the increasing tension between Peking and Hanoi was at least partly the cause of the sudden reversal of policy by Vietnam and the Soviet Union which first manifested itself in a more conciliatory attitude towards ASEAN. The Vietnamese Foreign Minister, N. Trinh, made his first official visit to ASEAN but deliberately ignored Singapore, where the Vice Premier, Phan Hien, then brought a message of peace directed at China.[78] Phan Hien stated several weeks later that Vietnam was prepared to engage in dialogue with ASEAN, and in November Phan Van Dong seemed to accept the idea of South-East Asian neutralisation. In opposition to Deng Xiao-ping, he promised not to support any internal Communist movement in the ASEAN region.[79]

---

77. Communiqué of the 8th meeting of ASEAN foreign ministers, Kuala Lumpur, 14 May 75; Young Mun Cheong, 'Indonesia-Vietnam relations and the recent Indochina conflict', *J. of the History Soc.* (Singapore), 1980, pp. 11–14.
78. *ST*, 7 Dec. & 25–27 July 78; *Bangkok Post*, 7 July 78.
79. *ST*, 11 Sept. 78. China agreed in 1981 to loosen its ties with the clandestine Communist parties of South-East Asia.

It came as a severe blow, at least for utopians, when in the same month the Soviet Union and Vietnam signed a treaty of friendship and cooperation, thus institutionalising the Soviet presence in Indochina. However, the Indonesian Foreign Minister said no more than that Vietnam's grave economic crisis alone could explain such an agreement and that he could understand such a motive.[80]

On the eve of the Vietnamese invasion of Kampuchea, ASEAN had no intention of getting further into the triangular conflict between Moscow, Hanoi and Peking which divided the Communist world. However, the Thai Prime Minister Kriangksak showed increasing anxiety over his country's security, and Lee Kuan Yew denounced the Vietnamese regional diplomatic offensives as a tactic directed against ASEAN. Hanoi's spectacular reversal of attitude in 1978 was analysed as a diplomatic charm campaign without any firm commitments, but with a remarkable aptitude for playing the ASEAN member-states off against each other. By visiting all ASEAN capitals except Bangkok, insisting that China and Singapore were in collusion, and flattering the regional ambitions of Jakarta or Kuala Lumpur, Vietnam sought to obtain a guarantee of ASEAN neutrality over China's support for the Pol Pot regime and over the next Vietnamese invasion of Kampuchea.

Singapore promoting ASEAN's anti-Vietnamese diplomacy. The entry of Vietnamese troops into Kampuchea in December 1978 only vindicated the unwavering mistrust felt by Singapore since the fall of Saigon.

It was to be expected that Bangkok, faced with its traditional enemy, would react strongly and seek to draw ASEAN into a policy of opposition to Hanoi. In reality, Thailand did not need the Kampuchea crisis in order to reaffirm and serve its national cohesion, the merit of its diplomacy, and the efficacy of its rather strong defence system backed by the United States. Certainly, Bangkok had no intention of remaining inactive — facing the problems of the influx of refugees, organising the Kampuchean resistance and the multiplication of clashes on the border but it wished to preserve Thailand's relative neutrality, inherited from not having experienced direct colonial rule in the past, and not to get involved in external conflict while there were so many development issues to be addressed at home.

On the other hand, the occupation of Kampuchea gave Singapore an ideal opportunity to articulate a more comprehensive regional policy, in order to have — despite its small population and physical size — a

80. *FEER*, 24 Nov. 78, p. 33.

more important voice in regional affairs, and to name Vietnam, and no longer China, as the principal danger in South-East Asia.[81] Because of the absolute need for regional stability in order for the emporium to survive, Singapore was able to fulfill a role as diplomatic middleman over the Indochinese crisis — between Indonesia, often followed by Malaysia, with their more favourable attitude towards Hanoi, and Thailand, threatened by the Vietnamese expansion and thus feeling close to the Kampuchean resistance and China's interests versus Vietnam. The city-state could also speak out publicly regarding Thailand's own position contiguous to Indochina with more freedom than was available to Bangkok.

Following the meeting between Lee and Kriangsak in December 1978, Singapore denounced in virulent terms Vietnam's imperialism and military expansionism which appeared to threaten Thailand as the likely next victim.[82] Lee obtained from his ASEAN colleagues, meeting in Bangkok on 12 January 1979 at Thailand's invitation, a collective demand for the immediate withdrawal of all foreign forces involved in Kampuchea. This statement seemed (for the satisfaction of Jakarta) sufficiently broad not to be directed at Vietnam exclusively, but also to include the Chinese backing of Pol Pot's partisans. This ASEAN diplomacy of the half-open door preceded by four weeks the Chinese attack on Vietnam's northern frontier on 17 February 1979.[83]

Following this military lesson which China wanted to impose on its neighbour, and which had come to an end by early March, Indonesia and Malaysia were obliged to adjust their Indochinese policy according to the position of Thailand as the ASEAN country most directly threatened by Vietnam. For similar reasons, Jakarta and Kuala Lumpur were not able either to contradict or to moderate Singapore's anti-Vietnamese policy. Rajaratnam boldly stated that an insidious war of destabilisation had started in South-East Asia, where hundreds of thousands of refugees had flowed in from Indochina.[84] Thailand had to

81. 'In face of the immediate threat from Vietnam, China and the ASEAN countries have a mutual interest in co-operation. While this will probably last for ever, the relationship could be extremely profitable – especially for Singapore' (*ST*, 26 Nov. 79).

82. 'It would be wise for non-communist countries in Southeast Asia not to work wholly on the assumption that the Vietnamese would stop at Kampuchea in their bid to extend their influence' (interview with Lee Kuan Yew by the BBC, 6 Feb. 79 [*ST*, 9 Feb. 79]); *Asiaweek*, 2 Feb. 79.

83. *ST*, 15 Jan. and 3 Feb. 79.

84. *ST*, 28 June 79.

bear the heavy burden of 600,000 in 1979–80, assembled in camps near the frontier; the Malaysian government came under attack from local Muslim political and/or religious groups who accused it of receiving Chinese immigrants from South Vietnam. Singapore asked whether ASEAN's good treatment of refugees did not act as an incentive to Vietnam to expel all its undesirables.

By the middle of 1979, the city-state was opting for a double diplomatic strategy of encouraging anti-Vietnamese resistance within Kampuchea and stirring up an international campaign of denunciation and defamation of Vietnam. At a new meeting in June, Lee and Kriangsak decided not to exclude the possibility of a military alliance: they refused to recognise Heng Samrin's new government installed by Vietnam in Phnom Penh and decided unofficially to make arms deliveries to certain factions of the Kampuchean resistance (excepting the troops of Pol Pot). Hanoi again criticised the collusion between Singapore, Bangkok and Peking, and launched its first military incursions into Thai territory in January 1980.[85]

Singapore condemned very vocally the Vietnamese occupation of Kampuchea at every international meeting it attended (e.g. the Commonwealth conference in August 1979 and the Non-Aligned conference in November). At the UN General Assembly, Singapore's ambassador Tommy Koh (later posted to Washington) coordinated the ASEAN delegations and intervened on behalf of the Five with remarkable authority. Resolutions 34/22 (Nov.1979) and 35/6 (Oct.1980) — the Soviets had invaded Afghanistan between those dates — were adopted with large majorities in favour of the non-recognition of Heng Samrin's government, the continuation of Democratic Kampuchea's representation at the UN, a demand for the withdrawal of all Vietnamese forces from Kampuchea, and the convening of a special UN conference on Kampuchea in the near future.[86]

Kuala Lumpur was asked by other ASEAN member-states to establish dialogue with Hanoi, and in March 1980 Indonesia and Malaysia published at Kuantan a joint declaration calling on the Vietnamese to reduce their links with Moscow, in exchange for China easing its

---

85. 'The reactionary allegations of the Singapore authorities and those of the Peking rulers are completely identical, so much so that we should wonder whether the Singaporean authorities now still represent an independent country in Southeast Asia' (Radio Hanoi, Nov. 79).

86. *ST*, 10 June and 2 July 79; 1 July, 1, 4, 5 & 21 Sept. 80; *ARB*, 9, 7 (31 Dec. 79), pp. 635–6, and 10, 6, pp. 747–8. J. Nishikawa (345).

pressure in both the north and west of the country (in the west through its support for the Kampuchean resistance). Indonesia's hope was to contribute to the freeing of Vietnam from the direct influence of the two Communist great powers, but this hope was of short duration: in June 1980, Hanoi launched a new offensive close to the Thai frontier, while its Foreign Minister, Thach, was still on an official visit to Jakarta![87]

Singapore's role in ASEAN's diplomatic successes over Kampuchea
The UN's special conference on Kampuchea, which was held in New York in July 1981, was a good example of Tommy Koh's assiduous anti-Vietnamese diplomacy. The objective was to rally the maximum number of votes in favour of Democratic Kampuchea keeping the official Kampuchean seat in the UN, and to promote international pressure for Vietnam's military disengagement. In spite of a boycott initiated by the Soviet Union and its allies, ninety-three states gave their support to Singapore and ASEAN.[88]

Of course, the potential withdrawal from Kampuchea through diplomatic negotiation between Vietnam and ASEAN remained a distant goal: in order to 'internalise' the Kampuchea issue, the Vietnamese responded by organising a series of conferences gathering the Indochinese states and based on a federal concept. These conferences would announce symbolically year after year the withdrawal of a part of the Vietnamese forces from Kampuchea. The Vietnamese hope was to convince those ASEAN countries which had been rather close to Hanoi during the previous years of Vietnam's goodwill and sincerity.[89]

Singapore and Bangkok fought against the very definite refusal of Malaysia to guarantee any concerted direct support from ASEAN for the Kampuchean resistance. In order to stress, formally at least, its policy of equidistance from Peking and Hanoi, Singapore made unofficial deliveries of arms to the Democratic Kampuchean resistance, and carried

---

87. Min. of Foreign Affairs, Thailand, 'The Vietnamese acts of aggression against Thailand's sovereignty and territorial integrity', Bangkok, 1980. R. Kershaw, 'Thailand after Vietnam . . .', *Asian Affairs*, Feb. 76, pp. 9–32; J. Kroef, 'Kampuchea, the diplomatic labyrinth', *Asian Survey*, Oct. 82, pp. 1009–33.
88. 'It is not our intention to bring Vietnam to its knees; we only want to bring it to its senses' (Dhanabalan, Chm. of ASEAN Standing Committee, *ARB*, 30.9.81, pp. 842–5).
89. *Le Monde*, 22 Mar., 15 & 24–25 Apr., 4 May 83.

on at the same time its active two-way trade with Vietnam — which even included rice from Thailand![90]

Singapore's second diplomatic success was the formation in June 1982 of a Kampuchean coalition government composed of the three principal groups resisting Phnom Penh and the Vietnamese. In September 1981 the city-state had received the three potential leaders of this coalition — Norodom Sihanouk, Son Sann and Khieu Sampan — for tripartite negotiations among themselves. Some ASEAN states felt embarrassed by this Singaporean initiative, and did not want to see the city-state acting too much alone. But from the very moment when Thailand approved it, in view of the Khmer Rouge and Peking agreeing to work together with the other resistance groups under Sihanouk's leadership and the absence of any Vietnamese signal to ease the situation, ASEAN's cohesion had to come into play by backing Thailand to the full.[91]

As successive UN resolutions showed later, Singapore and its ASEAN partners rallied, each year, an ever-increasing number of countries willing to condemn Vietnam, with the Kampuchea problem running in tandem for a long time with that of Afghanistan, and with the armed confrontations on the Thai frontier steadily increasing.[92] The government of Lee Kuan Yew, fortified by its longevity and stability, showed an invincible determination to erode Hanoi's belief that the West would quickly forget about the fate of Kampuchea. Precisely because of the impossibility for a small country of devoting attention to all the aspects and issues of international relations, Singapore has always preferred to select specific themes of direct interest and to work very hard on them — with the long-term objective of securing the island's viability and national identity. This was illustrated by the way it hammered away against Vietnam at the UN and in other international gatherings in order to keep the world community constantly alert to the danger of Communist expansion in South-East Asia.[93] From time to time, some

90. *ST*, 21 Sept. 80, 19 Dec. 81, 28 Jun. 82, 17 Mar. 84. *FEER*, 10 Dec. 81, pp. 44 & 67–8; 5 Apr. 84, pp. 54–6; 25 Nov. 84, pp. 52–3.
91. *ST*, 9 Dec. 81; *Indonesian Times*, 9 Aug. 84; *Le Monde*, 8 Sept. 81; *FEER*, 25 June 82, pp. 8–10, and 23 July 82, pp. 11–13; S.W. Simon, 'Cambodia and regional diplomacy', *Southeast Asian Affairs*, 1982, pp. 196–207.
92. *ST*, 27 Oct. 82; *FEER*, 20 Sept. 84, pp. 38–40, and 27 Sept. 84, pp. 40–2.
93. 'The ability to pay adequate attention to particular issues is also a power resource . . . Small states who are able to devote their full attention to a narrow range of issues can be quite influential on particular subjects' (Min. of Culture, *Issues facing Singapore in the 80s*, Singapore, 1981/2, pp. 13–14).

ASEAN partners disapprove of the form and/or content of the various positions taken by the city-state, yet they all somehow recognise their utility. They appreciated, with the partial exception of Indonesia, that Singapore would assume part of the heavy diplomatic burden of the Indochinese crisis, so freeing them to concentrate on other international problems facing ASEAN as a whole or some of the member-states individually.[94]

Indonesia, looking forward to taking over the regional leadership in South-East Asia together with Vietnam, tried — cautiously — to distance itself from Singapore and Bangkok as often as possible. Following the Kuantan declaration of 1980, leading government and military figures from Indonesia have visited Hanoi on many occasions since 1983–4, and Jakarta has tried hard to play a mediatory role between ASEAN and Vietnam. Hanoi answered, as usual, with the promise of a partial withdrawal from Kampuchea, only to launch in December and January 1984/5 its biggest offensive against the resistance: Thailand, once more directly threatened, renewed its protests at the UN.[95]

At the beginning of the 1990s it is difficult to predict whether or not the initial joint strategy of Singapore and Thailand, the restraining role of Jakarta, and some new initiatives from Bangkok to establish closer economic relations with Hanoi and Phnom Penh can bring about a political solution to the Kampuchean crisis by diplomatic negotiations alone. The numerous about-turns by Prince Sihanouk, as head of a coalition government consisting of resistance movements but hampered by its embarassing ally the Khmer Rouge, make it extremely difficult to prevent Vietnam from dominating the whole of Indochina. At the same time, Hanoi has cleverly used the potential withdrawal of its troops by 1989–90 as a pawn in the game. No one can yet be entirely sure whether it has any serious intention of loosening its alliance with the Soviet Union (less and less able to support Vietnam economically) and of opening up towards the West using the ASEAN countries, and Thailand in particular, as middlemen. It is not much easier to say whether an eventual disengagement by the superpowers from the

94. 'Singapore is a little like a small man who makes a lot of noise to divert your attention from his sixty-two inches' (Ronald McKie, quoted in George [432], 2nd edn, p. 72).
95. *FEER*, 9 Aug. 84, pp. 18–19; 8 Mar. 84, pp. 36–7; 22 Mar. 84, pp. 15–17; 26 July 84, pp. 32–3; 18 Jan. 85, pp. 5–8; 14 Feb. 85, p. 14; 21 Feb. 85, p. 16; 28 Feb. 85, pp. 32–3; 3 Oct. 85, p. 26. *Jakarta Post*, 13 Mar. and 4 & 8 May 84; 18 Feb., 6 Mar. & 16 July 85. *Asiaweek*, 18 Jan. 85, pp. 8–9.

Indochinese scene would make a useful contribution to direct negotiations between ASEAN and Vietnam, or whether it would automatically put the future of Kampuchea into the balance of gains and
losses the ASEAN countries might expect from dealing with Vietnam
bilaterally.

However, Singapore can be said to have won several points in political
and diplomatic terms. The anti-Vietnamese campaign which ASEAN
has waged since 1979 has contributed to an obvious decline in the
systematic anti-Chinese perception of some major regional actors like
Kuala Lumpur and Jakarta. The decision of Peking not to sacrifice
China's economic and social development on the altar of its conflict with
Hanoi, and the fact that it has not launched a second military 'lesson'
against the north of Vietnam, have emphasised China's relative weakness
in military terms, or at least its rejection of expansionist moves beyond
its borders.

In the economic field, the vast programme of internal liberalisation
initiated by Deng Xiao-ping up till 1989 has given ASEAN and the
world a glimpse of the formidable potential that China's decisive
industrial take-off could have over the years into the next century.
Neither Hanoi nor Jakarta — as they expressed their traditional defiance
of Peking for historical and political reasons already explained —
counted on this new idea of a China able to become, in the long run,
an economic giant, also helped throughout Asia and the Pacific (apart
from Japan) by the Overseas Chinese and the newly industrialised
economies of the region.[96]

Perhaps it falls to tiny Singapore, by virtue of its own economic
success, to make its neighbours Indonesia and Vietnam aware of the
Chinese ability to do business!

Through its highly diversified and dynamic functions as an international
crossroads, Singapore has become a magnetic pole of economic activity,
and, as has been illustrated in the last two chapters, it cannot remain
a political dwarf in the South-East Asian region. However, this
observation should not conceal the fact that there is no possibility of
ensuring the viability and prosperity of such a regional emporium

---

96. 'If by the 1990s or in the early decades of the 21st century the Communist system
in China were to produce a modern industrial state equipped with all the
technological advances, what will happen to the rest of Asia if it fails to achieve
similar progress?' (Wilairat [402], p. 515).

without a minimum of equilibrium and stability in the external environment. Faced with this harsh reality, the city-state has just one unique card to play: the island society has to be ordered and organised domestically with the most efficient and rational management possible. This card must be played by giving the Singaporean house enough cohesion and solidity to withstand the numerous uncertainties of regional and global international relations.

7

A CITY-STATE FACES THE CHALLENGES
OF SURVIVAL AND VIABILITY

After two decades of uninterrupted economic growth, Singaporeans experienced their Prime Minister's speech to the nation on 9 August 1985 as a psychological shock. Following its first economic recession in 1985 — which perhaps affected the city-state more severely than it did Asia's three other newly industrialised countries, without being anything more than the latest in a long series of challenges which the emporium has regularly had to face throughout history — Lee Kuan Yew's message was no different from what he had already said in 1965: national cohesion, economic and social rationalisation, maximisation of intellectual capacity and hard work, and the constant mobilisation of the whole population.

The comprehensive range of external conditions which have allowed the island emporium to develop are far beyond its own control, and Singapore has to work endlessly to lessen the numerous risks threatening its survival. Beyond its initial economic development, which was mainly due to large-scale foreign investment, and its political security which was tightly bound to its regional environment, its primary strategy is to multiply all kinds of interdependences through the city-state in order to become, and remain, useful and even indispensable to most actors on the regional and international scene. But it is also obvious that such a small state as Singapore will never be able to claim any significant influence on the pattern of world and even regional affairs.

In all this there is just one certainty. The mobilisation and fully coherent organisation of the island society is probably Singapore's only major independent resource. It has enabled the city-state to respond to the many challenges it has faced before and since 1965, and is one of the few keys to Singapore's future.

**Struggling for survival: the cornerstone concept of
nation-building since 1965**
Singapore's sudden independence in 1965 raised the problem of how the island-city, on becoming a sovereign state, could ensure its economic and political viability within the shortest possible time. Against the memories of 1963–5, a period punctuated by the most severe challenges

229

Singapore had had to endure since the Japanese attack in 1942, Lee Kuan Yew, Goh Keng Swee and Rajaratnam initiated mobilisation campaigns involving the whole population in the name of the necessary struggle for national survival.[1] This permanent effort for the defence of the emporium and its unflagging ability to adapt to outside events became transformed quickly into something of the nature of a national ideology. The syndrome of extreme vulnerability found a determined will among the Singaporean leaders to mobilize the island society using methods which, in some respects, are reminiscent of campaigns and mass rallies in China.[2]

After the crisis of 1963–5, the PAP continued to keep up an atmosphere of psychosis, in direct relation to the perpetual challenges of shaky external events: the communal violence in 1969 throughout the Malay Peninsula, the British military withdrawal from Singapore in 1971, the oil crisis in 1973–4, the Vietnamese expansion after 1975, the rise of protectionism and the international economic recession which affected the region from 1978–80 onwards. The concept of survival became the linch-pin of Singapore's internal cohesion and of its intangible independence, endlessly repeated in its foreign policy.[3] This strategy had three inseparable components: an iron will to live as an independent sovereign state, a determined capacity to make this a reality and compel respect for it, and a systematic adjustment to external fluctuations, with a maximum use of every opportunity to consolidate national security and viability.[4]

For Singapore the theme of economic survival regulates all domestic activities by virtue of a strict order of priorities according to which all demands and responses of the local society have to be canalised. This order varies according to the combination of internal and external variables, the external ones weighing with particular force in an

1. Chan Heng Chee (419); Morrison & Suhrke (335); Onn Wee-hock (179); Seah Chee Meow, 'The survival strategy: . . .' in Mauzy (ed.) (330), pp. 196–204.
2. 'Singapore's survival is the paramount concern of the PAP rulers. Everything else, including political norms, have to be subordinated to that' (R.K. Vasil, *Governing Singapore*, Singapore: Eastern UP, 1984, p. 143).
3. Seah Chee Meow, 'Singapore's foreign policy in Southeast Asia: . . .', *Pacific Community*, July 73, pp. 535–51, and 'Singapore 1979: . . .', *Asian Survey*, Feb. 1980, pp. 144–54.
4. Lee Kuan Yew, 'Survival for smaller nations' (speech), Canberra: National Press Club, 16 Mar. 65; G.G. Thompson (ed.) (395); 'Viability is not a simple or absolute concept, but a relative quality, which varies and fluctuates with circumstances' (E.C. Paul [355], p. 387).

emporium that relies so greatly on its regional neighbourhood, as on the rest of the world.[5] External challenges of one kind or another have justified and legitimised most of the measures decreed by the PAP, even those affecting the freedom and the conduct of individuals. The citizens of Singapore are first and foremost social beings, and their quest for excellence and the attainment of their maximum potential as individuals corresponds to the greater objective of making society also work to its greatest capacity. The working of every cog reflects the incessant struggle for survival; the social atmosphere produced is one of institutionalised urgency. And in order to anticipate any trouble or threat which could be damaging to the city-state's prosperity, the authorities and the whole population must always know where the 'devil' is likely to come from![6]

Because of its size, Singapore is undoubtedly right to prepare for every possible threat, but this attitude is not too well perceived by the neighbouring countries, which do not understand — or do not wish to understand — the motives behind the PAP's vocal campaigns to keep the islanders in a state of constant vigilance.[7] Malaysia has often been irritated by this attitude; on its part Singapore has seen itself as besieged in the midst of the Malay world, and has turned to Israeli advisers to organise its defence. At regular intervals Kuala Lumpur and Jakarta have reiterated their peaceful intentions, and have officially interpreted Singapore's survival policy as being addressed to potential threats from outside the region. However, the development of ASEAN cooperation and the impact of the crises in Indochina have contributed to a better understanding of the specific demands made by the island-state in relation to its own security.

Since 1978-9, Singapore's new economic strategy of moving into high-tech industrialisation has produced new requirements if its continued prosperity is to be guaranteed, and this move from quantitative

5. S.H. Alatas, 'Modernization and national consciousness' in Ooi Jin Bee (ed.) (457), pp. 216–32.
6. 'In the field of security, it is necessary to infuse a sense of urgency and preparation into the minds of the population to enable them to meet the challenges ahead, which can result from external developments beyond their control' (Lau Teik Soon, 'Singapore and political stability', *Pacific Community*, Jan. 72, p. 380). See also Lee Boon Hiok, 'Singapore: reconciling the survival ideology with the achievement concept', *Southeast Asian Affairs*, 1978, pp. 229–44.
7. 'Singapore may find itself surrounded by a hostile sea of obscurantist and xenophobic forces which will necessitate very dramatic measures for survival' (Lee Kuan Yew, 11 Dec. 65, in Josey [439], 1st edn, p. 293).

intensive development (in the 1970s) to more qualitative development today, combined with the arrival on the labour market of a young generation which has known nothing but the comforts of growth, could cause a certain weariness to affect the ideology of survival. The semi-reversal suffered by the PAP at the polls in the elections of December 1986, the delicate question of the succession to Lee Kuan Yew, and the economic recession of 1985–6 have together created the ideal conditions for the regime to renew its attachment to Singapore's survival ideology, notably on the occasion of the twentieth anniversary of independence and then in the run-up to the elections of September 1988. The PAP has strongly reaffirmed that Singapore's national wellbeing depends on its remaining in government. National and PAP ideologies are inextricably mixed, especially on the issue of the island's survival. Since 1965, the histories of the Singaporean 'nation' and of the PAP have become very closely associated with each other.[4]

Monopoly of power and dirigisme in the name of social welfare

Authoritarian economic and social planning

After 1963–5, the first generation of PAP leaders concentrated all power in their hands. They had just eliminated the main Communist-inspired opposition force, the Barisan Socialis, and now cultivate their image as the only political force able to tackle the dangers of stagnation or decline immediately after independence. Society had to yield to the absolute priority of the emporium's survival, and thus to the particular political entity — the PAP — which was its incarnation. The party's cohesion, discipline, centralisation and professional skills were indispensable if the vulnerability of such a small territory was to be overcome.

The economic successes achieved in the first years after independence rallied a large majority of the population to the regime, and it was a powerful incentive to the PAP to be able to implement whatever measures it judged appropriate for Singapore's development: hence the installation of a form of dirigisme and authoritarian planning. Economic growth and social transformation materialised so rapidly during the 1970s that the PAP's electorate and a majority of Singaporeans became convinced of the 'genius' of their Prime Minister and his government.[9]

8. Chang Heng Chee (420 and 421); Pang Chong Lian (460).
9. R.K. Vasil, *Governing Singapore*, op. cit., pp. 114–53.

The PAP has justified its monopoly of power up to the present time by the need to consolidate the city-state's initial achievements (still barely a quarter of a century old); by denying itself the right to commit errors (a luxury which no city-state can easily afford); by finding the optimum solution to every one of the challenges that have to be faced periodically; and by refusing to allow any questioning of the political order. The PAP has identified itself as the guarantor of stability and prosperity.[10]

The centralisation and consolidation of power by the PAP and its predilection for long-term action are the essence of Lee Kuan Yew's own political philosophy. Ever since his historic speech to the Malayan Forum in London in January 1950, Lee does not seem to have deviated from certain golden rules like pragmatic socialism, the rejection of Communism, multiracialism and a mode of government in which the leading figures are men inspired by a lofty view of the role of public authority, to the service of which they are completely devoted.[11] The decisive role of the small group of friends who have been close to Lee since the start of the PAP, and have been able to respond with tremendous success to the initial crises and challenges on both the internal and external fronts, could only lead to an extreme centralisation of power, where all important decisions, political and social control and the instruments of national mobilisation are in the hands of the Prime Minister and his closest advisers.[12]

The building of a technocratic state

The government of Singapore is based on a technocratic state apparatus ('administrative state') which clearly reflects those national priorities described above. The strong and coherent PAP élite is composed of senior civil servants and politicians, all carefully selected for their education and competence — and most of them are inspired by a true personal devotion to Lee Kuan Yew and his closest colleagues.[13] Lee himself estimated in 1967–8 that the ruling élite consisted of about 200 individuals, assisted at the managerial and operational level by 2,000

10. Goh Chok Tong, 'Importance of continued good government', *Coll. Speeches*, Singapore, Feb. 81, 4, 8. And see *ST*, 21 Aug. and 20, 23 & 25 Dec. 84.
11. Josey (439), 1st edn, p. 34, and (442), ch. 6.
12. The expulsion of the young Secretary-General of the NTUC, Lim Chee Onn, in Apr. 1983 and the dismissal of the President of the Republic, Devan Nair, in Apr. 1985 give further support to this contention.
13. P.S.J. Chen (423); G.W.H. Chen (422); Chen and Fawcett (424); K.E. Shaw (ed.) (471).

others. 'If', he added, 'you kill the 200 at the top and the 2,000 at the base with a single blow, you will have destroyed Singapore.'[14]

To have the freedom to put a planned welfare society in the place of the non-egalitarian laissez-faire policy of colonial times, and establish a charter for political stability leading to economic and social development, the PAP has considerably reduced both the possibility of social conflict and the resistance of the traditional élites. Government action and keeping the PAP in power do not depend so much on the leadership's capacity to respond to individual or particular demands from the island society; the PAP government promotes its own perception of the city-state's overall interests, both internal and external. The decision-making process has thus become, over the years, more 'administrative' than 'political'.[15]

The depoliticisation of Singapore's citizens was made possible by the elimination of the Barisan Socialis (the political party to the left of the PAP) and the consequent absence of an organised opposition, as a centre of trade unionism and of social and public expression. An obvious redistribution of the fruits of economic growth has also taken place, improving the collective social wellbeing of the population — the local human resources are the only capital which truly belong to a small city-state.[16] Such a redistribution of wealth has favoured the rise of a numerous middle class but may have brought less benefit to the grass-roots workers, who accepted low wages till the 1980s and have thus made an enormous contribution to the rapid industrialisation of Singapore. However, a majority of the population — the somewhat materialistic Chinese — have seemed well satisfied with the island's economic success and the spectacular improvement in their living standards over a span of less than twenty years.

At the top level of society, the political influence of old traditional business has also declined significantly. The slow-down of entrepot trade and the diversification of the economy have made necessary a rather large and interventionist state administration, which is more independent from the traditional Chinese commercial and banking community and from old colonial business interests than it was before 1965. The private

14. Josey (439), 1st edn, p. 381.
15. H. Crouch (278), pp. 13–23; Quah, Chang and Seah (466).
16. 'For such a small state, the goal of flexibility to external changes has meant the internal centralisation of power and control by one aggressive political party, and the close control of labour demands to ensure the continued attractiveness of Singapore to foreign capital' (P.D. Beaulieu [250], p. 276).

sector is dominated today by foreign and transnational companies whose activities usually embrace world markets and which therefore rely on looser political contacts and interaction with individual government administrations — in this Singapore is no exception.[17] Furthermore, the integrity of Singaporean civil servants and politicians has been elevated to the status of a dogma; this was the achievement of the first generation of PAP leaders, who included only very few businessmen. The city-state has been among the countries where institutionalised large or small-scale corruption is least prevalent. Remembering the troubled times of David Marshall's or Lim Yew Hock's governments, Lee Kuan Yew was persuaded that any development of corruption would undermine the foundations of the city-state's success and its international reputation.[18] The year 1960 saw the passing of the Prevention of Corruption Act and the setting up of the Corrupt Practices Investigation Bureau. For example, in 1975 the Minister of the Environment was severely condemned for a fraud which would have been considered normal in any other ASEAN country.[19]

Unlike in Hong Kong, daily life in Singapore feels the heavy hand of state authority. The Singapore Civil Service consisted in 1987 of fifteen ministries and more than eighty public agencies, employing 187,000 civil servants; this was equivalent to 14.9% of the active population, or about 7.1% of the total.[20] The constant problem is how to balance the smallness of the island's resources, how to remedy the very modest role of local private entrepreneurs and the enormous power of transnational companies, and how to create an instrument of efficient intervention in case of a recession or a needed restructuring of the economy. As in Korea or Taiwan, state initiative has played an important role in the industrialisation process: in Singapore, the state directly controls around 100 of the most important enterprises and about sixty others through holdings supported by the Development Bank of Singapore or the national trading company, Intraco. Senior civil servants, ministers and former ministers have seats on the boards of hundreds of public and private firms.[21]

17. Quah Jon Sien (465) and 'Public bureaucracy in Singapore' in You Poh Seng and Lim (239), pp. 295–8.
18. Quah (464).
19. Ong Pang Boon, Min. of Home Affairs, Prevention of Corruption Act, *Legislative Assembly Debates*, 1st Sess., vol. 12, 13 Feb. 60, cols 376–7. *FEER*, 6 Sept. 74, p. 123 ('The Mr Clean of Asia'). *FEER*, *Asia Yearbk*, 1976, p. 271.
20. Min. of Culture, Govt Directory, Singapore, 1984.
21. *ST*, 6 Apr. 85; Linda Low, 'Public enterprises in Singapore' in You Poh Seng and

Singapore and a convergence among ASEAN's political regimes

Is Singapore completely free to choose the nature of its political regime? If there is a certain convergence among the political systems of the ASEAN member-states, to what extent does the PAP contribute to it?

To the first of these questions events have already given an answer. The dangers of communalism and Communism are the two most obvious bottlenecks to the decision-making of the ASEAN governments, in both domestic and regional affairs. Neither Kuala Lumpur nor Jakarta would tolerate the destabilisation of Singaporean society by either of these two potential dangers: they would not accept for long any major political disorder in Singapore, because of the likelihood that it would spill over into their own countries. Reciprocally, Singapore could never immunise itself against any major political instability in Malaysia or Indonesia.

It is difficult to predict how these two countries, which share Singapore's basic hostility to communalism, would react if the island-state were to choose an ultra-democratic political system in contrast to the authoritarian regimes which have been dominant so far in ASEAN: for instance the PAP's multiracial policy and its battle against corruption have already indirectly exposed some of the more glaring defects of the regimes of its neighbours, and it is by no means certain that Singapore would benefit greatly from cultivating too strongly its own distinctive brand of politics if its neighbours do not move in the same direction. Singapore has already noted how its advanced economic development is able to breed resentments in the region.

As to the second question, a certain convergence among the political regimes of ASEAN, including Singapore, is indicated in several ways.[22]

First, the constraints on national self-determination are a common denominator of the declared policies of all ASEAN leaders. The PAP eliminated Communism within its national borders, as did Malaysia in 1948–60 and Indonesia in 1965–6. It then singled out the removal of the external Communist threat as the main target of its foreign policy, and became closer to Thailand than to its immediate neighbours because of the nature of their respective perceptions of China and Vietnam. Globally, the ideology of the struggle for survival embraced by Singapore is no different in essence from its ASEAN partners' domestic

---

Lim (239), pp. 253–87; Linda Seah, 'Public enterprise and economic development' in Chen (100), pp. 129–59.

22. E.D. Solidum (475).

policies, all of which value internal stability in defiance of any political or social disorder, whether inspired by Communism or by communalism, above all else. Only the ethnic and social balance varies from one ASEAN country to another, and the city-state differs from the rest in the intensity and systematic nature of the conditions and measures it imposes on itself for maintaining domestic stability because of its small size and the PAP's determination to keep control of all the levers of power in its own hands.

Secondly, priority is given to economic development in all ASEAN countries as the major long-term instrument for achieving internal stability and defeating Communism, whether internal or external. The recognition of this priority, at least in theory, makes for easier dialogue between Singapore and its partners, notably Indonesia, which was initially the most sensitive with regard to Singaporean independence. All proclaim in similar terms that they are building new societies — the PAP's 'new society' in Singapore, Golkar's New Order in Indonesia and the UMNO's New Economic Policy in Malaysia. The three countries are laying their bets on state capitalism and a mixed economy — even in Singapore, the most liberal among them — and on an industrialisation process which depends on massive foreign investment and the export of semi-processed and manufactured products.[23]

Thirdly, the city-state can be seen in the spectrum of ASEAN regimes ranging from 'guided' democracy in Malaysia and Singapore to different forms of constitutional authoritarianism in the three other states. Everywhere in ASEAN, the exercise of power is monopolised by a dominant movement or party (or by a single autocratic family, as in Brunei), with the army playing a more or less direct role (this is even the case in Singapore, where the PAP encourages the involvement of army cadres in politics), with an embryonic or residual opposition either muzzled altogether or barely tolerated, and with occasional recourse to emergency rule, which has again been used recently in both Singapore and Malaysia. The succession to the first generation of ASEAN's charismatic leaders is another major issue: changes are still too often brought about either by *coups* or by controlled elections and constitutional reforms. In Singapore, for instance, the PAP recently initiated the project of extending the constitutional powers of the Presidency, a post which could possibly fall to Lee Kuan Yew one day.[24]

23. H.U. Luther, 'The example of Singapore' in Dahm and Draguhn (428), pp. 113–34.
24. J.B. Abueva, 'Alternative priorities in development in ASEAN countries',

Power is highly personalised in all the ASEAN states. For Singaporeans of Chinese descent, Lee is a symbolic leader and guide in the loyalist and Confucianist sense of personifying the philosophy of good government, and any functional sense of his position as Prime Minister has only a secondary ranking in the Chinese collective mentality.[25] Since coming to power, and especially in recent years, he has revealed a political character different from what one might expect from such a brilliant politician, educated in Britain and exposed to Western legal systems and the concept of parliamentary democratic rule. His conception of power seems to be derived partly from Chinese tradition, based on the conviction of a certain superiority of the East to the West; he sees the West as going through a period of decline and decadence. He is attached to the one-party system related to a so-called purely 'Asian' concept of political power and social management. This goes so far as to reproduce in Singapore a form of nepotism not unknown in other parts of Asia. Lee Kuan Yew's son Brigadier-General Lee Hsien Loong, has been propelled to the front of the political stage, and could become Lee's true successor after Goh Chok Tong has served as a transitional Prime Minister in 1990–2.[26]

The mobilisation of Singaporean society

The political philosophy of total mobilisation

Sociologists could share with political scientists the analysis of the two interdependent factors which determined the appearance in Singapore of a dirigiste government driven by the will to mobilise all the potential strength of the island society. As we have just emphasised, the fragile geopolitical situation of the city-state, arising from the gross disproportion between its physical size and the immeasurable challenges to its survival, required a governing team whose first task would be to make the emporium permanently viable, and to obtain that goal, an optimally organised and rationalised society was needed in the domestic sector. On the other hand, little attention has been paid to the correlation between this task and the smallness of the population, its concentration within

Contemporary Southeast Asia, I, 1979, pp. 141–64, and Leifer (319). On the position of the President, see *ST*, 6 Sept. & 12 Oct. 84; *FEER*, 6 Sept. 84, pp. 25–6; 11 Apr. 85, pp. 10–11; 5 Sept. 85, pp. 10 & 13.

25. T.J.S. George (432), pp. 16–31; Josey (439), 1st edn. p. 607.
26. *ST*, 29 Nov. and 20 Dec. 84, 11 May 85; *FEER*, 24 Sept. 82, pp. 16–17; 4 Oct. 84, pp. 10–11; 12 July 84, pp. 12–13; 18 Oct. 84, pp. 32–33; 11 July 85, pp. 38–9.

an area smaller than that of a large European metropolis, the absence of any significant agricultural hinterland, and the existence of a dense urban-type communications network within the island, making it possible to supervise the actual impact of any government decision with the minimum of delay: an island space of this kind makes the process of national integration much easier, and enhances the effectiveness of governmental measures adopted for the promotion of social mobilisation. It is at this exact point that the so-called convergence of the ASEAN regimes reaches its limit: here one sees the radical difference and even opposition in the quality of geographical and social territory between a tiny island of 620 km.[2] and a giant country like Indonesia — and this is only to stress here the sharpest of the contrasts between any pair of ASEAN countries.[27] The PAP has succeeded in reconciling Singapore's domestic social order and its external vulnerability by subordinating the first to the second.

Most of the external parameters with a bearing on Singapore's viability are completely outside the control of the island authorities. The durability and reliability of the factors that govern its prosperity are related to the chronic fragility of the emporium: a kind of structural fragility that arises from the fact that it is an island with mainly external economic activities but without natural resources, an agrarian base or any large internal market on which it could fall back even briefly in times of emergency. This kind of conjunctural fragility depends on the relative stability of its regional environment, but it also remains at the mercy of unexpected and violent events. The external environment thus calls for constant vigilance and adaptability.

In view of the grave crises of 1957–65, the PAP probably had no choice but to make sure that it controlled every facet of social activity in the island. Its aim was thus to remove all elements of potential uncertainty and all internal weaknesses in society, which a destabilising force from outside could exploit. Parallel to the most judicious possible management of external dependences and of unforeseeable circumstances, the slogan of a 'rugged society' launched by the PAP made it clear that the survival of the city-state depended on the cohesiveness of its society and the infallibility of its government.[28] This strategy is all the more indispensable because up till 1965 any notion of state and nation had been lacking in an island populated by immigrants of

27. Quah Jon Sien in You Poh Seng and Lim (239), p. 307, and *Southeast Asian Affairs*, 1977, pp. 207–8. Seah Chee Meow in You Poh Seng (239).
28. P.A. Busch (418), pp. 33–4; C.E. Morrison (334), p. 230; M. & W. Neville (456).

different ethnic origins, who had never even considered the possibility of an independent Singapore. Lee Kuan Yew took up this theme when he declared on 13 July 1965: 'I would say that our best chance lies in a very rigorously organised society. There is no other outcome. Numerous small societies like ours have survived . . . what is necessary is a highly disciplined, determined and educated society, ready to work hard. Create such a community and you will see it survive and prosper for thousands of years.'[29]

Lee cannot be described as an ideologue, but the mobilisation of Singaporean society — given its exceptional geopolitical situation — was the result of his gift of persuasion. The psychosis of the critical period 1957–65 and the first economic successes of the post-independence years made this all the more persuasive.[30] Without using the whole panoply of means of coercion found in most other states of the region or in authoritarian regimes elsewhere — but keeping open the possibility of using the Internal Security Act at any time — the PAP quickly earned the reward of massive support and trust from the population. Under the banner of a so-called democratic, non-doctrinaire socialism,[31] its actions have been based on several simple underlying precepts.

First, external challenges of various kinds justify a permanent attitude of pragmatism and adaptability. Political dogmatism can result in paralysis when there is a need for action, and those in power should be able to revise their decisions if circumstances change. Secondly, through state authoritarian rule and intervention the appropriate responses could be found for national cohesion and for the reform of a society originally created to serve the interests of the colonial power. The authority of the virtuous government depends on the willingness of its citizens (the majority of whom are Chinese) to give their collective support to those who provide them with stability, employment, housing and social services, and these citizens might feel less attracted to individual freedoms as these are understood in parliamentary democracies.[32] Thirdly, the system of social mobilisation places a high value on work, effort,

---

29. Josey (439), 1st edn, pp. 486–7. See also Lee Khoon Choy, 'Creating a strong united community', *Coll. Speeches* (Singapore), 27 June 81, vol. 5, 1, and Tony Tan, 'A more cohesive and united nation', *Coll. Speeches*, 11 Apr. 81, vol. 4, 11.
30. Goh Chok Tong, 'Singapore must never allow anarchy to return', *Coll. Speeches*, 16 June 81, vol. 5, 3.
31. Goh Keng Swee (124); Devan Nair (453, 454, 455).
32. Clammer in Gosling and Lim (290), vol. 2, p. 280; T. Geiger (123).

ingenuity and talent — once again, the quintessential characteristics of the Chinese immigrant. In addition, it guarantees equality of duties and rights to all citizens, regardless of race, religion or social class, and here the divergence between theory and practice is certainly less evident in Singapore than it is elsewhere in the region. Finally, the construction of the Singaporean state produces technocrats who identify with the ideal of Confucianist ethics; in other words an administration which cares above all that the population should conform to the rules of good social conduct defined by the elders (Lee Kuan Yew and the first generation of PAP leaders). A Chinese cultural tradition of the mandarin type contributes to this regulation of daily life and of morality, which the great majority of Singaporeans seemed to accept so far. The PAP thus seeks to rally all the elements which make up the society, and the plan of Toh Chin Chye to transform the PAP into a national movement was a significant illustration of this.[33]

The organisation of public campaigns of mobilisation, which are held annually on the initiative of the Prime Minister's office, gives a vivid illustration of this will to organise the whole mass of the population. From 1958 to 1982, sixty-six such campaigns were launched, dealing with a wide variety of issues, and always emphasising certain weaknesses in the internal social order.[34] The purpose was to change collective behaviour and progressively create a Singaporean citizenship, using imagery and symbolism designed to suppress undesirable attitudes and promote a more disciplined and rational society.[35]

First application: a 'guided democracy'

Maintenance of political stability at any price, the controlled expression of any opposition, strict definition of social relations — these are some of the elements which best describe the PAP regime which has been in power now for a quarter of a century.

33. PAP, 'The party', 15th anniversary celebration souvenir, Singapore, 1969; 'PAP 1954–79', 25th anniversary, Singapore, 1979.
34. The themes were productivity, courtesy, public transport, cleanliness, family planning, health, work, speaking Mandarin, the economics of energy sources, the limitations of Western values, elderly people . . . Lee Kuan Yew, 'Courtesy, way to a better life', 27 June 81, *Speeches*, vol. 5, 1; S. Dhanabalan, 'Courtesy can succeed if sustained over time', *Speeches*, vol. 5, 3.
35. Quah in You Poh Seng and Lim (239), pp. 305–5 & 309–10. Tham Kok Weng, *National campaigns in Singapore politics*, Singapore: Nat. Univ. 1983.

Stability at home: a political priority

When the thirtieth anniversary of the PAP's foundation and the twentieth anniversary of independence were commemorated respectively in 1984 and 1985, the scourge of instability in an ethnically plural, politically divided and economically vulnerable society, which Singapore had suffered from before 1965, was deliberately recalled to public attention. According to Singapore's leaders, internal fragility is a luxury which the city-state cannot afford, except at the risk of sinking into decline or disappearing altogether; the social and political stability of the small republic, and of its neighbours, is seen as the best guarantee of long-term economic development and an indispensable element in the stability of the whole region. The stability of Malaysia cannot be separated from that of Singapore, and the social cohesion of the city-state could act as a safety-valve in the event of serious troubles erupting in its immediate neighbourhood, as occurred in Malaysia in 1969.

The primacy accorded to stability dominates the political life and social order of the island: Singapore has adopted a constitutional system close to the British model but limited by numerous restrictions implemented by the regime. As he explained in a well-known speech at London's Royal Institute of International Affairs (Chatham House) in 1962, Lee Kuan Yew does not believe that it is possible to transpose parliamentary democracy pure and simple to Asia.[36] At the end of the colonial period, civilian society had first of all to undergo a structural change to enable independence to become viable — in a way that would be credible both within and outside the island-state.

Are the majority of Singaporeans, being Chinese, less interested in individual political freedoms than in the ability of the government to assure them of a noticeable improvement in their living standards? It is open to anyone to believe or to disbelieve this analysis, but it is the philosophy of government which the PAP would have them accept, and which Lee Kuan Yew seems to have put into practice in a fairly reasonable and socially beneficial way, although the same philosophy has brought some other regimes to the threshhold of dictatorship.[37] Anyway, categorising the Singaporean regime is not one of the aims of this

---

36. George (432); Josey (438), pp. 46–53; G.G. Thompson (ed.) (395); R.K. Vasil (480), pp. 71–90.
37. 'It would probably be more correct to say that most Singaporeans of Chinese descent are much less interested in democracy than they are in humanistic reasonable government by a leadership elite' (Lee Kuan Yew in Josey (439, 1st edn, p. 605).

book. What is certain is that the emporium's chronic vulnerability, its delicate geopolitical position at the heart of the Malay world, and the very serious domestic political disturbances from 1957 till 1963, left the PAP governing team with almost no alternative but to go into high crisis management and form a kind of supreme command, as in the army, at least in the first years after independence.[38]

Did this reaction, amply justified at first, have to become institutionalised in an authoritarian style of government right up to the 1980s and perhaps even into the 1990s? Opinions differ. For some, the ideology of the permanent struggle for survival reflects the very real dangers which punctuate the life of any emporium; for others, it only symbolises the PAP's determination to stay in power by promoting its paramount ideology into something almost sacred.

The clear reverse suffered by the PAP in the 1984 elections, the problem of succession to the generation currently in power, and the economic recession of 1984–6 prodded Lee Kuan Yew into reasserting his own convictions on the limits to democracy: the Prime Minister and his closest colleagues often state that the so-called system of democratic representation — 'one person, one vote' — is ill-suited to the kinds of constraint bearing on the viability of the city-state.[39] Before and after the elections of 1988, this kind of utterance seemed genuinely to reflect the situation in the real world.

Control of the opposition
The elimination of the most radical opponents by applying special emergency measures in 1961–3, and the vigilance of the authorities against any signs of their re-emergence, discourage would-be detractors of the regime. The permanent need to defend the viability of the emporium and consolidate the economic and social success which were possible after 1965 motivated the rejection of every sign of opposition, which was systematically accused of risking the very basis of the city-state's prosperity and stability.

Each time it has had the chance to express itself through elections, about a quarter of the electorate has refused to give its endorsement

38. 'The Government will have to be strong and decisive with the right to pronounce unchallenged on a wide range of values. It is demanding that this be accepted as the core value', Asian Working Party on State and Nation Building, 1971, p. 56.
39. George (432), p. 114 (Chatham House lecture, 1962). *ST*, *Election 84*, Nov.–Dec. 84. *FEER*, 13 Dec. 84, p. 11; 27 Dec. 84, pp. 12–13; 21 Feb. 85, p. 23; 11 Apr. 85, p. 28; 15 Aug. 85, pp. 10–11.

to the PAP, but the political groups which the PAP had to face — the Workers' Party, the Singapore Democratic Party, the Barisan Socialis and the United People's Front — were and still are divided. Both the numbers of activists they can mobilise and the financial resources they can command are modest. None of them can appear very credible or constructive as long as the PAP government continues to be seen as the architect of two and a half decades of remarkable economic and social development.[40]

The leader of the Workers' Party, Jeyaratnam, entered parliament in 1981, and both he and the SDP leader, Chiam See Tong, were re-elected in 1984 — as representatives of the legal opposition. The 1984 result was accompanied by a loss for the PAP of 12% of the vote. Clearly things were not going well for the regime, and there was a need to evolve and abandon its rigidity. The younger generation, used to the economic success of the 1970s and early '80s, cannot be expected to spend their whole lives in a state of perpetual anxiety over the future of the city-state. Also society as a whole, which is experiencing the change-over of generations within the ruling élite and is looking, for a second and third industrial revolution, needs flexibility if imagination and innovation are to flourish.[41] On the eve of the 1984 elections, the PAP was keenly aware of this situation, and went so far as eventually to modify the electoral code to create an artificial parliamentary opposition through the expedient of two or three PAP-elected candidates withdrawing in favour of opposition candidates who had obtained the best results![42] All the same, the aggressive political campaign which the PAP waged against Jeyaratnam and Chiam showed that the Lee government was far from being well-disposed towards genuine opposition, small as it might be.[43] This impression seems to be confirmed by the disappearance in July 1985 of the newspaper, the *Singapore Monitor*, a further episode in the inexorable process of concentration in the local press, already heralded by the demise of the *Eastern Sun* and *Singapore Herald* in 1979 and the merging of the *Monitor* and *Straits Times* in

40. Seah Chee Meow in You Poh Seng and Lim (239), p. 245.
41. See also chapter 8.
42. *ST*, 25 Dec. 84. Such a withdrawal of candidates should have occurred in the December 1984 election, if the PAP had won 79 seats. Ch. Amendment to the Parliamentary Election Act, Sec. 51A.
43. *ST*, 29 Nov., 17 & 21–4 Dec. 84. *FEER*, 11 Apr. 85, p. 28; 30 May 85, p. 21; 3 Oct. 85, p. 8; 10 Oct. 85, p. 13; 11 July 85, pp. 38–9. *Asiaweek*, 4 Jan. 85, pp. 7–10; *Newsweek*, 11 Feb. 85, pp. 6–10.

1984.[44] Parallel with this, the government continued, through the Newspaper and Printing Press Act of 1974, to exert a direct control over the press by means of its right to inspect the financial management of newspapers and nominate some of their shareholders, and to withdraw the authorisation to print and publish without notice. Internal security and the defence of the national identity are among the reasons which the authorities invoke.

Periodically — and tirelessly — the PAP launches vigorous attacks against even the most embryonic show of opposition thought, rightly or wrongly, to be connected somehow with the pro-Communist agitation of the pre-independence period which those in power believe to be still latent today. As already noted in the previous section, the election campaign of 1987–8 was once again the occasion for violent and ingenious attacks by the PAP against the opposition and for the prolonged detention of several individuals under the Internal Security Act. Subsequently, the PAP started to enforce some legal restrictions against the foreign press. Some newspapers and periodicals like the *Asian Wall Street, Asiaweek* and the *Far Eastern Economic Review* have been accused of interfering in Singapore's domestic politics, and their circulation was suspended or limited within the city-state.

The control of social relations
Labour. Up till 1961–3, Malayan trade unionism was associated with the anti-colonial independence struggle, but had also fallen very much under the influence of the Malayan Communist Party. The official demise of the Barisan Socialis after 1961–3 and the end of its representation in Singapore's parliament was inevitably followed by a depoliticisation of local society and a lessening of conflict in social relations: on these possibly depended the success of the island's early industrialisation strategy, based as it was on labour discipline and modest wages in order to attract substantial foreign investment. To safeguard its viability at this stage, the city-state could not afford any political disorder as in the period before independence, or disruptive British-style trade unionism.[45]

The National Trade Union Congress (NTUC), which in 1965 replaced the Singapore Association of Trade Unions with its strong links

44. *AWSJ*, 28 Nov. 84. *FEER*, 21 May 85, p. 75; 26 July 84, 35–6; 18 Oct. 84, p. 83, 25 July 85, p. 14. Clutterbuck (274), pp. 341–3; Josey (438), 2nd edn, pp. 109–13.
45. N. Heyzer in Chen (ed.) (100), pp. 105–28; Pan Eng Fong and Tan Chwee Huat in ibid., pp. 227–39; Pan Eng Fong (182).

to the radical left, became from that time onwards a mere sub-organisation for the PAP as the party in power.[46] Possessing no freedom of action in the normal spheres such as wage negotiation, it sought to fill the void in developing various social services for the work-force, e.g. cooperatives, transport, insurance and travel. These restrictions on the social rights of labour seem to have been generally accepted by a majority of the active population for as long as the PAP has been able to get rid of unemployment (since 1971–3), to keep inflation very low, and to activate important social programmes which are accessible — and of benefit — to all: public housing, public health, schools and higher education.

Any disagreement with this new social system has been met with extreme inflexibility by the government. In 1969, workers in the naval dockyard slowed down production in a bid to retain their right to work overtime — Lee Kuan Yew did not hesitate to fire them all, citing charges of sabotage and high treason. In 1974, agitation once again flared up in this sector and received the support of the University Students' Union; arrests, trials and sanctions swiftly halted this supposed emergence of a new left wing.[47] Certain trade union leaders had made a show at the time of opposing the government's dirigisme in industrial relations: a reform in 1978 opened the control of the NTUC to non-trade unionists (in other words, to PAP cadres), and the NTUC secretary-general Devan Nair, a valued companion of Lee Kuan Yew up till his startling departure in 1985, was endowed with a power of veto over the appointment of future trade union leaders, sector by sector. The NTUC and its affiliated unions have become powerless to defy political decision-making. Lim Chee Onn, a young technocrat who was appointed to head the NTUC in place of Devan Nair in 1979, had to face this reality; in 1983 his rise was abruptly terminated when the government did not hesitate to dismiss him and appoint Ong Teong Cheong as his successor.[48] Another example was the authoritarian freezing of wage rises between 1985 and 1988. It was imposed by government decision following rapid wage rises in 1980–3 and the economic recession of 1984–6, to the dissatisfaction of many people.

46. NTUC, *Why labour must go modern*, Singapore: NTUC seminar, 1970; Nair (453, 454 and 455). See also various issues of the NTUC's publication *Perjuangan*.
47. *ST*, 25 Nov. 74.
48. 'If the union leadership challenges the political leadership, the political leadership must triumph, if necessary, by changing the ground rules to thwart the challenge' (Lee Kuan Yew, *FEER*, 30 Nov. 79).

The urban milieu. The drive to discipline and unify the whole of society is also found in the urban environment of the city-state itself. Before 1965, professional associations and Chinese secret societies had maintained sharp divisions between ethnic groups and social classes. After independence, their place has been taken — as in China — by some 175 Community Centres (Committees related exclusively to particular districts) and some 300 Residents' Committees (consultative committees of citizens).[49]

These committees, with permanent members nominated by the PAP, are the expression of 'democratic centralisation' of power rather than direct participation by the masses in the management of local and national affairs. They are firmly established in the HDB (Housing Development Board) public housing districts which provide homes for 75% of all Singaporeans.[50] They perform many civic and social activities, and play a role in the circulation, interpretation and implementation of the PAP's decisions. As grassroot units for the controlled organisation of society, they influence the social atmosphere and thus people's reactions. But their basic task is to cultivate in the population a strong identification with the fundamental values and rules for the island's survival and viability.

Singapore's internal and external security: the affirmation of a national identity

An emporium obviously does not have a national or 'state' identity of its own. It is an economic entity, artificially established in an alien territory and totally dedicated to its international, outward-looking vocation. Singapore was in no way predestined to become a sovereign state, and in its unique situation the PAP had few models to turn to for inspiration as to how best to make its independence truly effective. Rapid and sustained economic success was probably the only way to build up, in the long run, some kind of functional autonomy for such a special territory.

Having to govern a very heterogeneous society of immigrants without a common language, culture or political allegiance, the PAP could not in the long run rally the population under the 'welfare state' banner alone. Planning social order through material wellbeing does not

49. Peter Chen in You Poh Seng and Lim (239), pp. 315–38.
50. The 75% of Singaporeans, mainly of modest or middle incomes, who have acquired HDB apartments on preferential terms. P. Chen (100), pp. 315–38; R. Hassan (ed.) (434); G. Chen (422).

necessarily lead to a national cohesion which no power can destroy — i.e. to a code of collective values with which the whole population can voluntarily agree to identify. In the view of Lee Kuan Yew and his close cabinet friends, the struggle for survival, guided democracy and redistribution of growth had to serve as a key investment in the future in order to forge a national identity, a Singaporean citizenship.

The building of a multiracial society, which would assume responsibility for national defence, is seen as the ultimate key to securing the city-state internally and externally.

Multiracialism and national cohesion

Multiracialism as the cornerstone of the Singaporean nation
Chinese, Malays, Indians, Eurasians and Europeans have always been in continuous contact with eachother in the daily life of Singapore. Without a solid cohabitation of races, languages, cultures and creeds, social cohesion can run out of control in case of communal unrest whether of internal or external origin, as in 1964 and 1969 respectively.

The creation of a multiracial society is first and foremost an objective linked to internal security and stability. It also reflects the concern to make Singaporean society resistant to any new wave of communalist agitation in, or from, Malaysia. Any attempt at oppressive domination of the Malay minority in the island (15%) by the Chinese majority would be unacceptable to both Indonesia and Malaysia, and Singapore is very well aware of the acute anti-Chinese sensitivities of its two neighbours and their desire to protect the Malay populations and culture.[51] Finally, a frank and ambitious multiracial policy should be able to create a broad social consensus among the population at home, and somehow to challenge the communalist discrimination which it sees being practised in Indonesia or Malaysia. Multiracialism has become one of the major components of Singapore's efforts at national integration.[52]

Ever since the early 1950s, Lee Kuan Yew and his friends have repeatedly pointed at communalism as the most serious cause of conflict and division in Malaysia. The demand for an effective multiracial policy goes back to Lee's speech to the Malayan Forum in London in January 1950 and to the basic doctrine of the PAP enunciated in 1954. For ten years (1955–65) and above all while Singapore formed part of the

51. G. Benjamin (416); P.A. Busch (418).
52. J. Clammer (426), pp. 107–17.

Federation, the PAP never ceased to campaign for a Malaysian and not a Malay Malaysia, with no racial distinction or discrimination.[53]

Since 1966, the independent government of Singapore has opted for a very different road compared to Malaysia by promoting a multiracial society that would cut down any communalist or Communist revival locally. Unlike the legislation passed in Malaysia, a set of laws guarantees the same rights and obligations for all the ethnic, linguistic and religious elements in Singaporean society, and recognises no special privileges for any one of them. The strict equality of all citizens under the law has prevailed over racial discrimination, which is seen as an all too dangerous source of tension between the ethnic majority and the minorities. Furthermore, communalist agitation of any kind is considered as a direct threat to the security of Singapore, and severe penalties can await trouble-makers.[54] Having consolidated its grip on the levers of decision-making with the passage of time, the PAP has gambled on a transition to a multiracial society, at first glance legal and constitutional in character, but also using some more decisive instruments of national mobilisation.

Building a genuine multiracial society is a long and difficult process. If the Indian minority, small in numbers but strong in professional achievements is relatively well integrated into the island society, the Malays find themselves much more marginal: this is one major structural problem delaying a genuine social cohesion, and which is far from being resolved.

Multiracialism in the symbols of the nation
In creating a multiracial island society, Singapore has used both classic symbols of the nation-state and other key instruments of national cohesion, notably education and defence. All the national symbols —

53. 'The first problem we face is that of racial harmony between Chinese and Malays . . . The prerequisite of Malayan independence is the existence of a Malayan society, not Malay, not Malayan Chinese, not Malayan Indian, not Malayan Eurasian, but Malayan, one that embraces the various races already in the country' (Lee Kuan Yew, speech to the Malayan Forum, London, Jan. 1950). Rajaratnam, 'The cultural approach to politics', and Toh Chin Chye, 'Politics in plural societies', *Petir*, PAP, Sept. 58 & Aug. 60.
54. Sedition Ordinance, *Singapore Gazette* (Acts), Act no. 3, sec. 4, 14 Jan. 66. *Parliamentary Debates*, Singapore, vol. 25, 16 Mar. 67, cols 1257–60. Lee Khoon Choy, *National culture in a multiracial society*, Singapore: Min. of Culture, 1967. Rajaratnam, 'Building a genuinely Singapore community', *The Mirror*, 9 June 69, p. 1.

starting with the flag, the colours of which are inspired by those of its two neighbours — try to consolidate the city-state's multiracial identity and to counter-balance the preponderance of the Chinese in favour of the ethnic minorities. The first President of the Republic, Yusuf bin Iskak, was a Malay, and his two successors, Sheares and Nair, were respectively Eurasian and Indian. A Chinese, Wee Kim Wee, was appointed in September 1985. Of the four official languages, 'Bahasa Malaysia' figures as a sort of 'national' language because of its use in the Singapore anthem, which is not translated into the other local languages.

The Chinese have been deliberately under-represented in those government departments which contribute to the manufactured image of Singapore conveyed to the outside world. Malays are particularly numerous in the police, the army and the judiciary (a legacy from the colonial regime); however, following the communal troubles of 1969, the government has barred access for the Malays to key positions in the army and police; the PAP and the Chinese majority were unable to tolerate the idea that national security could be challenged by minority communalism which would eventually turn for support to Kuala Lumpur or Jakarta. Indians are over-represented in the diplomatic service, right up to the top most level: one outstanding example was Dhanabalan, who succeeded Rajaratnam as Minister of Foreign Affairs in the 1980s. Even if its ASEAN neighbours tend to regard Singapore as a Chinese emporium in a 'Malay ocean', they often have to negotiate with non-Chinese representatives of the Singapore government.

Education and multiracialism

It is more true in Singapore than in most other countries that the future depends on the young generation. More than half the population are under twenty-eight years old, and more than a quarter are still receiving education or a training of some kind. Education is one of the government's priorities and is the most important budget after defence.

The maximisation of its human resources and skills — the island's only asset — has a double dimension. First, there is the economic dimension, which is very much related to the necessarily rapid development and growth in the 1970s and '80s, and is linked too with the current transition to advanced services and high technologies through all kinds of labour training and upgrading programmes. Then there is a political dimension through the inculcation, from primary school onwards, of the essential national values as a guarantee for the long-term survival and secure viability of the city-state.[55]

Multilingualism and national cohesion

Multiracialism and multilingualism have evolved in a single direction, namely towards neither Communism nor communalism of Chinese inspiration, but an integration of all citizens trying to lead on to a true Singaporean national identity.

Bilingualism was introduced in schools in 1966. The core of instruction — at least 70% — is in English which, unlike the three other languages, has no ethnic flavour; it creates a more egalitarian means of communication between all Singaporeans, and of course is indispensable as a means of fulfilling the emporium's international vocation. On the other hand, each citizen's mother-tongue and its Asian cultural backing are not neglected: here the policy is to preserve a sense of Asian identity and self-expression for all, and to resist or reject certain decadent aspects of Western society transmitted by the English language and media.[56]

Outside the family circle and the most modest homes, English is dominant everywhere. This phenomenon is all the more marked since the authorities favoured, up till the beginning of the 1980s, a certain lessening in the use of the local Chinese dialects. Lee Kuan Yew had absorbed the lesson of the 1950s and '60s when the anglophone wing of the PAP had to fight against the pro-Communist opposition of the left wing, whose language and culture were purely Chinese. The PAP considered it too dangerous and destabilising in a plural society to leave the definition of the official languages and the content of education subject to communalist politicisation.[57] Through the promotion of bilingualism, the PAP set itself the task of tackling the ascendancy of Chinese dialects — Hokkien, Cantonese, Teochew, Hainanese — and

55. Lee Kuan Yew, *New bearings in our education system*, Singapore: Min. of Culture, 1966–7; Min. of Education, *Progress in education*, Singapore, 1959–65; Tan Peng Boo, *Education in Singapore*, Singapore: Educational Publication Bureau, 1969. See also John S. Quah, *Southeast Asian Affairs*, 1977, p. 212. The dozen manuals for the six primary school years expound all Singapore's nation building themes: Min. of Education, *Education for living*, Singapore, 1978.

56. Eddie Koa, *A sociolinguistic profile of Singapore*, Singapore: Nat. Univ., Dept. of Sociology, 1976; E. Afendras and E. Kuo (eds) (429); *FEER*, 22 Mar. 84, pp. 19–30.

57. Chiew Seen-kong, 'Ethnicity and national integration' and Seah Chee Meow & L. Seah, 'Educational reform and national integration' in Chen (ed.) (100), pp. 29–64 and 240–67.

of Chinese education imparted by institutions traditionally close to the Communists like Ngee Ann College and Nanyang University (closed in 1980). The PAP also wanted to play down the over-strong Chinese image of Singapore on the regional scene. The government campaigns in the early 1980s encouraging the Chinese population to give up dialects in favour of Mandarin (which is foreign to them) has also contributed to the decline in Singapore's Chinese cultures.

A certain anglophone assimilation has, to some degree and in different ways, been accepted by each ethno-linguistic group, and a kind of Singaporean identity has started to emerge.[58] More recently, the PAP has tried to restore some of the values and virtues of Confucian society, and to modernise them, especially among the young, in order to counter-balance the rapid moves towards a materialist Westernisation, which has been brought in by meteoric economic growth in less than two decades.

Multiracialism and meritocracy
The prosperity of Singapore depends on the best use being made of its human resources and on the high quality of its rulers. The deliberate élitism of Lee Kuan Yew and his government team is but one application of their strategy of social mobilisation to ensure survival for the emporium. The system of 'meritocracy', as enunciated by Rajaratnam, puts a premium on the social opportunities open to all citizens according to their intellectual skills and capacity for hard work; they can achieve high professional and social standing regardless of their ethnic, cultural or religious background.[59]

The universalisation of compulsory primary and secondary education, and the great increase in high-level university departments and specialised training programmes, combined with exceptional economic growth and full employment, have produced a well-educated generation of young people and dynamic new élites. However, even if it is impossible not to admire the policy and performance of the PAP and the results achieved in barely two decades, the system of meritocracy is questioned and even challenged, especially since the authorities tried to initiate a kind of 'brain planning' for the future. By giving preference to methods of assessment and selection of intellectual capacity based on some American systems of testing, sometimes as early as primary

58. G. Benjamin (416) and Chan Heng Chee (421).
59. The concept of meritocracy was invented by Rajaratnam in 1970: see *Straits Times*, 13 Apr. and 10 May 70.

school,[60] and by insisting on the priority of education and profession-alism, the educational machine has been producing a new generation of high quality graduates (almost all in economics and technology), but has often forgotten that academic knowledge and intelligence do not always go together. At the top levels of both the government administration and the national enterprises, the problem is quite similar: brilliant young technocrats are called on to succeed gradually — through a stage-by-stage period planned in advance — to those figures of the first generation who were the architects of independence and of two decades of Singapore's 'economic miracle'. Goh Chok Tong, who became Vice Premier after Goh Keng Swee went into semi-retirement at the end of 1984, is one of those technocrats who often address Singaporeans as if they were an administrative council. No one is able to see in him, so far, more than the makings of a transitional prime minister for a couple of years after Lee's resignation in November 1990, and all eyes turn insistently towards Lee's elder son, who will occupy the post of deputy prime minister.[61]

Meritocracy, as the expression of the best possible form of social organisation, runs the risk of branching off into rigid élitism (as with the *literati* in 18th–19th-century China) if it has to depend on a uniform mould for education and individual promotion. One of the PAP's most criticised projects at the 1984 election (since abandoned) was to encourage the best qualified professionals to marry and raise families together. Such 'scientifically' programmed élitism can prove counter-productive when it means government guiding and controlling people's private lives.[62] Excessive regulation of society, even if in the name of national survival, can stifle individual initiative, creativity, spontaneity, dedication and responsibility, especially among the young generation born in the 1960s. Human intelligence cannot be tamed, but Singapore has no choice but to rely on the ability and the response of its own people when it comes to taking up the challenges of post-industrial society.[63]

60. *FEER*, 20 Apr. 79, pp. 30–1.
61. Lee Lai To, 'Singapore's continuous search for quality', *Southeast Asian Affairs*, 1984, pp. 279–93; Shee Poon Kim, 'Political leadership and succession' in Chen (100), pp. 173–96; 'Don't talk down to us', *FEER*, 11 July 85, pp. 34–7.
62. *FEER*, 8 Sept. 83, pp. 23–4; 31 May 84, p. 7; 21 June 84, pp. 31–2; 23 May 85, p. 10. Concerning the book by Chee Heng Leng and Chan Chee Khoon, *Designer genes: IQ, ideology and sociology*, published in Singapore in 1984, see *FEER*, 20 Sept. 84, p. 53.
63. *FEER*, 17 Jan. 85, pp. 34–5; *Newsweek*, 9 Feb. 85, pp. 6–10.

In conclusion, the peculiar nature of the emporium condemns it to chart a course between the two inter-related necessities of cohesion and flexibility. Singapore can never rest: organisation is forever necessary for adaptation to changing domestic and external conditions, but it must always consist of flexible and imaginative rationalisation.

The ultimate leap for survival: from military defence to the concept of total defence

A well-equipped and structured defence does not automatically mean an absolute guarantee of Singapore's survival if conflict should occur: specialists in strategic studies are unable to state clearly how far an island territory of 620 km.[2] can be genuinely capable of defending itself or engaging in an armed dispute without the possibility of receiving a mortal blow at a very early stage of the conflict.[64]

Internal security: multiracialism and national defence

Rigorous national military service, and the parallel existence of a reserve corps of men aged up to fifty years, contribute to a decisive mixing of ethnic groups and cultures in all postings and grades, and foster a spirit of multiracialism and tolerance. All young males are obliged to serve between twenty-four and thirty months. National service generally has to be completed before one enters higher education, and it moulds the young generation through the ideology of Singapore's permanent mobilisation as a condition of survival and sustainable prosperity. At the end of his term, each serviceman receives a certificate which is, in a sense, also a certificate of good citizenship, before taking full responsibility for the future development of the city-state.[65]

The reservists and those holding senior rank in the army are those whose concern it is to preserve national cohesion, and they perform a function of social discipline largely derived from the example of the Swiss army.[66] As in other ASEAN countries, senior military figures are sometimes called upon — like Lee Kuan Yew's own son, who at one time ranked third in the army staff — to assume important national responsibilities outside the military sphere, and when this happens they

64. Josey (439), 1st edn, p. 180.
65. S.S. Bedlington (251); Lee Tzu Peng, 'Youth and the evolution of a Singaporean' in Min. of Education, *Youth in our society*, Singapore, May 1972, pp. 41–3.
66. 'The military and society in Switzerland', *Pioneer*, Singapore Armed Forces, Dec. 82, pp. 6–9; *ST*, 18 Mar. 84.

have to retire from the service. The presence of numerous reservists in the economic, political and social life of the city-state was seen by Rajaratnam as a supplementary guarantee of internal stability which would enable it to weather any period of external uncertainty (such as the economic recession in the mid-1980s, for example).[67]

External security: defence by deterrence

Under the Anglo-Malaysian Defence Agreement of 1957, Singapore never had an army of its own till 1965, except for two small infantry regiments and a civilian militia, the Singapore Volunteer Corps. Right after independence, the burden of defence fell squarely on the city-state as Britain announced its impending military withdrawal: Goh Keng Swee, one of Lee Kuan Yew's ablest and closest colleagues, was given the task of organising, with the minimum of delay, a credible defence to serve the island's fledgling sovereignty, and to be used as a catalyst in the process of nation-building.[68]

Goh Keng Swee had to move rapidly and effectively, but he also had to avoid too great a strain on the vulnerable economy of that time. In 1967, he opted for a system of conscription (the National Bill) and reservists (New Enlistment Bill) and turned for assistance to Israeli advisers. In less than ten years (1967–75) the Singapore Armed Forces (SAF) were operational on land with AMX 13 tanks, by sea with twelve patrol-boats and missile-launching vessels, and in the air with its first squadron of Hawker Hunter fighters. Up till 1971–2, defence represented nearly 40% of the government's annual budget and 11% of the Gross National Product.[69]

Faced with such formidable difficulties as its extreme vulnerability (its capture by the Japanese in 1942 was an ever-present memory), the initial hostility of its neighbours, the British military withdrawal and the loose structure of the ANZUK (Australia/New Zealand/United

---

67. 'If Singapore suffers a major economic crisis and the present PAP second leadership fails to overcome it, then an alternative to the PAP government under the tutelage of the military could become possible' (Shee Poon Kim in Chen [100], p. 195). See also *FEER*, 13 Jan. 83, pp. 26–32 ('The citizen soldier') and 18 Oct. 84, pp. 32–3.

68. *ST*, 25 Mar. 68, 22 Jan. 69; Goh Keng Swee, *Parliamentary Debates*, Singapore, 1969, vol. 29, col.1160.

69. Min. of Defence, Public Affairs Dept., The Singapore Armed Forces, Singapore, 1981; Moey Yue Ken (452); Yeo Nin Hong, 'The building of the Singapore armed forces' in J. Jayakumar (ed.) (437), pp. 36–43.

Kingdom) security agreement, Singapore concentrated its efforts on building up as credible a policy of deterrence as possible.[70] With a capacity for the lightning destruction of any potential aggressor launching a first strike, and a citizen-soldiers system operating through-out the whole population, as in Israel, Goh Keng Swee could demonstrate that the price of aggression would be too high.[71] He used the image of a 'poisoned fish' which the attacker would have to swallow before being able to set foot on the island. Besides, the enormous destruction that would be caused by any massive attack on Singapore's dense urban environment would nullify the very thing coveted by any potential enemy — the wealth of the city-state. Thus any major attack could only aim at the complete destruction of Singapore; otherwise it would be pointless.

Without sufficient resources or territory to resist a sustained attack or siege, the city-state has, since 1973–5, consolidated its strategy of deterrence by means of repeated qualitative upgrading. By opting for ultra-modern equipment and rigorous training to compensate for the negligible size of its geographical and human base, the city-state has become an impressive military-industrial centre in the region.[72]

Singapore's emergence as a military-industrial focus at the
heart of ASEAN
With its army of 50,000 and a pool of 200,000 reservists — more than in Malaysia or the Philippines — Singapore has notched up some out-standing achievements in terms of military preparedness in the context of the ASEAN region. With an annual defence budget of US$860 million (21% of public expenditure in 1987) — more in value than in the Philippines or New Zealand — the city-state stands on an equal footing with Sweden or Switzerland, and among the ASEAN countries makes the highest contribution per inhabitant (about US$330). Because it is an island, its major means of deterrence is the air force, which is

70. 'The nightmare that haunts even the Singapore leaders of today . . . is that one day they may wake up to find that they have been asked to go to Collyer Quay to hand over the city to an Indonesian admiral, or to the Johore Causeway to hand over the keys to a Malaysian general' (Dick Wilson [231], pp. 78–9).
71. Singapore speaks of the 'poisoned shrimp' system of deterrence: *The Mirror*, 8 Jan. 68; Goh Keng Swee, *Parliamentary Debates*, Singapore, 1966, vol. 26, col. 1162, and 1968, vol. 28, col. 36; Lee Kuan Yew, *Parliamentary Debates*, 1967, vol. 27, col. 39.
72. Wu Yuan Li, 'Planning security for a small nation: . . .', *Pacific Community*, July 72, pp. 661–74.

very close to the capacity of its Thai counterpart, and can also benefit from a strong local civil aviation industry.[73] Here Singapore has combined the sophistication of its defence with its strategy to develop high-tech industries, and it has already become a centre for light arms procurement and for maintenance and repair services for military hardware.[74] Since 1967, Chartered Industries of Singapore (CIS) has specialised in the production of munitions and small arms, and some other companies have more recently become manufacturers of military equipment under license; these also repair fighter and transport aircraft and small naval vessels.[75]

Singapore would have an important role to play if ASEAN were ever to consider harmonising arms procurement in the region, in the absence of a more general common defence agreement — something to which no member-state seems to aspire so far, even after several tense periods of confrontation with Indochina.[76] However this does not mean that the individual ASEAN members remain inactive. Since political dialogue was established between Singapore and its neighbours, and since the Vietnamese invaded Kampuchea, the city-state has regularly undertaken bilateral air force and/or naval exercises with Indonesia, Malaysia, Thailand and Brunei. ASEAN's unwritten rule implying that all member-states would help any of their number facing a sudden external attack or threat seems gradually to be gaining ground: Singapore and Malaysia somewhat timidly offered assistance to Thailand against Vietnam in 1984!

Probably because of its mistrust of the Chinese, Malaysia long refused to allow Singapore any facilities to organise joint air force exercises or set up training camps on its territory. This has made it necessary ever since for Singapore to carry out exercises in Brunei, Thailand and

---

73. In 1984, Singapore purchased three EE8C Hawkeye radar planes of US manufacture, and the entire control of the SAF was computerised. A decision to acquire eight F16 fighters, Super-Puma helicopters and French Mirages was taken in 1985. *Asian Defence J.*, Kuala Lumpur, Jan. 85, pp. 36–56; *ST*, 18 & 24 Mar. 84; *ARB*, 30 Nov. 80, pp. 742–6; *FEER*, 5 Apr. 84, p. 43.

74. Josey (439), 1st edn, p. 544; *ARB*, 30 Nov. 80, pp. 742–6; *FEER*, 13 Jan. 83, pp. 28–32; *FT*, 30 Nov. 83; *Pioneer* (SAF), July 83; *ST*, 28 Apr. & 18 June 83, 17 Nov. 84; *Singapore Econ. Bull.*, May 83, p. 12.

75. Examples are SAE (Singapore Automotive Engineering), SAI (Singapore Aircraft Industries), SSE (Singapore Shipbuilding and Engineering), ODE (Ordnance Dept. and Engineering) and SCS (Singapore Computer Systems).

76. *ST*, 24 Jan. 76 (standardisation of armaments); *FEER*, 13 Jan. 83, pp. 28–32.

Taiwan.[77] But here too there have been signs of change: the first Singaporean officers were accepted at the Johore War School in 1983, and Singapore assisted in the transfer of Malaysia's naval forces from the Woodlands base in Singapore to Lumut in Perak. Even with Indonesia Lee Kuan Yew is no longer unwilling to engage in free discussions on security questions, and memories of the confrontation are gradually fading. Exchange of information, anti-subversion intelligence, training of military personnel and joint exercises are contributing more and more to a kind of ASEAN zone of security. From 1987 onwards, the atmosphere of cooperation in security matters improved still further between Singapore and Malaysia, and in March 1988 the two countries took part in a 'first' joint naval exercise.[78] An important new stage was reached in the rapprochement between their two armies in 1989, when Malaysia allowed a bilateral joint exercise to be organised for the first time on its territory, in Sabah (East Malaysia), using live ammunition.[79]

This climate of confidence is something new but it still remains incomplete. Does it mean that Singapore has to abandon its deterrent strategy towards the rest of the region? At regular intervals the city-state, recalling its neighbours' criticism of its military cooperation with Israel, declares that there is no case for a 'siege city' strategy, and that its defence system is not directed against its partners. The spirit of détente was reaffirmed on a number of occasions, both by various leaders in Malaysia (including those of the PAS) and by numerous prominent figures in Singapore, most notably the Vice-Premier Goh Chok Tong in 1987–8.[80] However, the introduction of the concept of 'total

77. 'It is feared that the presence of Singapore forces in Malaysia might provoke a political backlash while the spectre of possible Singapore intervention in the event of a breakdown of communal relations in Malaysia continues to hover in the background' (*FEER*, 20 Oct. 83, p. 51). Also *ST*, 24 Sept. 79 and 6 Dec. 83; *NST*, 10 May 75.

78. *ST*, 4 Apr., 4 July & 20 July 87; 21 Mar. 88.

79. *ST*, 28 Jan. & 17 Mar. 89.

80. 'Where religious prejudice has to be stirred up against Singapore, then Singapore is Israel. Where social prejudices have to be stimulated, Singapore is depicted as a third China. Where anti-communist fears have to be used, then Singapore becomes Cuba . . .' (Rajaratnam in Chan Heng Chee, Asian Working Party on State and Nation Building, Singapore, 1971, p. 29). 'We are not Israel and Southeast Asia is not the Middle East' (Goh Keng Swee, *ST*, 27 Sept. 84). 'Singapore must pursue close ties with neighbours at every level. Deterrence has its limits . . . Deterrence needs to be supplemented by closer ties' (Goh Chok Tong, *ST*, 5 Dec. 88). In the same sense, see Dhanabalan, *ST*, 2 Aug 88; Goh Chok Tong, *ST*, 8 Feb. 88; and Lee Hsien Liong, *ST*, 10 Feb. 88.

defence' gives an impression that Singapore has latterly moved in the opposite direction. However, this new slogan is perhaps designed more to reinforce internal cohesion than to convey mistrust of the outside world.

Thus extended military cooperation between Singapore and its neighbours, which would have been inconceivable up till the late 1980s, has been quite firmly established. At the beginning of 1989, Indonesia followed Malaysia in agreeing to organise bilateral exercises with Singapore's land forces; and it seemed that Jakarta was willing to offer a site in northern Sumatra[81] as a training camp for use by Singapore's infantry.

The debate on Singapore's geostrategic situation in relation to its neighbours is far from being closed. For example, Singapore again 'put the boat out' on its own in late 1990 (the most recent case at the time of writing) by offering the United States military facilities in the city-state if the US army should ever withdraw from the Philippines. It did this without consulting the other ASEAN partners, and a hostile reaction was not long in coming, especially from Malaysia.

The struggle for survival as a sacred cause: total defence
Taking the civil-military defence systems of Switzerland, Sweden and Israel as its inspiration, the PAP has launched since 1983–4 a campaign of social mobilisation which, under the slogan 'total defence', intends to muster the entire population and every single sector of activity in the event of any acute external crisis.[82] In order to mobilise all Singaporeans within twenty-four hours, five areas of action were identified. First, military defence would continue to be based on conscripts and reservists, and information about the Singapore Armed Forces (SAF) would be fed to the public from primary school onwards.[83] Secondly, civil defence, which involved 34,000 men in 1987, would be concerned in case of war with the dead and wounded, and with huge material destruction. Tight organisation would be needed in view of the high density of the urban areas and the small area of the island.[84] Thirdly,

---

81. *FEER*, 13 Apr. 89, p. 260.
82. 'Total defence and you', *Pioneer*, Feb. 84; 'Sweden: they are totally prepared: are we?', *Pioneer*, Oct. 84; 'Blueprint for total defence', *ST*, 6 Mar. 84; *ST*, 23 Feb. & 1 May 84; *Asiaweek*, 7 Dec. 84.
83. *ST*, 22 Oct. 84; Yeo Ning Hong (Min. of Defence), 'Defence is every Singaporean's business' (speech), *Singapore Econ. Bull.*, May 83, p. 12.
84. *ST*, 14 Nov. 83 & 15 May 84.

economic defence would mean not only mobilising the whole machinery of industrial production in case of war, but also shaping in peace-time a strong linkage between all the civil and military applications of each branch of economic activity.[85] There are several possibilities of precise application to be distinguished here: easy conversion of civil infrastructures to military uses, development of high technology in arms procurement; and the exercise of civil responsibilities by the highest-ranking officers of the SAF. Fourthly, social defence should guarantee the internal invulnerability of Singapore by uniting the population around the dominant values affecting daily life and citizenship in the city-state, values with which most citizens should be able to identify. To this end a Consultative Council on Intra-social Relations has been working since 1984.[86] And, finally, psychological defence should protect the young from dogmatic ideology and subversion (mainly from Communism), from the potential danger of certain imported Western values (such as drug abuse and the relaxation of sexual morality), or from over-dependence on material comfort and welfare. When Rajaratnam declared in November 1984 that every Singaporean had to be prepared to face new crises, because these would be certain to arise in the future, he touched on the quintessential theme of survival and viability for the emporium city-state.[87]

The launching of the concept of total defence has coincided — not entirely by chance — with the onset of an important political and social transition for the city-state. Numerous challenges have come up, and have duly been magnified by the PAP to suit its long-term ambitions. These challenges are the ever-present themes of current political debate: the economic revival and reshuffle after the 1984–6 recession, the conditions of sustained economic growth, the political succession by the younger generation and the selection of new cadres, and the emergence

85. 'Plan to keep the economy going in case of war', *ST*, 25 Nov. 84.
86. *ST*, 18 Jan. 84.
87. 'There must be threats, and there will always be threats because history has always been of threats. So most important is . . . take precautions long before the threat becomes unmanageable . . . One lesson that Singaporeans must learn is please, don't build a philosophy that the world is fine, that it consists of saints, and therefore let's have a good life' (Rajaratnam in 'Prepare for new threats', *ST*, 20 Nov. 84). 'The people of Singapore must never assume that peace and prosperity such as they have enjoyed for the last 15 years will continue indefinitely, the volatility of the regional and international situation proves otherwise, and this nation must be prepared for any contingency' (Min. of Defence, *The Singapore Armed Forces*, 1981, p. 33).

of a legal opposition with the right of free expression. Total defence is a new global instrument serving the permanent mobilisation of society. It is also highly symptomatic of the political philosophy of the PAP, for whom not only the survival of the city-state but also its own retention of power are seen as inseparable.

8

CONCLUSION

The city-state is a form of political organisation of great antiquity, but there are few examples in the modern world. Because of its economic influence and the affirmation of an external diplomacy of its own, Singapore can be thought of as a twentieth-century Venice, which became a state purely by an accident of history in 1965. This Venice of South-East Asia corresponds closely to the definition of a politically independent society, set up in a small territory and dominated by commercial, financial and industrial activities. These are concentrated in a single urban centre, where the overwhelming majority of Singaporean citizens live and which is remarkable for its specific cultural and social identity, reacting primarily to the attitude and nature of the regimes and societies in the surrounding region. The birth, expansion and ultimate disappearance of particular city-states seem to have been closely related to their essential function of providing a bridge and an intersection between two external spheres of influence: the immediate and regional hinterland on the one hand and the wider international milieu on the other.

This book looks at the web of interrelationship between Singapore and the first of these spheres — the immediate region — and at the kind of implications this has for the internal organisation of the emporium. We have tried to determine and analyse some of the key variables governing the continued economic and political success of this city-state and thus affecting its long-term viability and survival. None the less, the often decisive contribution of the rest of the world outside the South-East Asian region, whether through the British colonial heritage or through the presence of vast Western economic interests at the present time, has not been overlooked. Singapore displays a genuine combination of regional and world inputs and its economic and political future depends as much on its immediate environment as on the rest of the world.

This study has identified so far the factors governing Singapore's economic and political life in its regional context. It would be appropriate now to review those factors in relation to certain key concepts which define the dependences and challenges which have affected the city-state in the past as they will continue to do in the future. 'Conflict versus cooperation' and 'cohesion versus flexibility' are the two concepts which form the basis of this final endeavour.

The concept of conflict versus cooperation

Before as well as after independence, the regional functions of Singapore evolved in the context of a long continuum of conflict and cooperation between the island emporium and its most immediate regional environment, namely Malaysia and Indonesia. This duality has always existed, sometimes threatening it and at other times increasing its chances of survival and long-term viability. Facing the immensity of Indonesia and the whole Malay world, Singapore is one of the keys to understanding the undercurrents of ASEAN development. It is an integral part of the tensions and complementarities within the region — by the history and nature of its bilateral relations with the neighbouring countries, by its dynamic networking role on behalf of the transnational Overseas Chinese business community, and by its original contributions to the institutional construction of ASEAN.

A reading of precolonial and colonial history strongly suggests that there has long been an unstable combination of conflict and cooperation between sea-based emporia (of which Singapore is the direct inheritor) and vast agrarian state formations occupying the hinterland (the Malay peninsula, Sumatra and Java). The British — predecessors of the Western investors who carried on the tradition after 1965 — were clever enough to place their colonial regime in a line of historical continuity and to create on Singapore island a new 'world-city' developing ties of economic complementarity between the region and the great powers outside. Singapore became like a flea in the fur of a large animal, representing the Malay world: a flea which, like a micro-chip in modern computer technology, concentrates within a tiny body a great range of services that are practically indispensable to its neighbours. At the same time, the flea disturbs its neighbours because it is mainly non-Malay (Overseas Chinese and Western-oriented) and is too successful economically.

The accumulation of wealth by and through this small emporium could not fail to arouse economic and political resistance from the adjacent countries, which aspired to control this strategic island which had been kept mainly under foreign rule since 1819. After decolonisation, the further success of Singapore and the continuation of its intimate links with the outside world were severely criticised by the young neighbouring independent states. The option was either to take it over (this came to the fore during the confrontation with Indonesia and after separation from Malaysia) or to accept a guarantee from the island-city that it would evolve from then on within the neighbours' sphere of influence and for their benefit.

The events of 1959–65 drove home the danger of the emporium being swiftly devoured by internal or external forces, or by both simultaneously. The flea has no choice but to be for ever exposed to the risk of being crushed, in one way or another, at any time and without warning!

Without the twofold trauma of the confrontation with Indonesia and the separation from Malaysia, the PAP leaders of independent Singapore would not have become so acutely aware of the city-state's extreme dependence on the immediate region, and the absolute necessity of reducing sources of tension with its neighbours so as to guarantee its viability and security.

In the economic sphere, the relative decline of the pure trading or re-export entrepot blunted the sharpest criticism formulated by Indonesia and Malaysia against the parasitic middleman's role of the Chinese city-state, and the diversification of Singapore's industrial and service-related activities multiplied the channels of cooperation and complementarity within the region. In the political sphere, its new economic power gained through rapid industrialisation enabled Singapore to assert its national identity on the world scene, but this had to be used with caution in view of the possible unfavourable perceptions and reactions from Kuala Lumpur and Jakarta. To dissipate the hostility inherited from the conflicts of 1963–5, Singapore preferred during the first phase, and thanks to large-scale foreign investment, to strengthen the foundations of a national economy more open to ASEAN, and then, from 1970–3 onwards, to deploy an active but gradual regional diplomacy that would be reasonably well received by its neighbours. Thanks to a sustained effort, the city-state has finally succeeded in skirting both the economic and the political obstacles to its complete incorporation within the regional community.

Its policy has contributed to a lessening of anti-Chinese communalist tendencies within ASEAN and to the neutralisation of the over-emotional and negative reaction of Indonesia and Malaysia to the domestic and regional role played by the Overseas Chinese. The contribution of the Singaporean and Overseas Chinese business circles to the development and internationalisation of the ASEAN economies has been progressively recognised, albeit unofficially.

The converging views of all the ASEAN countries regarding internal and external Communist threats have allowed Singapore to use the Indochinese crises of 1975 and 1978-9 to identify a new Communist scapegoat, namely Vietnam and not only China any more, and to play down the ASEAN perception of the Chinese identity of Singapore.

Time has blurred the tensions between Singapore and its neighbours, and strengthened the role played by the city-state in the region. No one any longer disputes the positive impact of Singapore's economic success and dynamism on the whole region. Even more important, the development of modern Singapore is tied to the region's own prosperity and stability. For example, Singapore's economic setbacks in 1984-6 coincided with a clear slowing-down of growth in Malaysia and Indonesia and with the beginning of similar succession problems in the ruling élites of several ASEAN states, including Singapore. This has shown the city-state to be much more securely integrated within the region than ever before, and there are no major signs that this situation might be disturbed, at least in the short and medium term.

The dilemma of cohesion versus flexibility

The history of Singapore can thus be summed up as a series of challenges to its survival and viability, which it was able to overcome precisely by mobilising all its internal resources and adapting itself permanently to a changing world.

Of these challenges few were mortal threats, contrary to the PAP's allegations propagated through its purpose-made survival ideology. Certainly this ideology is all-pervasive in Singapore and Israel (in the different cases of Sweden and Switzerland, it is used to justify the historic national policy of neutrality). But it is no less true that Singapore's prosperity has been at once threatened and stimulated many times both before and after 1965: the world crisis of 1929-32, the expansion of Japan in Asia and the building of the British naval base, the Japanese occupation in 1942-5 and the Pacific war, the anti-Communist emergency in 1948-60, the subversive pro-Communist labour and student activism in 1955-63, the merging with Malaya in 1963, the Indonesian confrontation, separation and independence in 1965, the sharp decline in entrepot trade and the increase in unemployment after 1965, the Vietnam war and Britain's military withdrawal from

Singapore in 1971, the oil crisis in 1973, the Indochinese crises of 1975 and 1978–9, protectionism and economic recessions in the 1980s. . . . The list is long, but each time Singapore was able to offer an appropriate response thanks to its finely-tuned policy of cohesion and flexibility. Both foreign investors and the business circles of the region find this a powerful attraction.

Under the banner of the permanent struggle for the survival and viability of the city-state, the PAP has given priority to the strengthening of internal cohesion at all costs. This takes the following specific forms:

– cohesion of Lee Kuan Yew's government team, who justify their image of good government and their long-term control of political power by the economic and social results registered during the last quarter-century and through the homogeneity, honesty and outstanding competence of its party cadres;
– cohesion to ensure political and social stability by eliminating all attempts — even suspected ones — to resume pro-Communist subversion, through the control of opposition movements and the instruments to promote national identity by absorbing the communal divisions of an originally plural society into a single unified society;
– cohesion of the social structures to serve economic growth by mobilising the population at all levels, and restraining the individual and collective freedoms of citizens;
– cohesion in the long-term industrialisation strategy by planning economic diversification and anticipating the future shape of external demand to derive maximum profit from the emporium's position as a crossroads and a supplier of goods and services to the region and the whole world.

Under the banner of 'struggling for survival', the PAP has staked everything on flexibility — a tireless striving to adapt the city-state to new challenges and to external events, however unpredictable:

– the flexibility of a society of immigrants prepared to shape their behaviour in conformity to the government's economic objectives, and regarding material and social achievement as the highest of individual values (at least-up to the present);
– a flexibility of government authority and public management trying to harness internal stability and the skills of the local workforce first to the rapidly growing Western economies (1965–73), then to the oil exploration and exploitation boom in South East Asia, and finally

to the progressive political stabilisation of the regional environment that followed the revival of ASEAN in 1975–6;

– flexibility in the priorities of Singapore's economic diplomacy both within ASEAN and in relation to the industrial countries, seeking non-institutional instruments of cooperation seeking efficient non-institutional and informal cooperation;

– flexibility of response to the most serious external challenges, playing as much on the opportunity they offer repeatedly to mobilise the whole of Singaporean society as on their real or fictitious threats to the future of the city-state.

The combination of cohesion and flexibility is not a paradox. Rather, it is a vicious circle. The rationalisation of society obviously makes it more capable of adapting to the external environment, but the erratic evolution of the outside world often leads to yet further rationalisation of internal order. Perhaps more than for any other form of state which wants to be active internationally, it is difficult to decide in the specific case of a city-state up to what point structures take precedence over circumstances, or vice versa. When trying to define the broad structural patterns which govern the working of the city-state, this type of approach might be somehow misleading. On the other hand the analysis of conjunctural facts and circumstances may not keep up with the rapid and irregular flow of events.

Thus, at the beginning of the 1980s, new challenges appeared. The authorities found themselves compelled to react before they were able to grasp all the implications, and they had to elaborate a new formula which balanced cohesion and flexibility. There were three categories of problems to which they had to respond. First, there was the inevitable change-over from the old to the new generation, and the rapid increase in the number of younger people. Secondly, adaptation was necessary in the face of two new factors: the relative decline in popularity of the PAP since the 1984 election, and the prospect of Lee Kuan Yew's gradual retirement. Then suddenly, in 1984–6, there occurred the first economic depression since independence, which could easily have nullified all the efforts to bring about a second industrial revolution based on high technology and advanced services.

These problems, unlike those of 1959–65, are clearly not so grave as to threaten survival itself, and the city-state's economic and political structures seem to be firmly consolidated, but the current challenges make a new set of appropriate answers very necessary. The Singapore government has to take some balanced measures designed to achieve cohesion and flexibility simultaneously, and which defines at once the range and the limits of its powers. The basic question is which of the two elements — cohesion or flexibility — has to be activated the more. Where is a balance struck that corresponds most closely to the true situation? The immediate reaction of Lee Kuan Yew and his associates was to reinforce national cohesion in order to avoid any harmful mismanagement of either economic or political affairs during the current delicate period of transition. Thus a new wave of state consolidation has been initiated since 1985. A gradual change-over of top administrative and political posts has been planned; the Prime Minister's son has been elected as a deputy and has subsequently made a meteoric rise through the government apparatus; Lee Kuan Yew stepped down as Prime Minister in November 1990, announcing at the same time his intention to remain the PAP's secretary-general for some time and to transform the regime into a semi-presidential one within a short time; the shortcomings of parliamentary democracy; and the opposition's lack of credibility have repeatedly been denounced; various individual and collective freedoms and rights have not yet been fully recognised or tolerated . . . Parallel to this, the PAP government has been aware that a greater spirit of creativity and flexibility is essential for a sustainable recovery of the economy and indeed for the whole future of the city-state, and it has tried to liberalise the mechanics of government and social control. While there have been some initiatives in that direction, they have remained tentative, piecemeal and on a modest scale: rapid promotion of young blood in the PAP, privatisation of certain national enterprises, diversification of Singapore's foreign investments, an increase in training programmes and in scientific and technical research, ...

The opinion of most foreign observers is that the PAP has not yet gone far enough in its moves to liberalise society, which are deemed to be necessary after two decades of uninterrupted rationalisation and semi-authoritarian rule which have undoubtedly changed Singapore from top to bottom. In the absence of a clearly identifiable system of island cohesion which could easily adapt to the future globalisation of world affairs, the PAP seems to be moving more hesitantly down the road of democratisation and liberalisation than its counterparts in Korea and Taiwan, such is its apparent fear of losing control, even partly, of the situation and thus of the conditions for national stability. The island-state has already reached a high degree of cohesion, and should surely protect itself against the suffocation which could result from excessive standardisation or social and cultural conformism, imposed jointly by the PAP and by the material achievements of the 1970s and 1980s. After Lee Kuan Yew and the old generation have stepped down, young technocrats could come to power who have had little opportunity to develop genuine political leadership qualities. The external world will always be unpredictable and likely to impinge on the city-state at more or less regular intervals. But should this justify a rigid regimentation of the island society? Since there are no economic, political and social solutions that can be scientifically programmed in advance, Singapore's best hope would seem to lie in following a middle way between rational organisation and flexibility for free initiative, creativity, cultural diversity and pluralism. Otherwise the long-term result could well be stagnation followed by decline.

After an independent existence of a quarter of a century, the young city-state should not miss the rendez-vous of its transition to maturity. There is no serious danger that it will disappear from the map of South-East Asia, having either been absorbed by its neighbours or succumbed to internal subversion. The city-state is expected to survive, for the benefit of the region, and, barring major accidents, it should be able to develop and consolidate further, as it has done since the recession of the middle 1980s.

A BIOGRAPHICAL SKETCH OF
LEE KUAN YEW

Harry Lee Kuan Yew ('the light which shines'), elder son of Lee Chin Koon, an oil company employee and jeweller, and Chua Jim Neo, was born in Singapore in 1923. His family, of Hakka origin from South China, settled in Singapore around the 1830s. A great-grandmother on his mother's side married a Malay and his paternal grandfather an Indonesian (Peranakan) Chinese. Lee's struggles against all forms of racial discrimination may owe something to his family background.

Lee Kuan Yew attended the anglophone primary school of Telok Kurau in order to become, as his grandfather wished, the equal of a British gentleman in terms of his professional status while retaining the Chinese tradition. From Telok Kurau he went on to Raffles College in Singapore, which was patronised by the local anglophone élite. The Great Depression of the 1930s ruined the families of both Lee's parents, thus in part laying the foundations for his later adoption of a pragmatic socialism.

The capitulation of Singapore, the pearl in Britain's Asian diadem, and the installation of the Japanese high command for South-East Asia in the island, made a profound impression on the young student, who escaped at the last minute being caught up in a series of summary executions ordered by the occupying power. He learned Japanese and worked for the Domei press agency, and became keenly aware during those dark years of the supremely vulnerable position of the island-city. At the liberation, Lee assisted Philip Hoalim, a close friend and founder of the Malayan Democratic Union, to prepare the early constitutional plan for self-government of Malaya.

Lee Kuan Yew now put forward the plans for his own career laid before the war, and left for Britain. At Fitzwilliam College, Cambridge, he obtained the highest honours in law, and became a junior barrister in London at the Middle Temple. It was also between 1946 and 1950 that his political career began through his active involvement in the Labour Club at Cambridge and the Malayan Forum in London, whose members included a number of his future political allies and enemies. It was to this audience that Lee delivered his celebrated speech on the future of Malaya shortly before returning home to Singapore.

In September 1950, Lee married Kwa Geok Choo, a brilliant fellow-student whom he had met in Cambridge, and with her set up a law firm. There were two sons (born in 1952 and 1957) and one daughter (born in 1955) of the marriage. The elder son, Lee Hsien Loong, after studying mathematics in the United States, became a brigadier-general at the age of thirty and a deputy in 1984 before taking on important ministerial functions. Many think he will step into the highest executive office after an interim period with Goh Chok Tong as premier.

From 1952 onwards, Lee Kuan Yew became the legal counsel to numerous local trade unions and, from that vantage point, listened in to the social agitation of the period, helped in this by his knowledge of Mandarin and Malay. This socio-political experience, acquired against the background of the anti-Communist emergency in force throughout Malaya from 1948, was a determining factor in the creation of the broadly social-democratic People's Action Party (PAP) in 1954, of which Lee became the first secretary-general. In 1955, the PAP won three seats in the Legislative Assembly, and Lee, now a deputy, was involved in the negotiations held in London on the independence of Malaya, during which his intelligence and the force of his personality greatly impressed the British authorities.

Catapulted into power in 1959 as Chief Minister of Singapore, following the abortive Communist attempts at destabilisation, Lee Kuan Yew managed to ensure that his party won every seat in the Assembly up till 1980. In 1963–5 he also sat in the parliament of the Federation of Malaya in Kuala Lumpur, and fought vigorously against communalist divisions between Malays and Chinese. It was on this question that he accepted — not without bitterness and regret — the separation of Singapore from the Federation on 9 August 1965: the definitive independence date of the city-state.

There is unanimous recognition of Lew Kuan Yew as one of the principal architects of Singapore's formidable economic achievements since 1965. He ranks as a leading world statesman because of the intermediary role he has frequently played in the Commonwealth, and the close relations he enjoys with numerous heads of state and government throughout the world.

In 1967 he was elected to the Bureau of the Socialist International, but resigned in 1976 following denunciation of the authoritarianism of the political regime in Singapore and the imprisonment of a number of opposition politicians. After the 1984 elections, in which the PAP lost some ground to a still embryonic opposition, Lee Kuan Yew has made efforts to prepare the ground for a political transition in which the younger generation will take over the reins of power. He announced his intention of giving up the premiership after his sixty-fifth birthday in 1988, but finally decided to step down only in November 1990 in favour of the Vice-Premier, Goh Chok Tong. He remains Secretary-General of the PAP and a senior minister in the Cabinet. Under a likely revision of the Constitution, he could also become a President with enlarged powers.

INFRASTRUCTURES AND DEVELOPMENT
IN BATAM

'I can visualise the day when Batam will be another Singapore, supplementing Singapore's present industrial, commercial and financial activities. What must be remembered is that both Batam and Singapore are in the centre of ASEAN, the largest region for potential economic growth in the world.' — Dr Radius Prawiro, Indonesian Minister for Trade and Cooperation, *The Batam Development Program*, p. 5.

Geographical situation
Batam is 20 km. south-east of Singapore, from which it is visible to the naked eye. The journey between them takes forty minutes by ferry and fifteen by helicopter. The island's area is 415 km.^{2}, i.e. two-thirds of Singapore, and in 1985 had 44,000 inhabitants (more than double the 1979 total of 20,000). It could only accommodate more than 700,000 with difficulty unless it brought in water from outside, since its local resources, like Singapore's, are limited.

Status
The island has been the subject of two presidential decrees — no. 41 (1973) and 45 (1978), and in 1976 was classed as a priority industrial development project.

The planning of the necessary infrastructures was set out in a first Master Plan in 1972 by the Indonesian national petroleum company, Pertamina, with the assistance of two consultancy firms, Pacific Bethel Co. (United States) and Nissho-Iwai (Japan); it was revised in 1977 by the American Cruk consultants. A second Master Plan, established in 1979 by the Batam Industrial Development Authority (BIDA) jointly with the Directorate-General of Planning of the Indonesian Ministry of Public Works, set out in detail the stages of development for the island envisaged over the period 1979–2004. BIDA, with its headquarters in Jakarta and the Minister of Research and Development, Habibie, as its president, had the responsibility for implementing the plan, along with an interministerial committee called the Supervisory Body of Batam

Industrial Zone, chaired by the Minister of Economy and Finance, and the Batam Industrial Corporation (PT Persero Batam, also with its headquarters in Jakarta).

The initial infrastructures (1973–80)
The road network is concentrated in the north of the island, and it is natural that this should be the side that faces Singapore. It links three urban centres — Batu Ampar to the north, Sekupang to the west and Kabil to the east. At Sekupang is a telecommunications centre, in constant touch with Singapore and including a satellite communications station. The aerodrome of Batu Besar is in the north-east of the island, close to Nongsa, which is destined ultimately to become a centre for tourism.

Three harbour zones have been laid down in the places already mentioned: Batu Ampar for industrial exports and passenger traffic, Sekupang for intra-regional trade and Kabil for oil tankers and containers. Teluk Tering will be called into service later to handle tourist transfers. Two ferry lines ply several times a day between Singapore and Batu Ampar (Batam Express) and Sekupang (Mirani Express).

Five industrial zones are planned: Batu Ampar for light industry and warehousing; Sekupang and, close by, Tanjung Uncang for processing of raw materials, timber and agricultural produce; Kabil and the east coast for refineries, steel works and heavy engineering; and Nongsa for tourism and hotels.

Longer-term objectives
On an infrastructural base requiring US$ 77 million of public investment annually, the island would need to have about half a million inhabitants by the year 2004 and to be capable of absorbing several hundred thousand tourists. An urbanisation plan for 1984–9, covering 1250 hectares divided into three districts, was set up by Atelier 6, an Indonesian company specialising in building design, together with Planning Research Corporation, based in Virginia, USA.

Batu Ampar, the administrative centre housing the local authorities and branches of BIDA and Persero, was to become Batam's principal town (its population estimated to reach 25,000 by 2004), embodying industry specialised in equipment for the oil industry and a deep-water harbour. Sekupang would be transformed into an agricultural and horticultural centre, and would have the management of four electricity generating stations, and of water treatment plants. Nongsa would have a heavy industrial zone of 4,000 ha., two large-capacity container terminals, four hotel complexes, an electricity generating station, a reservoir, and a plant for treating sea-water.

Hang Nadion airport at Batu Besar (800 ha.) would have to be developed rapidly in cooperation with the civil aviation authority in Singapore, with infrastructures capable of handling large-scale international traffic — the DC 10 and Airbus went into service on the Batam-Jakarta route in 1982–3.

Foreign investment policy

Batam enjoys a strategic position close to one of the world's busiest seaways, to the natural resources and markets of South-East Asia, and to the oil exploration and exploitation zones of the Indian Ocean, the China Sea and the Java Sea.

Every investment project approved by BIDA is exempted, for a negotiated period, from all taxes and import duties on equipment needed for its implementation. It benefits from complete managerial freedom and is also exempt from exchange control, in that it can repatriate profits. The price of land leased over a 25-30-year period ranged from 4 to 8 cents (US) per square metre where the use is agriculture, pasturage, food-processing and fishing, and $1.6–2.5 where it is industry, services or housing; payment is spread over five years. Two Indonesian banks, Bumi Daya and Dagang Negara, have a branch in Batam.

Labour is cheap but untrained, and the island is not the subject of any special programme of the Ministry of Transmigration. The tax of US$ 150 which normally applies to anyone wishing to travel abroad, whether a foreigner returning home or a permanent resident, is not levied on residents of Batam wishing to travel ιo Singapore, and those who regularly make the journey between the two islands. It is not necessary to obtain a visa in advance in order to visit Batam from Singapore.

Free trade zones are envisaged by Decrees 21 and 22 of 1978, which allow the free importation of all goods intended to be used in the island, even when it is intended to re-export them later to Singapore and the rest of the world. This legislation does not apply to exports from Batam to the rest of Indonesia, which are subject to the current national customs tariffs.

In 1989 Batam was declared a zone of priority economic expansion for both Indonesia and Singapore.

SELECT BIBLIOGRAPHY

The pre-colonial and colonial history of South-East Asia and the development of Singapore up till 1963–5.

1. ANDAYA, B.W., and L.Y. ANDAYA, *A history of Malaysia,* London: Macmillan, 1982.
2. ATTIWILL, Kenneth, *Fortress: The story of the siege and fall of Singapore,* New York, 1960.
3. BARBER, Noël, *Sinister twilight: The fall and rise of Singapore,* London: Collins, 1968.
4. ——, *The Singapore story: From Raffles to Lee Kuan Yew,* London: Collins (Fontana), 1978.
5. BELLWOOD, Peter, *Man's conquest of the Pacific: The prehistory of Southeast Asia and Oceania,* Auckland: Collins, 1978.
6. BENNETT, Henry G., *Why Singapore fell,* Sydney: Angus and Robertson, 1944.
7. BRADDEL, Sir Roland, *The lights of Singapore,* London: Methuen, 1935.
8. BRAUDEL, Fernand, *Civilisation matérielle, économie et capitalisme, XV–XVIIIe s.,* ('Le temps du monde') vol. 3, Paris: Armand Colin, 1979.
9. BRUHAT, Jean, *Histoire de l'Indonésie,* Paris: PUF, 1976.
10. BUCKLEY, C.B., *Anecdotal history of old times in Singapore (1819–1967),* Singapore, 1902, 2 vols.
11. CADY, John F., *Southeast Asia, its historical development,* New York: McGraw Hill, 1964.
12. CAFFRAY, K., *Out in the midday sun: Singapore 1941–45,* London, 1974.
13. CHAI HON-CHAN, *The development of British Malaya, 1896–1909,* London, Geo. Allen & Unwin, 1970.
14. CHEAH BOON KHENG, *Red star over Malaya: resistance and socialist conflict during and after the Japanese occupation, 1941–46,* Singapore UP, 1983.
15. CHIANG HAI DING, *A history of Straits Settlements foreign trade, 1870–1915,* Singapore: National Museum, 1978.
16. CHOO ENG-KANG, 'The Singapore trade depression, 1920–22', unpubl. thesis, Singapore National University, 1976.
17. COEDES, G., *Les Etats hindouisés d'Indochine et d'Indonésie,* Paris: Boccard, 1964.
18. COLLIS, Maurice, *Raffles,* London: Faber and Faber, 1966.
19. CONDOMINAS, George, *L'espace social à propos de l'Asie du sud-est,* Paris: Flammarion, 1980.
20. CUYLENBURG, John B. van, *Singapore through sunshine and shadow,* Singapore: Heinemann Asia, 1982.
21. DELVERT, Jean, *Géographie de l'Asie du sud-est,* Paris: PUF, 1974.

22. DEVILLERS, Philippe, *et al.*, *L'Asie du sud-est*, Paris: Sirey, 1970, 2 vols.
23. DUPUIS, Jacques. *Singapour et la Malaysia*, Paris: PUF, 1972.
24. DWYER, D.J., *The city as a center of change in Asia*, Hong Kong UP, 1972.
26. FISHER, Charles A., *Southeast Asia, a social, economic and political geography*, London: Methuen, 1964.
27. FUBER, Holden, *River empires of trade in the Orient, 1600–1800*, vol. 2 ('Europe and the world in expansion'), Minneapolis: Minnesota UP, 1976.
28. GERINI, G.E., *Researches on Ptolemy's geography of Eastern Asia*, London: Royal Asiatic Monographs no. 1, 1909.
29. GIBSON-HILL, C.A., *Singapore: old strait and new harbour, 1300–1870*. Singapore (Raffles Museum Memoirs, no. 3), 1956.
30. GILMOUR, Andrew, *My role in the rehabilitation of Singapore, 1946–53*. Singapore: ISEAS, 1973.
31. GOUROU, Pierre, *L'Asie*, Paris: Hachette, 1953.
32. GRAHAM, Gerald S., *Great Britain in the Indian Ocean: A study of maritime enterprise, 1810–1850*, Oxford, 1967.
33. HAHN, Emily, *Raffles of Singapore: A biography*, Singapore: Univ. of Malaya Press, 1968.
34. HALL, D.G.E., *A history of South-East Asia*, London: Macmillan, 1955.
35. HALL, Kenneth R., *Maritime trade and state development in early Southeast Asia*, Honolulu: Univ. of Hawaii Press, 1985.
36. HALL-JONES, John, *An early surveyor in Singapore: John Turnbull Thomson in Singapore, 1841–1853*, Singapore: National Museum, 1979.
37. HAMILL, Ian, *The strategic illusion: The Singapore strategy and the defence of Australia and New Zealand, 1919–1942*, Singapore UP, 1981.
38. HILL, R.D. (ed.), *South-East Asia: A systematic geography*, Kuala Lumpur: OUP, 1975.
39. HUTTERER, Karl L., *Economic exchange and social interaction in South-East Asia: Perspectives from prehistory, history and ethnography*, Ann Arbor: Univ. of Michigan, Center for South and Southeast Asian Studies, 1977.
40. *In search of Southeast Asia: A modern history*, ed. by David J. Steinberg, New York: Praeger, 1971.
41. ISOART, Paul, *Les Etats de l'Asie du sud-est*, Paris: Economica, 1978.
42. JOGINDER, Jessy S., *Malaysia, Singapore and Brunei, 1400–1965* (2nd edn), Kuala Lumpur: Longman, 1974.
43. KENG WONG LIM, 'The trade of Singapore, 1819–69', Singapore: *Journal of the Malayan Branch of the Royal Asiatic Society*, vol. 22, no. 192.
44. LEE YONG LENG, *Southeast Asia: Essays in political geography*, Singapore UP, 1982.
45. LEUR, Jacob C. van, *Indonesian trade and society*, The Hague: Van Hoeve, 1955.
46. LIM PHAI SOM, *The economic development of Malaya*, Washington: IBRD, 1955.

47. LOW NGIONG ING, *When Singapore was Syonan-to*, Singapore: Eastern UP, 1973.
48. MAKEPEACE, Walter, *One 100 years of Singapore 1819–1919* (2 vols), London: John Murray, 1921.
49. MARKS, Harry, *The first contest for Singapore, 1819–24*, The Hague: Martinus Nijhoff, 1959.
50. MARSHALL, David S., *Singapore's struggle for nationhood, 1945–59*, Singapore: Univ. Education Press, 1971.
51. MILLER, Eugene H., *The Singapore naval base*, Worcester: Clark University, 1940.
52. MOORE, Donald and Joanna, *The first 150 years of Singapore*, Singapore: Donald Moore, 1969.
53. MOORE, Donald, *The magic dragon: The story of Singapore*, St Albans: Panther Books, 1975.
54. NEIDPATH, James, *The Singapore naval base and the defence of Britain's Eastern Empire, 1919–41*, Oxford: Clarendon Press, 1981.
55. NEWBORD, T.J., *Political and statistical accounts of the British Settlements in the Straits of Malacca* (reprint), Kuala Lumpur: OUP, 1971.
56. OSBORNE, Milton, *Southeast Asia, an introductory history*, Sydney: Geo. Allen and Unwin, 1979.
57. OWEN, Frank, *The fall of Singapore*, London: Michael Joseph, 1960.
58. PEARSON, Harold F., *Stories of early Singapore*, London University Press, 1953.
59. PLUVIER, Jan, *Southeast Asia from colonialism to independence*, Kuala Lumpur: OUP, 1974.
60. REID, Anthony, and Lance CASTLES (eds), *Pre-colonial state systems in Southeast Asia*, Kuala Lumpur: Malaysian Council of the Asiatic Society, 1975.
61. RICHER, Philippe, *L'Asie du sud-est*, Paris: Imprimerie Nationale, 1981.
62. ROBEQUAIN, Charles, *Le monde malais*, Paris: Payot, 1946.
63. RYAN, N.J., *The making of modern Malaysia and Singapore: A history from earliest times to 1966*, Kuala Lumpur: OUP, 1969.
64. SARDESAI, D.R., *British trade and expansion in Southeast Asia, 1830–1914*, New Delhi: Allied Publishers, 1977.
65. SCHONENBERGER, Toni, *Der Britische Rückzug aus Singapore, 1945–76*, Zürich: Atlantis, 1981.
66. SHINOZAKI, Mamoru, *Syonan, my story: The Japanese occupation of Singapore*, Singapore: Asia Pacific Press, 1979.
67. SIMSON, Ivan, *Singapore: Too little, too late, the failure of Malaya's defences in 1942*, Singapore: Donald Moore for Asia Pacific Press, 1970.
68. SMITH, R.B. and W. WATSON, *Early Southeast Asia: Essays in archaeology, history and historical geography*, London: OUP (SOAS), 1979.
69. SMYTH, Sir John, *Percival and the Tragedy of Singapore*, London: Macdonald, 1971.

70. TAN DING EING, *A portrait of Malaysia and Singapore*, Singapore: OUP, 1979.

71. TARLING, Nicholas, *Anglo-Dutch rivalry in the Malay world, 1780–1824*, St Lucia: Univ. of Queensland Press, 1962.

72. — , *A concise history of Southeast Asia*. New York: Praeger, 1966.

73. — , *British policy in the Malay Peninsula and Archipelago, 1824–71*, London: OUP, 1969.

74. TEO, Celine Kiew-ting, 'The development of the port of Singapore, 1819–1959', unpubl. thesis, University of Singapore, 1962.

75. TREGONNING, Kennedy G., *Home port Singapore: A history of Straits Steamship Company, 1890–1965*, Singapore: OUP, 1967.

76. TROCKI, Carl A., *Prince of pirates: The Temenggongs and the development of Johor and Singapore, 1784–1885*, Singapore: ISEAS, 1979.

77. TURNBULL, Mary, *The Straits Settlements, 1826–67*, London: Athlone Press, 1972.

78. — , *A history of Singapore, 1819–1975*, Kuala Lumpur: OUP, 1977.

79. WALLERSTEIN, I., *Le système du monde du XVe s. à nos jours*, vol. 1: 'Capitalisme et économie-monde, 1450–1640', Paris: Flammarion, 1980.

80. WEE SIEW-RUN, 'The port of Singapore: Post-war development of its physical facilities', unpubl. thesis, University of Singapore, 1977.

81. WILLIAMS, Lea E., *Southeast Asia, a history*, New York: OUP, 1966.

82. WINSTEDT, Richard, *The Malays, a cultural history* (6th edn), London: Routledge and Kegan Paul, 1961, 198 p.

83. WOLTERS, O.W., *Early Indonesian commerce: A study of the origins of Srivijaya*, Ithaca, New York: Cornell UP, 1967.

84. WURZBURG, C.E., *Raffles of the Eastern Isles*, London: Hodder & Stoughton, 1954.

85. YEO ENG-LENG, 'Effects of great depression on Singapore', unpubl. thesis, National Univ. of Singapore, 1973.

The economy of Singapore and its contemporary international functions

86. ALEXANDER, Lewis M., *Marine regionalism in the Southeast Asian Seas*, Honolulu: East-West Center, 1982 (Research Report no. 11).

87. ALVIN, Tay Tuan H., *Asian dollar market mobilizing funds for regional development*, Singapore: National Univ., Dept of Economics and Statistics, 1980.

88. AMJAD Rashid, (ed.), *The development of labour-intensive industry in ASEAN countries*, Geneva: ILO, 1981.

89. ANG HUE-CHOO, 'Industrialization in Singapore, 1960–70', unpubl. thesis, National University, Singapore, 1974.

90. ARIEF, Sritua, *Banking and finance in Indonesia: An econometric study*, Jakarta: Sritua Arief Associates, 1978.

92. Asia Pacific Centre, *The markets of Asia-Pacific: Singapore*, London: Asia Pacific Centre, 1981.
93. AW BEE YAN, *Factor content of ASEAN trade*, Madison: University of Wisconsin Press, 1980.
94. Bank Negara Malaysia, *Money and Banking in Malaysia* (2nd edn), Kuala Lumpur, 1984.
95. BARLOW, Colin, *The natural rubber industry in Malaysia*, Kuala Lumpur: OUP, 1978.
96. BHATTACHARYA, Anindya K., *The Asian dollar market*, New York: Praeger, 1977.
97. BUCHANAN, Iain B.A., *Singapore in Southeast Asia: An economic and political appraisal*, London: Geo Bell, 1972.
98. CAIN, James M., *Funnel of trouble: The Straits of Malacca and Singapore*, US Army War College, 1975.
99. CHEN, Edward K.Y., *Hyper-growth in Asian economies*, London: Macmillan, 1979.
100. CHEN, Peter S.J. (ed.), *Singapore Development Policies and Trends*, Singapore: OUP, 1983.
101. CHIA SIOW YUE, 'Industrialization strategy and industrial performance in Singapore, 1960–73', unpubl. Ph. D. thesis, McGill University, Montreal.
102. —, *Export processing and industrialization: The case of Singapore*, Bangkok: ILO/ARTEP, 1982.
103. CHOW KIT BOEY, *External linkages and economic development: The Singapore experience*, Singapore: Chopmen, 1980.
104. CRONE, Donald K., *The ASEAN States: Coping with dependence*, New York: Praeger, 1983.
105. DANUSAPUTRO, St Munadjat, *The marine environment of Southeast Asia*, Bandung: Binacipta, 1981.
106. DEUTSCH, Antal and HANNA Zowall, *Compulsory savings and taxes in Singapore*, Singapore: ISEAS, 1988.
107. DIAMOND, J., *The economic impact of international tourism on the Singapore economy*, Cambridge, Mass.: Harvard Institute for International Development, 1979.
108. DJOJOHADIKUSUMO, Sumitromo, *Trade and aid in Southeast Asia: Malaysia and Singapore*, Melbourne: F.W. Cheshire for Committee for Economic Development, 1968.
109. DOSHI, Tilak, *The Singapore petroleum industry*, Singapore: ISEAS and Resource Systems Institute of the East-West Center (Honolulu), 1989.
110. DRAKE, Peter J., *Financial development in Malaya and Singapore*, Canberra: Australian National UP, 1969.
111. DRAPER, Charles, *Private foreign investment in ASEAN*, Bangkok: Economic Cooperation Centre for the Asian and Pacific Region, 1974.
112. — (ed.), *Essays in Southeast Asian trade and development*, Bangkok:

Economic Cooperation Centre for the Asian and Pacific Region, 1973.

116. Economist Intelligence Unit, *The ASEAN, Hong Kong, South Korea and Taiwan economies*, London: EIU, 1980.

117. EVERS, Hans-Dieter (ed.), *Modernisation in Southeast Asia*, London: OUP, 1975.

118. FISK, E.K. and H. OSMAN-RANI, *The political economy of Malaysia*, Kuala Lumpur: OUP, 1982.

119. FISTIE, Pierre, *La Thaïlande*, Paris: PUF, 1980.

120. FOUBERT, Charles H., *Les Philippines. Le réveil d'un archipel*, Paris: Eds l'Harmattan, 1980.

121. GALLEZ, A. and J.L. TROUPIN, *Les perspectives d'industrialisation des pays du sud-est asiatique*, Louvain: Institut d'Etudes des Pays en Développement, 1982, 2 vols.

122. GARNAUT, Ross (ed.), *ASEAN in a changing Pacific and world economy*, Canberra: Australian National UP, 1980.

123. GEIGER, Theodore, *Tales of two city-states: The development of Hong Kong and Singapore*, Washington, DC: National Planning Association, 1975.

124. GOH KENG SWEE, *The economics of modernization*, Singapore: Asia Pacific Press, 1972.

125. ——, *The practice of economic growth*, Singapore: Federal Publications, 1977.

126. GOLAY, Frank, *Underdevelopment and economic nationalism in Southeast Asia*, Ithaca: Cornell UP, 1982.

128. GULLICK, John M., *Malaysia: Economic expansion and national unity*, London: Benn, 1981.

129. HAKAM, A.N., *Government-induced technology upgrading in Asian NICs: The case of Singapore*, Singapore: National University, Dept. of Business Administration, 1982.

130. ——, *Deliberate restructuring in the NICs of Asia: The case of Singapore*, Singapore: National University, School of Management, 1983.

131. HAMZAH, B.A., *Oil and economic development issues in Brunei*, Singapore: ISEAS, 1980.

132. HARDSTONE, Peter C.N., *State viability and the size factor: The Singapore case*, Singapore: Nanyang University, Dept of Geography, 1977.

133. HERMANN, Michael, *Hong Kong versus Singapore*, Stuttgart: G. Fischer, 1970.

134. HIMAWAN, Charles, *The foreign investment process in Indonesia*, Jakarta/Singapore: Gunung Agung, 1980.

135. HONG HAI and SAW SWEE HOK (eds), *Growth and direction of ASEAN trade*, Singapore UP, 1982.

136. HORI-ANDROUAIS, Anne, *Les investissements japonais dans les pays de l'ASEAN*, Paris: PUF, 1979.

137. HUA PAK CHEONG, *Elements of banking in Singapore*, Singapore: Institute of Banking and Finance, 1978.

138. HUGHES, Helen and YOU POH SENG (eds), *Foreign investment and industrialization in Singapore*, Madison: Univ. of Wisconsin Press, 1969.
139. Industrial Market Research Ltd., *Singapore: A business appraisal*, London, 1978.
140. JAAFFAR ABU BAKAR, *Prospects for marine regionalism in the Malacca and Singapore Straits*, Honolulu: Univ. of Hawaii Press, 1984.
141. JAMES, Williams E., *By-passed areas: Regional inequalities and development policies in selected Southeast Asian countries*, Manila: Asian Development Bank, 1981.
142. JESUDASON, James V., *Ethnicity and the economy: The state, Chinese business and multinationals in Malaysia*, Singapore: OUP, 1989.
143. — *et al.*, *The Singapore economy reconsidered*, Singapore: ISEAS, 1987.
144. KER SIN TZE, *Public enterprises in ASEAN: Introductory survey*, Singapore: ISEAS, 1978.
145. KHOR KOK PENG, *The Malaysian economy: Structures and dependence*, Kuala Lumpur: Institut Masyarakat, 1983.
146. KRAUSE, Lawrence B. (ed.), *Economic interaction in the Pacific Basin*, Washington, DC: Brookings Institution, 1980.
147. KRISHNA, Kumar, and Maxwell G. LEOD (eds), *Multinationals from developing countries*, Lexington, Mass.: Lexington Books, 1981.
148. LEE SHENG YI, *The monetary and banking development of Malaysia and Singapore*, Singapore UP, 1974.
149. —, *Public finance and public investment in Singapore*, Singapore: Institute of Banking and Finance, 1978.
150. —, *Financial structure and monetary policy of Singapore*, Singapore: Nanyang University, IEBS, 1979.
151. —, *ASEAN industrial joint ventures in the private sector*, Vienna: UNIDO, 21 April 1982.
152. —, and Y.C. JAO, *Financial structures and monetary policy in Southeast Asia*, London: Macmillan, 1982.
153. LEE SOO ANN, *Industrialization in Singapore*, Melbourne: Longmans, 1973.
154. —, *Singapore goes transnational*, Singapore: Eastern UP, 1977.
155. — (ed.), *Highlights of the ASEAN economy*, Singapore Airlines, 1977.
156. LEIFER, Michael, *Malacca, Singapore and Indonesia*, Alphen aan den Rijn: Sijthoff and Noordhoff, 1978.
157. LEUNG CHIU-KEUNG (ed.), *Hong Kong, dilemmas of growth*, Canberra: Australian National University, and Centre of Asian Studies, University of Hong Kong, 1980.
158. LIM CHONG YAH, *Economic development in Singapore*, Singapore: Federal Publications, 1980.
159. —, *Education and national development*, Singapore: Federal Publications, 1983.

160. —, *Economic restructuring in Singapore*, Singapore: Federal Publications, 1984.

161. LIM LIN LEANS and CHEE PENG LIM (eds), *The Malaysian economy at the crossroads*, Kuala Lumpur: Malaysian Economic Association, 1984.

162. LIM, Linda, and YUEN CHINH, *Multinational firms and manufacturing for export in LDCs: The case of the electronics industry in Malaysia and Singapore*, (2 vols), Ann Arbor: University of Michigan Press, 1978.

163. LIM MAH HUI, *Ownership and control of the one hundred largest corporations in Malaysia*, Kuala Lumpur: OUP, 1981.

164. LIM JOO JOCK (ed.), *Foreign investment in Singapore: Economic and socio-political ramifications*, Singapore: ISEAS, 1977.

165. LIM JOO JOCK, *Geo-strategy and the South China Sea Basin*, Singapore UP, 1979.

166. LIM THEAN SOO, *The impact of customs*, Singapore: National Printers, 1974.

167. LUTHER, Hans U., *Ökonomie, Klassen und Staat in Singapur*, Frankfurt am Main: Metzner, 1980.

168. MANGLAPUS, Raul S., *Japan and Southeast Asia: Collision course*, New York: Carnegie Endowment for International Peace, 1976.

169. MCANDREWS, Colin, *Southeast Asia Seas: Frontiers for development*, Singapore: McGraw-Hill, 1981.

170. MEANS, Gordon P. (ed.), *Development and underdevelopment in Southeast Asia*, Ottawa: Canadian Society for Asian Studies, 1977.

171. MORALES SIDDAYAO, Corazon, *The off-shore petroleum resources of Southeast Asia*, Singapore: OUP, 1978.

172. MORGAN, Theodore (ed.), *Economic interdependence in Southeast Asia*, Bangkok: Conference, 1969.

173. NASUTION, Anwar, *Financial institutions and policies in Indonesia*, Singapore: ISEAS, 1983.

174. NG, Charles, and T.P.B. MENON (eds), *Singapore: A Decade of Independence*, Singapore: Alumni International, 1975.

175. NG CHIN KEONG, *The Chinese in Riau: A community on an unstable and restricted frontier*, Singapore: Nanyang Univ., Institute of Human and Social Studies, 1976.

176. NG KWAN-MENG, *Intra-ASEAN investments: A case study of Singapore*, Singapore National Univ., Dept of Economics, 1982.

177. NIKLAS, Klaus-Peter, *Singapur: Beispiel einer weltmarktorientierten Industrialisierungspolitik*, Stuttgart: Gustav Fischer, 1977.

178. NYAW MEE-KAU, *Export expansion and industrial growth in Singapore*, Hong Kong: Kingsway, 1979.

179. ONN WEE-HOCK, *The economics of growth and survival*, Singapore: NTUC, 1978.

180. OW CHWEE-HUAY, *Singapore's trade with West Malaysia, 1950–68*, Singapore: Min. of Finance, 1970.

181. Ow, Jerry POH-SONG, 'Trade patterns Singapore/West Malaysia, 1962–71', unpubl. thesis, National University, Singapore, 1973.
182. PANG ENG FONG, *Education, manpower and development in Singapore*, Singapore UP, 1982.
183. —— and Linda LIM, *The electronics industry of Singapore: Structure, technology and linkages*, Singapore: Chopmen, 1977.
184. ——, *Trade, employment and industrialization in Singapore*, Geneva: ILO/OIT, 1986.
185. ——, *Trade, employment and industrialisation in Singapore*, Geneva: ILO, 1986.
186. PANG ENG FONG and Rajah V. KOMARAN, *Hong Kong and Singapore multinationals: A comparison*, Paris: OECD Development Centre, May 1984.
187. PANG ENG FONG and CHOW KIT BOY (eds), *The new economic order: UNCTAD IV and Singapore*, Singapore: Stamford College Press, 1976.
188. PANGESTU, Mari, *Japanese and other foreign investment in the ASEAN countries*, Canberra: Australia-Japan Research Centre, 1977.
189. PANGLAYKIM, J., *Indonesia's economic and business relations with ASEAN and Japan*, Jakarta: Yayasan Proklamasi, Centre for Strategic and International Studies, 1977.
190. PAPANEK, Gustav F., *The Indonesian economy*, New York: Praeger, 1980.
191. PERRIN, Jean-Claude, *Le développement régional*, Paris: PUF, 1974.
192. *Pratique des marchés internationaux: Singapour*, ed. Eds du Moniteur, Paris, 1981.
193. RABUSHKA, Alvin, *Hong Kong: A study in economic freedom*, University of Chicago, Graduate School of Business, 1979.
194. RAO, Bhanoj, *Income inequality in Singapore: Impact of economic growth and structural change, 1966–75*, Singapore UP, 1980.
195. RIEGER, Hans C., *ASEAN trade directions: Trends and prospects*, Singapore: ISEAS, May 1983.
196. ROCHEGUDE, Anne, *L'Indonésie aujourd'hui*, Paris, 1981.
197. RODAN, Garry, *The political economy of Singapore's industrialisation: National, state and international capital*, London: Macmillan, 1989.
198. RUEFF, Jacques, *Report on the economic aspects of Malaysia,* Washington, DC: IBRD and Singapore Government Printing Office, 1963.
199. SALIM, Emil, *Hubungan ekonomi Indonesia dengan Singapura* (Relations between the Indonesian economy and Singapore), Jakarta: LEKNAS, 1966.
200. SAW SWEE HOCK (ed.), *ASEAN economies in transition*, Singapore National University Press, 1980.
201. —— and LIM CHOO PENG (eds), *Investment analysis in Singapore*, Singapore Securities Research Institute, 1979.
202. SCALAPINO, Robert A., and JUSUF Wanandi (eds), *Economic, political and security issues in Southeast Asia in the 1980s*, Berkeley: Univ. of California Press, 1982.

203. SEAH CHEE MEOW, *Singapore's position in ASEAN cooperation*, Singapore, National University, Dept of Political Science (Chopmen), 1979.

204. SEEPOH OI MOON, *Pattern of tourism in ASEAN*, Singapore National Univ., Dept of Geography, 1977–8.

205. SENKUTTUVAN, Arun (ed.), *Conference on MNCs and ASEAN Development in the 1980s*, Singapore: ISEAS, 1981.

206. SEOW, Greg F.H., *The service sector in Singapore's economy: performance and structure*, Singapore National University, Economic Research Centre (Chopmen), 1980.

207. SHAW, K.E., *Performance and perspectives of the Singapore economy*, Tokyo: Institute of Developing Economies, 1976.

208. SHEU JIA YOU, Joe, 'Dependency, development and state: Hong Kong, Singapore, South Korea and Taiwan', unpubl. Ph D. thesis, University of Indiana, 1980.

209. SIEH LEE MEI LING, *Ownership and control of Malaysian manufacturing corporations*, Kuala Lumpur: UMBC Publications, 1982.

210. SIRISENA, N.L., *Problems and prospects of cooperation in banking, finance and monetary policy in ASEAN*, Singapore: Nanyang University, Institute of Economics and Business Studies, 1977.

211. SKULLY, Michael T., *Merchant banking in ASEAN: A regional examination of its development and operations*, Kuala Lumpur: OUP, 1983.

212. SOK CHUN TANG, *International investments in Singapore*, Singapore: Malayan Law Journal, 1973.

213. *Southeast Asia: An emerging center of world influence*, ed. Raymond Wayne and K. Mulliner, Athens: Ohio University Press, 1977.

214. Southeast Asian Study Group (ed.), *Questioning development in Southeast Asia*, Singapore, 1977.

215. SUWIDJANA, Njoman, *Jakarta dollar market: A case of financial development in ASEAN*, Singapore: ISEAS, 1984.

216. TAN CHWEE HUAT, 'State enterprise and economic development in Singapore', unpubl. Ph.D. thesis, Univ. of Wisconsin, Madison, 1974.

217. —, *Financial institutions in Singapore* (2nd edn), Singapore UP, 1981.

218. TAN ENG HOO (ed.), *The Singapore business environment, a survey report*, Delft: Graduate School of Management, 1979.

219. TAN I. TJHIH, *Business-government relations in Southeast Asia: A study of Singapore and Malaysia*, New York University, Graduate School of Business Administration, 1972.

220. TAN YAM PIN and J.R. BOLTON (eds), *Investment in Singapore*, Singapore: LGPG, 1966.

221. TATE, D.J.M., *The making of modern Southeast Asia*, Kuala Lumpur: OUP, 1971.

222. TEH KOK PENG, *Protection, fiscal incentives and industrialization in West Malaysia since 1975*, Kuala Lumpur: Univ. of Malaysia, 1977.

223. TROLLIET, Pierre, and N. DE MITRY, *L'économie de Singapour*, Paris:

Documentation française, N.E.D. no. 4543–44, 14 Dec. 1979.

224. VAN LIEMT, Gijsbert, *Bridging the gap: Four newly industrialising countries and the changing international division of labour*, Geneva: ILO, 1988.

225. —— (ed.), *The ethnic Chinese in the ASEAN states*, Singapore: ISEAS, 1989.

226. VIKSNINS, Georg J., *Financial deepening in ASEAN countries*, Honolulu: Pacific Forum, 1981.

227. WAWN, Brian, *The economies of the ASEAN countries*, London: OUP 1982.

WAYNE, Raymond, *see* 213 above.

228. WEE MON CHENG, *The future of the Chinese in Southeast Asia as viewed from the economic angle*, Singapore: South Seas Society, 1970.

229. WEE TEONG-BOO (ed.), *The future of Singapore: The global city*, Singapore: University Education Press, 1977.

230. WILSON, Dick, *The future role of Singapore*, London: OUP, 1972.

231. ——, *East meets West: Singapore* (2nd edn), Singapore: Times Printers, 1975.

232. WONG, John, *ASEAN economies in perspective*, London: Macmillan, 1979.

234. WONG SAIK CHIN, *Public reaction to the oil crisis: The Singapore case*, Singapore: ISEAS, 1975.

235. WORONOFF, Jon, *Hong Kong: Capitalist paradise*, Hong Kong: Heinemann Asia, 1980.

236. WU YUAN-LI, *Economic development in Southeast Asia: The Chinese dimension*, Stanford, Calif.: Hoover Institution Press, 1982.

237. YAO, J.C. and S.Y. LEE (eds), *Financial structures and monetary policies in Southeast Asia*, London: Macmillan, 1982.

238. YOSIHARA, Kunio, *Japanese investment in Southeast Asia*, Honolulu: Univ. of Hawaii Press, 1978.

239. YOU POH SENG and LIM CHONG YAH (eds), *Singapore: 25 Years of Development*, Singapore: Nan Yang Zhou Lianhe Zaobao, 1984.

240. ——, *The Singapore economy*, Singapore: Eastern Universities Press, 1971.

The foreign policy of Singapore since independence (1965) and the creation of ASEAN (1967).

241. ABDUL RAHMAN, Putra Tunku, *As a matter of interest*, Kuala Lumpur: Heinemann Asia, 1981.

242. ABELL, Robyn, 'Philippine policy towards regional cooperation in Southeast Asia, 1961–69', unpubl. thesis, Australian National Univ., 1972.

243. ADULBHAN, Pakorn, *The role of the private sector in industrial and technological cooperation in ASEAN*, Vienna: UNIDO, July 1982.

244. AKRASANEE, Narongchaix, and V. Vichit-Vadakan (eds), *ASEAN*

cooperation in foreign investment and transnational corporations, Bangkok: Asian and Pacific Institute, 1979, 2 vols.

245. AMYOT, Jacques, *The Chinese and the national integration of Southeast Asia*, Bangkok: Chulalongkorn University, 1972.

246. ANAND, R.P. (ed.), *ASEAN: Identity, development and culture*, Quezon City: Univ. of the Philippines Law Center, 1981.

247. ANDERSEN, Robert A., *The separation of Singapore from Malaysia*, Washington, DC, 1973.

248. ARIEF, Sritua, *The Southeast Asian trade flows: A Statistical study of trade preference*, East Balmain (Australia): Rosecons, 1983.

249. ARIFF, Mohamed (ed.), *ASEAN cooperation in industrial projects*, Kuala Lumpur: Malaysian Economic Association, 1977.

250. BEAULIEU, Peter D., *Singapore: A case study of communalism and economic development*, Seattle: Univ. of Washington Press, 1975.

251. BEDLINGTON, Stanley S., *Malaysia and Singapore: The building of new states.*, Ithaca: Cornell UP, 1978.

252. BHATTACHARJEE, G.P., *Southeast Asian politics: Malaysia and Indonesia*, Calcutta: Minerva Associates, 1976.

253. BOLAND, B.J., *The struggle of Islam in modern Indonesia*, The Hague: Martinus Nijhoff, 1982.

254. BONNEFF, Marcel, *Pantjasila. 30 années de débats politiques en Indonésie*, Paris: CERI, Maison des Sciences de l'Homme, 1980.

255. BOYCE, Peter, *Malaysia and Singapore in international diplomacy*, Sidney Univ. Press, 1968.

256. BRACKMAN, Arnold C., *Indonesian communism: A history*, New York: Praeger, 1963.

257. —, *The communist collapse in Indonesia*, Singapore: Donald Moore, 1970.

258. —, *Indonesia: Suharto's road*, New York: American-Asian Educational Exchange, 1972.

259. BROINOWSKI, Alison (ed.), *Understanding ASEAN*, London: Macmillan, 1982.

260. BURCHETT, Wilfred G., *The China-Cambodia-Vietnam triangle*, Chicago: Vanguard Books, 1981.

261. CADY, John F., *The history of post-war Southeast Asia*, Athens: Ohio UP, 1974.

262. CAMILLERI, Joseph, *Southeast Asia in China's foreign policy*, Singapore: ISEAS, 1975.

263. CARSTENS, Sharon A., *Chinese associations in Singapore society*, Singapore: ISEAS, 1975.

264. CATTORI, Sylvia and Jean, *Asie du sud-est. L'enjeu thaïlandais*, Paris: L'Harmattan, 1979.

265. CAYRAC-BLANCHARD, Françoise, *Le parti communiste indonésien*, Paris: Armand Colin, 1973.

Select Bibliography

266. CHAWLA, Sudershan, *Southeast Asia under the new balance of nower*, New York: Praeger, 1974.
267. CHEAH BOON KHENG, *Red star over Malaya: Resistance and social conflict during and after the Japanese occupation, 1941–46*, Singapore UP, 1983.
268. CHIA SIOW YUE, *Singapore and ASEAN economic cooperation*, Bangkok: UN Asian and Pacific Development Institute, 1978.
269. — (ed.), *ASEAN economic cooperation*, Singapore: ISEAS, 1980.
270. CHONG LI CHOY, *Open self-regionalism: Power for ASEAN development*, Singapore: ISEAS, 1981.
271. CLAGUE, Peter, *Iron spearhead: The true story of a communist killer squad in Singapore*, Singapore: Heinemann, 1980.
272. CLAMMER, John R., *The ambiguity of identity: Ethnicity maintenance and change among the Chinese community of Malaysia and Singapore*, Singapore: ISEAS, 1979.
273. CLUTTERBUCK, Richard L., *The long, long war: The emergency in Malaya, 1948–60*. London: Cassell, 1967.
274. —, *Conflict and violence in Singapore and Malaysia, 1945–83* (2nd edn, revised), Singapore: Graham Brash, 1984.
275. COMBER, Leon, *13 May 1969: A historical survey of Sino-Malay relations*, Kuala Lumpur: Heinemann Asia, 1983.
276. COPPEL, Charles A., *Chinese in Indonesia, the Philippines and Malaysia*. London, Minority Rights Group, February 1982.
277. —, *Indonesian Chinese in crisis*, Kuala Lumpur: OUP, 1983.
278. CROUCH, Harold, *Domestic political structures and regional economic cooperation*, Singapore: ISEAS, 1984.
279. DRYSDALE, John, *Singapore: Struggle for success*, Singapore: Times, 1984.
281. FIFIELD, Russell H., *National and regional interests in ASEAN competition and cooperation*, Singapore: ISEAS, 1979.
282. FITZGERALD, C.P., *The third China: The Chinese communities in Southeast Asia*, Melbourne: Donald Moore, 1965.
283. —, *China and Southeast Asia since 1945*, Melbourne: Longman Australia, 1973.
284. FITZGERALD, Stephen, *China and the Overseas Chinese*, Cambridge UP, 1972.
285. FLETCHER, Nancy, *The separation of Singapore from Malaysia*, Ithaca: Cornell UP, 1967.
286. FUNSTON, N.J., *Malay politics in Malaysia: A study of the UMNO and Party Islam*, Kuala Lumpur: Heinemann, 1980.
287. GAGLIANO, Felix V., *Communal violence in Malaysia 1969: The political aftermath*, Athens: Ohio Univ. Center for International Studies, 1971.
288. GHAZALI, Muhammad bin Shafie, *Malaysia: International relations*, selected speeches, Kuala Lumpur: Creative Enterprise, 1982.
289. GOH CHENG TEIK, *Integration in a plural society: The Chinese in Malaysia*, Kuala Lumpur: Straits Echo Press, 1978.

290. GOSLING, L.A. Peter, and L. LIM (eds), *The Chinese in Southeast Asia* (2 vols), Singapore: Maruzen Asia, 1983.
291. GUILLOINEAU, Jean, *La Chine, l'URSS et les autres. L' Asie du sud-est et le conflit sino-soviétique*, Paris: Plon, 1980.
292. GULLICK, John M., *Malaysia: Economic expansion and national unity*, London: Benn, 1981.
293. GURTOV, MELVIN, *China and Southeast Asia: The politics of survival*, Lexington, Mass.: D.C Heath, 1975.
294. HASHIM, Wan, *Race relations in Malaysia*, Kuala Lumpur: Heinemann Asia, 1983.
295. HEIDHUES, Mary F.S., *Southeast Asia's Chinese minorities*, Hawthorn, Australia: Longman, 1974.
296. HUGHES, John, *Indonesia upheaval*, New York: David McKay, 1967.
297. HUNTER, Guy, *Southeast Asia: Race, culture and nation*, London: OUP, 1966.
298. INDORF, Hans H., *Impediments to regionalism in Southeast Asia: Bilateral constraints among ASEAN member states*, Singapore: ISEAS, 1984.
299. JAMAR, Joseph (ed.), *Intégrations régionales entre pays en voie de développement*, Bruges: College of Europe (Tempelhof), 1982.
300. JON QUAH, CHAN HENG CHEE and SEAH CHEE MEOW (eds), *Government and politics of Singapore*, Singapore: OUP, 1985.
301. JONES, Howard P., *Indonesia: The possible dream*, Singapore: Aryn Mas, 1977.
302. JØRGENSEN-DAHL, Arnfinn, *Regional organization and order in Southeast Asia*, London: Macmillan, 1982.
303. JOSEY, Alex, *Lee Kuan Yew and the Commonwealth*, Singapore: Donald Moore, 1969.
304. KAHIN, George McT., *Nationalism and revolution in Indonesia*, Ithaca: Cornell UP, 1966.
305. KHAW GUAT HOON, *Malaysian policies in Southeast Asia, 1957–70*, Singapore National Univ., 1976.
306. —, *An analysis of China's attitude towards ASEAN, 1967–76*, Singapore: ISEAS, 1977.
307. KAU MAU POHINI, *The Philippines and Southeast Asia*, New Delhi: Radiant, 1978.
308. KRAUSE, Lawrence B., *US economic policy toward the Association of Southeast Asian Nations*, Washington, DC: Brookings Institution, 1982.
309. KROEF, Justus M. van der, *Communism in Malaysia and Singapore: A contemporary survey*, The Hague: Martinus Nijhoff, 1967.
310. —, *Communism in Southeast Asia*, London: Macmillan, 1981.
311. LAU TEIK SOON, *Malaysia–Singapore foreign policies in Southeast Asia, 1965–70*, Canberra, Australian National UP, 1971.
312. LEE KUAN YEW, *The battle for a Malaysian Malaysia* (2 vols), Singapore: Min. of Culture, 1965.

313. LEE LAI-TO, *China's changing attitude towards Singapore, 1965–75*, Singapore National Univ., Dept of Political Science, 1975.
314. LEE POH PING, *Chinese society in 19th and early 20th century Singapore*, Ithaca: Cornell UP, 1974.
315. LEE, Raymond Lai Ming, *The social meaning of mass hysteria in West Malaysia and Singapore*, Boston: Univ. of Massachusetts Press, 1979.
316. LEE SHENG YI, *Asean industrial joint ventures in the private sector*, Vienna: UNIDO, 1982.
317. LEE TING HUI, *The communist organization in Singapore: Its techniques of manpower mobilization and management, 1948–66*, Singapore: ISEAS, 1976.
318. LEE YONG LENG, *Southeast Asia: Essays in political geography*, Singapore UP, 1982.
319. LEIFER Michel, *Dilemma of statehood in Southeast Asia*, Singapore: Asia Pacific Press, 1972.
320. —, *Indonesia's foreign policy*, London: Geo. Allen & Unwin for RIIA, 1983.
321. LIM CHONG YAH, *Singapore's position in ASEAN cooperation*, Tokyo: Institute of Developing Economies, 1979.
322. LIM JOO-JOCK, *Territorial power domains: Southeast Asia and China*, Singapore: ISEAS, 1984.
323. — and S. VANI, *Armed communist movements in Southeast Asia*, Singapore: ISEAS (Gower Publishing), 1984.
324. LOW LAI TENG, *Indonesian attitudes towards the Vietnamese war, 1965–75*, Singapore National Univ., Dept of History, 1981.
325. MACKIE, J.A.C., *Konfrontasi: The Indonesian-Malaysia dispute 1963–66*, Kuala Lumpur: OUP, 1974.
326. MALIK, Adam, *In the service of the Republic*, Singapore: Gunung Agung, 1980.
327. MARK LAU FONG, *The sociology of secret societies in Singapore and Peninsular Malaysia*, Kuala Lumpur: OUP, 1981.
328. MARTIN, Edwin W., *Southeast Asia and China: The end of containment*, Boulder, Colo.: Westview Press, 1977.
329. MCDOUGALL, John A., *Shared burdens: A study of communal discrimination by the political parties of Malaysia and Singapore*, Cambridge, Mass.: Harvard UP, 1968.
330. MAUZY, Diane (ed.), *Politics in the ASEAN states*, Kuala Lumpur: Marican, 1984.
331. MILNE, R.S. and D.K. MAUZY, *Politics and government in Malaysia*, Singapore: Federal Publications, 1978.
332. MOESE, Wolfgang (ed.), *Chinese regionalism in West Malaysia and Singapore*, Hamburg: Volkswagen Foundation, 1979.
333. MORELL, David, and Chai-Anan SAMUDAVANIJA, *Political conflict in Thailand: Reform, reaction, revolution*, Cambridge: Oelgeschlager, Gunn and Hain, 1981.

334. MORRISON, Charles E., *Southeast Asia in a changing international environment: A comparative foreign policy of four ASEAN member countries*, Baltimore: Johns Hopkins UP, 1976.

335. —, and SUHRKE, *Strategies of survival, the foreign policy dilemmas of smaller Asian states*, New York: St Martin's Press, 1978.

336. MORTIMER, Rex, *Indonesian communism under Sukarno: Ideology and politics, 1959–65*, Ithaca, Cornell UP, 1974.

337. MOZINGO, David P., *Sino-Indonesian relations: An overview, 1955–65*, Santa Barbara: Rand Corp., 1965.

338. —, *Chinese policy towards Indonesia, 1949–67*, Ithaca: Cornell UP, 1976.

339. NAM TAE YUL, *Malaysia and Singapore: The failure of an experiment*, Iowa City, 1969.

340. —, *Racism, nationalism and nation-building in Malaysia and Singapore*, Meerut, 1973.

341. NARONG CHAI, Akrasanee, *Thailand and ASEAN economic cooperation.* Singapore: ISEAS, 1980.

342. NAYA, Seiji (ed.), *ASEAN trade development and cooperation: PTA and trade liberalization*, New York: UN Report to ESCAP, 1980.

343. NEHER, Clark D., *Politics in Southeast Asia*, Cambridge: Schenkman, 1979.

344. NEO, Mary, *Intra-ASEAN cooperation: 1st summit to 2nd summit*, Singapore: National University, 1977.

345. NISHIKAWA, Jun, *ASEAN and the United Nations System*, New York: UNITAR, 1983.

346. NOORDIE, M.S., *From Malayan union to Singapore separation, 1945–65*, Kuala Lumpur: Univ. of Malaya, 1974.

347. O'BALLANCE, Edgar, *Malaya: The communist insurgent war, 1948–60*, London: Faber and Faber, 1966.

348. ONGKILI, James P., *Malaysia 1946–73: Nation building and the problem of communalism*, Kuala Lumpur: Univ. of Malaya, 1980.

349. OOI GUAT TIN, *The ASEAN preferential trade agreement: An analysis of potential effects on intra-ASEAN trade*, Singapore: ISEAS, 1981.

350. OSBORNE, Milton, *Singapore and Malaysia*, Ithaca: Cornell University Press, 1964.

351. OSTROM, Charles R., *A core interest analysis of the formation of Malaysia and the separation of Singapore*, Claremont, Graduate School, 1970.

352. PATERNO, Vicente T., *ASEAN industrial complementation*, Vienna: UNIDO, 1982.

353. PATHMANATHAN, Murugesu (ed.), *Readings in Malaysian foreign policy*, Kuala Lumpur: University of Malaya, 1976.

354. PAUKER, Guy J., F.H. GOLAY and C.H. ENLOE, *Diversity and development in Southeast Asia*, New York: McGraw-Hill, 1980.

355. PAUL, Erik C., *The viability of Singapore: An aspect of modern political geography*, Berkeley, Univ. of California Press, 1973.

292 *Select Bibliography*

356. PEACOCK, James L., *Muslim puritans: Reformist psychology in Southeast Asian Islam*, Berkeley: Univ. of California Press, 1978.
357. PETTMAN, Ralph, *Small power politics and international relations in Southeast Asia*, Sydney: Holt, Rinehart and Winston, 1976.
358. PFENNIG, Werner, and Mark SUH, *Aspects of ASEAN*, Cologne: Weltforum, 1984.
359. PHANIT, Thakur, *Regional integration attempts in Southeast Asia: A study of ASEAN's problems and progress*, Pennsylvania State Univ., Dept of Political Science, 1980.
360. PHUANGKASEM, Corinne, *Thailand's foreign relations, 1964–80*, Singapore: ISEAS.
362. PRINGLE, Robert, *Indonesia and the Philippines: US interests in island Southeast Asia*, New York: Columbia UP, 1980.
363. PURCELL, Victor, *The Chinese in Southeast Asia*, London: OUP 1965.
364. RAJENDRAN, Singhay G., *Singapore in ASEAN*, Singapore National University, Dept of Political Science, 1976.
365. RANJIT SINGH, D.S., *Brunei, 1839–1983: The problems of political survival*, Singapore: OUP, 1984.
366. RAU, Robert L., *Singapore's foreign relations 1965–72, with emphasis on the Five Power Commonwealth Group*, Ann Arbor: Univ. of Michigan Press, 1974.
367. REINHARDT, Jon M., *Foreign policy and national integration: The case of Indonesia*, New Haven: Yale University, Southeast Asian Studies, 1971.
368. RICHER, Philippe, *Jeu de quatre en Asie du sud-est*, Paris: PUF, 1982.
369. ROCHEGUDE, Anne, *L'Indonésie aujourd'hui*, Paris, 1981.
370. SANDHU, Kernial S., *A decade of ASEAN*, Singapore: Educational Publications, 1978.
371. SARAVANAMUTHU, J., *The dilemma of independence: Two decades of Malaysia's foreign policy, 1957–77*, Penang: Univ. Sains Malaysia, School of Social Sciences, 1983.
372. SARDESAI, D.R., *Southeast Asia past and present*, New Delhi: Vikas, 1981.
373. SEAH CHEE MEOW, *Singapore's position in ASEAN cooperation*, Singapore National Univ., Dept of Political Science, 1979.
374. SEAH, Tony Eng-wah, 'Problems and prospects of economic cooperation between Indonesia and other ASEAN members, with special reference to Singapore', National University Library, Singapore, 1977.
375. SHEE POON KIM, *The roots of sinophobia in the ASEAN countries*, Singapore: Nanyang University, 1977.
376. ——, *The ASEAN states relations with Vietnam*, Singapore National University, 1980.
377. SHORT, Anthony, *The communist insurrection in Malaysia, 1948–60*, London: Fredk Muller, 1975.

378. SIDDAYANO, Corazon (ed.), *ASEAN and the multinational corporations*, Singapore/Jakarta: ISEAS and CSIS, 1978.
379. SIMON, Sheldon W., *The ASEAN states and regional security*, Stanford: Hoover Institution Press, 1982.
380. SINAGA, Janner, *ASEAN: Economic, political and defense problems and prospects in regional cooperation with reference to major powers in Southeast Asia*, Washington, DC: Georgetown Univ., 1974.
381. SINGHAM, Geoffrey R., 'Singapore in ASEAN', unpubl. thesis, National Univ., Singapore, 1977.
382. SIOW, Moli, *Conflict, consensus and political change: Case-study of intra-ethnic divisions in West Malaysia*, Ann Arbor: Michigan UP, 1980.
383. SKULLY, Michael T., *ASEAN regional financial cooperation*, Singapore: ISEAS, 1979.
384. SNOW, Roger W., *A comparative analysis of confrontation as an instrument of Indonesian foreign policy*, Seattle: Univ. of Washington Press, 1973.
385. SONG ONG SIANG, *One hundred years' history of the Chinese in Singapore*, Singapore: Univ. of Malaya Press, 1967.
386. SUH, Mark (ed.), *The ASEAN: Regional cooperation in the ascendant*, Berlin: FGS AP, 1983.
387. SURYADINATA, Leo, *Indigeneous Indonesian, the Chinese minority and China*. Washington, DC: American University, 1975.
388. — (ed.), *Political Thinking of the Indonesian Chinese, 1900–1977*, Singapore University Press, 1979.
389. TAJIMA, Takashi., *China and Southeast Asia: Strategic interest and policy prospects*, London: Institute for Strategic Studies, 1981.
390. TALABOT, Marcel, *Singapour, troisième Chine*, Paris: Robert Laffont, 1974.
391. TAN, Gerald, *Trade liberalization in ASEAN*, Singapore: ISEAS, 1982.
392. TAN FUH GIH, *ASEAN monetary and banking cooperation from the standpoint of Singapore and Malaysia*, Singapore: Nanyang Univ., 1977.
393. TARNTHONG, Thongswasdi, *ASEAN after the Vietnam war*, Claremont: California Graduate School, 1979.
394. TAYLOR, Jay., *China in Southeast Asia: Peking's relations with revolutionnary movements*, New York: Praeger, 1974.
395. THOMPSON, George G. (ed.), *Singapore's international relations*, Singapore: Education Board, 1966.
396. TILMAN, Robert O., *The enemy beyond: External threat perceptions in the ASEAN region*, Singapore: ISEAS, 1984.
397. VIRAPHOL, S. (ed.), *The ASEAN: Problems and prospects in a changing world*, Bangkok: Chulalongkorn Univ., 1975.
398. WANG GUNGWU, *Community and nation: essays on Southeast Asia and the Chinese*, Singapore: Heinemann Asia, 1981.
399. WARSHAWSKY, Howard, 'From confrontation to cooperation: The influence of domestic forces on Indonesian foreign policy', unpubl. Ph.D. thesis, Univ. of Virginia, Charlottesville, 1974.

400. WEINSTEIN, Franklin B., *The uses of foreign policy in Indonesia*, Ithaca: Cornell UP, 1972.
401. ——, *Indonesian foreign policy and the dilemma of dependence: From Sukarno to Suharto*, Ithaca: Cornell UP, 1976.
402. WILAIRAT, Kawin, 'Singapore's foreign policy: a study of the foreign policy system of a city-state', unpubl Ph. D. thesis, Georgetown Univ., Washington, DC, 1975.
403. ——, *Singapore's foreign policy*, Singapore: ISEAS, 1975.
404. WILLIAMS, Lea E., *The future of the Overseas Chinese in Southeast Asia*, Washington DC, US Council on Foreign Relations, 1966.
405. WILSON, Dick, *The neutralization of Southeast Asia.*, New York: Praeger, 1975.
406. WU TEH YAO, *Southeast Asia and China: Asian neighbours*, Singapore National University, Dept of Political Science, 1974.
407. ——, *Politics East, politics West*, Singapore: Pan Pacific, 1979.
408. WU YUAN LI, *Economic development in Southeast Asia: The Chinese dimension*, Stanford: Hoover Institution Press, 1980.
409. WONG, John, *The political economy of China's changing relations with Southeast Asia*, Singapore National Univ, 1984.
410. YONG, C.P. (ed.), *Ethnic Chinese in Southeast Asia*, Singapore University Press, 1981.
411. ZACHER, Mark W., and MILNE, R.S., *Conflict and stability in Southeast Asia*, New York: Anchor Books, 1974.
412. ZAGORIA, Donald S., *Vietnam triangle: Moscow, Peking, Hanoi*, New York: Pegasus, 1968.

Singapore: Internal politics and society

413. BEDLINGTON, Stanley S., *The Singapore Malay community: The politics of state integration*, Ithaca: Cornell UP, 1974.
414. BELL, David S., *Unity in diversity: Education and political integration in an ethnically pluralistic society*, Indiana Univ., Dept of Political Science, 1972.
415. BELLOWS, Thomas J., *The Singapore party system: The first two decades*, New Haven: Yale UP, 1978.
416. BENJAMIN, Geoffrey, *The cultural logic of Singapore's multiracialism*, Singapore National Univ., Dept of Sociology, 1975.
417. BETTS, Russel H., *Multiracialism, meritocracy and the Malays of Singapore*, Ann Arbor: Univ. of Michigan Press, 1978.
418. BUSCH, Peter A., *Political unity and ethnic diversity: A case study of Singapore*, New Haven: Yale UP, 1972.
419. CHAN HENG CHEE, *Singapore: the politics of survival, 1965–67*, Singapore: OUP, 1971.
420. ——, *The dynamics of one party dominance: The PAP at the grass roots*. Singapore, Univ. Press, 1976.
421. ——, *In middle passage: The PAP faces the 80s*, Singapore NU, 1979.

422. CHEN, George W.H., *The social bases of political development and integration: The case of Singapore*, Eugene: Univ. of Oregon, 1974.
423. CHEN, Peter S.J., *Elites and national development in Singapore*, Singapore National Univ., Dept. of Sociology, 1975.
424. —, and James T. Fawcett, *Public Policy and Population Change in Singapore*, New York: The Population Council, 1979.
425. CHIN KIN WAH, *The defence of Malaysia and Singapore: The transformation of a security system, 1957–71*, Cambridge UP, 1983.
426. CLAMMER, John, *Singapore: Ideology, society and culture*, Singapore: Chopmen, 1985.
427. CRAIG, Jo Ann, *Culture shock! What not to do in Malaysia and Singapore, how and why not to do it*, Singapore: Times International, 1979.
428. DAHM, Bernhard, and W. DRAGUHN (eds), *Politics, society and economy in the ASEAN states*, Wiesbaden: Harrassowitz, 1975.
430. FIC Victor H. Fic (ed.), *Strategies for social change: from upon Malaysia and Singapore*, St Catherines: Brock Univ., Canadian Society for Asian Studies, 1974.
431. FONG SIP CHEE, *The PAP story: The pioneering years*, Singapore: Times, 1979.
432. GEORGE, T.J.S., *Lee Kuan Yew's Singapore*, Singapore: Eastern Univ. Press, 1984 (1st edn 1973).
433. GIRLING, John L.S., *The bureaucratic policy in modernizing societies: Similarities, differences and prospects in the ASEAN region*, Singapore: ISEAS, 1981.
434. HASSAN, Riaz (ed.), *Singapore society in transition*, Kuala Lumpur: OUP, 1976.
435. HOADLEY, J. Stephen, *The military in the politics of South East Asia*, Cambridge, Mass.: Schenkman, 1975.
436. ISEAS (ed.), *Political and social change in Singapore*, Singapore: ISEAS, 1975.
437. JAYAKUMAR, J. (ed.), *Our heritage and beyond, a collection of essays on Singapore, its past, present and future*, Singapore: NTUC, 1982.
438. JOSEY, Alex, *Singapore, its past, present and future*, Singapore: Eastern University Press, 1980 (1st edn 1973).
439. —, *Lee Kuan Yew*, Singapore: Times International, 1980, 2 vols (1st edn 1968, 1 vol.).
440. —, *Industrial relations: labour laws in a developing Singapore*, Singapore: Federal Publications, 1976.
441. —, *Personal opinion*, Singapore: Federal Publications, 1978.
442. —, *Lee Kuan Yew: The struggle for Singapore*, Sydney: Angus and Robertson, 1980.
443. KASSIM, Ismail, *Problems of élite cohesion: A perspective from a minority community*, Singapore University Press, 1974.
444. RUO Eddie C.Y., and E.A. AFENDRAS (eds), *Language and society in Singapore*, Singapore UP, 1980.

296 *Select Bibliography*

445. KUO, Eddie, and Aline WONG (eds), *The contemporary family in Singapore: Structure and changes*, Singapore UP, 1979.
446. LEONG CHOON CHEONG, *Youth in the army*, Singapore: Federal Publications, 1978.
447. LEONG, Peter Hu-weng, 'Business élites in Singapore with special reference to the Chinese case', Singapore: National Library, 1977.
448. LIM CHONG YAH, *Education and national development*, Singapore: Federal Publ., 1983.
449. MARGOLIN, Jean-Louis, 'Singapour, 1954–80. Économie, politique, société, une dialectique' (2 vols), unpubl. thesis, Univ. of Paris VII, 1982.
450. ——, *Singapour, 1959–1987. Genèse d'un nouveau pays industriel*, Paris: L'Harmattan, 1989.
451. MILNE, R.S., and Diane K. Mauzy, *Singapore: The legacy of Lee Kuan Yew*, Boulder: Westview Press, 1990.
452. MOEY YUE KEN, 'The defence policy of Singapore, 1965–72', unpubl. thesis, National University, Singapore, 1974.
453. NAIR, Devan, *Tomorrow, the peril and the promise*, Singapore: NTUC, 1976.
454. ——, *Socialism that works ... the Singapore way*, Singapore: Federal Publications, 1976.
455. ——, *Not by wages alone*, Singapore: NTUC, 1982.
456. NEVILLE, Mollie and Warwick, *Singapore, a disciplined society*, Auckland: Heinemann, 1980.
457. OOI JIN BEE and CHIANG HAI DING (eds), *Modern Singapore*, Singapore University Press, 1969.
458. ONG TENG CHEONG, *Report on moral education, 1979*, Singapore: Moral Education Committee, 1979.
459. ONG WEE HOCK, *Job creation or job loss? What every Singaporean should know about the economics of survival*, Singapore: NTUC, 1977.
460. PANG CHONG LIAN, *Singapore's PAP: Its history, organization and leadership*, Singapore: OUP, 1971.
461. PERITZ, René, *The evolving politics of Singapore: A study of trends and issues*, Philadelphia: Univ. of Pennsylvania Press, 1964.
462. PLATT, John T., *English in Singapore and Malaysia,* Kuala Lumpur: OUP, 1980.
463. PRANEE, Saipiroon, *ASEAN governments' attitudes towards regional security, 1975–79*, Bangkok: Chulalongkorn Univ., Institute of Asian Studies, 1982.
464. QUAH JON SIEN, T., *Administrative and legal measures for combating bureaucratic corruption in Singapore*, Singapore, National Univ., Dept. of Political Science, 1978.
465. ——, The origins of the public bureaucracies in the ASEAN countries. Singapore National Univ., Dept. of Political Science, 1978.

466. ——, CHANG HENG CHEE and SEAH CHEE MEOW (eds), *Government and politics in Singapore*, Singapore: OUP, 1985.

467. SAW SWEE HOCK and R.S. BHATAL (eds), *Singapore towards the year 2000*, Singapore UP, 1981.

468. SEAH CHEE MEOW, *The Singapore bureaucracy and issues of transition*, Singapore National Univ., Dept. of Political Science, 1975.

469. ——, *Higher education in the changing environment, case study of Singapore and Indonesia*, Singapore: Regional Institute for Higher Education and Development, 1979.

470. SEAH CHEE MEOW (ed.), *Trends in Singapore*, Singapore: ISEAS, 1975.

471. SHAW, K.E. (ed.), *Elites and national development in Singapore*, Tokyo: Institute of Developing Economies, 1977.

472. SIDDIQUE, Sharon, *Singapore's little India*, Singapore: ISEAS, 1982.

473. SIMON, Sheldon, *The ASEAN states and regional security*, Stanford: Hoover Institution Press, 1982.

474. SINGH Sandhu, Kernial, and Paul WHEATLEY, *Management of success: The moulding of Singapore*, Singapore: ISEAS, 1989.

475. SOLIDUM, Estrella D., *Towards a Southeast Asian community*, Quezon City: Univ. of the Philippines Press, 1974.

476. SOON TECK WONG, *Singapore's new education system: Education reform for national development*, Singapore: ISEAS, 1988.

477. TAN TAI WEI, *Our social framework and its ethical basis*, Singapore: Oriental UP, 1973.

478. THOMPSON, George G. (ed.), *The concept of democracy*, Singapore: Adult Education Board, 1964.

479. TYRES, Ray, *Singapore then and now* (2 vols), Singapore: Univ. Education Press, 1976.

480. VASIL, Raj K., *Governing Singapore*, Singapore: Eastern Universities Press, 1984.

481. WALTER, Michael A., and Riaz HASSAN, *An island community in Singapore: A characterization of a marginal society*. Singapore National Univ., Dept of Sociology, 1977.

482. WIMALASARI, Jayantha, *Correlates of work values of Singapore employees*, Singapore National Univ., School of Managment, 1983.

483. WONG, Evelyne Sue, *Industrial relations in Singapore: Challenge of the 1980s*, Singapore National Univ., Dept of Business Administration, 1982.

484. WU TEH YAO, *Political and social change in Singapore*, Singapore: ISEAS, 1975.

485. YEO KIM WAH, *Political development in Singapore, 1945–55*, Singapore UP, 1973.

486. YEO MUI KIN, *Some aspects of the population and urban geography of an island republic: The case study of Singapore since 1957*, London: SOAS, 1974.

INDEX

Australia, 70, 83, 86, 93, 99, 109, 112, 115, 123, 132, 137, 141, 191, 255
ASEAN, 1, 3, 11, 15, 18, 27, 36–8, 41, 47, 55–6, 62–5, 69, 74, 80, 82–4, 90–3, 97, 99, 103, 106, 107, 109–15, 117–19, 121, 123–6, 128–9, 131, 133–6, 138–9, 144–6, 148–50, 152–5, 157–8, 162–3, 165–89, 191–3, 210, 213–16, 218–27, 231, 235–9, 250, 254, 256, 259, 263, 264–5, 267

Bandung, 200, 217
Bangkok, 69, 86, 107, 146, 165–6, 171, 221
Barisan Socialis, 207–8, 213, 232–4, 244–5
Batam, 75–80, 85, 98–9, 157, 161–3, 273–5
Borneo, 18, 23, 45, 75, 118
Britain, *see* United Kingdom
Brunei, Sultanate of, 10, 39, 41, 84–5, 87, 110, 112, 115, 117, 124–6, 129–31, 133–5, 144, 147–8, 150, 177, 207, 209–10, 237, 257
Bumiputra, 71, 190, 198
Burma (Myanmar), 41, 84, 87, 115

Cambodia, 109, 158, 210, 213, 215–16, 221, 223–8, 257
Causeway, 73, 127, 151–2, 159–60, 163
Celebes, 18, 48, 105
Changi, 73, 107–9
China (People's Republic of), 4, 6–8, 11, 15, 17–20, 27, 76, 86, 90, 99, 113, 116, 123, 134–5, 140–1, 151, 157, 162, 189–91, 194, 203–4, 210–18, 220–3, 236, 238, 240–1, 247, 253, 257, 265
Communism, 51, 143, 154–5, 157–8, 162–6, 189–92, 201, 203–28, 236–7, 245–6, 249, 251, 260, 265–6, 270–2

Dhanabalan, 158, 250
defence, 20–2, 141, 154–6, 160, 163, 167, 217, 220, 230–1, 238, 248, 250, 254–261, 265

Deng Xiao Ping, 215, 216, 220, 227

Europe, 15, 17, 19–20, 36–8, 46, 62, 109, 112, 118–19, 126, 129, 142, 168, 239, 248

Goh Chok Tong, 217, 233, 238, 253, 258
Goh Keng Swee, 52, 142, 216, 230, 253, 255–6

Habibie, 76, 78–9, 105, 161
Hong Kong, 11, 15, 18–19, 21, 27, 36–7, 42, 46, 52, 58, 64–6, 68–70, 90, 93, 95, 100, 103, 111, 113–16, 118, 120, 122–3, 124–9, 132–5, 137, 151, 190–2, 201, 212–13, 216, 235

India, 4, 16, 17, 197, 248, 250
Indochina, 1, 3, 6, 37, 41, 55, 144, 154, 158, 162, 165, 204, 213, 218–28, 257, 265–6
Indonesia, 2, 3, 11, 14, 18, 23, 25, 38–41, 43–9, 51, 54, 57, 62, 64–6, 68, 70, 74–81, 83–6, 88–90, 92–3, 97, 102–5, 108, 110, 112–13, 115, 123–126, 129, 131–4, 138–40, 143–8, 150–4, 156–7, 160–5, 168, 170–1, 175–7, 179–80, 183–91, 194–5, 200–3, 207, 211–13, 215, 217, 218, 220–7, 231, 236, 237, 239, 248, 250, 257–9, 263–5
Islam, 7–10, 115, 142, 146, 149, 159, 162–4, 195–6, 199–202, 215, 223, 249
Israel, 72, 109, 149, 159, 256

Jakarta, 48–9, 67, 74, 76, 105, 108, 112, 115, 122, 131–3, 140, 145, 149, 152–3, 155, 157, 161–3, 168, 196, 200, 212, 217, 224
Japan, 15, 20–22, 36–37, 39, 41, 46, 56, 59, 62, 66, 70, 74, 76, 80, 86–9, 91–2, 102–3, 105–7, 110, 114, 120–1, 123, 129, 132, 135, 137, 142–3, 179, 182–4, 191, 204, 227, 230, 265